# Social Problems     *05/06*

*Thirty-Third Edition*

**EDITOR**

**Kurt Finsterbusch**

*University of Maryland, College Park*

Kurt Finsterbusch received a bachelor's degree in history from Princeton University in 1957 and a bachelor of divinity degree from Grace Theological Seminary in 1960. His Ph.D. in sociology, from Columbia University, was conferred in 1969. Dr. Finsterbusch is the author of several books, including *Understanding Social Impacts* (Sage Publications, 1980), *Social Research for Policy Decisions* (Wadsworth Publishing, 1980, with Annabelle Bender Motz), and *Organizational Change as a Development Strategy* (Lynne Rienner Publishers, 1987, with Jerald Hage). He is currently teaching at the University of Maryland, College Park, and, in addition to serving as editor for *Annual Editions: Social Problems*, he is also editor of *Annual Editions: Sociology*, McGraw-Hill/Dushkin's *Taking Sides: Clashing Views on Controversial Social Issues*, and *Sources: Notable Selections in Sociology*.

*McGraw-Hill/Dushkin*

2460 Kerper Blvd., Dubuque, Iowa 52001

Visit us on the Internet
*http://www.dushkin.com*

# Credits

1. **Introduction: The Nature of Social Problems and General Critiques of American Society**
   Unit photo—© PhotoDisc, Inc.
2. **Problems of the Political Economy**
   Unit photo—Getty Images/ Ryan McVay.
3. **Problems of Poverty and Inequality**
   Unit photo—© Getty Images/ McDaniel Woolf.
4. **Institutional Problems**
   Unit photo—© Getty Images/ PhotoLink.
5. **Crime, Violence, and Law Enforcement**
   Unit photo—© PhotoDisc, Inc.
6. **Problems of Population, Environment, Resources, and the Future**
   Unit photo—© Getty Images/ Neil Beer.

# Copyright

Cataloging in Publication Data
Main entry under title: Annual Editions: Social Problems. 2005/2006.
1. Social Problems—Periodicals. I. Finsterbusch, K, *comp.* II. Title: Social Problems.
ISBN 0–07–310830–8      658'.05      ISSN 0272–4464

Thirty-Third Edition

Cover image © Photos.com
Printed in the United States of America    1234567890QPDQPD98765    Printed on Recycled Paper

# Editors/Advisory Board

Members of the Advisory Board are instrumental in the final selection of articles for each edition of ANNUAL EDITIONS. Their review of articles for content, level, currentness, and appropriateness provides critical direction to the editor and staff. We think that you will find their careful consideration well reflected in this volume.

# Preface

In publishing ANNUAL EDITIONS we recognize the enormous role played by the magazines, newspapers, and journals of the public press in providing current, first-rate educational information in a broad spectrum of interest areas. Many of these articles are appropriate for students, researchers, and professionals seeking accurate, current material to help bridge the gap between principles and theories and the real world. These articles, however, become more useful for study when those of lasting value are carefully collected, organized, indexed, and reproduced in a low-cost format, which provides easy and permanent access when the material is needed. That is the role played by ANNUAL EDITIONS.

The reason we study social problems is so that we can do something about them. Corrective action, however, is not taken until the situation is seen as a problem and the fire of concern is kindled in a number of citizens. A democratic country gives those citizens means for legally trying to change things, and this freedom and opportunity is a great pride for our country. In fact, most college students have already given some time or money to a cause in which they believe. This is necessary because each generation will face struggles for justice and rights. Daily forces operate to corrupt, distort, bias, exploit, and defraud as individuals and groups seek their own advantage at the expense of others and the public interest. Those dedicated to a good society, therefore, constantly struggle against these forces. Furthermore, the struggle is often complex and confusing. Not always are the defenders of the status quo in the wrong and the champions of change in the right. Important values will be championed by both sides. Today there is much debate about the best way to improve education. Opposing spokespersons think they are serving the good of the children and of America. In a similar manner, conscientious students in the same college class and reading the same material will hotly disagree. Therefore, solving problems is usually not a peaceful process. First it requires information and an understanding of the problem, and we can expect disagreements on both the facts and the interpretations. Second, it requires discussion, compromises, and a plan with majority support or at least the support of the powerful groups. Third, it requires action. In a democratic society this process should involve tolerance and even goodwill toward one's opponents as long as they act honestly, fairly, and democratically. Class discussions should involve respect for each others' opinions.

In some ways the study of social problems is easy and in some ways it is hard. The easy aspect is that most people know quite a lot about the problems that this book addresses; the hard part is that solving the problems is very difficult. If the solutions were easy, the problems would have been solved by now, and we would not be studying these particular issues. It may be easy to plan solutions, but it is hard to implement them. In general, however, Americans are optimistic and believe in progress; we learn by our mistakes and keep trying until conditions are acceptable. For instance, the members of Common Cause, including myself, have worked for campaign finance reform since 1970. Our efforts failed until Watergate created a huge public demand for it, and both campaign finance reform and public-right-to-know laws were passed. The reform, however, led to the formation of PACs (Political Action Committees) to get around the law and buy influence legally. Recently new campaign finance reform laws were passed. Nevertheless, I would speculate that while they will somewhat reduce the influence of money on politics, sooner or later moneyed interests will find a way to continue to have inordinate influence on policy decisions and eventually precipitate yet another reform effort. It could be that at the end of the twenty-first century Americans will be struggling with many of the same problems as today, but it is reasonable to believe that things will be somewhat better at that point because throughout this century people will mobilize again and again to improve our society; some will do this at considerable cost to themselves.

The articles presented here were selected for their attention to important issues, the value of the information and ideas that they present, and/or their ability to move the reader to concern and possibly even action toward correcting social problems. This edition of *Annual Editions: Social Problems* begins in unit 1 by defining social problems and presenting a general critique of American society. In unit 2 it examines some big issues in the political and economic systems that have society-wide impacts. Next, unit 3 examines issues of inequality and injustice that challenge basic American values. Unit 4 considers how well the various institutions of society work. Most are being heavily criticized. Why? Then, unit 5 studies the traditional problem of crime and law enforcement. Fortunately, there is some good news here. Finally, unit 6 confronts the issue of sustainability in a world experiencing serious environmental decline.

To assist the reader in identifying issues covered in the articles, the topic guide lists the topics in alphabetical order and the articles in which they are discussed. A reader doing research on a specific topic is advised to check this guide first. A valuable resource for users of this book is the *World Wide Web sites* that can be used to further explore article topics.

*Annual Editions: Social Problems 05/06* depends upon reader response to develop and change. You are encouraged to return the postpaid article rating form at the back of the book with your opinions about existing articles, recommendations of articles for subsequent editions, and advice on how the anthology can be made more useful as a teaching and learning tool.

Kurt Finsterbusch

*Editor*

*Dedicated to my students who have taught me to be more concerned about many social problems*

# Contents

Preface                                                    iv
Topic Guide                                                xi
Selected World Wide Web Sites                             xiv

## UNIT 1
## Introduction: The Nature of Social Problems and General Critiques of American Society

Unit Overview                                            xvi

1. **Social Problems: Definitions, Theories, and Analysis,** Harold A. Widdison and H. Richard Delaney, *McGraw-Hill/Dushkin,* 1995
   This essay, written specifically for this volume, explores the complexities associated with defining, studying, and attempting to resolve "social" problems. The three major theoretical approaches—*symbolic interactionism, functionalism, and conflict*—are summarized.                                    2

2. **The Fragmentation of Social Life,** D. Stanley Eitzen, *Vital Speeches of the Day,* July 1, 2000
   In this essay about America, Stanley Eitzen addresses a crucial problem: the *fragmentation of social life.* He suggests that America could come apart in the future. Eitzen discusses excessive *individualism,* heightened personal *isolation,* increasing inequality, and the deepening *racial/ethnic/religious/sexuality divide.*                                          11

3. **How to Re-Moralize America,** Francis Fukuyama, *The Wilson Quarterly,* Summer 1999
   Recently many of the indicators of *moral decline* have started to show improvement. Francis Fukuyama reports the changes and accepts the challenge of explaining how moral regeneration occurs generally and what caused a potential *moral regeneration* in the 1990s. In the process he explores the basic sociological questions: What are the sources of *value systems*? How do they arise and change? In his search for an answer he leads the reader through a sociological detective story.                                        16

## UNIT 2
## Problems of the Political Economy

Unit Overview                                            23

*Part A.    The Polity*

4. **Who Rules America?,** G. William Domhoff, from *Who Rules America? Power and Politics in the Year 2000,* The McGraw-Hill Companies/Mayfield, 1997
   G. William Domhoff is the leading proponent of the *power elite* view of American Politics as it applies to *political influence* in America today.              25

5. **Rights, Liberties, and Security: Recalibrating the Balance After September 11,** Stuart Taylor Jr., *Brookings Review,* Winter 2003
   A rule of government is that when dangers increase, liberties shrink. Yes, but how much? Where should the balance be? Stuart Taylor Jr. analyzes the problem starting with the premise that today we face *dangers without precedent:* a mass movement of militant Islamic terrorists who crave martyrdom, hide in shadows, are fanatically bent on slaughtering as many of us as possible. Taylor calls for a reassessment of the *civil liberties rules* that restrict the government's investigative powers.                                                   29

The concepts in bold italics are developed in the article. For further expansion, please refer to the Topic Guide and the Index.

6. **How the Little Guy Gets Crunched,** Donald L. Barlett and James B. Steele, *Time,* February 7, 2000

Politics means a win for some and a loss for others. The authors show that the **campaign contributions** of powerful **special interests** provide gains for the contributor but losses for the little guy.

35

### Part B.    The Economy

7. **Surveying the Global Marketplace,** Murray Weidenbaum, *USA Today,* January 2004

According to Murray Weidenbaum the global economy is very mixed up and that is a good thing. The Honda has more parts made in America than the Pontiac. Half of Xerox's employees work abroad. More than half of the revenues of many multinational American companies orginate overseas. Globalization lowers the prices that we pay in the stores but also creates problems and calls for new institutions to manage it.

38

8. **Evaluating Economic Change,** Joseph E. Stiglitz, *Daedalus,* Summer 2004

Joseph E. Stiglitz evaluates the costs and benefits of the momentous changes involved in the precesses of globalization. These processes have greatly benefitted some countries and hurt other countries. Surprisingly his economic analysis leads him into an extended discussion of morals.

41

9. **Shopping and Prosperity: The Consumer Economy,** Robert J. Samuelson, *Current,* March/April 2004

The consumption side of the economy gets little attention in academia and the media but it is a big part of our lives and the economy. Robert J. Samuelson tells its story including its historical roots, its consequences, and its psychological dimensions.

46

10. **Is Your Job Going Abroad?,** Jyoti Thottam, *Time,* March 1, 2004

Part of the debate in the last election was about the shortage of jobs and the number of jobs that are going overseas. Jyoti Thottam provides the data and the issues behind this debate. While politicians argue, however, college students wonder if their future job is about to be given to college graduates in India. According to Thottam they have reason to worry.

49

### Part C.    Problems of Place

11. **A Broken Heartland,** Jeff Glasser, *U.S. News & World Report,* May 7, 2001

Stories of **economic decline** are grim. Such is the situation today in many midwest **rural** counties that are distant from cities. They are dying economically and many residents are moving away, making it harder for those who remain to survive economically. Their history includes heroic struggles against economic hardships but today they fight a losing battle.

54

12. **The Longest Journey,** *The Economist,* November 2–8, 2002

Are immigrants on average a drain on the American economy or net contributors? *The Economist* cites studies showing that in the long run they pay more in taxes than they draw out in expenditures. Some economists even argue that many immigrants are necessary to support the increasing numbers of elderly. But immigration issues are complex and have no easy answers.

57

# UNIT 3
# Problems of Poverty and Inequality

Unit Overview

62

### Part A.    Inequality and the Poor

13. **For Richer: How the Permissive Capitalism of the Boom Destroyed American Equality,** Paul Krugman, *The New York Times Magazine,* October 20, 2002

The American economy has made the rich very rich in the past three decades but has not been nearly as generous to the poor. As a result the **income gap** has widened considerably. Paul Krugman details the facts about the growing inequality and explains how it happened.

65

The concepts in bold italics are developed in the article. For further expansion, please refer to the Topic Guide and the Index.

14. **The Real Face of Homelessness,** Joel Stein, *Time,* January 20, 2003

The bum sleeping on the park bench is not the new face of homelessness. Increasingly the homeless are ***mothers with children***. Joel Stein points out why this is the case and tells the painful stories of some homeless families. **73**

*Part B.   Welfare*

15. **Requiem for Welfare,** Evelyn Z. Brodkin, *Dissent,* Winter 2003

The old welfare system has been buried. What is the ***new welfare system*** and what has happened to the people who were on the old welfare system? Evelyn Z. Brodkin tackles these issues and criticizes some aspects of the transformed welfare system. **77**

*Part C.   Racial and Ethnic Inequality and Issues*

16. **What's At Stake,** Barbara Kantrowitz and Pat Wingert, *Newsweek,* January 27, 2003

The issue of ***affirmative action*** is in confusion today. It was definitely a badly needed policy in the beginning, and it has accomplished much, and made our society much more fair and just. But is it needed now and is it unfair now? This article clarifies what affirmative action is, where it stands legally today, and how universities should handle the issue. **83**

17. **Why We Hate,** Margo Monteith and Jeffrey Winters, *Psychology Today,* May/June 2002

The authors demonstrate the prevalence of ***prejudice and hatred*** in America and explain this in terms of ***social identity theory.*** Whenever people are divided into groups, negative attitudes develop toward the out group. **91**

*Part D.   Gender Inequalities and Issues*

18. **Human Rights, Sex Trafficking, and Prostitution,** Alice Leuchtag, *The Humanist,* January/February 2003

One of the evil plagues haunting the world today is ***sex slavery*** and it is getting worse. It is the product of extreme poverty and considerable profits. The exploitation involved is horrendous. ***Human rights*** groups are trying to stop the practice. Alice Leuchtag covers many aspects of this issue. **95**

19. **The Battle Over Gay Marriage,** John Cloud, *Time,* March 22, 2004

The legal definition of marriage is one of the hot topics of today since Massachusetts has legalized gay marriages. John Cloud reviews the history of and contested viewpoints on this issue. **101**

20. **Reversing the "Gender Gap",** Joel Wendland, *Political Affairs,* March 2004

Joel Wendland counters the recent magazine articles announcing a gender gap that favors women. Yes girls do better in school than boys and graduate from high school and college in greater numbers, but on many other dimensions of inequality women still substantially trail men. **106**

# UNIT 4
# Institutional Problems

**Unit Overview** **108**

*Part A.   The Family*

21. **The American Family,** Stephanie Coontz, *Life,* November 1999

Stephanie Coontz explains that ***modern families*** are better than the way the media portray them and that families of the past were probably worse. She corrects myths about the modern family with many underreported facts. **110**

22. **Living Better: Get Wed,** Amy M. Braverman, *Current,* January 2004

Amy Braverman reports on the latest research on the many benefits of marriage that include better physical and mental health, sex life, financial stability for parents, and many benefits for the kids. **115**

The concepts in bold italics are developed in the article. For further expansion, please refer to the Topic Guide and the Index.

23. **We're Not in the Mood,** Kathleen Deveny, *Newsweek,* June 30, 2003

Kathleen Deveny discusses a problem that has not received much attention: that **overworked married couples** do not have energy for much of a **sex life**. "Their once steamy love life slowly cooled" sums up her analysis. She also describes ways that couples are trying to resist this trend.　　　　**119**

*Part B.*　*Education*

24. **Against School: How Public Education Cripples Our Kids, and Why,** John Taylor Gatto, *Harper's,* September 2003

John Taylor Gatto attacks the American school system for preventing children from growing up and for being boring. He suspects that this result is exactly what those who control the school system want schools to be. In arguing his radical thesis, he presents a very provocative history of the evolution of the American school system.　　　　**124**

25. **How I Joined Teach for America—and Got Sued for $20 Million,** Joshua Kaplowitz, *City Journal,* Winter 2003

Most parents think favorably of the schools that their children attend, although some inner city schools are bad. Joshua Kaplowitz' personal story sheds much light on some of the problems.　　　　**129**

*Part C.*　*Health*

26. **Whose Hospital Is It?,** Arthur Allen, *Mother Jones,* May/June 2004

One aspect of the current health care crisis in the U.S. is the closing of many hospitals because they are not making enough profit for the corporations that own them. Arthur Allen reports on this trend along with other health care problems.　　　　**135**

27. **Death Stalks a Continent,** Johanna McGeary, *Time,* February 12, 2001

One of the greatest and most painful crises in the world today is the **AIDS epidemic in Africa.** Johanna McGeary's report on this crisis reveals shocking behavior by families and others toward victims and points out **cultural and structural factors** which contribute to the crisis.　　　　**139**

# UNIT 5
# Crime, Violence, and Law Enforcement

**Unit Overview**　　　　**148**

*Part A.*　*Crime*

28. **The Criminal Menace: Shifting Global Trends,** Gene Stephens, *The Futurist,* May/June 2003

Gene Stephens describes crime trends throughout the world. Overall crime rates in the United States were the highest in the Western world in 1980 but have fallen in the United States and increased in many other nations. Now several Western countries have higher rates. Nevertheless, the U.S. murder rate is still the highest. The author also reviews the competing explanations for the decline of crime in the U.S.　　　　**150**

29. **The Aggregate Burden of Crime,** David A. Anderson, *Journal of Law and Economics,* October 1999

David Anderson makes a valiant effort to compute the annual costs of major types of crime and the net annual total costs of all crime that he claims exceeds $1 trillion or over $4000 per capita. Fraud and cheating on taxes costs Americans over 20 times the costs of theft, burglary, and robbery.　　　　**154**

*Part B.*　*Law Enforcement*

30. **Reasonable Doubts,** Stephen Pomper, *The Washington Monthly,* June 2000

Stephen Pomper critically assesses the **criminal justice system** and recommends strong, badly needed **reforms**.　　　　**158**

The concepts in bold italics are developed in the article. For further expansion, please refer to the Topic Guide and the Index.

31. **On Patrol,** Eli Lehrer, *The American Enterprise,* June 2001
The police have been both strongly praised and strongly criticized this past decade. Now it is time to get up close and personal as the police do their work. Eli Lehrer follows a policewoman on her patrol and lets us see how extremely varied *police work* is.

**163**

### Part C.   Terrorism

32. **The Terrorism to Come,** Walter Laqueur, *Policy Review,* August/ September 2004
Walter Laqueur provides a rich lesson on terrorism from the left-wing revolutionary terrorism of several decades ago to the religiously inspired terrorism of today, which is not a response to poverty conditions. Currently the terrorist war is more cultural than political.

**169**

33. **Understanding the Terrorist Mind-Set,** Randy Borum, *The FBI Law Enforcement Bulletin,* July 2003
How do terrorists think? If terrorists are our greatest threat today—we need to understand their beliefs, values, and motives. This is what Randy Borum teaches us in this article.

**177**

# UNIT 6
# Problems of Population, Environment, Resources, and the Future

Unit Overview

**180**

### Part A.   Two Descriptions of the State of the Planet: Population and the Environment

34. **Rescuing a Planet Under Stress,** Lester R. Brown, *The Humanist,* November/December 2003
Lester Brown summarizes the state of the planet's environment that he portrays as under significant stress, and therefore, requires that significant changes occur throughout the world in how humans use the environment. He proposes solutions that involve "rapid systemic change."

**182**

35. **The Pentagon and Climate Change,** *Monthly Review,* May 2004
The climate change problem has been raised to a higher level of concern because of a Pentagon study of the possible social impacts—including economic and political instability and even war—of an abrupt climate change. In addition to this story this article assesses the seriousness of the negative impacts of global warming, the possibility of abrupt climate change, and some of the hindrances to addressing the problems.

**187**

### Part B.   Technological Issues

36. **The Future of Humanity,** Colin Tudge, *New Statesman,* April 8, 2002
*DNA research* has opened up breathtaking possibilities and excrutiating *moral dilemmas* at the same time. Now society has to decide whether to continue to leave the creation of humans to providence or evolution, or to genetically engineer our offspring. In this article, Colin Tudge presents the issues, options, and debates.

**194**

37. **The Secret Nuclear War,** Eduardo Goncalves, *The Ecologist,* April 2001
An extremely consequential technology is nuclear. The energy it produces has greatly benefited mankind, but at what price? Eduardo Goncalves reports on all the *nuclear accidents*, testings, experiments, leaks, production, cover-ups, and storage and reuse materials that he can find out about. The *death toll* could be as high as 175 million, and the shameful behavior of countless agencies that he reports on is shocking.

**198**

### Part C.   The Future

38. **The Globalization of Politics: American Foreign Policy for a New Century,** Ivo H. Daalder and James M. Lindsay, *Brookings Review,* Winter 2003
Since the Berlin wall came down the bipolar world power arrangement disintegrated and the new world power arrangement is not entirely clear. The authors focus on the globalization of politics and the appropriate role of the United States.

**205**

The concepts in bold italics are developed in the article. For further expansion, please refer to the Topic Guide and the Index.

39. **Community Building: Steps Toward a Good Society,** Amitai Etzioni, *Current,* January 2001

As America becomes more diverse and more unequal, can we build community? Identity politics have partly corrected past injustices, "but have also divided the nation along group lines." According to Amitai Etzioni a new thrust is needed. He reviews the threats to community and recommends communitarian solutions including ways to curb inequality, ways to increase *bonding,* and ways to increase value *commitments.*                209

40. **Sleepwalking Through the Apocalypse,** William Van Dusen Wishard, *Vital Speeches of the Day,* September 1, 2003

William Van Dusen Wishard is president of a firm that does research on trends and he begins this article by describing ten key world-wide trends that suggest "we've come to the end of the world, as we've known it." The world is becoming global economically, socially, and psychologically. The growth of international travel, migration, and communication are transforming world institutions and cultures. To cope we need a world consciousness.                213

**Index**                219

**Test Your Knowledge Form**                222

**Article Rating Form**                223

The concepts in bold italics are developed in the article. For further expansion, please refer to the Topic Guide and the Index.

# Topic Guide

This topic guide suggests how the selections in this book relate to the subjects covered in your course. You may want to use the topics listed on these pages to search the Web more easily.

On the following pages a number of Web sites have been gathered specifically for this book. They are arranged to reflect the units of this *Annual Edition*. You can link to these sites by going to the DUSHKIN ONLINE support site at *http://www.dushkin.com/online/*.

## ALL THE ARTICLES THAT RELATE TO EACH TOPIC ARE LISTED BELOW THE BOLD-FACED TERM.

### Abuse
18. Human Rights, Sex Trafficking, and Prostitution
28. The Criminal Menace: Shifting Global Trends

### Aggression
17. Why We Hate
28. The Criminal Menace: Shifting Global Trends
32. The Terrorism to Come
33. Understanding the Terrorist Mind-Set

### Assimilation
12. The Longest Journey
39. Community Building: Steps Toward a Good Society

### Business and the market
7. Surveying the Global Marketplace
8. Evaluating Economic Change
9. Shopping and Prosperity: The Consumer Economy
10. Is Your Job Going Abroad?
23. We're Not in the Mood
26. Whose Hospital Is It?

### Capitalism
7. Surveying the Global Marketplace
8. Evaluating Economic Change
13. For Richer: How the Permissive Capitalism of the Boom Destroyed American Equality

### Children and childhood
12. The Longest Journey
22. Living Better: Get Wed
24. Against School: How Public Education Cripples Our Kids, and Why
25. How I Joined Teach for America—and Got Sued for $20 Million

### Civil rights
5. Rights, Liberties, and Security: Recalibrating the Balance After September 11
16. What's At Stake
18. Human Rights, Sex Trafficking, and Prostitution
19. The Battle Over Gay Marriage
20. Reversing the "Gender Gap"

### Community
11. A Broken Heartland
12. The Longest Journey
39. Community Building: Steps Toward a Good Society

### Conflict
1. Social Problems: Definitions, Theories, and Analysis
2. The Fragmentation of Social Life
6. How the Little Guy Gets Crunched
16. What's At Stake
17. Why We Hate
19. The Battle Over Gay Marriage
32. The Terrorism to Come
33. Understanding the Terrorist Mind-Set

### Corporate welfare
6. How the Little Guy Gets Crunched

### Crime
18. Human Rights, Sex Trafficking, and Prostitution
28. The Criminal Menace: Shifting Global Trends
29. The Aggregate Burden of Crime
30. Reasonable Doubts
31. On Patrol
32. The Terrorism to Come
33. Understanding the Terrorist Mind-Set

### Culture
3. How to Re-Moralize America
19. The Battle Over Gay Marriage
20. Reversing the "Gender Gap"
21. The American Family
22. Living Better: Get Wed
24. Against School: How Public Education Cripples Our Kids, and Why
25. How I Joined Teach for America—and Got Sued for $20 Million
33. Understanding the Terrorist Mind-Set
39. Community Building: Steps Toward a Good Society

### Demography
11. A Broken Heartland
36. The Future of Humanity

### Discrimination
16. What's At Stake
17. Why We Hate
18. Human Rights, Sex Trafficking, and Prostitution
19. The Battle Over Gay Marriage
20. Reversing the "Gender Gap"

### Disintegration and integration
2. The Fragmentation of Social Life
11. A Broken Heartland
27. Death Stalks a Continent
39. Community Building: Steps Toward a Good Society

### Disorganization and organization
2. The Fragmentation of Social Life
11. A Broken Heartland
27. Death Stalks a Continent
39. Community Building: Steps Toward a Good Society

### Ecology and environment
34. Rescuing a Planet Under Stress
35. The Pentagon and Climate Change

### Economy
6. How the Little Guy Gets Crunched
7. Surveying the Global Marketplace
8. Evaluating Economic Change
9. Shopping and Prosperity: The Consumer Economy
10. Is Your Job Going Abroad?
11. A Broken Heartland

13. For Richer: How the Permissive Capitalism of the Boom Destroyed American Equality
14. The Real Face of Homelessness

## Education

24. Against School: How Public Education Cripples Our Kids, and Why
25. How I Joined Teach for America—and Got Sued for $20 Million

## Family

14. The Real Face of Homelessness
19. The Battle Over Gay Marriage
20. Reversing the "Gender Gap"
21. The American Family
22. Living Better: Get Wed
23. We're Not in the Mood
37. The Secret Nuclear War

## Future

2. The Fragmentation of Social Life
23. We're Not in the Mood
32. The Terrorism to Come
34. Rescuing a Planet Under Stress
35. The Pentagon and Climate Change
36. The Future of Humanity
40. Sleepwalking Through the Apocalypse

## Gender roles

19. The Battle Over Gay Marriage
20. Reversing the "Gender Gap"
21. The American Family
22. Living Better: Get Wed
23. We're Not in the Mood

## Globalization

7. Surveying the Global Marketplace
8. Evaluating Economic Change
10. Is Your Job Going Abroad?
38. The Globalization of Politics: American Foreign Policy for a New Century
40. Sleepwalking Through the Apocalypse

## Government

4. Who Rules America?
5. Rights, Liberties, and Security: Recalibrating the Balance After September 11
6. How the Little Guy Gets Crunched
13. For Richer: How the Permissive Capitalism of the Boom Destroyed American Equality
14. The Real Face of Homelessness
16. What's At Stake
30. Reasonable Doubts
32. The Terrorism to Come
38. The Globalization of Politics: American Foreign Policy for a New Century

## Health

2. The Fragmentation of Social Life
26. Whose Hospital Is It?
27. Death Stalks a Continent

## Immigration

12. The Longest Journey
39. Community Building: Steps Toward a Good Society

## Law enforcement

5. Rights, Liberties, and Security: Recalibrating the Balance After September 11
16. What's At Stake
18. Human Rights, Sex Trafficking, and Prostitution
28. The Criminal Menace: Shifting Global Trends

29. The Aggregate Burden of Crime
30. Reasonable Doubts
31. On Patrol
32. The Terrorism to Come
33. Understanding the Terrorist Mind-Set

## Lifestyles

13. For Richer: How the Permissive Capitalism of the Boom Destroyed American Equality
14. The Real Face of Homelessness
19. The Battle Over Gay Marriage
20. Reversing the "Gender Gap"
21. The American Family
22. Living Better: Get Wed
23. We're Not in the Mood

## Lower class

14. The Real Face of Homelessness

## Marriage and divorce

19. The Battle Over Gay Marriage
21. The American Family
22. Living Better: Get Wed
23. We're Not in the Mood

## Multiculturalism

16. What's At Stake
17. Why We Hate
39. Community Building: Steps Toward a Good Society

## Politics

4. Who Rules America?
5. Rights, Liberties, and Security: Recalibrating the Balance After September 11
6. How the Little Guy Gets Crunched
15. Requiem for Welfare
16. What's At Stake
18. Human Rights, Sex Trafficking, and Prostitution
32. The Terrorism to Come
38. The Globalization of Politics: American Foreign Policy for a New Century

## Poverty

14. The Real Face of Homelessness
15. Requiem for Welfare
18. Human Rights, Sex Trafficking, and Prostitution

## Race and ethnic relations

2. The Fragmentation of Social Life
16. What's At Stake
17. Why We Hate

## Sexism

18. Human Rights, Sex Trafficking, and Prostitution
20. Reversing the "Gender Gap"

## Social change

2. The Fragmentation of Social Life
3. How to Re-Moralize America
7. Surveying the Global Marketplace
8. Evaluating Economic Change
9. Shopping and Prosperity: The Consumer Economy
10. Is Your Job Going Abroad?
11. A Broken Heartland
13. For Richer: How the Permissive Capitalism of the Boom Destroyed American Equality
14. The Real Face of Homelessness
15. Requiem for Welfare
16. What's At Stake
19. The Battle Over Gay Marriage
20. Reversing the "Gender Gap"

21. The American Family
22. Living Better: Get Wed
23. We're Not in the Mood
28. The Criminal Menace: Shifting Global Trends
32. The Terrorism to Come
33. Understanding the Terrorist Mind-Set
36. The Future of Humanity
38. The Globalization of Politics: American Foreign Policy for a New Century
40. Sleepwalking Through the Apocalypse

## Social control

28. The Criminal Menace: Shifting Global Trends
29. The Aggregate Burden of Crime
30. Reasonable Doubts
33. Understanding the Terrorist Mind-Set

## Socialization

17. Why We Hate
25. How I Joined Teach for America—and Got Sued for $20 Million
33. Understanding the Terrorist Mind-Set

## Social relationships

2. The Fragmentation of Social Life
17. Why We Hate
19. The Battle Over Gay Marriage
20. Reversing the "Gender Gap"
21. The American Family
22. Living Better: Get Wed
23. We're Not in the Mood
39. Community Building: Steps Toward a Good Society

## Social stratification and inequality

2. The Fragmentation of Social Life
4. Who Rules America?
13. For Richer: How the Permissive Capitalism of the Boom Destroyed American Equality
14. The Real Face of Homelessness
15. Requiem for Welfare
16. What's At Stake
18. Human Rights, Sex Trafficking, and Prostitution
19. The Battle Over Gay Marriage
20. Reversing the "Gender Gap"
39. Community Building: Steps Toward a Good Society

## Social theory

1. Social Problems: Definitions, Theories, and Analysis
4. Who Rules America?
39. Community Building: Steps Toward a Good Society

## Technology

36. The Future of Humanity
37. The Secret Nuclear War

## Terrorism

5. Rights, Liberties, and Security: Recalibrating the Balance After September 11
17. Why We Hate
32. The Terrorism to Come
33. Understanding the Terrorist Mind-Set

## Upper class

4. Who Rules America?
13. For Richer: How the Permissive Capitalism of the Boom Destroyed American Equality

## Values

3. How to Re-Moralize America
19. The Battle Over Gay Marriage
21. The American Family
22. Living Better: Get Wed

33. Understanding the Terrorist Mind-Set
36. The Future of Humanity
39. Community Building: Steps Toward a Good Society
40. Sleepwalking Through the Apocalypse

## Violence

28. The Criminal Menace: Shifting Global Trends
29. The Aggregate Burden of Crime
32. The Terrorism to Come
33. Understanding the Terrorist Mind-Set
37. The Secret Nuclear War

## Wealth

4. Who Rules America?
8. Evaluating Economic Change
9. Shopping and Prosperity: The Consumer Economy
13. For Richer: How the Permissive Capitalism of the Boom Destroyed American Equality

## Welfare

15. Requiem for Welfare

## Women

18. Human Rights, Sex Trafficking, and Prostitution
20. Reversing the "Gender Gap"
23. We're Not in the Mood

## Work and employment

7. Surveying the Global Marketplace
8. Evaluating Economic Change
10. Is Your Job Going Abroad?
14. The Real Face of Homelessness
15. Requiem for Welfare
16. What's At Stake
20. Reversing the "Gender Gap"
21. The American Family
23. We're Not in the Mood

# World Wide Web Sites

The following World Wide Web sites have been carefully researched and selected to support the articles found in this reader. The easiest way to access these selected sites is to go to our DUSHKIN ONLINE support site at *http://www.dushkin.com/online/*.

# AE: Social Problems 05/06

The following sites were available at the time of publication. Visit our Web site—we update DUSHKIN ONLINE regularly to reflect any changes.

## General Sources

### The Gallup Organization
*http://www.gallup.com*

Open this Gallup Organization home page for links to an extensive archive of public opinion poll results and special reports on a huge variety of topics related to American society.

### Library of Congress
*http://www.loc.gov*

Examine this extensive Web site to learn about resource tools, library services/resources, exhibitions, and databases in many different fields related to social problems.

### National Geographic Society
*http://www.nationalgeographic.com*

This site provides links to National Geographic's huge archive of maps, articles, and other documents. There is a great deal of material related to social and cultural topics that will be of great value to those interested in the study of cultural pluralism.

## UNIT 1: Introduction: The Nature of Social Problems and General Critiques of American Society

### American Studies Web
*http://www.georgetown.edu/crossroads/asw/*

This eclectic site provides links to a wealth of resources on the Internet related to social issues, from gender studies to education to race and ethnicity. It is of great help when doing research in demography and population studies.

### Anthropology Resources Page
*http://www.usd.edu/anth/*

Many cultural topics can be accessed from this site from the University of South Dakota. Click on the links to find information about differences and similarities in values and lifestyles among the world's peoples.

### Social Science Information Gateway
*http://sosig.esrc.bris.ac.uk*

SOSIG is an online catalog of Internet resources relevant to social science education and research. Every resource is selected by a librarian or subject specialist.

## UNIT 2: Problems of the Political Economy

### National Center for Policy Analysis
*http://www.ncpa.org*

Using these Policy Digest Archives, you can link to discussions on an array of topics that are of major interest in the study of American politics and government from a sociological perspective, from regulatory policy, to affirmative action, to income.

### Penn Library: Sociology
*http://www.library.upenn.edu/*

This site provides a number of indexes on culture and ethnic studies, population and demographics, and statistical sources that are of value in studying social problems.

## UNIT 3: Problems of Poverty and Inequality

### grass-roots.org
*http://www.grass-roots.org*

Various resources and models for grassroots action and a summary and samples of Robin Garr's book, *Reinvesting in America,* are provided at this site.

### Immigration Facts
*http://www.immigrationforum.org*

The pro-immigrant National Immigration Forum offers this page to examine the effects of immigration on the U.S. economy and society. Click on the links for discussion of underground economies, immigrant economies, and other topics.

### Joint Center for Poverty Research
*http://www.jcpr.org*

Open this site to find research information related to poverty. The site provides working papers, answers to FAQs, and facts about who is poor in America. Welfare reform is also addressed.

### SocioSite
*http://www.pscw.uva.nl/sociosite/TOPICS/Women.html*

This sociology site from the University of Amsterdam's Sociology Department provides links to affirmative action, family and children's issues, and much more.

### William Davidson Institute
*http://www.wdi.bus.umich.edu*

Access the University of Michigan Business School's site for topics related to the changing global economy and the effects of globalization in general.

### WWW Virtual Library: Demography & Population Studies
*http://demography.anu.edu.au/VirtualLibrary/*

Here is a definitive guide to demography and population studies. A multitude of important links to information about global poverty and hunger can be found here.

## UNIT 4: Institutional Problems

### The Center for Education Reform
*http://edreform.com/school_choice/*

Visit this site to view current opinions and concerns related to school choice and school reform.

### Go Ask Alice!
*http://www.goaskalice.columbia.edu*

This interactive site provides discussion and insight into a number of personal issues of interest to college-age people and those younger and older. Questions about physical and emotional health and well-being in the modern world are answered.

# www.dushkin.com/online/

### The National Academy for Child Development (NACD)
*http://www.nacd.org*

This international organization is dedicated to helping children and adults to reach their full potential. Its home page presents links to various programs, research, and resources into topics related to the family and society.

### National Council on Family Relations (NCFR)
*http://www.ncfr.com*

This NCFR home page will lead you to valuable links to articles, research, and other resources on important issues in family relations, such as stepfamilies, couples, and divorce.

### National Institute on Aging (NIA)
*http://www.nih.gov/nia/*

The NIA presents this home page to lead you to a variety of resources on health, lifestyle, and social issues that are of concern to people as they grow older.

### National Institute on Drug Abuse (NIDA)
*http://165.112.78.61*

Use this site index of the U.S. National Institute on Drug Abuse for access to NIDA publications, information on drugs of abuse, and links to other related Web sites.

### National Institutes of Health (NIH)
*http://www.nih.gov*

Consult this site for links to extensive health information and scientific resources. Comprised of 24 institutes, centers, and divisions, including the Institute of Mental Health, the NIH is one of eight health agencies of the Public Health Service.

### Parenting and Families
*http://www.cyfc.umn.edu/features/index.html*

The University of Minnesota's Children, Youth, and Family Consortium site leads to many organizations and other resources related to divorce, single parenting, and stepfamilies, and to information about other topics about the family.

### A Sociological Tour Through Cyberspace
*http://www.trinity.edu/~mkearl/index.html*

This extensive site provides valuable essays, commentaries, data analyses, and links on every aspect of social problems, including such topics as death and dying, family, social gerontology, and social psychology.

### World Health Organization (WHO)
*http://www.who.int/home-page/*

The World Health Organization will provide you with links to a wealth of statistical and analytical information about health and the environment in the developing world.

## UNIT 5: Crime, Violence, and Law Enforcement

### ACLU Criminal Justice Home Page
*http://aclu.org/CriminalJustice/CriminalJusticeMain.cfm*

This Criminal Justice page of the American Civil Liberties Union Web site highlights recent events in criminal justice, addresses police issues, lists important resources, and contains a search mechanism.

### Terrorism Research Center
*http://www.terrorism.com*

The Terrorism Research Center features definitions and original research on terrorism, counterterrorism documents, a comprehensive list of Web links, and monthly profiles of terrorist and counterterrorist groups.

## UNIT 6: Problems of Population, Environment, Resources, and the Future

### Human Rights and Humanitarian Assistance
*http://www.etown.edu/vl/humrts.html*

Through this part of the World Wide Web Virtual Library, you can conduct research into a number of human-rights concerns around the world. The site also provides links to many other subjects related to important social issues.

### The Hunger Project
*http://www.thp.org*

Browse through this nonprofit organization's site to explore how it tries to achieve its goal: the end to global hunger through leadership at all levels of society. The Hunger Project contends that the persistence of hunger is at the heart of the major security issues threatening our planet.

**We highly recommend that you review our Web site for expanded information and our other product lines. We are continually updating and adding links to our Web site in order to offer you the most usable and useful information that will support and expand the value of your Annual Editions. You can reach us at:** *http://www.dushkin.com/annualeditions/.*

# UNIT 1

# Introduction: The Nature of Social Problems and General Critiques of American Society

## Unit Selections

1. **Social Problems: Definitions, Theories, and Analysis**, Harold A. Widdison and H. Richard Delaney
2. **The Fragmentation of Social Life**, D. Stanley Eitzen
3. **How to Re-Moralize America**, Francis Fukuyama

## Key Points to Consider

- What are your first five choices for the major social problems of America? In what ways does your list seem to reflect one of the three major approaches to social problems?

- How much distance do you feel from people with very different interests, values, lifestyles, religion, race or ethnicity, and class? What kinds of bonds do you feel with them?

- What signs of moral decay in America do you observe? What signs of moral strength do you observe?

- Describe what you imagine the re-moralization of society would be like?

 **Links: www.dushkin.com/online/**
These sites are annotated in the World Wide Web pages.

**American Studies Web**
*http://www.georgetown.edu/crossroads/asw/*
**Anthropology Resources Page**
*http://www.usd.edu/anth/*
**Social Science Information Gateway**
*http://sosig.esrc.bris.ac.uk*

What is a social problem? There are several different definitions of social problems and many different lists of serious social problems today. As editor of the 05/06 edition of *Annual Editions: Social Problems*, I have tried to provide valuable articles on all of the topics that are covered in most social problems textbooks.

Three articles are included in this introductory unit. The first deals with the issue of the definition of "social problems" and the major approaches to understanding these problems in a larger theoretical framework. The second is my selection for an article that provides a thoroughgoing broad critique of American society. It does not address one social problem but presents the author's view of what is wrong with America in general. Its main theme is that social life in America is extremely fragmented, so individual well-being suffers. The third accepts the moral decline thesis and analyzes how America could re-moralize.

Harold Widdison and H. Richard Delaney, in the first article, introduce the reader to sociology's three dominant theoretical positions and give examples of how those espousing each theory would look at specific issues. The three theories—symbolic interactionism, functionalism, and conflict theory—represent three radically different approaches to the study of social problems and their implications for individuals and societies. The perceived etiology of problems and their possible resolutions reflect the specific orientations of those studying them. As you read the subsequent articles, try to determine which of the three theoretical positions the various authors seem to be utilizing. Widdison and Delaney conclude this article by suggesting several approaches that students may wish to consider in defining conditions as "social" problems and how they can and should be analyzed.

In the second article, D. Stanley Eitzen admits that some social indicators are quite positive, such as low unemployment, but chooses to focus on some social problems. He cites several and then explores the fragmentation of social life. His question is, "Will society continue to cohere or will new crises pull us apart?"

He discusses excessive individualism, heightened personal isolation, the widening income and wealth gaps, and the deepening racial/ethnic/religious/sexuality divide. He shows that these divisions are deep. The next issue is "whether the integrative societal mechanisms that have served us well in the past will save us again or whether we will continue to fragment." He does not answer this question, but he worries that the answer may be no.

Francis Fukuyama, in the third article, points out that recently many of the indicators of moral decline have started to improve. They are still far worse than three decades ago, but further decline does not seem likely. This raises an interesting sociological question: Can America re-moralize? And if so, how? Fukuyama tries to answer these questions. He must first explain the sources of value systems and then explain how they arise and change. Finally, he must extrapolate from these analyses a theory of value transformation that can explain the potential for moral regeneration in the 1990s. He sets for himself a daunting intellectual challenge and leads the reader through a sociological detective story as he takes on the task.

# SOCIAL PROBLEMS:

## *Definitions, Theories, and Analysis*

Harold A. Widdison and H. Richard Delaney

## INTRODUCTION AND OVERVIEW

When asked, "What are the major social problems facing humanity today?" college students' responses tend to mirror those highlighted by the mass media—particularly AIDS, child abuse, poverty, war, famine, racism, sexism, crime, riots, the state of the economy, the environment, abortion, euthanasia, homosexuality, and affirmative action. These are all valid subjects for study in a social problems class, but some give rise to very great differences of opinion and even controversy. Dr. Jack Kevorkian in Michigan and his killing machine is one example that comes to mind. To some he evokes images of Nazi Germany with its policy of murdering the infirm and helpless. Others see Kevorkian's work as a merciful alternative to the slow and agonizing death of individuals with terminal illnesses. In the latter light, Kevorkian is not symbolic of a potentially devastating social issue, but of a solution to an escalating social problem.

The same controversy exists at the other end of life—specifically, what obligations do pregnant women have to themselves as opposed to the unborn? Some individuals see abortion as a solution to the problems of population, child abuse, disruption of careers, dangers to the physical and emotional health of women, as well as the prevention of the birth of damaged fetuses, and they regard it as a right to self-determination. Others look at abortion as attacking the sanctity of life, abrogating the rights of a whole category of people, and violating every sense of moral and ethical responsibility.

Affirmative action is another issue that can be viewed as both a problem and a solution. As a solution, affirmative action attempts to reverse the effects of hundreds of years of discrimination. Doors that have been closed to specific categories of people for many generations are, it is hoped, forced open; individuals, regardless of race, ethnicity, and gender, are able to get into professional schools, and secure good jobs, with the assurance of promotion. On the other hand, affirmative action forces employers, recruiting officers, and housing officials to give certain categories of individuals a preferred status. While affirmative action is promoted by some as a necessary policy to compensate for centuries of exclusion and discrimination, others claim that it is discrimination simply disguised under a new label but with different groups being discriminated against. If race, sex, age, ethnicity, or any other characteristic other than merit is used as the primary criterion for selection or promotion, then discrimination is occurring. Discrimination hurts both sides. William Wilson, an African American social scientist, argues that it is very damaging to the self-esteem of black individuals to know that the primary reason they were hired was to fill quotas.

Both sides to the debate of whether these issues themselves reflect a social problem or are solutions to a larger societal problem have valid facts and use societal-level values to support their claims. Robin William Jr. in 1970 identified a list of 15 dominant value orientations that represent the concept of the good life to many Americans:

1. Achievement and success as major personal goals.
2. Activity and work favored above leisure and laziness.
3. Moral orientation—that is, absolute judgments of good/bad, right/wrong.
4. Humanitarian motives as shown in charity and crisis aid.
5. Efficiency and practicality: a preference for the quickest and shortest way to achieve a goal at the least cost.
6. Process and progress: a belief that technology can solve all problems and that the future will be better than the past.
7. Material comfort as the "American dream."
8. Equality as an abstract ideal.
9. Freedom as a person's right against the state.
10. External conformity: the ideal of going along, joining, and not rocking the boat.
11. Science and rationality as the means of mastering the environment and securing more material comforts.

12. Nationalism: a belief that American values and institutions represent the best on earth.
13. Democracy based on personal equality and freedom.
14. Individualism, emphasizing personal rights and responsibilities.
15. Racism and group-superiority themes that periodically lead to prejudice and discrimination against those who are racially, religiously, and culturally different from the white northern Europeans who first settled the continent.

This list combines some political, economic, and personal traits that actually conflict with one another. This coexistence of opposing values helps explain why individuals hold contradictory views of the same behavior and why some issues generate such intensity of feelings. It is the intent of this article and the readings included in this book to attempt to help students see the complex nature of a social problem and the impact that various values, beliefs, and actions can have on them.

In the next segment of this article, the authors will look at specific examples of values in conflict and the problems created by this conflict. Subsequently the authors will look at the three major theoretical positions that sociologists use to study social problems. The article will conclude with an examination of various strategies and techniques used to identify, understand, and resolve various types of social problems and their implications for those involved.

As noted above, contemporary American society is typified by values that both complement and contradict each other. For example, the capitalistic free enterprise system of the United States stresses rugged individualism, self-actualization, individual rights, and self-expression. This economic philosophy meshes well with Christian theology, particularly that typified by many Protestant denominations. This fact was the basis of German sociologist Max Weber's "The Protestant Ethic and the Spirit of Capitalism" (1864). He showed that the concepts of grace (salvation is a gift—not something you can earn), predestination (the fact that some people have this gift while others do not), and a desire to know if the individual has grace gave rise to a new idea of what constitutes success. Whereas, with the communitarian emphasis of Catholicism where material success was seen as leading to selfishness and spiritual condemnation, Protestantism viewed material success as a sign of grace. In addition, it was each individual's efforts that resulted in both the economic success and the spiritual salvation of the individual. This religious philosophy also implied that the poor are poor because they lack the proper motivation, values, and beliefs (what is known as the "culture of poverty") and are therefore reaping the results of their own inadequacies. Attempts to reduce poverty have frequently included taking children from "impoverished" cultural environments and placing them in "enriched" environments to minimize the potentially negative effects

parents and a bad environment could have on their children. These enrichment programs attempt to produce attitudes and behaviors that assure success in the world but, in the process, cut children off from their parents. Children are forced to abandon the culture of their parents if they are to "succeed." Examples of this practice include the nurseries of the kibbutz in Israel and the Head Start programs in America. This practice is seen by some social scientists as a type of "cultural genocide." Entire cultures were targeted (sometimes explicitly, although often not intentionally) for extinction in this way.

This fact upsets a number of social scientists. They feel it is desirable to establish a pluralistic society where ethnic, racial, and cultural diversity exist and flourish. To them attempts to "Americanize" everyone are indicative of racism, bigotry, and prejudice. Others point to the lack of strong ethnic or racial identities as the unifying strength of the American system. When immigrants came to America, they put ethnic differences behind them, they learned the English language and democratic values, and they were assimilated into American life. In nations where immigrants have maintained their ethnic identities and held to unique cultural beliefs, their first loyalty is to their ethnic group. Examples of the destructive impact of strong ethnic loyalties can be seen in the conflict and fragmentation now occurring in the former Soviet Union, Czechoslovakia, and Yugoslavia.

James Q. Wilson (1994:54–55) noted in this regard:

> We have always been a nation of immigrants, but now the level of immigration has reached the point where we have become acutely conscious, to a degree not seen, I think, since the turn of the century, that we are a nation of many cultures. I believe that the vast majority of those who have come to this country came because they, too, want to share in the American Dream. But their presence here, and the unavoidable tensions that attend upon even well-intentioned efforts at mutual coexistence, makes some people—and alas, especially some intellectuals in our universities—question the American Dream, challenge the legitimacy of Western standards of life and politics, and demand that everybody be defined in terms of his or her group membership. The motto of this nation—*E pluribus unum*, out of the many, one—is in danger of being rewritten to read, *Ex uno plures*—out of the one, many.

# THEORETICAL EXPLANATIONS: SYMBOLIC INTERACTION, FUNCTIONALISM, CONFLICT

In their attempts to understand social phenomena, researchers look for recurring patterns, relationships between observable acts, and unifying themes. The particular way in which researchers look at the world reflects not only their personal views and experiences, but their professional perspective as well. Sociologists focus on interactions between individuals, between individuals and groups, between groups, and between groups and the larger society in which they are located. They try to identify those things that facilitate or hinder interaction, and the consequences of each. But not all sociologists agree as to the most effective/appropriate approach to take, and they tend to divide into three major theoretical camps: symbolic interactionism, functionalism, and conflict theory. These three approaches are not mutually exclusive, but they do represent radically different perspectives of the nature of social reality and how it should be studied.

## Symbolic Interaction

This theoretical perspective argues that no social condition, however unbearable it may seem to some, is inherently or objectively a social problem until a significant number of politically powerful people agree that it is contrary to the public good. Scientists, social philosophers, religious leaders, and medical people may "know" that a specific action or condition has or will eventually have a devastating effect on society or a specific group in society, but until they can convince those who are in a position to control and perhaps correct the condition, it is not considered a social problem. Therefore it is not the social condition, but how the condition is defined and by whom, that determines if it is or will become a social problem. The social process whereby a specific condition moves from the level of an individual concern to a societal-level issue can be long and arduous or very short. An example of the latter occurred in the 1960s when some physicians noticed a significant increase in infants born with severe physical deformities. Medical researchers looking into the cause made a connection between the deformities and the drug thalidomide. Pregnant women suffering from severe nausea and health-threatening dehydration were prescribed this drug, which dramatically eliminated the nausea and appeared to have no bad side effects. But their babies were born with terrible deformities. Once the medical researchers discovered the connection, they presented their findings to their colleagues. When the data were reviewed and found to be scientifically valid, the drug was banned immediately. Thus a small group's assessment of an issue as a serious problem quickly was legitimized by those in power as a societal-level social problem and measures were taken to eliminate it.

Most situations are not this clear-cut. In the mid-1960s various individuals began to question the real reason(s) why the United States was involved in the war in Southeast Asia. They discovered data indicating that the war was not about protecting the democratic rights of the Vietnamese. Those in power either ignored or rejected such claims as politically motivated and as militarily naive. Reports from the Vietcong about purported U.S. mil-

itary atrocities were collected and used as supportive evidence. These claims were summarily dismissed by American authorities as Communistic propaganda. Convinced of the validity and importance of their cause, the protesters regrouped and collected still more evidence including data collected by the French government. This new information was difficult for the U.S. government to ignore. Nevertheless, these new claims were rejected as being somewhat self-serving since the Vietcong had defeated the French in Indochina and presumably the French government could justify its own failure if the United States also failed.

Over the years the amount of data continued to accumulate augmented by new information collected from disenchanted veterans. This growing pool of evidence began to bother legislators who demanded an accounting from the U.S. government and the Department of Defense, but none was forthcoming. More and more students joined the antiwar movement, but their protests were seen as unpatriotic and self-serving—that is, an attempt to avoid military service. The increasing numbers of protesters caused some legislators to look more closely at the claims of the antiwar faction. As the magnitude of the war and the numbers of American servicemen involved grew, the numbers of people affected by the war grew as well. Returning veterans' reports of the state of the war, questionable military practices (such as the wholesale destruction of entire villages), complaints of incompetent leadership in the military, and corrupt Vietnamese politicians gave greater credibility to the antiwar movement's earlier claims and convinced additional senators and representatives to support the stop-the-war movement, even though those in power still refused to acknowledge the legitimacy of the movement.

Unable to work within the system and convinced of the legitimacy of their cause, protesters resorted to unconventional and often illegal actions, such as burning their draft cards, refusing to register for the draft, seeking refuge in other countries, attacking ROTC (Reserve Officers' Training Corps) buildings on college campuses, and even bombing military research facilities. These actions were initially interpreted by government officials as criminal activities of self-serving individuals or activities inspired by those sympathetic with the Communist cause. The government engaged in increasingly repressive efforts to contain the movement. But public disaffection with the war was fueled by rising American casualties; this, coupled with the discontent within the ranks of the military, eventually forced those in power to acquiesce and accept the claims that the war was the problem and not the solution to the problem. Reaching this point took nearly 15 years.

For the symbolic interactionist, the fact that socially harmful conditions are thought to exist is not the criterion for what constitutes a social problem. Rather the real issue is to understand what goes into the assessment of a specific condition as being a social problem. To the symbolic interactionist, the appropriate questions are, (a) How is it that some conditions become defined as a social problem while others do not? (b) Who, in any society, can legitimate the designation of a condition as a social problem? (c) What solutions evolve and how do they evolve for specific social problems? (d) What factors exist in any specific society that inhibit or facilitate resolution of social problems?

In summary, symbolic interactionists stress that social problems do not exist independently of how people define their world. Social problems are socially constructed as people debate whether or not some social condition is a social problem and decide what to do about it. The focus is on the meanings the problem has for those who are affected by it and not on the impact it is having on them.

## Functionalism

A second major theory sociologists use to study social problems is functionalism. Functionalists argue that society is a social system consisting of various integrated parts. Each of these parts fulfills a specific role that contributes to the overall functioning of society. In well-integrated systems, each part contributes to the stability of the whole. Functionalists examine each part in an attempt to determine the role it plays in the operation of the system as a whole. When any part fails, this creates a problem for the whole. These failures (dysfunctions) upset the equilibrium of the system and become social problems. To functionalists, anything that impedes the system's ability to achieve its goals is, by definition, a social problem. Unlike the symbolic interactionists, the functionalists argue that for itself that must necessarily be at the expense of other groups. It is this consistent conflict over limited resources that threatens societal peace and order.

Whereas the functionalists try to understand how different positions of power came into existence (Davis & Moore 1945), the conflictists show how those in power attempt to stay in power (Mills 1956). The conflict theorists see social problems as the natural and inevitable consequences of groups in society struggling to survive and gain control over those things that can affect their ability to survive. Those groups that are successful then attempt to use whatever means they must to control their environment and consolidate their position, thus increasing their chances of surviving. According to conflict theorists, those in power exploit their position and create poverty, discrimination, oppression, and crime in the process. The impact of these conditions on the exploited produces other pathological conditions such as alienation, alcoholism, drug abuse, mental illness, stress, health problems, and suicide. On occasions, such as that which occurred in Los Angeles in the summer of 1991 when policemen were found innocent of the use of excessive force in the beating of Rodney King, the feelings of helplessness and hopelessness can erupt as rage against the system in the form

of violence and riots or as in Eastern Europe as rebellion and revolution against repressive governments.

The conflict theorists argue that drug abuse, mental illness, various criminal behaviors, and suicide are symptoms of a much larger societal malaise. To understand and eliminate these problems, society needs to understand the basic conflicts that are producing them. The real problems stem from the implications of being exploited. Being manipulated by the powerful and denied a sense of control tends (a) to produce a loss of control over one's life (powerlessness), (b) to lead to an inability to place one's productive efforts into some meaningful context (meaningless), (c) not to being involved in the process of change but only in experiencing the impact resulting from the changes (normlessness), and (d) to cause one to find oneself isolated from one's colleagues on the job (self-isolation). Conflictists see all of these problems as the product of a capitalistic system that alienates the worker from himself and from his or her fellow workers (Seeman 1959).

To protect their positions of power, privilege, prestige, and possessions, those in power use their wealth and influence to control organizations. For example, they manipulate the system to get key individuals into positions where they can influence legislation and decisions that are designed to protect their power and possessions. They might serve on or appoint others to school boards to assure that the skills and values needed by the economy are taught. They also assure that the laws are enforced internally (the police) or externally (the military) to protect their holdings. The war in the Persian Gulf is seen by many conflict theorists as having been fought for oil rather than for Kuwait's liberation. When the exploited attempt to do something about their condition by organizing, protesting, and rebelling, they threaten those in power. For example, they may go on a strike that might disrupt the entire nation. Under the pretext that it is for the best good of society, the government may step in and stop the strike. Examples are the air-traffic-controllers strike of 1987 and the railroad strike in 1991. In retaliation the workers may engage in work slow-down, stoppage, and even sabotage. They may stage protests and public demonstrations and cast protest votes at the ballot boxes. If these do not work, rebellions and revolutions may result. Those in power can respond very repressively as was the case in Tiananmen Square in China in 1989, threaten military force as the Soviet Union did with the Baltic countries in 1990, or back down completely as when the Berlin Wall came down. Thus reactions to exploitation may produce change but inevitably lead to other social problems. In Eastern Europe and the former Soviet Union, democracy has resulted in massive unemployment, spiraling inflation, hunger, crime, and homelessness.

Sometimes those in power make concessions to maintain power. Conflict theorists look for concessions and how they placate the poor while still protecting the privileged and powerful. The rich are viewed as sharing power only if forced to do so and only to the extent absolutely necessary.

Robert Michels (1949), a French social philosopher, looked at the inevitable process whereby the members of any group voluntarily give their rights, prerogatives, and power to a select few who then dominate the group. It may not be the conscious decision of those who end up in positions of power to dominate the group, but, in time, conscious decisions may be made to do whatever is necessary to stay in control of the group. The power, privilege, and wealth they acquire as part of the position alter their self-images. To give up the position would necessitate a complete revision of who they are, what they can do, and with whom they associate. Their "selves" have become fused/confused with the position they occupy, and in an attempt to protect their "selves," they resist efforts designed to undermine their control. They consider threats to themselves as threats to the organization and therefore feel justified in their vigorous resistance. According to Michels, no matter how democratic an organization starts out to be it will always become dominated and controlled by a few. The process whereby this occurs he labeled the "Iron Law of Oligarchy." For example, hospitals that were created to save lives, cure the sick, and provide for the chronically ill, now use the threat of closure to justify rate increases. The hospital gets its rate increase, the cost of health goes up, and the number of individuals able to afford health care declines, with the ultimate result being an increase in health problems for the community. Although not explicitly stated, the survival of the organization (and its administrators) becomes more important than the health of the community.

In summary, the conflict theoretical model stresses the fact that key resources such as power and privilege are limited and distributed unequally among the members/groups in a society. Conflict is therefore a natural and inevitable result of various groups pursuing their interests and values. To study the basis of social problems, researchers must look at the distribution of power and privilege because these two factors are always at the center of conflicting interests and values. Moreover, whenever social change occurs, social problems inevitably follow.

## Conflict and Functionalism: A Synthesis

While conflict theorists' and functionalists' explanations of what constitutes the roots of social problems appear to be completely contradictory, Dahrendorf (1959) sees them as complementary. "Functionalism explains how highly talented people are motivated to spend twenty-five years of study to become surgeons; conflict theory explains how surgeons utilize their monopoly on their vital skills to obtain rewards that greatly exceed that necessary to ensure an adequate supply of talent." (See also Ossowski 1963; van de Berghe 1963; Williams 1966; Horowitz 1962; and Lenski 1966 for other attempts at a synthesis between these two theoretical models.)

# SOCIAL PROBLEMS: DEFINITION AND ANALYSIS

## Value Conflicts

It is convenient to characterize a social problem as a conflict of values, a conflict of values and duties, a conflict of rights (Hook, 1974), or a social condition that leads to or is thought to lead to harmful consequences. Harm may be defined as (a) the loss to a group, community, or society of something to which it is thought to be entitled, (b) an offense perceived to be an affront to our moral sensibilities, or (c) an impoverishment of the collective good or welfare. It is also convenient to define values as individual or collective desires that become attached to social objects. Private property, for example, is a valued social object for some while others disavow or reject its desirability; because of the public disagreement over its value, it presents a conflict of values. A conflict of values is also found in the current controversy surrounding abortion. Where pro-life supporters tend to see life itself as the ultimate value, supporters of pro-choice may, as some have, invoke the Fourteenth Amendment's right-to-privacy clause as the compelling value.

## Values-versus-Duties Conflicts

A second format that students should be aware of in the analysis of social problems is the conflict between values and obligations or duties. This approach calls our attention to those situations in which a person, group, or community must pursue or realize a certain duty even though those participating may be convinced that doing so will not achieve the greater good. For example, educators, policemen, bureaucrats, and environmentalists may occupy organizational or social roles in which they are required to formulate policies and follow rules that, according to their understanding, will not contribute to the greater good of students, citizens, or the likelihood of a clean environment. On the other hand, there are situations in which we, as individuals, groups, or communities, do things that would not seem to be right in our pursuit of what we consider to be the higher value. Here students of social problems are faced with the familiar problem of using questionable, illogical, or immoral means to achieve what is perhaps generally recognized as a value of a higher order. Police officers, for example, are sometimes accused of employing questionable, immoral, or deceptive means (stings, scams, undercover operations) to achieve what are thought to be socially helpful ends and values such as removing a drug pusher from the streets. Familiar questions for this particular format are, Do the ends justify the means? Should ends be chosen according to the means available for their realization? What are the social processes by which means themselves become ends? These are questions to which students of social problems and social policy analysis should give attention since immoral, illegal, or deceptive means can themselves lead to harmful social consequences.

Max Weber anticipated and was quite skeptical of those modern bureaucratic processes whereby means are transformed into organizational ends and members of the bureaucracy become self-serving and lose sight of their original and earlier mission. The efforts of the Central Intelligence Agency (CIA) to maintain U.S. interests in Third World countries led to tolerance of various nations' involvement in illicit drugs. Thus the CIA actually contributed to the drug problem the police struggle to control. A second example is that of the American Association of Retired Persons (AARP). To help the elderly obtain affordable health care, life insurance, drugs, and so forth, the AARP established various organizations to provide or contract for services. But now the AARP seems to be more concerned about its corporate holdings than it is about the welfare of its elderly members.

## RIGHTS IN CONFLICT

Finally, students of social problems should become aware of right-versus-right moral conflicts. With this particular format, one's attention is directed to the conflict of moral duties and obligations, the conflict of rights and, not least, the serious moral issue of divided loyalties. In divorce proceedings, for example, spouses must try to balance their personal lives and careers against the obligations and duties to each other and their children. Even those who sincerely want to meet their full obligations to both family and career often find this is not possible because of the real limits of time and means.

Wilson (1994:39, 54) observes that from the era of "Enlightenment" and its associated freedoms arose the potential for significant social problems. We are seeing all about us in the entire Western world the working out of the defining experience of the West, the Enlightenment. The Age of Enlightenment was the extraordinary period in the eighteenth century when individuals were emancipated from old tyrannies—from dead custom, hereditary monarchs, religious persecution, and ancient superstition. It is the period that gave us science and human rights, that attacked human slavery and political absolutism, that made possible capitalism and progress. The principal figures of the Enlightenment remain icons of social reform: Adam Smith, David Hume, Thomas Jefferson, Immanuel Kant, Isaac Newton, James Madison. The Enlightenment defined the West and set it apart from all of the other great cultures of the world. But in culture as in economics, there is no such thing as a free lunch. If you liberate a person from ancient tyrannies, you may also liberate him or her from familiar controls. If you enhance his or her freedom to create, you will enhance his or her freedom to destroy. If you cast out the dead hand of useless custom, you may also cast out the living hand of essential tradition. If you give an individual freedom of expres-

sion, he or she may write *The Marriage of Figaro* or he or she may sing "gangsta rap." If you enlarge the number of rights one has, you may shrink the number of responsibilities one feels.

There is a complex interaction between the rights an individual has and the consequences of exercising specific rights. For example, if an individual elects to exercise his or her right to consume alcoholic beverages, this act then nullifies many subsequent rights because of the potential harm that can occur. The right to drive, to engage in athletic events, or to work, is jeopardized by the debilitating effects of alcohol. Every citizen has rights assured him or her by membership in society. At the same time, rights can only be exercised to the degree to which they do not trample on the rights of other members of the group. If a woman elects to have a baby, must she abrogate her right to consume alcohol, smoke, consume caffeine, or take drugs? Because the effects of these substances on the developing fetus are potentially devastating, is it not reasonable to conclude that the rights of the child to a healthy body and mind are being threatened if the mother refuses to abstain during pregnancy? Fetal alcohol effect/syndrome, for instance, is the number-one cause of preventable mental retardation in the United States, and it could be completely eliminated if pregnant women never took an alcoholic drink. Caring for individuals with fetal alcohol effect/syndrome is taking increasingly greater resources that could well be directed toward other pressing issues.

Rights cannot be responsibly exercised without individuals' weighing their potential consequences. Thus a hierarchy of rights, consequences, and harms exists and the personal benefits resulting from any act must be weighed against the personal and social harms that could follow. The decision to use tobacco should be weighed against the possible consequences of a wide variety of harms such as personal health problems and the stress it places on society's resources to care for tobacco-related diseases. Tobacco-related diseases often have catastrophic consequences for their users that cannot be paid for by the individual, so the burden of payment is placed on society. Millions of dollars and countless health care personnel must be diverted away from other patients to care for these individuals with self-inflicted tobacco-related diseases. In addition to the costs in money, personnel, and medical resources, these diseases take tremendous emotional tolls on those closest to the diseased individuals. To focus only on one's rights without consideration of the consequences associated with those rights often deprives other individuals from exercising their rights.

The Constitution of the United States guarantees individuals rights without clearly specifying what the rights really entail. Logically one cannot have rights without others having corresponding obligations. But what obligations does each right assure and what limitations do these obligations and/or rights require? Rights for the collectivity are protected by limitations placed on each individual, but limits of collective rights are also mandated by laws assuring that individual rights are not infringed upon. Therefore, we have rights as a whole that often differ from those we have as individual members of that whole. For example, the right to free speech may impinge in a number of ways on a specific community. To the members of a small Catholic community, having non-Catholic missionaries preaching on street corners and proselytizing door-to-door could be viewed as a social problem. Attempts to control their actions such as the enactment and enforcements of "Green River" ordinances (laws against active solicitation), could eliminate the community's problem but in so doing would trample on the individual's constitutional rights or religious expression. To protect individual rights, the community may have to put up with individuals pushing their personal theological ideas in public places. From the perspective of the Catholic community, aggressive non-Catholic missionaries are not only a nuisance but a social problem that should be banned. To the proselytizing churches, restrictions on their actions are violations of their civil rights and hence a serious social problem.

Currently another conflict of interests/rights is dividing many communities, and that is cigarette smoking. Smokers argue that their rights are being seriously threatened by aggressive legislation restricting smoking. They argue that society should not and cannot legislate morality. Smokers point out how attempts to legislate alcohol consumption during the Prohibition of the 1920s and 1930s was an abject failure and, in fact, created more problems than it eliminated. They believe that the exact same process is being attempted today and will prove to be just as unsuccessful. Those who smoke then go on to say that smoking is protected by the Constitution's freedom of expression and that no one has the right to force others to adhere to his or her personal health policies, which are individual choices. They assert that if the "radicals" get away with imposing smoking restrictions, they can and will move on to other health-related behaviors such as overeating. Therefore, by protecting the constitutional rights of smokers, society is protecting the constitutional rights of everyone.

On the other hand, nonsmokers argue that their rights are being violated by smokers. They point to an increasing body of research data that shows that secondhand smoke leads to numerous health problems such as emphysema, heart disease, and throat and lung cancer. Not only do nonsmokers have a right not to have to breathe smoke-contaminated air, but society has an obligation to protect the health and well-being of its members from the known dangers of breathing smoke.

These are only a few examples of areas where rights come into conflict. Others include environmental issues, endangered species, forest management, enforcement of specific laws, homosexuality, mental illness, national health insurance, taxes, balance of trade, food labeling and packaging, genetic engineering, rape, sexual devia-

tion, political corruption, riots, public protests, zero population growth, the state of the economy, and on and on. It is notable that the degree to which any of these issues achieves widespread concern varies over time. Often, specific problems are given much fanfare by politicians and special interests groups for a time, and the media try to convince us that specific activities or behaviors have the greatest urgency and demand a total national commitment for a solution. However, after being in the limelight for a while, the importance of the problem seems to fade and new problems move into prominence. If you look back over previous editions of this book, you can see this trend. It would be useful to speculate why, in American society, some problems remain a national concern while others come and go.

## The Consequences of Harm

To this point it had been argued that social problems can be defined and analyzed as (a) conflicts between values, (b) conflicts between values and duties, and (c) conflicts between rights. Consistent with the aims of this article, social problems can be further characterized and interpreted as social conditions that lead, or are generally thought to lead, to harmful consequences for the person, group, community, or society.

Harm—and here we follow Hyman Gross's (1979) conceptualization of the term—can be classified as (a) a loss, usually permanent, that deprives the person or group of a valued object or condition it is entitled to have, (b) offenses to sensibility—that is, harm that contributes to unpleasant experiences in the form of repugnance, embarrassment, disgust, alarm, or fear, and (c) impairment of the collective welfare—that is, violations of those values possessed by the group or society.

Harm can also be ranked as to the potential for good. Physicians, to help their patients, often have to harm them. The question they must ask is, "Will this specific procedure, drug, or operation, produce more good than the pain and suffering it causes?" For instance, will the additional time it affords the cancer patient be worth all the suffering associated with the chemotherapy? In Somalia, health care personnel are forced to make much harder decisions. They are surrounded by starvation, sickness, and death. If they treat one person, another cannot be treated and will die. They find themselves forced to allocate their time and resources, not according to who needs it the most, but according to who has the greatest chance of survival.

Judges must also balance the harms they are about to inflict on those they must sentence against the public good and the extent to which the sentence might help the individual reform. Justice must be served in that people must pay for their crimes, yet most judges also realize that prison time often does more harm than good. In times of recession employers must weigh harm when they are forced to cut back their workforce: Where should the cuts occur? Should they keep employees of long standing and cut those most recently hired (many of which are nonwhites hired through affirmative action programs)? Should they keep those with the most productive records, or those with the greatest need for employment? No matter what employers elect to do, harm will result to some. The harm produced by the need to reduce the workforce must be balanced by the potential good of the company's surviving and sustaining employment for the rest of the employees.

The notion of harm also figures into the public and social dialogue between those who are pro-choice and those who are pro-life. Most pro-lifers are inclined to see the greatest harm of abortion to be loss of life, while most pro-choicers argue that the compelling personal and social harm is the taking away of a value (the right to privacy) that everyone is entitled to. Further harmful consequences of abortion for most pro-lifers are that the value of life will be cheapened, the moral fabric of society will be weakened, and the taking of life could be extended to the elderly and disabled, for example. Most of those who are pro-choice, on the other hand, are inclined to argue that the necessary consequence of their position is that of keeping government out of their private lives and bedrooms. In a similar way this "conflict of values" format can be used to analyze, clarify, and enlarge our understanding of the competing values, harms, and consequences surrounding other social problems. We can, and should, search for the competing values underlying such social problems as, for example, income distribution, homelessness, divorce, education, and the environment.

Loss, then, as a societal harm consists in a rejection or violation of what a person or group feels entitled to have. American citizens, for example, tend to view life, freedom, equality, property, and physical security as ultimate values. Any rejection or violation of these values is thought to constitute a serious social problem since such a loss diminishes one's sense of personhood. Murder, violence, AIDS, homelessness, environmental degradation, the failure to provide adequate health care, and abortion can be conveniently classified as social problems within this class of harms.

Offenses to our sensibilities constitute a class of harm that, when serious enough, becomes a problem affecting moral issues and the common good of the members of a society. Issues surrounding pornography, prostitution, and the so-called victimless crimes are examples of behaviors that belong to this class of harm. Moreover some would argue that environmental degradation, the widening gap between the very rich and the very poor, and the condition of the homeless also should be considered within this class of harm.

A third class of harm—namely impairments to the collective welfare—is explained, in part, by Gross (1979:120) as follows:

> Social life, particularly in the complex forms of civilized societies, creates many dependencies among members of a community. The welfare of each member depends upon the exercise of restraint and precaution by others in the pursuit of their legitimate activities, as well as upon cooperation toward certain common objectives. These matters of collective welfare involve many kinds of interests that may be said to be possessed by the community.

In a pluralistic society, such as American society, matters of collective welfare are sometimes problematic in that there can be considerable conflict of values and rights between various segments of the society. There is likely to remain, however, a great deal of agreement that those social problems whose harmful consequences would involve impairments to the collective welfare would include poverty, poor education, mistreatment of the young and elderly, excessive disparities in income distribution, discrimination against ethnic and other minorities, drug abuse, health and medical care, the state of the economy, and environmental concerns.

## BIBLIOGRAPHY

Dahrendorf, R. (1959). *Class and class conflict in industrial society.* Stanford, CA: Stanford University Press.

Davis, Kingsley, & Moore, Wilbert E. (1945). Some principles of stratification. *American Sociological Review, 10,* 242–249.

Gans, Herbert J. (1971). The uses of poverty: The poor pay all. *Social Policy.* New York: Social Policy Corporation.

Gross, Hyman. (1979). *A theory of criminal justice.* New York: Oxford University Press.

Hook, Sidney. (1974). *Pragmatism and the tragic sense of life.* New York: Basic Books.

Horowitz, M. A. (1962). Consensus, conflict, and cooperation. *Social Forces, 41,* 177–188.

Lenski, G. (1966). *Power and privilege.* New York: McGraw-Hill.

Michels, Robert. (1949). *Political parties: A sociological study of the oligarchical tendencies of modern democracy.* New York: Free Press.

Mills, C. Wright. (1956). *The power elite.* New York: Oxford University Press.

Ossowski, S. (1963). *Class structure in the social consciousness.* Translated by Sheila Patterson. New York: The Free Press.

Seeman, Melvin. (1959). On the meaning of alienation. *American Sociological Review, 24,* 783–791.

Van den Berghe, P. (1963). Dialectic and functionalism: Toward a theoretical synthesis. *American Sociological Review, 28,* 695–705.

Weber, Max. (1964). *The protestant ethic and the spirit of capitalism*. Translated by Talcott Parson. New York: Scribner's.

William, Robin, Jr. (1970). *American society: A sociological interpretation*, 3rd. ed. New York: Alfred A. Knopf.

Williams, Robin. (1966). Some further comments on chronic controversies. *American Journal of Sociology, 71*, 717–721.

Wilson, James Q. (1994, August). The moral life. *Brigham Young Magazine*, pp. 37–55.

Wilson, William. (1978). *The declining significance of race*. Chicago: University of Chicago Press.

## CHALLENGE TO THE READER

As you read the articles that follow, try to determine which of the three major theoretical positions each of the authors seems to be using. Whatever approach the writer uses in his or her discussion suggests what he or she thinks is the primary cause of the social problem/issue under consideration.

Also ask yourself as you read each article, (1) What values are at stake or in conflict? (2) What rights are at issue or in conflict? (3) What is the nature of the harm in each case, and who is being hurt? (4) What do the authors suggest as possible resolutions for each social problem?

Written by Harold A. Widdison and H. Richard Delaney for *Annual Editions: Social Problems.* © 1995 by McGraw-Hill/Dushkin, Guilford, CT 06437.

# The Fragmentation of Social Life

## SOME CRITICAL SOCIETAL CONCERNS FOR THE NEW MILLENNIUM

*Address by* **D. STANLEY EITZEN**, *Emeritus Professor of Sociology, Colorado State University*
*Delivered to the Life Enrichment Series, Bethel, North Newton, Kansas, April 12, 2000*

## D. STANLEY EITZEN

For many observers of American society this is the best of times. The current economic expansion is the longest in U.S. history. Unemployment is the lowest in three decades. Inflation is low and under control. The stock market has risen from 3500 to over 11,000 in eight years. The number of millionaires has more than doubled in the past five years to 7.1 million. The Cold War is over. The United States is the dominant player in the world both militarily and economically. Our society, obviously, is in good shape.

But every silver lining has a cloud. While basking in unprecedented wealth and economic growth, the U.S. has serious domestic problems. Personal bankruptcies are at a record level. The U.S. has the highest poverty rate and the highest child poverty rate in the Western world. We do not have a proper safety net for the disadvantaged that other countries take for granted. Hunger and homelessness are on the rise. Among the Western nations, the U.S. has the highest murder rate as well as the highest incarceration rate. Also, we are the only Western nation without a universal health care system, leaving 44 million Americans without health insurance.

I want to address another crucial problem that our society faces—the fragmentation of social life. Throughout U.S. history, despite a civil war, and actions separating people by religion, class, and race, the nation has somehow held together. Will society continue to cohere or will new crises pull us apart? That is the question of the morning. While there are many indicators of reduced societal cohesion, I will limit my discussion to four: (1) excessive individualism; (2) heightened personal isolation; (3) the widening income and wealth gap; and (4) the deepening racial/ethnic/religious/sexuality divide.

## EXCESSIVE INDIVIDUALISM

We Americans celebrate individualism. It fits with our economic system of capitalism. We are self-reliant and responsible for our actions. We value individual freedom, including the right to choose our vocations, our mates, when and where to travel, and how to spend our money. At its extreme, the individualistic credo says that it is our duty to be selfish and in doing so, according to Adam Smith's notion of an "invisible hand," society benefits. Conservative radio commentator Rush Limbaugh said as much in his response to an initiative by President Clinton to encourage citizen volunteerism: "Citizen service is a repudiation of the principles upon which our country was based. We are here for ourselves."

While Rush Limbaugh may view rugged individualism as virtuous, I do not. It promotes inequality; it promotes the tolerance of inferior housing, schools, and services for "others"; and it encourages public policies that are punitive to the disadvantaged. For example, this emphasis on the individual has meant that, as a society, the United States has the lowest federal income tax rates in the Western world. Our politicians, especially Republicans, want to lower the rates even more so that individuals will have more and governments, with their presumed interest in the common good, will have less. As a result, the United States devotes relatively few resources to help the disadvantaged and this minimal redistribution system is shrinking.

In effect, our emphasis on individualism keeps us from feeling obligated to others.

Consider the way that we finance schools. Schools are financed primarily by the states through income taxes and local school districts through property taxes. This means that wealthy states and wealthy districts have more money to educate their children than the less advantaged states and districts. The prevailing view is that if my community or state is well-off, why should my taxes go to help children from other communities and other states?

The flaw in the individualistic credo is that we cannot go it alone—our fate depends on others. Paradoxically, it is in our individual interest to have a collective interest. We deny this at our peril for if we disregard those unlike ourselves, in fact doing violence to them, then we invite their hostility and violence, and, ultimately, a fractured society.

# HEIGHTENED PERSONAL ISOLATION

There are some disturbing trends that indicate a growing isolation as individuals become increasingly isolated from their neighbors, their co-workers, and even their family members. To begin, because of computers and telecommunications there is a growing trend for workers to work at home. While home-based work allows flexibility and independence not found in most jobs, these workers are separated from social networks. Aside from not realizing the social benefits of personal interaction with colleagues, working from home means being cut off from pooled information and the collective power that might result in higher pay and better fringe benefits.

Our neighborhoods, too, are changing in ways that promote isolation. A recent study indicates that one in three Americans has never spent an evening with a neighbor. This isolation from neighbors is exacerbated in the suburbs. Not only do some people live in gated communities to physically wall themselves off from "others" but they wall themselves off from their neighbors behaviorally and symbolically within gated and nongated neighborhoods alike. Some people exercise on motorized treadmills and other home exercise equipment instead of running through their neighborhoods. Rather than walking to the corner grocery or nearby shop and visiting with the clerks and neighbors, suburbanites have to drive somewhere away from their immediate neighborhood to shop among strangers. Or they may not leave their home at all, shopping and banking by computer. Sociologist Philip Slater says that "a community life exists when one can go daily to a given location at a given time and see many of the people one knows." Suburban neighborhoods in particular are devoid of such meeting places for adults and children. For suburban teenagers almost everything is away—practice fields, music lessons, friends, jobs, school, and the malls. Thus, a disconnect from those nearby. For adults many go through their routines without sharing stories, gossip, and analyses of events with

friends on a regular basis at a coffee shop, neighborhood tavern, or at the local grain elevator.

Technology also encourages isolation. There was a major shift toward isolation with the advent of television as people spent more and more time within their homes rather than socializing with friends and neighbors. Now, we are undergoing a communications revolution that creates the illusion of intimacy but the reality is much different. Curt Suplee, science and technology writer for the Washington Post, says that we have seen "tenfold increases in 'communication' by electronic means, and tenfold reductions in person-to-person contact." In effect, as we are increasingly isolated before a computer screen, we risk what Warren Christopher has called "social malnutrition." John L. Locke, a professor [of] communications argues in The De-Voicing of Society that e-mail, voice mail, fax machines, beepers, and Internet chat rooms are robbing us of ordinary social talking. Talking, he says, like the grooming of apes and monkeys, is the way we build and maintain social relationships. In his view, it is only through intimate conversation that we can know others well enough to trust them and work with them harmoniously. In effect, Locke argues that we are becoming an autistic society, communicating messages electronically but without really connecting. Paradoxically, then, these incredible communication devices that combine to connect us in so many dazzling ways also separate us increasingly from intimate relationships.

Fragmentation is also occurring within many families, where the members are increasingly disconnected from each other. Many parents are either absent altogether or too self-absorbed to pay very much attention to their children or each other. On average, parents today spend 22 fewer hours a week with their children than parents did in the 1960s. Although living in the same house, parents or children may tune out each other by engaging in solitary activities. A survey by the Kaiser Family Foundation found that the average child between 2 and 18, spends 5 and one-half hours a day alone watching television, at a computer, playing video games, on the Internet, or reading. Many families rarely eat together in an actual sit-down meal. All too often material things are substituted for love and attention. Some children even have their own rooms equipped with a telephone, television, VCR, microwave, refrigerator, and computer, which while convenient, isolates them from other family members. Such homes may be full of people but they are really empty.

The consequences of this accelerating isolation of individuals are dire. More and more individuals are lonely, bitter, alienated, anomic, and disconnected. This situation is conducive to alcohol and drug abuse, depression, anxiety, and violence. The lonely and disaffected are ripe candidates for membership in cults, gangs, and militias where they find a sense of belonging and a cause to believe in but in the process they may become more paranoid and, perhaps, even become willing terrorists. At a less extreme level, the alienated will disengage from society by shunning voluntary associations, by home schooling their children, and by not participating in elections. In short, they will become increasingly individualistic, which compounds their problem and society's problem with unity.

## THE WIDENING INEQUALITY GAP

There is an increasing gap between the rich and the rest of us, especially between the rich and the poor. Data from 1998 show that there were at least 268 billionaires in the United States, while 35 million were below the government official poverty line.

Timothy Koogle, CEO of Yahoo made $4.7 million a day in 1999, while the median household income in that year was $110 a day. Bill Gates, CEO of Microsoft is richer than Koogle by far. He is worth, depending on [the] stock market on a given day, around $90 billion or so. Together, eight Americans—Microsoft billionaires Bill Gates, Paul Allen, and Steve Ballmer plus the five Wal-Mart heirs—have a net worth of $233 billion, which is more than the gross domestic product of the very prosperous nation of Sweden. The Congressional Budget Office reports that in 1999, the richest 2.7 million Americans, the top 1 percent of the population, had as many aftertax dollars to spend as the bottom 100 million put together.

Compared to the other developed nations, the chasm between the rich and the poor in the U.S. is the widest and it is increasing. In 1979, average family income in the top 5 percent of the earnings distribution was 10 times that in the bottom 20 percent. Ten years later it had increased to 16:1, and in 1999 it was 19:1, the biggest gap since the Census Bureau began keeping track in 1947.

The average salary of a CEO in 1999 was 419 times the pay of a typical factory worker. In 1980 the difference was only 42 times as much. This inequality gap in the United States, as measured by the difference in pay between CEOs and workers, is by far the highest in the industrialized world. While ours stands at 419 to 1, the ratio in Japan is 25 to 1, and in France and Germany it is 35 to 1.

At the bottom end of wealth and income, about 35 million Americans live below the government's official poverty line. One out of four of those in poverty are children under the age of 18. Poor Americans are worse off than the poor in other western democracies. The safety net here is weak and getting weaker. We do not have universal health insurance. Funds for Head Start are so inadequate that only one in three poor children who are eligible actually are enrolled in the program. Welfare for single mothers is being abolished, resulting in many impoverished but working mothers being less well-off because their low-wage work is not enough to pay for child care, health care, housing costs, and other living expenses. Although the economy is soaring, a survey of 26 cities released by the U.S. Conference on Mayors shows that the numbers of homeless and hungry in the cities have risen for 15 consecutive years. The demand for emergency food

is the highest since 1992 and the demand for emergency shelter is the largest since 1994. According to the U.S. Department of Agriculture, there were about 36 million, including 14 million children living in households afflicted with what they call "food insecurity," which is a euphemism for hunger.

Of the many reasons for the increase in homelessness and hunger amidst increasing affluence, three are crucial. First, the government's welfare system has been shrinking since the Reagan administration with the support of both Republicans and Democrats. Second, the cost of housing has risen dramatically causing many of the poor to spend over 50 percent of their meager incomes for rent. And, third, charitable giving has not filled the void, with less than 10 percent of contributions actually going to programs that help the poor. In effect, 90 percent of philanthropy is funneled to support the institutions of the already advantaged—churches (some of which trickles down to the poor), hospitals, colleges, museums, libraries, orchestras, and the arts.

The data on inequality show clearly, I believe, that we are moving toward a two-tiered society. Rather than "a rising tide lifting all boats," the justification for capitalism as postulated by President John Kennedy, the evidence is that "a rising tide lifts only the yachts." The increasing gap between the haves and the have-nots has crucial implications for our society. First, it divides people into the "deserving" and the "undeserving." If people are undeserving, then we are justified in not providing them with a safety net. As economist James K. Galbraith says: "A high degree of inequality causes the comfortable to disavow the needy. It increases the psychological distance separating these groups, making it easier to imagine that defects of character or differences of culture, rather than an unpleasant turn in the larger schemes of economic history, lie behind the separation." Since politicians represent the monied interests, the wealthy get their way as seen in the continuing decline in welfare programs for the poor and the demise of affirmative action. Most telling, the inequality gap is not part of the political debate in this, or any other, election cycle.

A second implication is that the larger the gap, the more destabilized society becomes.

In this regard economist Lester Thurow asks: "How much inequality can a democracy take? The income gap in America is eroding the social contract. If the promise of a higher standard of living is limited to a few at the top, the rest of the citizenry, as history shows, is likely to grow disaffected, or worse." Former Secretary of Labor, Robert Reich, has put it this way: "At some point, if the trends are not reversed, we cease being a society at all. The stability of the country eventually is threatened. No country can endure a massive gap between people at the top and people at the bottom." Or, as economist Galbraith puts it: "[Equality] is now so wide it threatens, as it did in the Great Depression, the social stability of the country. It has come to undermine our sense of ourselves as a nation of equals. Economic inequality, in this way, challenges the essential unifying myth of American national life."

## THE DEEPENING RACIAL/ETHNIC/ RELIGIOUS/SEXUALITY DIVIDE

The United States has always struggled with diversity. American history is stained by the enslavement of Africans and later the segregated and unequal "Jim Crow" south, the aggression toward native peoples based on the belief in "Manifest Destiny," the internment of Japanese Americans during World War II, episodes of intolerance against religious minorities, gays and lesbians, and immigrants. In each instance, the majority was not only intolerant of those labeled as "others," but they also used the law, religious doctrine, and other institutional forms of discrimination to keep minorities separate and unequal. Despite these ongoing societal wrongs against minorities, there has been progress culminating in the civil rights battles and victories of the 1950s, 1960s, and early 1970s.

But the civil rights gains of the previous generation are in jeopardy as U.S. society becomes more diverse. Currently, the racial composition of the U.S. is 72 percent white and 28 percent nonwhite. In 50 years it will be 50 percent nonwhite. The racial landscape is being transformed as approximately 1 million immigrants annually set up permanent residence in the United States and another 300,000 enter illegally and stay. These new residents are primarily Latino and Asian, not European as was the case of earlier waves of immigration. This "browning of America" has important implications including increased division.

An indicator of fragmentation along racial lines is the "White flight" from high immigration areas, which may lead to what demographer William Frey has called the "Balkanization of America." The trends toward gated neighborhoods, the rise of private schools and home schooling are manifestations of exclusiveness rather than inclusiveness and perhaps they are precursors to this "Balkanization."

Recent state and federal legislation has been aimed at reducing or limiting the civil rights gains of the 1970s. For example, in 1994 California passed Proposition 187 by a 3- to 2-popular vote margin, thereby denying public welfare to undocumented immigrants. Congress in 1996 voted to deny most federal benefits to legal immigrants who were not citizens. A number of states have made English the official state language. In 1997 California passed Proposition 209, which eliminated affirmative action (a policy aimed at leveling the playing field so that minorities would have a fair chance to succeed). Across the nation, Congress and various state legislatures, most recently Florida, have taken measures to weaken or eliminate affirmative action programs.

Without question racial and ethnic minorities in the U.S. are the targets of personal prejudicial acts as well as pervasive institutional racism. What will the situation be like by 2050 when the numbers of Latinos triple from their present population of 31.4 million, and the Asian population more than triples from the current 10.9 million, and the African American population increases 70 percent from their base of 34.9 million now?

Along with increasing racial and ethnic diversity, there is a greater variety of religious belief. Although Christians are the clear majority in the United States, there are also about 7 million Jews, 6 million Muslims (there are more Muslims than Presbyterians), and millions of other non-Christians, including Buddhists, and Hindus, as well as atheists.

While religion often promotes group integration, it also divides. Religious groups tend to emphasize separateness and superiority, thereby defining "others" as infidels, heathens, heretics, or nonbelievers. Strongly held religious ideas sometimes split groups within a denomination or congregation. Progressives and fundamentalists within the same religious tradition have difficulty finding common ground on various issues, resulting in division. This has always been the case to some degree, but this tendency seems to be accelerating now. Not only are there clashes within local congregations and denominational conferences but they spill out into political debates in legislatures and in local elections, most notably school board elections, as religious factions often push their narrow, divisive sectarian policies. These challenges to religious pluralism are increasing, thus promoting fragmentation rather than unity.

There is also widespread intolerance of and discrimination toward those whose sexual orientation differs from the majority. The behaviors of gay men and lesbian women are defined and stigmatized by many members of society as sinful; their activities are judged by the courts as illegal; and their jobs and advancement within those jobs are often restricted because of their being different sexually. As more and more homosexuals become public with their sexuality, their presence and their political agenda are viewed as ever more threatening and must be stopped.

My point is this: diversity and ever increasing diversity are facts of life in our society. If we do not find ways to accept the differences among us, we will fragment into class, race, ethnic, and sexual enclaves.

Two social scientists, John A. Hall and Charles Lindholm, in a recent book entitled Is America Breaking Apart? argue that throughout American history there has been remarkable societal unity because of its historically conditioned institutional patterns and shared cultural values. Columnist George Will picked up on this theme in a Newsweek essay, postulating that while the U.S. has pockets of problems, "American society is an amazing machine for homogenizing people." That has been the case but will this machine continue to pull us together? I believe, to the contrary, that while the U.S. historically has overcome great obstacles, a number of trends in contemporary society have enormous potential for pulling us apart. Our society is moving toward a two-tiered society with the gap between the haves and the have-nots, a withering bond among those of different social classes, and a growing racial, ethnic, and sexuality divide. The critical question is whether the integrative societal mechanisms that have served us well in the past will save us again or whether we will continue to fragment?

The challenge facing U.S. society as we enter the new millennium is to shift from building walls to building bridges. As our society is becoming more and more diverse, will Americans feel empathy for, and make sacrifices on behalf of, a wide variety of people who they define as different? The answer to this crucial question is negative at the present time. Social justice seems to be an outmoded concept in our individualistic society.

I shall close with a moral argument posed by one of the greatest social thinkers and social activists of the 20th century, the late Michael Harrington. Harrington, borrowing from philosopher John Rawls, provides an intuitive defi-nition of a justice. A just society is when I describe it to you and you accept it even if you do not know your place in it. Harrington then asks (I'm paraphrasing here): would you accept a society of 275 million where 44 million people do not have health insurance, where 35 million live in poverty including one-fifth of all children? Would you accept a society as just where discrimination against minorities is commonplace, even by the normal way society works? Would you accept a society where a sizable number of people live blighted lives in neighbor-hoods with a high concentration of poverty, with inferior schools, with too few good jobs? You'd be crazy to accept such a society but that is what we have. Harrington concludes: "If in your mind you could not accept a society in which we do unto you as we do unto them, then isn't it time for us to change the way we are acting towards them who are a part of us?" If, however, we accept an unjust society, then our society will move inexorably toward a divided and fortress society.

---

From *Vital Speeches of the Day*, July 1, 2000, pp. 563-566. © 2000 by D. Stanley Eitzen. Reprinted by permission of the author.

# How to Re-Moralize America

## by Francis Fukuyama

In 1994, William J. Bennett published a book called *The Index of Leading Cultural Indicators*, which brought together a variety of statistics about American social trends. Between the mid-1960s and the early 1990s, Bennett showed, there was a shocking deterioration of America's social health. By the 1990s, one American child out of three was being born to an unmarried mother, nearly a third of African American men between the ages of 20 and 29 were involved in some way with the criminal justice system, and scores on standardized tests of educational achievement had dropped America to the bottom of the pack among industrialized countries. While we were materially richer than at any time in history, Bennett argued, we were becoming morally poorer at an alarming rate.

In the brief period since Bennett's *Index* appeared, we have experienced what seems to be a remarkable turnaround. Crime, including violent crimes and those against property, has decreased by more than 15 percent nationally; the murder rate in New York City has declined to levels not seen since the mid-1960s. Divorce rates, which had already begun a downward trend in the 1980s, continue on that path. Starting in 1995, the illegitimacy rate ceased its upward climb and began to decline slightly. The teenage pregnancy rate dropped eight percent between 1991 and 1996; among black teenagers, it fell 21 percent. Welfare caseloads have dropped by as much as a quarter nationally, and states at the forefront of welfare reform, such as Wisconsin, have seen astonishing reductions of up to 75 percent. Americans' general level of

trust in their institutions and in one another, though difficult to gauge, has risen. In 1991, for example, only 15 to 20 percent of Americans said they trusted the federal government to do the right thing most of the time; by the end of the decade that percentage had rebounded to between 25 and 30 percent.

What are we to make of these improvements? Are Americans at century's end being blessed not only with a booming stock market and a near full-employment economy but a restoration of cultural health as well? Many conservatives, notably social scientist Charles Murray and historian Gertrude Himmelfarb, don't think so. The changes, they argue, are too shallow and recent; they may be the product of more jails and stiffer sentencing rather than any true improvement in moral behavior. One conservative activist, Paul Weyrich of the Free Congress Foundation, was thrown into such despair last summer by the public's refusal to repudiate President Bill Clinton despite a sex scandal and impeachment proceedings that he publicly declared that Americans have never been more degenerate than they are today.

But conservatives are wrong to dismiss the good news contained in the social statistics. In fact, there has been a shift back to more traditional social values, and they should take credit for helping to bring it about. It would be a mistake to become complacent, or to think that our social and cultural problems are now behind us. But there is good reason to think that American society is undergoing a degree of moral regeneration. There is still a great deal of confusion over the sources of moral decline, however, and over the nature of moral renewal. Liberals need to confront the reality of moral decline and the importance of socially beneficial, less self-centered values. Conservatives have to be realistic and recognize that many of the developments they dislike in contemporary society are driven by economic and technological change—change brought about by the same dynamic capitalist economy they so often celebrate.

Moral decline is not a myth or a figment of the nostalgic imagination. Perhaps the most important conservative achievement over the past couple of decades was to convince the rest of American society that these changes had occurred, that they reflected a disturbing shift in values, and that consequently not every social problem could be addressed by creating a new federal program and throwing money at it.

This reconception of social problems began with two large government-funded studies published in the mid-1960s: Daniel Patrick Moynihan's report, *The Negro Family: The Case for National Action* (1965), and James Coleman's *Equality of Educational Opportunity* (1966). Moynihan, then working for the U.S. Department of Labor, argued that family structure, and in particular the absence of fathers in many African American homes, was directly related to the incidence of crime, teenage pregnancy, low educational achievement, and other social pathologies. Coleman's study showed that student educational achievement was most strongly affected not by the tools of public policy, such as teacher salaries and classroom size, but by the environment a child's family and peers create. In the absence of a culture that emphasizes self-discipline, work, education, and other middle-class values, Coleman showed, public policy can achieve relatively little.

Once published, the Moynihan report was violently attacked. Moynihan was accused of "blaming the victim" and seeking to impose white values on a community that had different but not necessarily inferior cultural norms. Liberals at first denied the reality of massive changes in family structure, and then fell back on the argument that single-parent households are no worse from the standpoint of child welfare than traditional ones—the kind of argument Moynihan was later to label "defining deviancy down." By the early 1990s, however, conservatives had largely won the argument. In 1994, the publication of Sara McLanahan and Gary Sandefur's book *Growing Up with a Single Parent* (1994) made the social science community's shift more or less official. The two well-respected sociologists found that a generation's worth of empirical research supported Moynihan's basic conclusion: growing up in a single-parent family is correlated with a life of poverty and a host of other social ills.

Few Americans understand that they were not alone in experiencing these changes. All of the industrialized countries outside Asia experienced a massive increase in social disorder between the 1960s and '90s—a phenomenon that I have called the Great Disruption of Western social values. Indeed, by the 1990s Sweden, the United Kingdom, and New Zealand all had higher rates of property crime than the United States. More than half of all Scandinavian children are born to unmarried mothers, compared with one-third of American children. In Sweden, so few people bother to get married that the institution itself probably is in long-term decline.

While conservatives won their case that values had changed for the worse, they were on shakier ground in their interpretation of why this shift had occurred. There were two broad lines of argument. The first, advanced by Charles Murray in his landmark book *Losing Ground* (1984), argued that family breakdown, crime, and other social pathologies were ultimately the result of mistaken government policies. Chief among them was Aid to Families with Dependent Children (AFDC), which in effect subsidized illegitimacy by paying welfare benefits only to single mothers. But there were other causes, such as new court-imposed constraints on police departments won by civil libertarians. In this interpretation, any improvement in social indicators today must be the result of the unwinding of earlier social policies through measures such as the 1996 welfare reform bill.

The second conservative line of argument held that moral decline was the result of a broad cultural shift. Former federal judge Robert Bork, for example, blamed the 1960s counterculture for undermining traditional values and setting the young at war with authority. Others, such as philosopher John Gray, reached further back in time. They revived the arguments of Edmund Burke and Joseph de Maistre, tracing moral decay to an Enlightenment commitment to replacing tradition and religion with reason and secular humanism.

While there is more than a germ of truth in each of these interpretations, neither is adequate to explain the shift in values that occurred during the Great Disruption. Detailed econometric studies seeking to link AFDC to illegitimacy have shown that although there is some causal connection, the relationship is not terribly strong. More important, illegitimacy is only part of a much broader story of family breakdown that includes divorce, cohabitation in place of marriage, declining fertility, and the separation of cohabiting couples. These ills cut across the socioeconomic spectrum and can hardly be blamed on a federal poverty program.

The second line of argument, which sees moral breakdown as a consequence of a broad cultural shift, is not so much wrong as inadequate. No one who has lived through the last several decades can deny that there has been a huge shift in social values, a shift whose major theme has been the rise of individualism at the expense of communal sources of authority, from the family and neighborhood to churches, labor unions, companies, and the government. The problem with this kind of broad cultural explanation is that it cannot explain timing. Secular humanism, for example, has been in the works for the past four or five hundred years. Why all of a sudden in the last quarter of the 20th century has it produced social chaos?

The key to the timing of the Great Disruption, I believe, is to be found elsewhere, in changes that occurred in the economy and in technology. The most important social values that were shaken by the Great Disruption are those having to do with sex, reproduction, and the family. The reason the disruption happened when and where it did can be traced to two broad technological changes that began in the 1960s. One is the advent of birth control. The other is the shift from industrial to information-based economies and from physical to mental labor.

The nuclear family of the 1950s was based on a bargain that traded the husband's income for the wife's fertility: he worked, she stayed home to raise the family. With the economy's shift from manufacturing to services (or from brawn to brains), new opportunities arose for women. Women began entering the paid labor force in greater numbers throughout the West in the 1960s, which undid the old arrangement. Even as it liberated women from complete dependence on their husbands, it freed many men from responsibility for their families. Not surprisingly, women's participation in the labor force correlates strongly with divorce and family breakdown throughout the industrialized world.

The Pill reinforced this trend by shifting the burden of responsibility for the consequences of sex to women. No longer did men need to worry greatly if their adventures led to pregnancy. One sign of this change was found by economists Janet Yellen, George Akerlof, and Michael Katz. Between the 1960s and '90s, the number of brides who were pregnant at the altar declined significantly. The shotgun wedding, that ultimate symbol of male accountability, is increasingly a thing of the past.

Humans share a fundamental trait with other animal species: males are less selective in their choice of sexual partners than females, and less attached to their children. In humans, the role that fathers play in the care and nurture of their children tends to be socially constructed to a significant degree, shaped by a host of formal and informal controls that link men to their families. Human fatherhood is therefore more readily subject to disruption. The sexual revolution and the new economic and cultural independence of women provided that disruption. The perfectly reasonable desire of women to increase their autonomy became, for men, an excuse to indulge themselves. The vastly increased willingness of men to leave

behind partners and children constitutes perhaps the single greatest change in moral values during the Great Disruption. It lies at the core of many of the period's social pathologies.

What are the chances of a moral renewal? What are its potential sources? Renewal must be possible. While conservatives may be right that moral decline occurred over the past generation, they cannot be right that it occurs in every generation. Unless we posit that all of human history has been a degeneration from some primordial golden age, periods of moral decline must be punctuated by periods of moral improvement.

Such cycles have occurred before. In both Britain and the United States, the period from the end of the 18th century until approximately the middle of the 19th century saw sharply increasing levels of social disorder. Crime rates in virtually all major cities increased. Illegitimacy rates rose, families dissolved, and social isolation increased. The rate of alcohol consumption, particularly in the United States, exploded. But then, from the middle of the century until its end, virtually all of these social indicators reversed direction. Crime rates fell. Families stabilized, and drunkards went on the wagon. New voluntary associations—from temperance and abolitionist societies to Sunday schools—gave people a fresh sense of communal belonging.

The possibility of re-moralization poses some large questions: Where do moral values come from, and what, in particular, are the sources of moral values in a postindustrial society? This is a subject that, strangely, has not received much attention. People have strong opinions about what moral values ought to be and where they ought to come from. If you are on the left, you are likely to believe in social equality guaranteed by a welfare state. If you are a cultural conservative, you may favor the authority of tradition and religion. But how values actually are formed in contemporary societies receives little empirical study. Most people would say that values are either passed along from previous generations through socialization (which fails to explain how change occurs) or are imposed by a church or other hierarchical authority. With the exception of a few discredited theories, sociologists and cultural anthropologists haven't had much to contribute. They have had much more success in describing value systems than in explaining their genesis.

Into this breach in the social sciences have stepped the economists, who have hardly been shy in recent years about applying their formidable methodological tools to matters beyond their usual realm. Economists tend to be opponents of hierarchy and proponents of bargaining—individuals, they say, act rationally on their own to achieve socially productive ends. This describes the market. But Friedrich A. Hayek (among others) suggested that moral rules—part of what he called the "extended order of human cooperation"—might also be the product of a similar decentralized evolutionary bargaining process.

Take the virtues of honesty and reliability, which are key to social cooperation and that intangible compound of mutual trust and engagement called "social capital." Many people have argued that such virtues have religious sources, and that contemporary capitalist societies are living off the cultural capital of previous ages—in America, chiefly its Puritan traditions. Modern capitalism, in this view, with its amoral emphasis on profits and efficiency, is steadily undermining its own moral basis.

Such an interpretation, while superficially plausible, is completely wrong. A decentralized group of individuals who have to deal with one another repeatedly will tend as a matter of self-interest to evolve norms of honesty and reliability. That is, reputation, whether for honesty or fair dealing or product quality, is an asset that self-interested individuals will seek to acquire. While religion may encourage them, a hierarchical source of rules is not necessary. Given the right background conditions—especially the need for repeated dealings with a particular group of people—order and rules will tend to emerge spontaneously from the ground up.

The study of how order emerges spontaneously from the interaction of individual agents is one of the most interesting and important intellectual developments of the late 20th century. One reason it is interesting is that the study is not limited to economists and other social scientists. Scientists since Charles Darwin have concluded that the high degree of order in the biological world was not the creation of God or some other creator but rather emerged out of the interaction of simpler units. The elaborate mounds of some species of African termites, taller than a human being and equipped with their own heating and air conditioning systems, were not designed by anyone, much less by the neurologically simple creatures that built them. And so on, throughout the natural world, order is created by the blind, irrational process of evolution and natural selection. (In the 1980s, the now famous Santa Fe Institute was created to support studies of just this type of phenomenon, so-called complex adaptive systems, in a wide variety of fields.)

Indeed, there is a good deal more social order in the world than even the economists' theories would suggest. Economists frequently express surprise at the extent to which supposedly self-interested, rational individuals do seemingly selfless things: vote, contribute to charities, give their loyalty to employers. People do these things because the ability to solve repeated dilemmas of social cooperation is genetically coded into the human brain, put there by an evolutionary process that rewarded those individuals best able to generate social rules for themselves. Human beings have innate capabilities that make them gravitate toward and reward cooperators who play by the community's rules, and to ostracize and isolate opportunists who violate them. When we say that human beings are social creatures by nature, we mean not that they are cooperative angels with unlimited resources for altruism but that they have built-in capabilities for perceiving the moral qualities of their fellow humans. What James Q. Wilson calls the "moral sense" is put there by nature, and will operate in the absence of either a law-giver or a prophet.

If we accept the fact that norms have spontaneous as well as hierarchical sources, we can place them along a continuum that extends from hierarchical and centralized types of authority at one end to the completely decentralized and spontaneous interactions of individuals at the other. But there is a second dimension. Norms and moral rules can be the product of rational bargaining and negotiation, or they can be socially inherited or otherwise a-rational in origin.

In order to clarify the origins of re-moralization, I have constructed a matrix (next page) that organizes these alternatives along two axes. Different types of moral rules fall into different quadrants. Formal laws handed down by governments belong in the rational/hierarchical quadrant; common law and spontaneously generated rules concerning, say, honesty in market relations, fall in the rational/spontaneous quadrant. Because, according to most recent research, incest taboos have biological origins, they are a spontaneous, a-rational norm. Revealed religion—Moses bringing the Ten Commandments down from Mount Sinai, for example—occupies the a-rational hierarchical quadrant. But folk religions—a cult of rock worshipers, for example–may be a species of spontaneous, a-rational order.

This taxonomy gives us a basis for at least beginning a discussion of where norms in a postindustrial society come from. Economists, following their rational, nonhierarchical bent, have been busy populating the upper-right quadrant with examples of spontaneously generated rules. A case in point is the database of more than 5,000 cases of so-called common pool resource problems compiled by Elinor Ostrom. Such problems confront communities with the need to determine rules for sharing common resources such as fisheries or pastureland. Contrary to the expectation that the self-interest of each individual will lead to the depletion of the resources—the famous "tragedy of the commons"—Ostrom finds many cases in which communities were able to spontaneously generate fair rules for sharing that avoided that result.

Max Weber, the founder of modern sociology, argued that as societies modernize, the two rational quadrants, and particularly the hierarchical quadrant, tend to play a strong role in the creation of norms. Rational bureaucracy was, for him, the essence of modernity. In postindustrial societies, however, all four quadrants continue to serve as

# The Universe of Norms

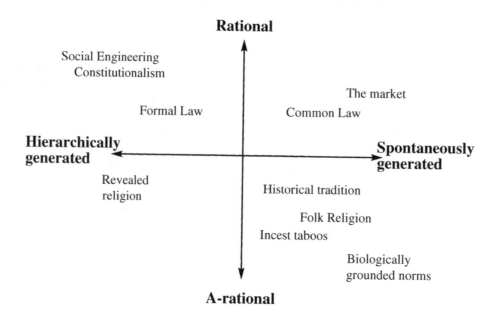

important sources of norms. Modern corporations, for example, have discovered that they cannot organize complex activities and highly skilled workers in a centralized, formal, top-down system of bureaucratic rules. The trend in management is to reduce formal bureaucracy in favor of informal norms that link a variety of firms and individuals in networks.

**W**e now have a framework in which to discuss how the socially corrosive effects of the Great Disruption are being overcome, and what continuing possibilities for change there might be. In the quest for the source of authoritative new rules, one starting point is the rational-hierarchical quadrant, which is the sphere of public policy. Crime rates are down across the United States today in no small measure because government is embracing better policies, such as community policing, and spending more on law enforcement, prisons, and punishment.* But the fact that tougher policies have brought crime rates down would not be regarded by most people as evidence of moral renewal. We want people to behave better not because of a crackdown but because they have internalized certain standards. The question then becomes, Which of the three remaining quadrants can be the source of moral behavior?

**M**any cultural conservatives believe that religion is the sine qua non of moral values, and they blame the Great Disruption on a loss of religious values. Religion played a powerful role in the Victorian upsurge during

the second half of the 19th century, they note, and, therefore, any reversal of the Great Disruption must likewise depend on a religious revival. In this view, the cultural conservatives are supported (in a way) by Friedrich Nietzsche, who once denounced the English "flathead" John Stuart Mill for believing that one could have something approximating Christian values in the absence of a belief in the Christian God.

Nietzsche famously argued that God was on his deathbed and incapable, in Europe at least, of being resuscitated. There could be new religions, but they would be pagan ones that would provoke "immense wars" in the future. Religious conservatives can reply that, as an empirical matter, God is not dead anywhere but in Europe itself. A generation or two ago, social scientists generally believed that secularization was the inevitable byproduct of modernization, but in the United States and many other advanced societies, religion does not seem to be in danger of dying out.

Some religious conservatives hope, and many liberals fear, that the problem of moral decline will be resolved by a large-scale return to religious orthodoxy—a transformation as sudden as the one Ayatollah Khomeini wrought 20 years ago by returning to Iran on a jetliner. For a variety of reasons, this seems unlikely. Modern societies are so culturally diverse that it is not clear whose version of orthodoxy would prevail. Any true form of orthodoxy is likely to be seen as a threat to important groups and hence would neither get very far nor serve as a basis for widening the radius of trust. Instead of integrating society, a conservative religious revival might only increase social discord and fragmentation.

It is not clear, moreover, that the re-moralization of society need rely on the hierarchical authority of revealed religion. Against Nietzsche's view that moral behavior inevitably rests on dogmatic belief, we might counterpose Adam Smith, the Enlightenment philosopher with perhaps the most realistic and highly developed theory of moral action. Harking back to a kind of Aristotelian naturalism, Smith argued that human beings are social and moral creatures by nature, capable of being led to moral behavior both by their natural passions and by their reason. The Enlightenment has been justly criticized for its overemphasis on human reason. But reason does not have to take the form of a bureaucratic state seeking to engineer social outcomes through the wholesale rearrangement of society. It can also take the form of rational individuals interacting with one another to create workable moral rules, or, in Smith's language, being led from a narrowly selfish view of their interests to the view of an "impartial spectator" exercising reasoned moral judgment.

Religious conservatives, in other words, underestimate the innate ability of human beings to evolve reasonable moral rules for themselves. Western societies underwent an enormous shock during the mid-20th century, and it is not surprising that it has taken a long time to adjust. The process of reaching a rational set of norms is not easy or automatic. During the Great Disruption, for example, large numbers of men and women began to behave in ways that ended up hurting the interests of children. Men abandoned families, women conceived children out of wedlock, and couples divorced for what were often superficial and self-indulgent reasons. But parents also have a strong interest in the well-being of their children. If it can be demonstrated to them that their behavior is seriously injuring the life chances of their offspring, they are likely to react rationally and want to alter that behavior in ways that help their children.

During the Great Disruption, there were many intellectual and cultural currents at work obscuring from people the consequences of their personal behavior for people close to them. They were told by social scientists that growing up in a single-parent family was no worse than growing up in an intact one, reassured by family therapists that children were better off if the parents divorced, and bombarded by images from the popular culture that glamorized sex. Changing these perceptions requires discussion, argument, even "culture wars." And we have had them. Today Barbara Dafoe Whitehead's controversial 1993 assertion that "Dan Quayle was right" about the importance of families no longer seems radical.

What would the re-moralization of society look like? In some of its manifestations, it would represent a continuation of trends that have already occurred in the 1990s, such as the return of middle-class people from their gated suburban communities to downtown areas, where a renewed sense of order and civility once again makes them feel secure enough to live and work. It would show up in increasing levels of participation in civil associations and political engagement. And it would be manifest in more civil behavior on college campuses, where a greater emphasis on academics and more carefully codified rules of behavior are already apparent.

The kinds of changes we can expect in norms concerning sex, reproduction, and family life are likely to be more modest. Conservatives need to be realistic in understanding how thoroughly the moral and social landscapes have been altered by powerful technological and economic forces. Strict Victorian rules concerning sex are very unlikely to return. Unless someone can figure out a way to un-invent birth control, or move women out of the labor force, the nuclear family of the 1950s is not likely to be reconstituted in anything like its original form.

Yet the social role of fathers has proved very plastic from society to society and over time, and it is not unreasonable to think that the commitment of men to their families can be substantially strengthened. This was the message of two of the largest demonstrations in Washington during the 1990s, the Nation of Islam's Million Man March and the Promise Keepers' rally. People were rightly suspicious of the two sponsors, but the same message about male responsibility can and should be preached by more mainstream groups.

There is also evidence that we are moving into a "post-feminist" age that will be friendlier to families and children. Feminism denigrated the work of raising children in favor of women's paid labor—an attitude epitomized by Hillary Clinton's dismissive response to questions about her Arkansas legal career that she could have just "stayed home and baked cookies." Many women are indeed now working—not as lawyers or policymakers but as waitresses and checkers at Wal-Mart, away from the children they are struggling to raise on their own after being abandoned by husbands or boyfriends. Many women like these might choose to stay at home with their children during their early years if the culture told them it was okay, and if they had the financial means to do so. I see anecdotal evidence all around me that the well-to-do are already making this choice. This does not represent a return of the housewife ideal of the 1950s, just a more sensible balancing of work and family.

Women might find it more palatable to make work and career sacrifices for the sake of children if men made similar sacrifices. The postindustrial economy, by undermining the notion of lifetime employment and steady movement up a career ladder for men, may be abetting just such a social change. In the industrial era, technology encouraged the separation of a male-dominated workplace from a female-dominated home; the information age may reintegrate the two.

Religion may serve a purpose in reestablishing norms, even without a sudden return to religious orthodoxy. Religion is frequently not so much the product of dogmatic belief as it is the provider of a convenient language that allows communities to express moral beliefs that they would hold on entirely secular grounds. A young woman I know does not want to have sex until she is married. She tells her suitors that she follows this rule out of religious conviction, not so much because she is a believer but because this is more convincing to them than a utilitarian explanation. In countless ways, modern, educated, skeptical people are drawn to religion because it offers them community, ritual, and support for values they otherwise hold. Religion in this sense is a form of a-rational, spontaneous order rather than a hierarchical alternative to it.

**R**e-moralizing a complex, diverse society such as the United States is not without pitfalls. If a return to broad orthodoxy is unlikely, re-moralization for many will mean dropping out of mainstream society—for example, by home-schooling one's children, withdrawing into an ethnic neighborhood or enclave, or creating one's own limited patch of social order. In his science fiction novel *The Diamond Age*, Neal Stephenson envisions a future world in which a group of computer programmers, realizing the importance of moral values for economic success, create a small community called New Atlantis. There they resurrect Victorian social values, complete with top hats and sexual prudery. The "Vickies" of New Atlantis do well for themselves but have nothing to say to the poor, disorganized communities that surround them. Re-moralization may thus go hand in hand with a sort of miniaturization of community, as it has in American civil society over the past generation. Conversely, if these small communities remain reasonably tolerant and open, they may light the way to a broader moral revival, just as Granges, Boy Scout troops, immigrant ethnic associations, and the other myriad small communities of the late 19th century did.

The reconstruction of values that has started in the 1990s, and any renorming of society that may happen in the future, has and will be the product of political, religious, self-organized, and natural norm building. The state is neither the source of all our troubles nor the instrument by which we can solve them. But its actions can both deplete and restore social capital in ways large and small. We have not become so modern and secularized that we can do without religion. But we are also not so bereft of innate moral resources that we need to wait for a messiah to save us. And nature, which we are constantly trying to evict with a pitchfork, always keeps running back.

## Note

\* A highly salient issue often is not what the government does, but what it refrains from doing, since an overly large and centralized state can rob individuals and communities of initiative and keep them from setting norms for themselves. During the 1960s and '70s, the American court system decriminalized many forms of petty deviance such as panhandling and public drunkenness. By limiting the ability of urban middle-class neighborhoods to set norms for social behavior, the state indirectly encouraged suburban flight and the retreat of the middle class into gated communities. To the extent that these kinds of policies can be limited or reversed, social order will increase.

FRANCIS FUKUYAMA *is Hirst Professor of Public Policy at George Mason University and former deputy director of the policy planning staff at the U.S. State Department. He is the author of* The End of History and the Last Man *(1992) and* Trust: The Social Virtues and the Creation of Prosperity *(1995). His new book, published by the Free Press, is* The Great Disruption: Human Nature and the Reconstitution of Social Order *(1999).*

# UNIT 2
# Problems of the Political Economy

## Unit Selections

4. **Who Rules America?**, G. William Domhoff
5. **Rights, Liberties, and Security: Recalibrating the Balance After September 11**, Stuart Taylor Jr.
6. **How the Little Guy Gets Crunched**, Donald L. Barlett and James B. Steele
7. **Surveying the Global Marketplace**, Murray Weidenbaum
8. **Evaluating Economic Change**, Joseph E. Stiglitz
9. **Shopping and Prosperity: The Consumer Economy**, Robert J. Samuelson
10. **Is Your Job Going Abroad?**, Jyoti Thottam
11. **A Broken Heartland**, Jeff Glasser
12. **The Longest Journey**, The Economist

## Key Points to Consider

- How could the political decision-making process be made more fair and democratic? How can the influence of money on politics be reduced?

- Where would you strike the balance between security and civil rights?

- What are the impacts of globalization that concern you the most?

- Can American capitalism reform itself or are extensive new government regulations necessary?

- What are the strengths and weaknesses of American capitalism? What are some of the major problems that now face American businesses and workers and how can they be solved?

- What are the pros and cons of immigration today? What should our immigration policy be?

 **Links: www.dushkin.com/online/**
These sites are annotated in the World Wide Web pages.

**National Center for Policy Analysis**
*http://www.ncpa.org*
**Penn Library: Sociology**
*http://www.library.upenn.edu/*

Since the political system and the economy interpenetrate each other to a high degree, it is now common to study them together under the label *political economy*. Since the political economy is the most basic aspect of society, it should be studied first. The way it functions affects how problems in other areas can or cannot be addressed. Here we encounter issues of power, control, and influence. It is in this arena that society acts corporately to address the problems that are of concern. It is important, therefore, to ascertain the degree to which the economic elite controls the political system. The answer determines how democratic America is. Next we want to know how effective the American political economy is. Can government agencies be effective? Can government regulations be effective? Can the economy be effective? Can the economy make everyone prosper and not just the owners and top administrators?

The first subsection of unit 2 includes three articles on the political system. In the first, G. William Domhoff examines the extent of the control that the economic elite has over the government. He concludes that its control is so great that it functions as a ruling class. Its control is decisive on policies concerning income, taxes, property rights, regulations, and other economic matters on which the economic elites are not deeply divided. It is in matters that do not concern them as a class that democratic processes work best. The second article reviews the political impact of September 11, 2001. Stuart Taylor, Jr. points out that the extensive U.S. civil rights have to be curtailed to increase the investigative and detention powers of the government—to assist it in protecting us from terrorism. But what is the right balance between civil rights and protection against terrorism? Taylor favors public protection over civil rights because of his dark assessment of our present situation. "Today we face dangers without precedent: a mass movement of militant Islamic terrorists who crave martyrdom, hide in shadows, are fanatically bent on slaughtering as many of us as possible and—if they can—using nuclear truck bombs to obliterate New York or Washington or both. The third article examines the campaign process and shows that the campaign contributions of powerful special interests bias the process. They provide gains for the contributor but losses for the little guy.

The next subsection deals with major problems and issues of the economy. The first article deals with globalization, which is often praised by many economists and politicians for stimulating economic growth and criticized by many on moral grounds for harming the poor and lower classes around the world. Murray Weidenbaum sidesteps this debate and shows that globalization is blurring the distinctions between national and foreign companies and that national and foreign economies are blending together. Honda has more parts made in America than Pontiac and many large American companies make more money abroad than at home. Weidenbaum argues that globalization is good for America. In the next article Joseph Stiglitz does take up the debate and evaluates the costs and benefits of globalization. The results are mixed. Some countries benefit and other countries are hurt. He extends his cost-benefit analysis to other recent

economic changes and concludes that it is not clear whether the U.S. is better off now than a decade or two ago. It turns out that the issue revolves around how people's morals define the situation. In the next article Robert J. Samuelson focuses on the consumption side of the economy. Analysts view America as the first consumerist society and still the society most devoted to consumerism and most given to the "urge to splurge." Samuelson provides plenty of data to support these statements. The last economic issue reviewed in this section is about the migration of American jobs to overseas as described by Jyoti Thottam. Blue-collar jobs have been going abroad for decades. Now white-collar jobs are increasingly migrating overseas. The numbers are small today but rising very rapidly.

The final subsection looks at issues of place. Cities have been the trouble spots of America. They are famous for crime, high unemployment for unskilled workers, poor government, failing schools, racial and ethnic tensions, and troubled neighborhoods. But the rural scene also has problems of its own. In "A Broken Heartland," Jeff Glasser grimly describes the decline of many Midwest rural counties. As manufacturing or other sources of economic activity decline or move, people drift away, making it hard for the remainder to survive economically. Public spirit, generous effort, and commitment cannot reverse the decline. Noble communities are dying. The final article in this unit is about a different migration. It analyzes whether current immigration into the United States is on average a drain on the American economy or a net contribution. It concludes that on average immigrants contribute more than they take from our economy in the long run. In fact immigrants will be needed to help pay for the growing number of elderly.

# Who Rules America?

## G. William Domhoff

### Power and Class in the United States

*Power* and *class* are terms that make Americans a little uneasy, and concepts like *power elite* and *dominant class* immediately put people on guard. The idea that a relatively fixed group of privileged people might shape the economy and government for their own benefit goes against the American grain. Nevertheless,... the owners and top-level managers in large income-producing properties are far and away the dominant power figures in the United States. Their corporations, banks, and agribusinesses come together as a *corporate community* that dominates the federal government in Washington. Their real estate, construction, and land development companies form *growth coalitions* that dominate most local governments. Granted, there is competition within both the corporate community and the local growth coalitions for profits and investment opportunities, and there are sometimes tensions between national corporations and local growth coalitions, but both are cohesive on policy issues affecting their general welfare, and in the face of demands by organized workers, liberals, environmentalists, and neighborhoods.

As a result of their ability to organize and defend their interests, the owners and managers of large income-producing properties have a very great share of all income and wealth in the United States, greater than in any other industrial democracy. Making up at best 1 percent of the total population, by the early 1990s they earned 15.7 percent of the nation's yearly income and owned 37.2 percent of all privately held wealth, including 49.6 percent of all corporate stocks and 62.4 percent of all bonds. Due to their wealth and the lifestyle it makes possible, these owners and managers draw closer as a common social group. They belong to the same exclusive social clubs, frequent the same summer and winter resorts, and send their children to a relative handful of private schools. Members of the corporate community thereby become a *corporate rich* who create a nationwide *social upper class* through their social interaction.... Members of the growth coalitions, on the other hand, are *place entrepreneurs,* people who sell locations and buildings. They come together as local upper classes in their respective cities and sometimes mingle with the corporate rich in educational or resort settings.

The corporate rich and the growth entrepreneurs supplement their small numbers by developing and directing a wide variety of nonprofit organizations, the most important of which are a set of tax-free charitable foundations, think tanks, and policy-discussion groups. These specialized nonprofit groups constitute a *policy-formation network* at the national level. Chambers of commerce and policy groups affiliated with them form similar policy-formation networks at the local level, aided by a few national-level city development organizations that are available for local consulting.

Those corporate owners who have the interest and ability to take part in general governance join with top-level executives in the corporate community and the policy-formation network to form the *power elite,* which is the leadership group for the corporate rich as a whole. The concept of a power elite makes clear that not all members of the upper class are involved in governance; some of them simply enjoy the lifestyle that their great wealth affords them. At the same time, the focus on a leadership group allows for the fact that not all those in the power elite are members of the upper class; many of them are high-level employees in profit and nonprofit organizations controlled by the corporate rich....

The power elite is not united on all issues because it includes both moderate conservatives and ultraconservatives. Although both factions favor minimal reliance on government on all domestic issues, the moderate conservatives sometimes agree to legislation advocated by liberal elements of the society, especially in times of social upheaval like the Great Depression of the 1930s and the Civil Rights Movement of the early 1960s. Except on defense spending, ultraconservatives are characterized by a complete distaste for any kind of government programs under any circumstances—even to the point of opposing government support for corporations on some issues. Moderate conservatives often favor foreign aid, working through the United Nations, and making attempts to win over foreign enemies through patient diplomacy, treaties, and trade agreements. Historically, ultraconservatives have opposed most forms of foreign involvement, although they have become more tolerant of foreign trade agreements over the past thirty or forty years. At the same time, their hostility to the United Nations continues unabated.

Members of the power elite enter into the electoral arena as the leaders within a *corporate-conservative coalition,* where they are aided by a wide variety of patriotic, antitax, and other single-issue organizations. These conservative advocacy organizations are funded in varying degrees by the corporate rich, direct-mail appeals, and middle-class conservatives. This coalition has played a large role in both political parties at the presidential level and usually succeeds in electing a conservative majority to both houses of Congress. Historically, the conservative majority in Congress was made up of most Northern Republicans and most Southern Democrats, but that arrangement has been changing gradually since the 1960s as the conservative Democrats of the South are replaced by even more conservative Southern Republicans. The corporate-conservative coalition also has access to the federal government in Washington through lobbying and the appointment of its members to top positions in the executive branch....

Despite their preponderant power within the federal government and the many useful policies it carries out for them, members of the power elite are constantly critical of government as an alleged enemy of freedom and economic growth. Although their wariness toward government is expressed in terms of a dislike for taxes and government regulations, I believe their underlying concern is that government could change the power relations in the private sphere by aiding average Americans through a number of different avenues: (1) creating government jobs for the unemployed; (2) making health, unemployment, and welfare benefits more generous; (3) helping employees gain greater workplace rights and protections; and (4) helping workers organize unions. All of these initiatives are opposed by members of the power elite because they would increase wages and taxes, but the deepest opposition is toward any government support for unions because unions are a potential organizational base for advocating the whole range of issues opposed by the corporate rich....

## Where Does Democracy Fit In?

...[T]o claim that the corporate rich have enough power to be considered a dominant class does not imply that lower social classes are totally powerless. *Domination* means the power to set the terms under which other groups and classes must operate, not total control. Highly trained professionals with an interest in environmental and consumer issues have been able to couple their technical information and their understanding of the legislative and judicial processes with well-timed publicity, lobbying, and lawsuits to win governmental restrictions on some corporate practices. Wage and salary employees, when they are organized into unions and have the right to strike, have been able to gain pay increases, shorter hours, better working conditions, and social benefits such as health insurance. Even the most powerless of people—the very poor and those discrim-

inated against—sometimes develop the capacity to influence the power structure through sit-ins, demonstrations, social movements, and other forms of social disruption, and there is evidence that such activities do bring about some redress of grievances, at least for a short time.

More generally, the various challengers to the power elite sometimes work together on policy issues as a *liberal-labor coalition* that is based in unions, local environmental organizations, some minority group communities, university and arts communities, liberal churches, and small newspapers and magazines. Despite a decline in membership over the past twenty years, unions are the largest and best-financed part of the coalition, and the largest organized social force in the country (aside from churches). They also cut across racial and ethnic lines more than any other institutionalized sector of American society....

The policy conflicts between the corporate-conservative and liberal-labor coalitions are best described as *class conflicts* because they primarily concern the distribution of profits and wages, the rate and progressivity of taxation, the usefulness of labor unions, and the degree to which business should be regulated by government. The liberal-labor coalition wants corporations to pay higher wages to employees and higher taxes to government. It wants government to regulate a wide range of business practices, including many that are related to the environment, and help employees to organize unions. The corporate-conservative coalition resists all these policy objectives to a greater or lesser degree, claiming they endanger the freedom of individuals and the efficient workings of the economic marketplace. The conflicts these disagreements generate can manifest themselves in many different ways: workplace protests, industrywide boycotts, massive demonstrations in cities, pressure on Congress, and the outcome of elections.

Neither the corporate-conservative nor the liberal-labor coalition includes a very large percentage of the American population, although each has the regular support of about 25–30 percent of the voters. Both coalitions are made up primarily of financial donors, policy experts, political consultants, and party activists....

*Pluralism.* The main alternative theory [I] address.... claims that power is more widely dispersed among groups and classes than a class-dominance theory allows. This general perspective is usually called *pluralism,* meaning there is no one dominant power group. It is the theory most favored by social scientists. In its strongest version, pluralism holds that power is held by the general public through the pressure that public opinion and voting put on elected officials. According to this version, citizens form voluntary groups and pressure groups that shape public opinion, lobby elected officials, and back sympathetic political candidates in the electoral process....

The second version of pluralism sees power as rooted in a wide range of well-organized "interest groups" that are often based in economic interests (e.g., industrialists, bankers, labor unions), but also in other interests as well (e.g., environmental, consumer, and civil rights groups). These interest groups join together in different coalitions depending on the specific issues. Proponents of this version of pluralism sometimes concede that public opinion and voting have only a minimal or indirect influence, but they see business groups as too fragmented and antagonistic to form a cohesive dominant class. They also claim that some business interest groups occasionally join coalitions with liberal or labor groups on specific issues, and that business-dominated coalitions sometimes lose. Furthermore, some proponents of this version of pluralism believe that the Democratic Party is responsive to the wishes of liberal and labor interest groups.

In contrast, I argue that the business interest groups are part of a tightly knit corporate community that is able to develop classwide cohesion on the issues of greatest concern to it: opposition to unions, high taxes, and government regulation. When a business group loses on a specific issue, it is often because other business groups have been opposed; in other words, there are arguments within the corporate community, and these arguments are usually settled within the governmental arena. I also claim that liberal and labor groups are rarely part of coalitions with business groups and that for most of its history the Democratic Party has been dominated by corporate and agribusiness interests in the Southern states, in partnership with the growth coalitions in large urban areas outside the South. Finally, I show that business interests rarely lose on labor and regulatory issues except in times of extreme social disruption like the 1930s and 1960s, when differences of opinion between Northern and Southern corporate leaders made victories for the liberal-labor coalition possible....

## How the Power Elite Dominates Government

This [section] shows how the power elite builds on the ideas developed in the policy-formation process and its success in the electoral arena to dominate the federal government. Lobbyists from corporations, law firms, and trade associations play a key role in shaping government on narrow issues of concern to specific corporations or business sectors, but their importance should not be overestimated because a majority of those elected to Congress are predisposed to agree with them. The corporate community and the policy-formation network supply top-level governmental appointees and new policy directions on major issues.

Once again, as seen in the battles for public opinion and electoral success, the power elite faces opposition from a minority of elected officials and their supporters in labor unions and liberal advocacy groups. These opponents are sometimes successful in blocking ultra-conservative initiatives, but most of the victories for the liberal-labor coalition are the result of support from moderate conservatives....

## Appointees to Government

The first way to test a class-dominance view of the federal government is to study the social and occupational backgrounds of the people who are appointed to manage the major departments of the executive branch, such as state, treasury, defense,

and justice. If pluralists are correct, these appointees should come from a wide range of interest groups. If the state autonomy theorists are correct, they should be disproportionately former elected officials or longtime government employees. If the class-dominance view is correct, they should come disproportionately from the upper class, the corporate community, and the policy-formation network.

There have been numerous studies over the years of major governmental appointees under both Republican and Democratic administrations, usually focusing on the top appointees in the departments that are represented in the president's cabinet. These studies are unanimous in their conclusion that most top appointees in both Republican and Democratic administrations are corporate executives and corporate lawyers—and hence members of the power elite....

## Conclusion

This [section] has demonstrated the power elite's wide-ranging access to government through the interest-group and policy-formation processes, as well as through its ability to influence appointments to major government positions. When coupled with the several different kinds of power discussed in earlier [sections] this access and involvement add up to power elite domination of the federal government.

By *domination,* as stated in the first [section], social scientists mean the ability of a class or group to set the terms under which other classes or groups within a social system must operate. By this definition, domination does not mean control on each and every issue, and it does not rest solely on involvement in government. Influence over government is only the final and most visible aspect of power elite domination, which has its roots in the class structure, the corporate control of the investment function, and the operation of the policy-formation network. If government officials did not have to wait for corporate leaders to decide where and when they will invest, and if government officials were not further limited by the general public's acceptance of policy recommendations from the policy-formation network, then power elite involvement in elections and government would count for a lot less than they do under present conditions.

Domination by the power elite does not negate the reality of continuing conflict over government policies, but few conflicts, it has been shown, involve challenges to the rules that create privileges for the upper class and domination by the power elite. Most of the numerous battles within the interest-group process, for example, are only over specific spoils and favors; they often involve disagreements among competing business interests.

Similarly, conflicts within the policy-making process of government often involve differences between the moderate conservative and ultraconservative segments of the dominant class. At other times they involve issues in which the needs of the corporate community as a whole come into conflict with the needs of specific industries, which is what happens to some extent on tariff policies and also on some environmental legislation. In neither case does the nature of the conflict call into question the domination of government by the power elite.

...Contrary to what pluralists claim, there is not a single case study on any issue of any significance that shows a liberal-labor victory over a united corporate-conservative coalition, which is strong evidence for a class-domination theory on the "Who wins?" power indicator. The classic case studies frequently cited by pluralists have been shown to be gravely deficient as evidence for their views. Most of these studies reveal either conflicts among rival groups within the power elite or situations in which the moderate conservatives have decided for their own reasons to side with the liberal-labor coalition....

More generally, it now can be concluded that all four indicators of power introduced in [the first section] point to the corporate rich and their power elite as the dominant organizational structure in American society. First, the wealth and income distributions are skewed in their favor more than in any other industrialized democracy. They are clearly the most powerful group in American society in terms of "Who benefits?" Second, the appointees to government come overwhelmingly from the corporate community and its associated policy-formation network. Thus, the power elite is clearly the most powerful in terms of "Who sits?"

Third, the power elite wins far more often than it loses on policy issues resolved in the federal government. Thus, it is the most powerful in terms of "Who wins?" Finally, as shown in reputational studies in the 1950s and 1970s,... corporate leaders are the most powerful group in terms of "Who shines?" By the usual rules of evidence in a social science investigation using multiple indicators, the owners and managers of large income-producing properties are the dominant class in the United States.

Still, as noted at the end of the first [section], power structures are not immutable. Societies change and power structures evolve or crumble from time to unpredictable time, especially in the face of challenge. When it is added that the liberal-labor coalition persists in the face of its numerous defeats, and that free speech and free elections are not at risk, there remains the possibility that class domination could be replaced by a greater sharing of power in the future.

# Rights, Liberties, AND Security

## Recalibrating the Balance after September 11

by Stuart Taylor, Jr.

When dangers increase, liberties shrink. That has been our history, especially in wartime. And today we face dangers without precedent: a mass movement of militant Islamic terrorists who crave martyrdom, hide in shadows, are fanatically bent on slaughtering as many of us as possible and—if they can—using nuclear truck bombs to obliterate New York or Washington or both, without leaving a clue as to the source of the attack.

How can we avert catastrophe and hold down the number of lesser mass murders? Our best hope is to prevent al-Qaida from getting nuclear, biological, or chemical weapons and smuggling them into this country. But we need be unlucky only once to fail in that. Ultimately we can hold down our casualties only by finding and locking up (or killing) as many as possible of the hundreds or thousands of possible al-Qaida terrorists whose strategy is to infiltrate our society and avoid attention until they strike.

The urgency of penetrating secret terrorist cells makes it imperative for Congress—and the nation—to undertake a candid, searching, and systematic reassessment of the civil liberties rules that restrict the government's core investigative and detention powers. Robust national debate and deliberate congressional action should replace what has so far been largely ad hoc presidential improvisation. While the USA-PATRIOT Act—no model of careful deliberation—changed many rules for the better (and some for the

worse), it did not touch some others that should be changed.

Carefully crafted new legislation would be good not only for security but also for liberty. Stubborn adherence to the civil liberties status quo would probably damage our most fundamental freedoms far more in the long run than would judicious modifications of rules that are less fundamental. Considered congressional action based on open national debate is more likely to be sensitive to civil liberties and to the Constitution's checks and balances than unilateral expansion of executive power. Courts are more likely to check executive excesses if Congress sets limits for them to enforce. Government agents are more likely to respect civil liberties if freed from rules that create unwarranted obstacles to doing their jobs. And preventing terrorist mass murders is the best way of avoiding a panicky stampede into truly oppressive police statism, in which measures now unthinkable could suddenly become unstoppable.

This is not to advocate truly radical revisions of civil liberties. Nor is it to applaud all the revisions that have already been made, some of which seem unwarranted and even dangerous. But unlike most in-depth commentaries on the liberty-security balance since September 11—which argue (plausibly, on some issues) that we have gone too far in expanding government power—this article contends that in important respects we have not gone far enough. Civil libertarians have underestimated

the need for broader investigative powers and exaggerated the dangers to our fundamental liberties. Judicious expansion of the government's powers to find suspected terrorists would be less dangerous to freedom than either risking possibly preventable attacks or resorting to incarceration without due process of law—as the Bush administration has begun to do. We should worry less about being wiretapped or searched or spied upon or interrogated and more about seeing innocent people put behind bars—or about being blown to bits.

### Recalibrating the Liberty-Security Balance

The courts, Congress, the president, and the public have from the beginning of this nation's history demarcated the scope of protected rights "by a weighing of competing interests... the public-safety interest and the liberty interest," in the words of Judge Richard A. Posner of the U.S. Court of Appeals for the Seventh Circuit. "The safer the nation feels, the more weight judges will be willing to give to the liberty interest."

During the 1960s and 1970s, the weight on the public safety side of the scales seemed relatively modest. The isolated acts of violence by groups like the Weather Underground and Black Panthers—which had largely run their course by the mid-1970s—were a minor threat compared with our enemies today. Suicide bombers were virtually unheard of. By contrast, the threat to civil liberties posed by broad governmental investigative and detention powers and an imperial presidency had been dramatized by Watergate and by disclosures of such ugly abuses of power as FBI Director J. Edgar Hoover's spying on politicians, his wiretapping and harassment of the Rev. Martin Luther King, Jr., and the government's disruption and harassment of antiwar and radical groups.

To curb such abuses, the Supreme Court, Congress, and the Ford and Carter administrations placed tight limits on law enforcement and intelligence agencies. The Court consolidated and in some ways extended the Warren Court's revolutionary restrictions on government powers to search, seize, wiretap, interrogate, and detain suspected criminals (and terrorists). It also barred warrantless wiretaps and searches of domestic radicals. Congress barred warrantless wiretaps and searches of suspected foreign spies and terrorists—a previously untrammeled presidential power—in the 1978 Foreign Intelligence Surveillance Act. And Edward Levi, President Ford's attorney general, clamped down on domestic surveillance by the FBI.

We are stuck in habits of mind that have not yet fully processed how dangerous our world has become or how ill-prepared our legal regime is to meet the new dangers.

As a result, today many of the investigative powers that government could use to penetrate al-Qaida cells—surveillance, informants, searches, seizures, wiretaps, arrests, interrogations, detentions—are tightly restricted by a web of laws, judicial precedents, and administrative rules. Stalked in our homeland by the deadliest terrorists in history, we are armed with investigative powers calibrated largely for dealing with drug dealers, bank robbers, burglars, and ordinary murderers. We are also stuck in habits of mind that have not yet fully processed how dangerous our world has become or how ill-prepared our legal regime is to meet the new dangers.

## Rethinking Government's Powers

Only a handful of the standard law-enforcement investigative techniques have much chance of penetrating and defanging groups like al-Qaida. The four most promising are: infiltrating them through informants and undercover agents; finding them and learning their plans through surveillance, searches, and wiretapping; detaining them before they can launch terrorist attacks; and interrogating those detained. All but the first (infiltration) are now so tightly restricted by Supreme Court precedents (sometimes by mistaken or debatable readings of them), statutes, and administrative rules as to seriously impede terrorism investigators. Careful new legislation could make these powers more flexible and useful while simultaneously setting boundaries to minimize overuse and abuse.

## Searches and Surveillance

The Supreme Court's case law involving the Fourth Amendment's ban on "unreasonable searches and seizures" does not distinguish clearly between a routine search for stolen goods or marijuana and a preventive search for a bomb or a vial of anthrax. To search a dwelling, obtain a wiretap, or do a thorough search of a car or truck, the government must generally have "probable cause"—often (if incorrectly) interpreted in the more-probable-than-not sense—to believe that the proposed search will uncover evidence of crime. These rules make little sense when the purpose of the search is to prevent mass murder.

Federal agents and local police alike need more specific guidance than the Supreme Court can quickly supply. Congress should provide it, in the form of legislation relaxing for terrorism investigations the restrictions on searching, seizing, and wiretapping, including the undue stringency of the burden of proof to obtain a search warrant in a terrorism investigation.

Search and seizure restrictions were the main (if widely unrecognized) cause of the FBI's famous failure to seek a warrant during the weeks before September 11 to search the computer and

other possessions of Zacarias Moussaoui, the alleged "20th hijacker." He had been locked up since August 16, technically for overstaying his visa, based on a tip about his strange behavior at a Minnesota flight school. The FBI had ample reason to suspect that Moussaoui—who has since admitted to being a member of al-Qaida—was a dangerous Islamic militant plotting airline terrorism.

Congressional and journalistic investigations of the Moussaoui episode have focused on the intelligence agencies' failure to put together the Moussaoui evidence with other intelligence reports that should have alerted them that a broad plot to hijack airliners might be afoot. Investigators have virtually ignored the undue stringency of the legal restraints on the government's powers to investigate suspected terrorists. Until these are fixed, they will seriously hobble our intelligence agencies no matter how smart they are.

From the time of FDR until 1978, the government could have searched Moussaoui's possessions without judicial permission, by invoking the president's inherent power to collect intelligence about foreign enemies. But the 1978 Foreign Intelligence Security Act (FISA) bars searches of suspected foreign spies and terrorists unless the attorney general could obtain a warrant from a special national security court (the FISA court). The warrant application has to show not only that the target is a foreign terrorist, but also that he is a member of some international terrorist "group."

Coleen Rowley, a lawyer in the FBI's Minneapolis office, argued passionately in a widely publicized letter last May 21 to FBI Director Robert S. Mueller III that the information about Moussaoui satisfied this FISA requirement. Congressional investigators have said the same. FBI headquarters officials have disagreed, because before September 11 no evidence linked Moussaoui to al-Qaida or any other identifiable terrorist group. Unlike their critics, the FBI headquarters officials were privy to any relevant prior decisions by the FISA court, which cloaks its proceedings and decisions in secrecy. In addition, they were understandably gun-shy about going forward with a legally shaky warrant application in the wake of the FISA court's excoriation of an FBI supervisor in the fall of 2000 for perceived improprieties in his warrant applications. In any event, even if the FBI had done everything right, it was and is at least debatable whether its information about Moussaoui was enough to support a FISA warrant.

More important for future cases, it is clear that FISA—even as amended by the USA-PATRIOT Act—would not authorize a warrant in any case in which the FBI cannot tie a suspected foreign terrorist to one or more confederates, whether because his confederates have escaped detection or cannot be identified or because the suspect is a lone wolf.

Congress could strengthen the hand of FBI terrorism investigators by amending FISA to include the commonsense presumption that any foreign terrorist who comes to the United States is probably acting for (or at least inspired by) some international terrorist group. Another option would be to lower the burden of proof from "probable cause" to "reasonable suspicion." A third option—which could be extended to domestic as well as international terrorism investigations—would be to authorize a warrantless "preventive" search or wiretap of anyone the government has reasonable grounds to suspect of preparing or helping others prepare for a terrorist attack. To minimize any temptation for government agents to use this new power in pursuit of ordinary criminal suspects, Congress could prohibit the use in any prosecution unrelated to terrorism of any evidence obtained by such a preventive search or wiretap.

The Supreme Court seems likely to uphold any such statute as consistent with the ban on "unreasonable searches and seizures." While the Fourth Amendment says that "no warrants shall issue, but upon probable cause," warrants are not required for many types of searches, are issued for administrative searches of commercial property without probable cause in the traditional sense, and arguably should never be required. Even in the absence of a warrant or probable cause, the justices have upheld searches based on "reasonable suspicion" of criminal activities, including brief "stop-and-frisk" encounters on the streets and car

stops. They have also upheld mandatory drug-testing of certain government employees and transportation workers whose work affects the public safety even when there is no particularized suspicion at all. In the latter two cases, the Court suggested that searches designed to prevent harm to the public safety should be easier to justify than searches seeking evidence for criminal cases.

## Exaggerated Fear of Big Brother

Proposals to increase the government's wiretapping powers awaken fears of unleashing Orwellian thought police to spy on, harass, blackmail, and smear political dissenters and others. Libertarians point out that most conversations overheard and e-mails intercepted in the war on terrorism will be innocent and that the tappers and buggers will overhear intimacies and embarrassing disclosures that are none of the government's business.

Such concerns argue for taking care to broaden wiretapping and surveillance powers only as much as seems reasonable to prevent terrorist acts. But broader wiretapping authority is not all bad for civil liberties. It is a more accurate and benign method of penetrating terrorist cells than the main alternative, which is planting and recruiting informers—a dangerous, ugly, and unreliable business in which the government is already free to engage without limit. The narrower the government's surveillance powers, the more it will rely on informants.

Moreover, curbing the government's power to collect information through wiretapping is not the only way to protect against misuse of the information. Numerous other safeguards less damaging to the counterterrorism effort—inspectors general, the Justice Department's Office of Professional Responsibility, congressional investigators, a gaggle of liberal and conservative civil liberties groups, and the news media—have become extremely potent. The FBI has very little incentive to waste time and resources on unwarranted snooping.

To keep the specter of Big Brother in perspective, it's worth recalling that the president had unlimited power to wiretap suspected foreign spies and terrorists un-

til 1978 (when FISA was adopted); if this devastated privacy or liberty, hardly anyone noticed. It's also worth noting that despite the government's already-vast power to comb through computerized records of our banking and commercial transactions and much else that we do in the computer age, the vast majority of the people who have seen their privacy or reputations shredded have not been wronged by rogue officials. They have been wronged by media organizations, which do far greater damage to far more people with far less accountability.

Nineteen years ago, in *The Rise of the Computer State*, David Burnham wrote: "The question looms before us: Can the United States continue to flourish and grow in an age when the physical movements, individual purchases, conversations and meetings of every citizen are constantly under surveillance by private companies and government agencies?" It can. It has. And now that the computer state has risen indeed, the threat of being watched by Big Brother or smeared by the FBI seems a lot smaller than the threat of being blown to bits or poisoned by terrorists.

## The Case for Coercive Interrogation

The same Zacarias Moussaoui whose possessions would have been searched but for FISA's undue stringency also epitomizes another problem: the perverse impact of the rules—or what are widely assumed to be the rules—restricting interrogations of suspected terrorists.

"We were prevented from even attempting to question Moussaoui on the day of the attacks when, in theory, he could have possessed further information about other co-conspirators," Coleen Rowley complained in a little-noticed portion of her May 21 letter to Mueller. The reason was that Moussaoui had requested a lawyer. To the FBI that meant that any further interrogation would violate the Fifth Amendment "*Miranda* rules" laid down by the Supreme Court in 1966 and subsequent cases.

It's not hard to imagine such rules (or such an interpretation) leading to the loss of countless lives. While interrogating Moussaoui on September 11 might not have yielded any useful information, suppose that he had been part of a team planning a second wave of hijackings later in September and that his resistance could have been cracked. Or suppose that the FBI learns tomorrow, from a wiretap, that another al-Qaida team is planning an imminent attack and arrests an occupant of the wiretapped apartment.

We all know the drill. Before asking any questions, FBI agents (and police) must warn the suspect: "You have a right to remain silent." And if the suspect asks for a lawyer, all interrogation must cease until the lawyer arrives (and tells the suspect to keep quiet). This seems impossible to justify when dealing with people suspected of planning mass murder. But it's the law, isn't it?

Actually, it's not the law, though many judges think it is, along with most lawyers, federal agents, police, and cop-show mavens. You do *not* have a right to remain silent. The most persuasive interpretation of the Constitution and the Supreme Court's precedents is that agents and police are free to interrogate any suspect without *Miranda* warnings; to spurn requests for a lawyer; to press hard for answers; and—at least in a terrorism investigation—perhaps even to use hours of interrogation, verbal abuse, isolation, blindfolds, polygraph tests, death-penalty threats, and other forms of psychological coercion short of torture or physical brutality. Maybe even truth serum.

The Fifth Amendment self-incrimination clause says only that no person "shall be compelled in any criminal case to be a witness against himself." The clause prohibits forcing a defendant to testify at his trial and also making him a witness against himself indirectly by using compelled pretrial statements. It does not prohibit compelling a suspect to talk. *Miranda* held only that in determining whether a defendant's statements (and information derived from them) may be used against him at his trial, courts must treat all interrogations of arrested suspects as inherently coercive unless the warnings are given.

Courts typically ignore this distinction because in almost every litigated case the issue is whether a criminal defendant's incriminating statements should be suppressed at his trial; there is

no need to focus on whether the constitutional problem is the conduct of the interrogation, or the use at trial of evidence obtained, or both. And as a matter of verbal shorthand, it's a lot easier to say "the police violated *Miranda*" than to say "the judge would be violating *Miranda* if he or she were to admit the defendant's statements into evidence at his trial."

> You do *not* have a right to remain silent. The Fifth Amendment self-incrimination clause does not prohibit compelling a suspect to talk; it limits what can be used at trial.

But the war against terrorism has suddenly increased the significance of this previously academic question. In terrorism investigations, it will often be more important to get potentially life-saving information from a suspect than to get incriminating statements for use in court.

Fortunately for terrorism investigators, the Supreme Court said in 1990 that "a constitutional violation [of the Fifth Amendment's self-incrimination clause] occurs only at trial." It cited an earlier ruling that the government can obtain court orders compelling reluctant witnesses to talk and can imprison them for contempt of court if they refuse, if it first guarantees them immunity from prosecution on the basis of their statements or any derivative evidence. These decisions support the conclusion that the self-incrimination clause "does not forbid the forcible extraction of information but only the use of information so extracted as evidence in a criminal case," as a federal appeals court ruled in 1992.

Of course, even when the primary reason for questioning a suspected terrorist is prevention, the government could pay a heavy cost for ignoring *Miranda* and using coercive interrogation techniques, because it would sometimes find it difficult or impossible to prosecute extremely dangerous terrorists. But terrorism investigators may be

able to get their evidence and use it too, if the Court—or Congress, which unlike the Court would not have to wait for a proper case to come along—extends a 1984 precedent creating what the justices called a "public safety" exception to *Miranda*. That decision allowed use at trial of a defendant's incriminating answer to a policeman's demand (before any *Miranda* warnings) to know where his gun was hidden.

Those facts are not a perfect parallel for most terrorism investigations, because of the immediate nature of the danger (an accomplice might pick up the gun) and the spontaneity of the officer's question. And as Rowley testified, "In order to give timely advice" about what an agent can legally do, "you've got to run to a computer and pull it up, and I think that many people have kind of forgotten that case, and many courts have actually limited it to its facts."

But when the main purpose of the interrogation is to prevent terrorist attacks, the magnitude of the danger argues for a broader public safety exception, as Rowley implied in her letter.

Congress should neither wait for the justices to clarify the law nor assume that they will reach the right conclusions without prodding. It should make the rules as clear as possible as soon as possible. Officials like Rowley need to know that they are free to interrogate suspected terrorists more aggressively than they suppose. While a law expanding the public safety exception to *Miranda* would be challenged as unconstitutional, it would contradict no existing Supreme Court precedent and—if carefully calibrated to apply only when the immediate purpose is to save lives—would probably be upheld.

Would investigators routinely ignore *Miranda* and engage in coercive interrogation—perhaps extorting false confessions—if told that the legal restraints are far looser than has been supposed? The risk would not be significantly greater than it is now. Police would still need to comply with *Miranda* in almost all cases for fear of jeopardizing any prosecution. While that would not be true in terrorism investigations if the public safety exception were broadened, extreme abuses such as beatings and torture would violate the due process clause of the Fifth Amendment (and of the Fourteenth Amendment as well), which has been construed as barring interrogation techniques that "shock the conscience," and is backed up by administrative penalties and the threat of civil lawsuits.

## Bringing Preventive Detention inside the Law

Of all the erosions of civil liberties that must be considered after September 11, preventive detention—incarcerating people because of their perceived dangerousness even when they are neither convicted nor charged with any crime—would represent the sharpest departure from centuries of Anglo-American jurisprudence and come closest to police statism.

But the case for some kind of preventive detention has never been as strong. Al-Qaida's capacity to inflict catastrophic carnage dwarfs any previous domestic security threat. Its "sleeper" agents are trained to avoid criminal activities that might arouse suspicion. So the careful ones cannot be arrested on criminal charges until it is too late. And their lust for martyrdom renders criminal punishment ineffective as a deterrent.

Without preventive detention, the Bush administration would apparently have no solid legal basis for holding the two U.S. citizens in military brigs in this country as suspected "enemy combatants"—or for holding the more than 500 noncitizens at Guantanamo Bay. Nor would it have had a solid legal basis for detaining any of the 19 September 11 hijackers if it had suspected them of links to al-Qaida before they struck. Nor could it legally have detained Moussaoui—who was suspected of terrorist intent but was implicated in no provable crime or conspiracy—had he had not overstayed his visa.

What should the government do when it is convinced of a suspect's terrorist intent but lacks admissible evidence of any crime? Or when a criminal trial would blow vital intelligence secrets? Or when ambiguous evidence makes it a tossup whether a suspect is harmless or an al-Qaidan? What should it do with suspects like Jose Padilla, who was arrested in Chicago and is now in military detention because he is suspected of (but not

charged with) plotting a radioactive "dirty-bomb" attack on Washington, D.C.? Or with a (hypothetical) Pakistani graduate student in chemistry, otherwise unremarkable, who has downloaded articles about how terrorists might use small planes to start an anthrax epidemic and shown an intense but unexplained interest in crop-dusters?

Only four options exist. Let such suspects go about their business unmonitored until (perhaps) they commit mass murders; assign agents to tail them until (perhaps) they give the agents the slip; bring prosecutions without solid evidence and risk acquittals; and preventive detention. The latter could theoretically include not only incarceration but milder restraints such as house arrest or restriction to certain areas combined with agreement to carry (or to be implanted with) a device enabling the government to track the suspect's movements at all times.

As an alternative to preventive detention, Congress could seek to facilitate prosecutions of suspected "sleepers" by allowing use of now-inadmissible and secret evidence and stretching the already broad concept of criminal conspiracy so far as to make it almost a thought crime. But that would have a harsher effect on innocent terrorism suspects than would preventive detention and could weaken protections for all criminal defendants.

As Alan Dershowitz notes, "[N]o civilized nation confronting serious danger has ever relied exclusively on criminal convictions for past offenses. Every country has introduced, by one means or another, a system of preventive or administrative detention for persons who are thought to be dangerous but who might not be convictable under the conventional criminal law."

The best argument against preventive detention of suspected international terrorists is history's warning that the system will be abused, could expand inexorably—especially in the panic that might follow future attacks—and has such terrifying potential for infecting the entire criminal justice system and undermining our Bill of Rights that we should never start down that road. What is terrorist intent, and how may it be proved? Through a suspect's advocacy of a ter-

rorist group's cause? Association with its members or sympathizers? If preventive detention is okay for people suspected of (but not charged with) terrorist intent, what about people suspected of homicidal intent, or violent proclivities, or dealing drugs?

These are serious concerns. But the dangers of punishing dissident speech, guilt by association, and overuse of preventive detention could be controlled by careful legislation. This would not be the first exception to the general rule against preventive detention. The others have worked fairly well. They include pretrial detention without bail of criminal defendants found to be dangerous, civil commitment of people found dangerous by reason of mental illness, and medical quarantines, a practice that may once again be necessary in the event of bioterrorism. All in all, the danger that a preventive detention regime for suspected terrorists would take us too far down the slippery slope toward police statism is simply not as bad as the danger of letting would-be mass murderers roam the country.

In any event, we already have a preventive detention regime for suspected international terrorists—three regimes, in fact, all created and controlled by the Bush administration without congressional input. First, two U.S. citizens—Jose Padilla, the suspected would-be dirty bomber arrested in Chicago, and Yaser Esam Hamdi, a Louisiana-born Saudi Arabian captured in Afghanistan and taken first to Guantanamo—have been in military brigs in this country for many months without being charged with any crime or allowed to see any lawyer or any judge. The administration claims that it never has to prove anything to anyone. It says that even U.S. citizens arrested in this country—who may have far stronger grounds than battlefield detainees for denying that they are enemy combatants—are entitled to no due process whatever once the government puts that label on them. This argument is virtually unprecedented, wrong as a matter of law, and indefensible as a matter of policy.

Second, Attorney General John Ashcroft rounded up more than 1,100 mostly Muslim noncitizens in the fall of 2001, which involved preventive detention in many cases although they were charged with immigration violations or crimes (mostly minor) or held under the material witness statute. This when-in-doubt-detain approach effectively reversed the presumption of innocence in the hope of disrupting any planned followup attacks. We may never know whether it succeeded in this vital objective. But the legal and moral bases for holding hundreds of apparently harmless detainees, sometimes without access to legal counsel, in conditions of unprecedented secrecy, seemed less and less plausible as weeks and months went by. Worse, the administration treated many (if not most) of the detainees shabbily and some abusively. (By mid-2002, the vast majority had been deported or released.)

Third, the Pentagon has incarcerated hundreds of Arab and other prisoners captured in Afghanistan at Guantanamo, apparently to avoid the jurisdiction of all courts—and has refused to create a fair, credible process for determining which are in fact enemy combatants and which of those are "unlawful."

These three regimes have been implemented with little regard for the law, for the rights of the many (mostly former) detainees who are probably innocent, or for international opinion. It is time for Congress to step in—to authorize a regime of temporary preventive detention for suspected international terrorists, while circumscribing that regime and specifying strong safeguards against abuse.

## Civil Liberties for a New Era

It is senseless to adhere to overly broad restrictions imposed by decades-old civil-liberties rules when confronting the threat of unprecedented carnage at the hands of modern terrorists. In the words of Harvard Law School's Laurence H. Tribe, "The old adage that it is better to free 100 guilty men than to imprison one innocent describes a calculus that our Constitution—which is no suicide pact—does not impose on government when the 100 who are freed belong to terrorist cells that slaughter innocent civilians, and may well have access to chemical, biological, or nuclear weapons." The question is not whether we should increase governmental power to meet such dangers. The question is how much.

---

*Stuart Taylor, Jr., is a senior writer for* National Journal.

# HOW THE LITTLE GUY GETS CRUNCHED

When powerful interests shower Washington with millions in campaign contributions, they often get what they want. But it's ordinary citizens and firms that pay the price—and most of them never see it coming

### By Donald L. Barlett and James B. Steele

IT WAS JUST YOUR TYPICAL PIECE OF congressional dirty work. As 1999 wound down, the House and Senate passed the District of Columbia Appropriations Act. You might think that would be a boring piece of legislation. You would be wrong. For buried in the endless clauses authorizing such spending items as $867 million for education and $5 million to promote the adoption of foster children was Section 6001: Superfund Recycling Equity. It had nothing to do with the District of Columbia, nor appropriations, nor "equity" as it is commonly defined.

Instead Section 6001 was inserted in the appropriations bill by Senator Trent Lott of Mississippi, the Senate majority leader, to take the nation's scrap-metal dealers off the hook for millions of dollars in potential Superfund liabilities at toxic-waste sites. In doing so, Lott had the support of colleagues in both parties.

This early Christmas present to the scrap-metal dealers—who contributed more than $300,000 to political candidates and committees during the 1990s—made them very happy. Others in the recycling chain were not so happy. All of a sudden, they were potentially responsible for millions of dollars in damages the junkmen might otherwise have had to pay.

While clever in its obscurity, Section 6001 is not an especially big giveaway by Capitol Hill standards. Rather, it is typical among the growing litany of examples of how Washington extends favorable treatment to one set of citizens at the expense of another. It's a process that frequently causes serious, sometimes fatal economic harm to unwary individuals and businesses that are in the way.

How do you get that favorable treatment? If you know the right people in Congress and in the White House, you can often get anything you want. And there are two surefire ways to get close to those people:

- Contribute to their political campaigns.
- Spend generously on lobbying.

If you do both of these things, success will maul you like groupies at a rock concert. If you do neither—and this is the case with about 200 million individuals of voting age and several million corporations—those people in Washington will treat you accordingly. In essence, campaign spending in America has divided all of us into two groups: first- and second-class citi-

zens. This is what happens if you are in the latter group:

You pick up a disproportionate share of America's tax bill.

You pay higher prices for a broad range of products, from peanuts to prescription drugs.

You pay taxes that others in a similar situation have been excused from paying.

You are compelled to abide by laws while others are granted immunity from them.

You must pay debts that you incur while others do not.

You are barred from writing off on your tax return some of the money spent on necessities while others deduct the cost of their entertainment.

You must run your business by one set of rules while the government creates another set for your competitors.

In contrast, first-class citizens—the fortunate few who contribute to the right politicians and hire the right lobbyists—enjoy all the benefits of their special status. Among them:

If they make a bad business decision, the government bails them out.

If they want to hire workers at below-market wage rates, the government provides the means to do so.

If they want more time to pay their debts, the government gives them an extension.

If they want immunity from certain laws, the government gives it.

If they want to ignore rules their competitors must comply with, the government gives its approval.

If they want to kill legislation that is intended for the public good, it gets killed.

Call it government for the few at the expense of the many. Looked at another way, almost any time a citizen or a business gets what it wants through campaign contributions and lobbying, someone else pays the price for it. Sometimes it's a few people, sometimes millions. Sometimes it's one business, sometimes many. In short, through a process often obscured from public view, Washington anoints winners and creates losers. Among the recent winners and the wannabes, who collectively have contributed millions of dollars to candidates and their parties and spent generously on lobbying:

• **TAX-FREE PROFITS** Last December, President Clinton signed into law the Ticket to Work and Work Incentives Improvement Act, hailing the legislation as providing "the most significant advancement for people with disabilities since the Americans with Disabilities Act almost a decade ago." He called it "a genuinely American bill."

Indeed so. For it also provided something quite unrelated to disabilities: a lucrative tax break for banks, insurers and financial-service companies. A provision woven into the legislation allowed the foreign subsidiaries of these businesses to extend the income-tax-free status of foreign earnings from the sale of securities, annuities and other financial holdings. Among the big winners: American International Group Inc., an insurance giant, as well as the recently formed Citigroup. Overall, the tax break will cost the U.S. Treasury $1.5 billion in the next two years, just as it did

in the past two years. The amount is equivalent to all the income taxes paid over four years by 300,000 individuals and families that earn between $25,000 and $30,000 a year.

• **THE GREAT S&L GIVEBACK** Owners of savings and loan associations, many of whom are suing the Federal Government for clamping down on them during the S&L crisis in the 1980s, will benefit from a one-paragraph clause that was slipped into legislation that will hold the U.S. government liable for billions of dollars in damage claims because federal regulators nixed certain accounting practices. As is typical with special-interest measures, there were no hearings or estimates of the cost before the clause mysteriously showed up in the Omnibus Consolidated and Emergency Supplemental Appropriations Act of 1998. Among the potential beneficiaries: billionaires Ron Perelman and the Pritzker and Bass families. The losers: all other taxpayers, who will have to pick up the tab.

THE FUTURE PROMISES MUCH MORE OF THE same. In this presidential election year, companies and industries that hope for special treatment in the new decade are busy making their political contributions and their connections. Examples:

• **A LONGER LIFE FOR GOLDEN DRUGS** Major pharmaceutical companies will seek legislation to extend the patent life on their most valuable drugs. In the past, such giveaways were often inserted into unrelated legislation and covered a single drug or two. But this year, watch for heavy lobbying for the granddaddy of all patent extenders. It would protect pharmaceutical company sales of $3 billion annually and add years to the profitable life of at least seven expensive drugs, such as Schering-Plough's Claritin for allergies and Eulexin for prostate cancer, SmithKline Beecham's Relafen for arthritis and G.D. Searle's Daypro for arthritis. The big losers: patients, especially senior citizens on fixed incomes, who must buy expensive prescription drugs instead of cheaper generic versions. Estimates of the added cost run from $1 billion to $11 billion over the next decade.

• **CARS WITH A CHECKERED PAST** The National Automobile Dealers Association is pushing for a federal law regulating the sale of rebuilt wrecked cars. Like a lot of special-interest legislation, the Na-

tional Salvage Motor Vehicle Consumer Protection Act, as it's called, sounds good. No one is likely to argue with its call for federal standards to govern the sale of "nonrepairable and rebuilt vehicles." But look closely. The fine print actually provides minimal standards, gives states the option of ignoring these, applies to only half the cars on the road and keeps secret the history of near totaled vehicles. Sponsored by majority leader Lott, the bill has cleared the Senate Commerce Committee, whose chairman, presidential candidate John McCain, is a co-sponsor. Losers: consumers who unknowingly buy rebuilt wrecks at inflated prices.

---

**Over and over, Washington extends favored treatment to those who pay up—at the expense of those who don't.**

---

BOTH THE RECIPIENTS OF CAMPAIGN CONtributions and the givers insist that no public official is for sale, that no favors are granted in exchange for cash. Few people believe that; U.S. Supreme Court Justice David Souter summed up the prevailing public attitude during arguments in a case that led the Justices last week to uphold the current $1,000 limit on individual campaign contributions. (Donations to parties are still unlimited.) Said Souter:

"I think most people assume—I do, certainly—that someone making an extraordinarily large contribution is going to get some kind of an extraordinary return for it. I think that is a pervasive assumption. And… there is certainly an appearance of, call it an attenuated corruption, if you will, that large contributors are simply going to get better service, whatever that service may be, from a politician than the average contributor, let alone no contributor."

Campaign-finance reform has emerged as an issue during the budding presidential race. Three of the four leading candidates are for it; one is against. McCain has made limiting campaign contributions his defining issue, although the Arizona Republican has accepted contributions from corporations seeking favors from his Commerce committee. Bill Bradley has also spoken out for reform, calling for public financing of elections. Vice President Gore, although involved in the Clinton Administration's 1996 fund-raising scandals, also advocates publicly funded campaigns. Only Texas Governor George W. Bush favors the status quo.

Just how obsessed with raking in cash are the 535 members of Congress?

A veteran Washington lawyer who once served an apprenticeship with a prominent U.S. Senator relates a telling experience. The lawyer, who represents an agency of a state government, visited the home office of a Congressman in that state to discuss a national issue affecting the agency and, indirectly, the Congressman's constituents. After an effusive greeting, the Congressman's next words were brief and to the point:

"How much money can you contribute?"

The stunned lawyer explained that he represented a state agency and that state governments do not contribute to political candidates. As if in response to hearing some programmed words that altered his brain circuitry, the Congressman changed his tone and demeanor instantly. Suddenly, he had more pressing obligations. He would be unable to meet with the lawyer. Rather, he said, an aide would listen to whatever it was the lawyer had to say.

Of course, those who give money to political candidates or their parties don't necessarily get everything they seek. Often the reason is that their opponents are just as well connected. But they do get access—to the Representative or Senator, the White House aide or Executive Branch official—to make their case.

Try it yourself. You won't get it.

Bits and pieces of the story of those who give the money and what they get in return have been told, here and elsewhere. But who gets hurt—the citizens and businesses that do not play the game—remains an untold story.

Over the next nine months, continuing until the presidential election in November, TIME will publish periodic reports examining the anonymous victims of big money and politics.

---

**Editor's note:** In early 2002, Congress considered the Shays-Meehan campaign finance reform bill. It passed in the House, but it was delayed in the Senate.

---

# Surveying the Global Marketplace

*"Half of Xerox's employees work on foreign soil and less than half of Sony's employees are Japanese. More than 50% of IBM's revenues originate overseas; the same is true for Citigroup, ExxonMobil, DuPont, Procter & Gamble, and many other corporate giants."*

By Murray Weidenbaum

A FEW YEARS AGO, an overnight frost occurred in Brazil. What followed may remind us of the lyrics to the old song: "The ankle bone is connected to the leg bone. The leg bone is connected to the knee bone...." The global economy truly is interconnected. An official in Brasilia that morning announced an expected decline in coffee production. The news instantly reached the Chicago Options Exchange. The price of coffee futures began to rise. Traders in other agricultural products responded by bidding up their futures prices. Forecasts of commodity prices jumped around the world, triggering concern over rising inflation—and tightening by central banks. Traders started selling off bonds, driving yields and interest rates higher. Finally, stock prices fell. Just another day in the global economy.

The global marketplace has been around since ancient times. The Greeks and the Phoenicians traded all over their known world and invested abroad heavily. They called the results colonies. What is different today is more advanced technology and more open economies. It took explorer Marco Polo years to travel to China and back. Today, one can fly the round trip in a couple of days. Information can flow in a fraction of a second. In 1980, 3,000,000,000 minutes of international phone calls were made into and out of the U.S. Currently, the annual total is over 30,000,000,000.

Globalization—the increased movement of goods, services, people, information, and ideas across national borders and around the world—no longer is just a buzzword; it has arrived. There is substantial evidence for an increasingly global marketplace. World trade is expanding much faster than world production and crossborder investments are growing at a more rapid rate than trade. People in one country are more likely to be affected by economic actions in other nations in many capacities: as customers, entrepreneurs and investors, managers and workers, taxpayers, and citizens.

An example of the global economy is illustrated in a cartoon of an auto show. The customer asks, "Is this car made in the United States?" The dealer responds, "Which part?" The Pontiac with a General Motors nameplate was sold through the Pontiac dealer network. However, the car was assembled in Korea using components made mainly in Asia. In contrast, Honda models, produced in Marysville, Ohio, have many more U.S.-made parts—but they have a Japanese brand nameplate and are sold through the Honda dealer network. Which is the American car? Another example of globalization is furnished by the shipping label used by a U.S. firm: "Made in one or more of the following countries: Korea, Hong Kong, Malaysia, Singapore, Taiwan, Mauritius, Thailand, Indonesia, Mexico, Philippines." The label continues, "Exact country of origin is unknown."

Yet another way of looking at the international marketplace is to examine the flow of imports and exports, not just in and out of the U.S., but in and out of the European Union and Japan. Almost half of what we call foreign trade actually involves transactions between different parts of the same company—between a domestic firm and its overseas subsidiaries or between a foreign firm and its domestic subsidiaries. In a geopolitical sense, this is foreign commerce. To the company, however, these international flows of goods and services are internal transfers.

Globalization, though, does not mean a unified global economy. Not every product is "tradable" internationally. Cement and haircuts are produced and consumed locally. Even most international trade stays in the region where it originates. Three vast regions are now economically dominant and are likely to remain so far into the 21st century: North America, Europe, and East Asia. In North America, Canada is the U.S.'s number-one customer and Mexico is number two. The integration of other national economies is a continuing process. In the case of the European Union (EU), economic integration seems quite secure. Nevertheless, the EU's most important accomplishment is not economic. Rather, for the first time since the days of the Frankish king Charlemagne, war between France and Germany is unthinkable. The EU is reducing restrictions on business, trade, and labor. People as well as goods, services, and investments increasingly are able to move freely from one EU nation to another. This trend makes European businesses more efficient as they achieve greater economies of scale.

For countries outside the EU, however, serious disadvantages result. The EU has reduced the internal trade barriers, but it has common external trade restrictions against nonmembers. In 1960, before the European Common Market gained momentum, more than 60% of the foreign trade of the 15 member nations was outside the EU. At present, about 70-80% stays in the EU. This is not particularly good news for American companies that are trying to export to Europe.

Nevertheless, the EU is not a static concept. Originally, it comprised six countries: Germany, France, Italy, Belgium, the Netherlands, and Luxembourg. Gradually, it expanded to 15 nations to include the United Kingdom, Ireland, Denmark, Greece, Spain, Portugal, Austria, Sweden, and Finland. Who is missing? Norway, Switzerland, and Eastern Europe. Ten Eastern European countries are scheduled to join May 1, 2004—subject to national vote: Hungary, the Czech Republic, Slovakia, Poland, Slovenia, Latvia, Lithuania, Estonia, Malta, and Cyprus. Poland, Slovenia, and Slovakia already have voted yes. Add up all those gross domestic products and Europe becomes the world's largest marketplace. Yet, there are limits to economic unification. Each member nation retains its own tax system, language, and culture. Different national growth rates place stress on the European Monetary System and not all EU countries have adopted the euro as their currency.

East Asian growth has come in three waves. First was Japan. Although its dominance over Asia is weakening, it still is a world powerhouse. The second wave—albeit slowed by the 1997-98 financial crisis—included Taiwan, South Korea, Hong Kong, Singapore, Thailand, and Malaysia. The new tier of rapidly developing nations—composed of low-cost industrial suppliers—is dominated by China. However, most of East Asia's "foreign" trade is with other Asian countries, as is most of the foreign investment in the region.

## Impact on business

Globalization is producing fundamental changes in business. The consequences for many firms are profound. Half of Xerox's employees work on foreign soil and less than half of Sony's employees are Japanese. More than 50% of IBM's revenues originate overseas; the same is true for Citigroup, Exxon-Mobil, DuPont, Procter & Gamble, and many other corporate giants. Joint ventures no longer are merely a domestic decision. Coming obtains one-half of its profits from foreign joint ventures with Samsung in Korea, Asahi Glass in Japan, and Ciba-Geigy in Switzerland. Strategic alliances increasingly have shifted overseas. They now involve previously competitive companies on different continents.

The automotive and electronics industries provide numerous examples. Boeing and British Aerospace have teamed up for military projects. Volkswagen produces cars with Ford for the Brazilian market, while General Motors and Toyota operate a major joint venture in the U.S. In today's global marketplace, the same companies often are suppliers, customers, and competitors for and to each other. Whatever approach is used, becoming an internationally oriented company usually pays off. Sales by American firms with no foreign activities grow at half the rate of those with international operations. Companies with international business grow faster in every industry and their profits are higher.

While private enterprise increasingly is global, government policy often is extremely parochial. Voters care about their jobs and locality, and politicians readily exploit those concerns. Consider Pres. Bush's steel protection plan. It benefits steel producing industries in a few states—but it hurts steel-using industries far more. However, the effects are spread out over all 50 states. Remember, consumers, who think more about price and quality than country of origin, vote every day—in dollars, yen, euros, and pounds. They buy products and services made anywhere in the world. I recently saw a bumper sticker that proclaimed, "Save whales, boycott Japanese products." It was on a Toyota.

The extremists on both sides of the debate should be ignored. Many proglobalization proponents are true believers, urging government to get out of the way entirely, thus allowing the marketplace to work its magic. At the same time, antiglobalization critics also are dedicated to their beliefs. They want to eliminate the entire capitalistic system. Let us try to develop a high middle ground. The serious views on globalization can be divided into a bright side and a dark side. As to the former, international cooperation increases economic growth and living standards—but not uniformly. It offers consumers greater variety of products and lower prices while raising the number of jobs and wage levels. Improvements in overall working conditions, however, do not occur for every worker.

Globalization keeps business on its toes, although firms unable to compete wind up on their backs. A global economy encourages a greater exchange of information and use of technology. Yet, terrorists take advantage of that. Global economic development provides wealth for environmental cleanup, but there is no guarantee that the resources will be used for that purpose. The record shows it helps developing nations and lifts millions of people out of poverty by creating a new middle class, although not every poor country develops. For example, globalization has bypassed central Africa. International economic development extends business and political freedom, yet corruption can be rampant. Finally, the result of a more global economy is longer life expectancy, improved health standards, and higher literacy rates.

On the dark side, widespread poverty occurs in the midst of global prosperity. The critics assert that is caused by globalization. International income disparity tends to increase, but fewer people remain in poverty. On balance, the rich are getting richer faster than the poor. In terms of geographical differences, eastern and southern Asia are developing much faster than Africa and western Asia.

Critics contend that globalization moves jobs to low-wage factories that abuse workers' rights. True,

many children work in sweatshops, but few of them are employed by the large multinational corporations. Overwhelmingly, the poor working conditions are found in indigenous firms, producing goods for local markets. When we ask why children work, the response is troublesome—because their families are in poverty. In many cases, the entire region has been left behind by globalization, which is why low-income countries welcome foreign investment, a process that exerts an upward force on wages, production, and national income. A basic economic principle is at work here: raise the demand for labor and wages will rise.

The puppet-parading protesters at the World Trade Organization meetings in Seattle and Mexico were wrong. On balance, globalization—warts and all—is working. Those "terrible" multinational enterprises are creating widespread wealth. In recent years, the poorer countries have been growing at a 50% faster rate than the more developed nations. More people have moved out of poverty in the last two decades than ever before. Economic development is far from complete, though. Many societies are not participating in the world economy, especially in Africa. They need the opportunity to reap the benefits achieved by other hitherto undeveloped economies, such as South Korea.

Finally, we should not ignore the challenges that arise in a dynamic global economy, notably, the development of China as an industrial power and the rise of India as a major service center. Their growing economic strength is generating

problems as well as opportunities for business firms, workers, and consumers everywhere. History provides examples of such basic changes. In the 19th century, Europe dominated the world economy. That monopoly ended with the rise of the U.S. as a major industrial power. Europe's share of world commerce declined, but the absolute results were very positive. Total world trade rose. So did living standards in each nation. A similar situation is developing in Asia. Japan emerged as a major economic power in the 20th century—and the pace of economic development accelerated. A comparable result occurred in the 19th century. The American economy in effect was the new boy on the block. In the 21st century, we can expect China and India to fill that role.

Much will depend on the policies they pursue. History demonstrates that six factors are key to global economic success: an economy open to foreign trade and investment; minimal government controls over business, but the effective supervising of financial institutions; an uncorrupt judicial system; economic information that is transparent and readily available; high labor mobility; and easy entry into the marketplace by new businesses. These six points underscore an even more basic notion: Vigorous competition is the key to long-term international economic success.

*Murray Weidenbaum,* Ecology Editor of *USA Today,* is Mallinckrodt Distinguished University Professor, Washington University, St. Louis, Mo.

# Evaluating economic change

Joseph E. Stiglitz

In recent years there have been enormous changes in our technology, our economy, and our society. But has there been progress?

From most economists the first reaction to this question is: Of course there must have been progress! After all, the growth of new technologies expands opportunity sets, what we can do, the amount of output per unit input. We can choose either to have more output, more goods and services, or to work less. However we make the choice, surely we are better off.

But what, then, about the sweeping changes we associate with the phenomenon of globalization? For several years I have been actively involved in debates around the world about the costs and benefits of this phenomenon. As a result of globalization, the countries of the world are more closely integrated. Goods and services move more freely from one country to another. This is the result of the lowering of transportation and communication costs through changes in technology, and of the elimination or reduction of many man-made barriers such as tariffs. The countries that have been most successful at both increasing incomes and reducing poverty—the countries of East Asia—have grown largely because of globalization. They took advantage of global markets for their goods; they recognized that what separates developed from less developed countries is a disparity not only in resources but also in knowledge; they tapped into the pool of global knowledge to close that gap; and most even opened themselves up to the flow of international capital.

But in the countries that have been less successful, globalization is often viewed with suspicion. As I have argued elsewhere, there is a great deal of validity to the complaints of those who are discontent. In much of the world, there has been in recent years a slowing of growth, an increase in poverty, a degradation of the environment, and a deterioration of national cultures and of a sense of cultural identity. Globalization proves that change does not invariably produce progress.

In America we have also seen change, and seemingly at an ever faster pace—but here, too, it is not clear if most Americans are better off. Recent numbers suggest that productivity growth is increasing at the impressive speed of over 4 percent per annum. Americans who work are working longer hours, while more and more Americans are not working: some are openly unemployed; some are so discouraged by the lack of jobs that they have stopped looking (and therefore are no longer included in the unemployment statistics); and some have even applied for, and have begun to receive, disability payments that they would not have sought had there been a job available. Recent decades have seen a concomitant change in values. Forty years ago, the best graduating students sought jobs in which they could work to ensure the civil rights of all Americans, to fight the war on poverty both within the United States and abroad, or to pursue the advance of knowledge; in the 1990s, the best students wanted jobs on Wall Street or with the big law firms. No doubt this shift was brought about in large part by the disproportionate salaries of that decade; these seemed to say, in effect, how much more society valued the work of corporate executives over that of the researchers whose high-tech, biotech, and Internet innovations helped fuel the boom.

Many are concerned, moreover, by the seeming erosion of moral values, exhibited so strikingly in the corporate scandals that rocked the country in the last few years, from Enron to Arthur Andersen, from WorldCom to the New York Stock Exchange—scandals that involved virtually all our major accounting firms, most of our major banks, many of our mutual funds, and a large proportion of our major corporations.

Of course, every society has its rotten apples.[1] But when such apples are so pervasive, one has to look for systemic problems. This seeming erosion of moral values is just one change (the increasing bleakness of the suburban landscape in which so many Americans live is another) that does not seem to indicate progress.

How can this happen? How can improvements in technology, which seemingly increase opportunities, and therefore should also increase societal well-being, so often have adverse consequences, bringing about change that is not progress? In the way that I have posed the question, I have implicitly defined what I mean as progress: an improvement in well-being, or at least in the perception of well-being. But that begs part of the question: whose well-being, and in whose perception?

An economy is a complicated system. The price of steel, for instance, depends on wages, interest rates, and the price of iron ore, coke, and limestone. Each of these in turn depends on the prices of other goods and services, in one vast, complicated, and interrelated system. The marvel of the market is that, somehow, it has solved this system of simultaneous equations—solved it before there were any computers that could even approach a problem of such mathematical complexity.

A disturbance to any one part of the system causes ripples throughout it. While improvements in technology improve opportunity sets and in principle could make everyone better off, in practice they often do not. A change in technology that enables a machine to replace an unskilled worker reduces the demand for unskilled workers, thereby lowering their wages and increasing income inequality. Poverty may also increase. Of course, the gains of those who are better off may be greater than the losses of those who are worse off; if so, the government may tax the new gains and redistribute the proceeds to those who lose, in such a way as to make everyone better off. Making everyone better off is what I mean by progress.

But ideology and interests may preclude that. Conservative philosophers will say that it is the right of each individual to keep the produce of his own efforts. But this is a misleading argument, because the notion of individual labor and effort is not well defined. The tools and technology that an individual uses, for instance, are probably not the result of his own labor. They may well be the result instead of public expenditures, of the kind of government investments in research and technology that created the Internet. And, in the first place, government-financed advances in biomedical research may have resulted in the individual even being alive and able to produce anything at all.

Interests buttress ideologies. While some conservatives may resort to philosophical arguments for why there should not be redistribution, those at the top of the income distribution—who have seen their incomes rise much in recent years—have a self-interest in arguing against progressivity. They are unlikely to approach the question from any of the perspectives from which the issue of social justice has been posed—such as that of Rawls, who asks, in effect, what would be a fair tax system, were we to have to decide such a question from behind a veil of ignorance, before we knew whether we were to end up rich or poor, skilled or unskilled? But, of course, people know how the dice has been rolled, so they argue for what is right from the perspective of their current advantage.

Economists have traditionally been loath to talk about morals. Indeed, traditional economists have tried to argue that individuals pursuing their self-interest necessarily advance the interests of society. This is Adam Smith's fundamental insight, summed up in his famous analogy of the invisible hand: Markets lead individuals, in the pursuit of their own self-interest, as if by an invisible hand, to the pursuit of the general interest. Selfishness is elevated to a moral virtue.

Much of the research of the two centuries following Smith's original insight has been devoted to understanding the sense in which, and the conditions under which, he was right. His insight grew into, among other things, the idea that the pursuit of self-interested profit-maximizing activity leads to an economic efficiency in which no one can be made better off without making someone else better off. (This concept is called Paretian efficiency, after the great Italian economist Vilfredo Pareto.) It took a long time before the assumptions underlying the theory—perfect competition, perfect markets, perfect information, etc.—were fully understood.

By focusing on the consequences of imperfect information, my own research (with Bruce Greenwald of Columbia University) has challenged the Smithian conclusion.[2] We have showed that when information is imperfect, and especially when there are asymmetries of information (that is, different individuals knowing different things), then the economy is essentially never Pareto efficient. Sometimes, in other words, the invisible hand is not visible simply because it is simply not there. Markets do not lead to efficient outcomes, let alone outcomes that comport with social justice. As a result, there is often good reason for government intervention to improve the efficiency of the market.[3]

Just as the Great Depression should have made it evident that the market often does not work as well as its advocates claim, our recent Roaring Nineties should have made it self-evident that the pursuit of self-interest does not necessarily lead to overall economic efficiency. The executives of Enron, Arthur Andersen, WorldCom, etc. were rewarded with stock options, and they did everything they could to pump up the price of their shares and maximize their own returns; and many of them managed to sell while the prices remained pumped up. But those who were not privy to this kind of inside information held on to their shares, and when the stock prices collapsed, their wealth was wiped out. At Enron, workers lost not only their jobs but their pensions. It is hard to see how the pursuit of self-interest—the corporate greed that seemed so unbridled—advanced the general interest.

Advances in the economics of information (especially in that branch that deals with the problem that is, interestingly, referred to as 'moral hazard') help explain the seeming contradiction. Problems of information mean that decisions inevitably have to be delegated. The shareholders have to delegate responsibility for making decisions, but their lack of information makes it virtually impossible for them to ensure that the managers to whom they have entrusted their wealth and the care of the company will act in their best interests. The manager has a *fiduciary responsibility*. He is supposed to act on *behalf of others*. It is his *moral* obligation. But standard economic theory says that he should act in *his own interests*. There is, accordingly, a *conflict of interest*.

In the 1990s, as I have argued elsewhere, such conflicts became rampant. Accounting firms that made more money in providing consulting services than in providing good accounts no longer took as seriously their responsibility to provide accurate accounts. Analysts made more money by touting stocks they knew were far overvalued than by providing accurate information to their unwary customers who depended on them.

Consciences may be salved by the doctrine that the pursuit of self-interest will in fact make everyone better off. But the pursuit of self-interest does not in general lead to economic well-being, and societies in which there are high levels of trust, loyalty, and honesty actually perform better economically than those in which these virtues are absent. Economists are just beginning to discover how non-economic values, or 'good norms,' actually enhance economic performance.

But some economic changes may corrode these values, for several reasons. We have already drawn attention to two: Such changes may produce new conflicts of interest and new contexts in which the pursuit of self-interest clashes with societal well-being. When people see others benefiting from such conditions, a new norm of greed emerges. CEOs defend their rapacious salaries by referring to what others are getting; some even argue that such salaries are required to provide them the appropriate incentives for making 'the hard decisions.'

There is a third way in which economic change may undermine norms, particularly in developing countries. To be maintained, norms have to be enforced; there have to be consequences for violating them. Greater mobility typically weakens social mechanisms for the enforcement of norms. Even when there is not greater mobility, greater societal change and uncertainty results in putting less weight on the future, more weight on the short-run benefits from violating a norm than on the long-run costs. In many Western societies this shift, with its increased emphasis on the individual, has undermined many social norms, along with the sense of community.

**C**hanges in technology, in laws, and in norms may all exacerbate conflicts of interest, and, in doing so, may actually impair the overall efficiency of the economy. The notion that change is necessarily welfare enhancing is typically supported by the same simplistic notions, sometimes referred to as market fundamentalism, that assert that markets necessarily lead to efficient outcomes. If the economy is always efficient, then any change that increases the output per unit input must enhance welfare.

But if the economy is not necessarily efficient, then there can be changes that exacerbate the inefficiencies. For instance, the presence of competition is one of the requirements for market efficiency; if changes in technology result in one firm's dominating the market, competition is reduced, and with it, welfare.

More generally, there is no theorem that ensures the efficiency of the economy in the production of innovations. The theorems concerning the efficiency of the economy are all predicated on the assumption that there is no change in technology, or at least no change in technology that is the result of deliberate actions on the part of firms or individuals. In short, standard economic theory is of little relevance in discussions about the efficiency of markets in the production of knowledge. This itself should come as no surprise, for knowledge can be viewed as a special form of information, and the general result referred to earlier about the lack of efficiency of markets with imperfect information extends to this case.

To take another example, there have been notable innovations in financial markets. These have some important advantages. For instance, they enable risks to be shifted from those less able to bear them to those more able to do so. But some financial innovations have made it more difficult to monitor what a firm and its managers are doing, thus worsening the information problem. Many of these innovations were the result of a corporate desire to minimize tax burdens; companies did not want to bear their fair share, so they devised ways of hiding, legally, income from the tax authorities. One of the big intellectual breakthroughs of the 1990s was the realization that these same techniques could be used to provide distorted information to investors; costs could be hidden, and revenues increased. With *reported* profits thereby enhanced, share prices also increased. But because share prices were based on distorted information, resources were misallocated. And when the bubble to which this misinformation contributed broke, the resulting downturn was greater than it otherwise would have been.

Curiously, stock options, which underlay many of these problems, were at one time viewed as an innovation; they were heralded as providing better incentives for managers to align their interests with those of the shareholders. This argument was more than a little disingenuous: in fact, the typical stock-option package, especially as it was put into practice, did not provide better incentives. While pay went up when stock prices went up, much of the increase in the stock price had nothing to do with the managers' performance; it just reflected overall movements in the market. It would have been better to base pay on relative performance. Moreover, when, as in 2000 and 2001, share prices fell, management pay did not fall. It simply took on other forms. This is another example of an innovation that was not, in any real sense, progress.

Now consider some examples of putative reforms. Especially in the area of economic policy, a combination of misguided economic analysis, ideology, and special interests often results in reforms that are not, in fact, welfare enhancing—even though they are billed as progress. For instance, in Mexico tax revenues as a share of GDP are so small that the public sector cannot perform many of its essential functions; there is underinvestment in science and technology, education, health, and infrastructure. Among the reforms the Fox government has advocated are tax changes that would increase revenues—but whether society as a whole would benefit depends in part on how the tax revenues are increased. Conservatives have long advocated the VAT (a uniform tax, common in Europe, that is levied at each stage of production), but within the Clinton administration it was summarily dismissed because it is not a progressive tax, a matter of particular concern in a country like Mexico with such a high level of inequality. There were alternative proposals for raising taxes—such as on the profits of the oligopolies and monopolies—that would have been more efficient and equitable.

Elsewhere, policies sold as 'reform'—opening up markets to destabilizing speculative short-term capital flows—have exposed countries to huge risks. The East Asian crisis of 1997, the global financial crisis of 1998, the Latin American crises of recent years—all are at least partly attributable to these short-term flows. Just as there is no general theorem assuring us that changes in technology produced by the economy are welfare enhancing, so too there is no general theorem assuring us that the policy reforms that emerge out of the political process—whether at the national or international level—are welfare enhancing. There are, in fact, numerous analyses that suggest quite the opposite.

In economics, the dominant strand of thinking has evolved out of physics. And so economies are analyzed in terms of equilibrium. The consequence of change is to move an economy from one equilibrium to another. Much of what I have said so far can be summarized as follows: Once we recognize that the equilibrium that naturally emerges in an economy may not be efficient, then a change that moves us from one equilibrium to a new equilibrium may not be welfare enhancing.

Another strand of thought in economics owes its origins to a misunderstanding of evolutionary biology. Darwin's notion of natural selection was not teleological, but some of those who extended Darwinian ideas to the social context argued as if it were. If only the fittest survived, then society, reasoned such social Darwinists, must also be increasingly fit. This misunderstanding of Darwin became central to the Spencerian doctrines of social Darwinism. Darwin himself was far more subtle. He realized that one could not define 'fit' in isolation of the elements of the ecological system; that different species occupy different niches; that there are, in effect, multiple equilibria. He realized that the species that survive on one of the Galapa-

gos Islands are not necessarily better or worse in any sense than those that survive on other islands.[4]

Indeed, there is again no theorem that assures us that evolutionary processes are, in any sense, welfare enhancing. They may, in fact, be highly myopic. A species that might do well in the long run may not borrow against its future prosperity, and hence may be edged out in the competition for survival by a species that is better suited for the environment of the moment.[5]

Precisely this kind of myopia was evidenced in the competitive struggles of the 1990s. Those investment banks whose analysts provided distorted information to their customers did best. Repeatedly, the investment banks explained that they had no choice but to engage in such tactics if they were to survive. While the most egregious corporations and accountants—the Enrons, Arthur Andersens, Tycos, and WorldComs—had their comeuppances, others survived, even prospered. And many continue to defend their practices and tactics, opposing fair disclosure of information and accounting procedures that would allow ordinary shareholders to ascertain both the levels of executive compensation and the extent of the dilution of share value through stock options.

The connection between technology and the evolution of society has long been recognized. The innovations that led to the assembly line increased productivity, but almost surely reduced individual autonomy. The movement from an agrarian, rural economy to an urban, industrial economy caused enormous societal change. While this Great Transformation is often viewed as progress, it did not leave everyone better off;[6] so too with the transformations that the New Economy and globalization are bringing about in the societies of the advanced industrial countries and, even more so, of the developing world. While some of these changes open up the possibility of greater individual autonomy, others simultaneously presage a weakening of the sense of community. Even the community of the workplace may be weakened.

Still, I do not believe in either economic or technological determinism. The adverse consequences of some of the changes that I have noted are not inevitable. We have followed one evolutionary path; there are others. Much of the political and social struggle going on today is an attempt to change that path. Those in positions of political power in fact play an important role in shaping the evolution both of society and technology—for instance, by creating within the tax system rewards and incentives for certain business practices.

At the global level, America's status as the sole superpower has allowed it to stymie progress to greater democracy within the international arena. Globalization has entailed the closer economic integration of the countries of the world, and with that closer integration there is a need for more collective action, as global public goods and externalities have taken on increasing importance.

But political globalization has not kept pace with economic globalization. Rather than engaging in democratic processes of decision making, America has repeatedly attempted to impose its views on the rest of the world unilaterally.

In this essay, I have challenged the thesis that improvements in, say, technology necessarily result in an enhancement of well-being. Increases in income can enrich individual lives. They can enable individuals access to more knowledge. They can reduce the corrosive anxieties associated with insecurities about well-being—one of the problems repeatedly noted in surveys attempting to ascertain the dimensions of poverty. In doing all this, improvements in technology can help free individuals from the bonds of materialism.

But unfortunately, all that goes under the name of progress does not truly represent progress, even in the narrow economic sense of the term. I have emphasized that there are innovations, changes in technology, that, while they represent increases in efficiency, lower economic well-being, at least for a significant fraction of the population.

In the end, every change ought to be evaluated in terms of its consequences. Neither economic theory nor historical experience assures us that the changes that get adopted during the natural evolution of society and of the economy necessarily constitute progress. Moreover, neither political theory nor historical experience can assure us that attempts to redirect development will necessarily guarantee better outcomes. A recognition of this is, in my mind, itself progress, and lays the foundation for attempts to structure economic and political processes in ways that make it more likely that the changes we face will in fact constitute meaningful progress.

## Notes

1. See Joseph E. Stiglitz, *The Roaring Nineties: A New History of the World's Most Prosperous Decade* (New York: W. W. Norton, 2003).

2. See, in particular, Bruce Greenwald and Joseph E. Stiglitz, "Externalities in Economies with Imperfect Information and Incomplete Markets," *Quarterly Journal of Economics* 101 (2) (May 1986): 229-264.

3. Of course, it should have been obvious that something was wrong with Smith's conclusions. The Great Depression, during which a very large fraction of the country's resources were left idle, at great social cost, seemed to demonstrate that sometimes the market economy did not work well. Nevertheless, supporters of free markets claimed that the Great Depression was caused not by the failure of markets, but of government.

4. For an elaboration of these ideas, see Karla Hoff and Joseph E. Stiglitz, "Modern Economic Theory and Development," in *Frontiers of Development Economics: The Future in Perspective*, ed. Gerald Meier and Joseph E. Stiglitz (Oxford: Oxford University Press, 2000), 389-459.

5. These ideas are discussed briefly in Joseph E. Stiglitz, *Whither Socialism?* (Cambridge, Mass.: MIT Press, 1994).

6. See Karl Polanyi, *The Great Transformation: The Political and Economic Origins of Our Time* (Boston: Beacon Press, 2001), with a foreword by Joseph E. Stiglitz, vii-xvii.

Joseph E. Stiglitz, a Fellow of the American Academy since 1983, is University Professor at Columbia University. He won the Nobel Prize in economic science in 2001. His recent books include "Globalization and Its Discontents" (2002) and "The Roaring Nineties: A New History of the World's Most Prosperous Decade" (2003). He is indebted to the MacArthur, Mott, and Ford Foundations for financial support.

# SHOPPING AND PROSPERITY

## *THE CONSUMER ECONOMY*

### ROBERT J. SAMUELSON

We shop, therefore we are. This is not exactly the American credo, but it comes close to being the American pastime. Even infants and toddlers quickly absorb the consumer spirit through television and trips to the supermarket ("I want *that*" is a common refrain). As we age, consumption becomes an engine of envy, because in America the idea is that everyone should have everything—which means that hardly anyone ever has enough. The notion that wants and needs have reached a limit of material and environmental absurdity, though preached fervently by some social activists and intellectuals, barely influences ordinary Americans. They continue to flock to shopping malls, automobile dealers, cruise ships, and health clubs. There are always, it seems, new wants and needs to be satisfied.

Although consumerism now defines all wealthy societies, it's still practiced most religiously in its country of origin. Indeed, Americans have rarely so indulged the urge to splurge as in the past decade. Look at the numbers. In 2002, consumer spending accounted for 70 percent of U.S. national income (gross domestic product), which is a modem American record, and a much higher figure than in any other advanced nation. In Japan and France, consumer spending in 2002 was only 55 percent of GDP; in Italy and Spain, it was 60 percent. These rates are typical elsewhere. Even in the United States, consumer spending was only 67 percent of GDP as recently as 1994. Three added percentage points of GDP may seem trivial, but in today's dollars they amount to an extra $325 billion annually.

This spending spree has, in some ways, been a godsend. Without it, the U.S. and world economies would recently have fared much worse. During the 1997-98 Asian financial crisis, the irrepressible buying of American consumers cushioned the shock to countries that, suddenly unable to borrow abroad had to curb their domestic spending. Roughly half of U.S. imports consist of consumer goods, automobiles, and food (oil, other raw materials, and industrial goods make up the balance). By selling Americans more shoes, toys, clothes, and electronic gadgets, Asian countries partially contained higher unemployment. U.S. trade deficits exploded. From 1996 to 2000, the deficit of

the current account (a broad measure of trade) grew from $177 billion to $411 billion.

## *SPENDING FOR AMERICA*

Later, the buying binge sustained the U.S. economy despite an onslaught of bad news that, by all logic, should have been devastating: the popping of the stock market "bubble" of the 1990s; rising unemployment (as dot-com firms went bankrupt and business investment—led by telecommunications spending—declined); 9/11; and a string of corporate scandals (Enron, WorldCom, Tyco). But American consumers barely paused, and responded to falling interest rates by prolonging their binge. Car and light-truck sales of 17.1 million units in 2001 gave the automobile industry its second-best year ever, after 2000. The fourth- and fifty-best years were 2002 (16.8 million units) and 2003 (an estimated 16.6 million units). Strong home sales buoyed appliance, furniture, and carpet production.

To some extent, the consumption boom is old hat. Acquisitiveness is deeply embedded in American culture. Describing the United States in the 1830s, Alexis de Tocqueville marveled over the widespread "taste for physical gratification." Still, the ferocity of the latest consumption outburst poses some interesting questions. Why do Americans spend so much more of their incomes than other peoples? How can we afford to do that? After all, economic theory holds that societies become wealthier only by sacrificing some present consumption to invest in the future. And if we aren't saving enough, can the consumer boom continue?

Let's start with why Americans spend so much. One reason is that our political and cultural traditions differ from those of other nations. We do some things in the private market that other societies do through government. Health care, education, and social welfare are good examples. Most middle-class Americans under 65 pay for their own health care, either directly or through employer-provided health insurance (which reduces their take-home pay). That counts as private consumption. In countries with government-run health care systems, similar medical costs are classified as government spending. The same thing is true of education. Although U.S. public schools involve government spending, college tuition (or tuition for private school or pre-school) counts as personal consumption. Abroad, governments often pay more of total educational costs.

## INVESTMENT

It's also true that the United States saves and invests less than other nations—investment here meaning money that, though initially channeled into stocks, bonds, or bank deposits, ultimately goes into new factories, machinery, computers, and office buildings. Low U.S. saving and investment rates have often inspired alarm about America's future. In 1990, for instance, Japan's national savings rate was 34 percent of GDP, more than double the U.S. rate of 16 percent. By out-investing us, Japan (it was said) would become the world's wealthiest nation. That hasn't happened, in part because what matters is not only how much countries invest but how well they invest it. And Americans generally are better investors than others.

Of course, there's waste. The hundreds of billions of dollars invested in unneeded dot-com and telecom networks in the late 1990s are simply the latest reminder of that. But the American business system corrects its blunders fairly quickly. If projects don't show signs of becoming profitable, they usually don't get more capital. Wall Street's obsession with profits—though sometimes deplored as discouraging long-term investment—compels companies to cut costs and improve productivity. If bankrupt firms (Kmart and United Airlines are recent examples) can't improve efficiency, their assets (stores, planes) are sold to others who hope to do better. American banks, unlike Japanese banks, don't rescue floundering companies. Neither (usually) does the government, unlike governments in Europe. Getting more bang from our investment buck, we can afford to invest less and consume more.

Our privileged position in the world economy reinforces the effect. Since the 1970s, we've run trade deficits that have allowed us to have our cake and eat it too: All those imports permit adequate, investment rates without crimping consumption. We send others dollars; they send us cars, clothes, and computer chips. It's a good deal as long as we're near full employment (when we're not, high imports add to unemployment). The trade gap—now about five percent of GDP—persists in part because the dollar serves as the major global currency. Foreigners—companies and individuals—want dollars so they can conduct trade and make international investments. Some governments hoard dollars because they'd rather export than import. The strong demand for dollars props up the exchange rate, making our imports less expensive and our exports more expensive. Continuous trade deficits result.

All this suggests that the consumer boom could go on forever, because Americans always feel the need to outdo the Joneses—or at least to stay even with them. No level of consumption ever suffices, because the social competition is con-

stant. The surge in prosperity after World War II briefly fostered the illusion that the competition was ebbing because so many things that had once been restricted (homes, cars, televisions) became so widely available. "If everyone could enjoy the good things of life—as defined by mass merchandisers—the meanness of class distinctions would disappear," Vance Packard wrote in his 1959 classic *The Status Seekers*. Instead, he found, Americans had developed new distinctions, including bigger homes and flashier clothes.

Four decades later, little has changed. Americans constantly pursue new markets of success and status. In 2002, the median size of a new home was 20 percent larger than in 1987, even though families had gotten smaller. Luxury car sales have soared. According to the marketing research firm of J. D. Power and Associates, in 1980 luxury brands—mainly Cadillacs and Lincolns, along with some Mercedes—accounted for only 4.5 percent of new-vehicle sales. By 2003, luxury brands—a category that now includes Lexus, Infinity, and Acura, along with Hummers and more BMWs and Mercedes—exceeded 10 percent of sales. Second homes are another way that people separate themselves from the crowd. Perhaps 100,000 to 125,000 such homes are built annually, says economist Gopal Ahluwalia of the national Association of Homebuilders. In the 1990s, comparable figures were between 75,000 and 100,000.

## OVER-CONSUMPTION

To critics, this "consumption treadmill" is self-defeating, as Cornell University economist Robert H. Frank put it in his 1999 book *Luxury Fever: Money and Happiness in an Era of Excess*. People compete to demonstrate their superiority, but most are frustrated because others continually catch up. Meanwhile, over-consumption—homes that are too big, cars that are too glitzy—actually detracts from people's happiness and society's well-being, Frank argued. Striving to maximize their income, workers sacrifice time with family and friends—time that, according to surveys, they would prize highly. And society's "reluctance to take money out of consumers' pockets through taxation means too little is spent to solve collective problems such as poverty and pollution.

As a cure, Frank proposed a progressive consumption tax. People would be taxed only on what they spent, at rates rising to 70 percent above $500,000. Savings (put, for example, into stocks, bonds, and bank deposits) would be exempt. The tax would deter extravagant spending and encourage saving, Frank contended. Total consumption spending would be lower, government spending could be higher, and the competition for status would simply occur at lower levels of foolishness. The "erstwhile Ferrari driver … might turn instead to [a] Porsche," he wrote. Whatever their merits, proposals such as this lack political support. Indeed, they do not differ dramatically—except for high tax rates—from the present income tax, which allows generous deductions for savings, through vehicles such as 401 (k) plans and individual retirement accounts.

Still, America's consumption boom could falter, because it faces three powerful threats: debt, demographics, and the dollar.

## CREDIT AND DEBT

Over six decades, we've gone from being a society uneasy with credit to a society that rejoices in it. In 1946, household debt was 22 percent of personal disposable income. Now, it's roughly 110 percent. Both business and government have promoted more debt. In 1950, Diners Club introduced the modern credit card, which could be used at multiple restaurants and stores. (Some department stores and oil companies were already offering cards restricted to their outlets.). New laws—the Fair Housing Act of 1968, the Equal Credit Opportunity Act of 1974—prohibited discriminatory lending. One result was the invention of credit-scoring formulas that evaluate potential borrowers on their past payment of bill, thereby reducing bias against women, the poor, and minorities. Similarly, the federal government encourages home mortgages through Fannie Mae and Freddie Mac, government-created companies that buy mortgages.

This "democratization of credit" has enabled consumer spending to grow slightly faster than consumer income. People simply borrow more. Economist Thomas Durkin of the Federal Reserve notes the following: In 1951, 20 percent of U.S. households had a mortgage, compared with 44 percent in 2001; in 1970, only 16 percent of households had a bank credit card, compared with 73 percent in 2001. The trouble is that this accumulation of debt can't continue forever. Sooner or later, Americans will decide that they've got as much as they can handle. Or lenders will discover that they've exhausted good and even mediocre credit risks. No one knows when that will happen, but once it occurs, consumer spending may rise only as fast as consumer income—and slower still if borrowers collectively repay debts.

What could hasten the turning point is the baby boom. We're now on the edge of a momentous generational shift. The oldest baby boomers (born in 1946) will be 58 in 2004; the youngest (born in 1964) will be 40. For most Americans, peak spending occurs between the ages of 35 and 54, when household consumption is about 20 percent above average, according to Susan Sterne, an economist with Economic Analysis Associates. Then it gradually declines. People don't buy new sofas or refrigerators. They pay off debts. For 15 years or so, the economy has benefited from baby boomers' feverish buying. It may soon begin to suffer from their decreased spending.

## THE DOLLAR

Finally, there's the dollar. Should foreign demand for U.S. investments wane—or should American politicians, worried about jobs, press other countries to stop accumulating U.S. Treasury securities—the dollar would decline on foreign exchange markets. There would simply be less demand, as foreigners sold dollars for other currencies. Then our imports could become more expensive while our exports could become cheaper. Domestic supplies might tighten. Price pressures on consumer goods—cars, electronics, clothes—could intensify. This might cause Americans to buy a little less. But if they continued buying as before, the long-heralded collision between consumption and investment might materialize. (As this article goes to press, the dollar has dropped from its recent highs. The ultimate effects remain to be seen.)

Little is preordained. Sterne thinks retired baby boomers may defy history and become spendthrifts. "They don't care about leaving anything to their kids," she says. "There's no reluctance to go into debt." Their chosen instrument would be the "reverse mortgage," which unlocks home equity. (Under a reverse mortgage, a homeowner receives a payment from the lender up to some percentage of the home's value; upon the owner's death, the loan is repaid, usually through sale of the house.) Maybe. But maybe the post-World War II consumption boom has reached its peak. If the retreat occurs gently, the consequences, at least on paper should be painless and imperceptible. We'll spend a little less of our incomes and save a little more. We'll import a little less and export a little more. These modest changes shouldn't hurt, but they might. The U.S. and world economies have grown so accustomed to being stimulated by the ravenous appetite of ordinary Americans that you can't help but wonder what will happen if that appetite disappears.

---

*Mr. Samuelson is a columnist for Newsweek. From "Shop 'til We Drop?" by Robert J. Samuelson, Wilson Quarterly, Winter 2004, pages 24–29.*

# Is Your Job Going Abroad?

**As the debate about exporting work from America dominates the presidential campaign, voters need to separate myth from reality. A TIME guide to how we got here—and why short-term pain might translate into long-term gain**

## By Jyoti Thottam

ROSEN SHARMA is sure about one thing. His nine-month-old company, Solidcore, a start-up that makes backup security systems for computers, could not survive without outsourcing. By lowering his development costs, the 18 engineers who work for him in India for as little as one-fourth the salary of their American counterparts allow him to spend money on 13 senior managers, engineers and marketing people in Silicon Valley. If he doesn't outsource, in fact, the venture capitalists who fund start-ups like his won't give him a nickel. Sharma's Indian-American team, tethered by a broadband connection, gets his product in front of customers faster and cheaper. "As a business, you have to stay competitive," he says. "If we don't do it, our competitors will, and they're going to blow us away."

But Sharma's sharp analysis loses its edge when he thinks about what decisions like his will mean someday for his children, a 2-year-old daughter and another on the way. "As a father, my reaction is different than my reaction as a CEO," he says. He believes that companies like his will always need senior people in the U.S., like the systems architects who design new products and the experienced salespeople who close deals. "But if you're graduating from college today, where are the entry-level jobs?" Sharma asks quietly. How do you get to that secure, skilled job when the path that leads you there has disappeared?

That's an issue that economists, politicians and workers are struggling with as the U.S. finds itself in the middle of a structural shift in the economy that no one quite expected. There must be a mix-up here. We ordered a recovery, heavy on the jobs, please. What we're getting is a new kind of homeland insecurity powered by the rise of outsourcing, a bland yet ominous piece of business jargon that seems to imply that every call center, insurance-claims processor, programming department and Wall Street back office is being moved to India, Ireland or some other place thousands of miles away.

To be sure, public anxiety and election-year finger pointing have blurred some important distinctions. To set them straight: most of the jobs that have shifted to places like Mexico and China in the past several decades have been in manufacturing, which is being done with ever increasing sophistication in low-wage countries. Some have also blamed trade-liberalization deals like the North American Free Trade Agreement (NAFTA), which the Labor Department estimates was responsible for the loss of more than 500,000 U.S. jobs between 1994 and 2002. That's a significant number but modest in comparison with the millions of jobs that are created and lost annually in the constant churn of the U.S. economy. Indeed, much of the job loss during the recent U.S. recession was cyclical in nature. But in recent years, one noteworthy segment of the economy began suffering from the permanent change of outsourcing (or offshoring), particularly the movement of service-industry, technology-oriented jobs to overseas locations with lower salaries. What puts teeth into the buzz word is the sense that getting outsourced could happen to almost anyone.

## OUTSOURCING IS ACCELERATING, AND QUICKLY BECOMING THE DEFINING ECONOMIC ISSUE OF THE 2004 CAMPAIGN

Outsourcing, primarily to India, accounts for less than 10% of the 2.3 million jobs lost in the U.S. over the past three years. But the trend is speeding up, and it is quickly becoming the defining economic issue of the election campaign. The Administration learned that the hard way a few weeks ago, when President Bush's chief economic adviser suddenly found himself on the wrong side of the issue. In a casually imperious tone worthy of Martha Stewart, Gregory Mankiw declared, "Outsourcing is just a new way of doing international trade ... More things are tradable than were tradable in the past, and that's a good thing."

Many economists agree with him. Anything that makes an economy more efficient tends to help in the long run. But in reducing job losses to macroeconomic landfill, Mankiw handed Democrats an issue. His words, accompanied by an ominous drumbeat, are now immortalized on the AFL-CIO's website, just before an image of a beaming John Kerry, who won the union's endorsement last week.

Kerry is taking the opportunity to paint Bush as insensitive to middle-class job anxieties. "I don't think the Bush Administration has ever felt this or had a sense of it," Kerry told TIME. "And I think the No. 1 major issue facing the country right now is, How do you really create the jobs that we want?" With a touch of demagoguery, John Edwards has sought to get an edge on Kerry by reviving the unresolved battle over NAFTA, which Kerry voted to approve a decade ago. "When it comes to bad trade agreements, I know what they do to people," Edwards said last week. "I have seen it with my own eyes what happens when the mill shuts down." Kerry points out that at the time Edwards was in no position to put anything on the line over NAFTA: "I don't know where he registered his vote, but it wasn't in the Senate."

Unfortunately for Bush, outsourcing has become Exhibit A in any gripe session about why the economic recovery has been weak in creating new jobs. To some extent, he succeeded in making a plausible connection between his tax cuts and the robust pace of economic growth. "People have more money in their pocket to spend, to save, to invest," he has said. "[Tax relief] is helping the economy recover from tough times." But his efforts to sell a pastiche of programs to help the unemployed have had a tougher time punching through. When it comes to jobs, the numbers fail him. On the basis of previous recoveries, Bush was promising to add 2.6 million new jobs this year. That pledge is starting to look like fantasy, and the Administration has distanced itself from its own predictions.

In crafting an effective response to outsourcing, all the candidates face the same challenge: dealing with a relatively new phenomenon. Their responses are a work in progress, ranging from mild proposals of dubious effectiveness to ideas that sound vaguely like protectionism. In the meantime, voters are left to separate the myths from the realities. Some answers:

## • FROM MEXICO TO INDIA: HOW DID WE GET THERE?

BEFORE ACQUIRING ITS CURRENT incendiary meaning, outsourcing referred to the practice of turning over noncritical parts of a business to a company that specialized in that activity. At first it was ancillary functions like running the cafeteria or cleaning the offices. Then it started moving up to corporate-service functions. Why operate a call center if what you really do, your core competence, is run a credit-card business? So credit-card companies hired independent call centers to take over the phones,

and that industry put down roots in places like Omaha, Neb., which early on had a fiber-optic hub. But as the price of information technology fell and the Internet exploded, capacity began popping up around the world. Which meant that all you needed to run a call center, or a customer-service center, was information technology (IT) and employees who spoke English. Hello, India.

From there, multinational companies began moving up the food chain. Silicon Valley, which for years had been importing highly educated Indian code writers—driving up wage and real estate costs—discovered it was a lot cheaper to export the work to the same highly educated folks over there. So did Wall Street, which employs an army of accountants, analysts and bankers to pore over documents, do deal analysis and maintain databases. The potential list gets longer: medical technicians to read your X rays, accountants to prepare your taxes, even business journalists to interpret companies' financial statements.

Jared Bernstein, senior economist at the Economic Policy Institute, says the frustration of these educated workers is what gives the debate over outsourcing such intensity. "There is no safety net for $80,000-a-year programmers," he says, and perhaps there shouldn't be. Their education is supposed to provide that. Bernstein says that after the factory closings of the 1980s and the emergence of the "knowledge economy," many liberals and conservatives alike had reached a consensus that manufacturing jobs could not be saved but the "lab coat" jobs would always stay here. "Now that vision is under siege," Bernstein says. And the white-collar middle class is feeling the sting of insecurity that manufacturing workers know so well.

## • WHY SO FAST?

IT'S DOUBLY DIFFICULT FOR PEOPLE to watch outsourcing accelerate as the economy improves. The stock market had a strong 2003, and corporate profits in many industries exceeded expectations, so why haven't companies that started outsourcing as a way to cut costs reversed course and brought the jobs back home? That might have happened after other recessions, but this shift is different. To some extent, companies are gun-shy about committing to full-time workers and the attendant fringe benefits. Instead of rushing to expand their computer systems and hiring people to maintain them, firms are keeping their outsourcing companies on speed dial.

That's why outsourcing to India has exploded during the recovery. It jumped 60% in 2003 compared with the year before, according to the research magazine Dataquest, as corporations used some of their profits (not to mention tax breaks) to expand overseas hiring. That translates to 140,000 jobs outsourced to India last year. Vivek Paul, president of Wipro, one of India's leading outsourcing companies (it handles voice and data processing for Delta Airlines, for instance), says its service business grew 50% in the last quarter of 2003. "Companies that are emerging from the slowdown are beginning to invest some of that in India," he says. John McCarthy, author of the Forrester Research landmark study that predicted 3.3 million jobs would move overseas by 2015 (there are about 130 million jobs in the U.S. today), says last year's gains in outsourcing didn't come from new companies jumping on the bandwagon. The most dramatic changes came from outsourcing dabblers who finally made a commitment and now allocate as much as 30% of their IT budgets offshore.

Another factor speeding things up is the development of an industry devoted to making outsourcing happen, thanks to entrepreneurs like Randy Altschuler and Joe Sigelman. Just five years ago, they were junior investment bankers at the Blackstone Group and Goldman Sachs, one in New York City, the other in London. During one particularly long night of proofreading PowerPoint slides and commiserating by phone about finding yet another error courtesy of their companies' in-house document service, they had an epiphany. They would find a better way of doing that work. This was at the height of the dot-com boom, and everyone they knew was trying to figure out a way to Silicon Valley. These two had a different idea. They would go to India, set up a team of accountants and desktop-publishing experts and persuade investment banks in New York to outsource their confidential financial documents and client presentations halfway around the world.

The entrepreneurs' families, not to mention Silicon Valley's venture capitalists, "were looking at us in a crazy way," Sigelman says, especially when he relocated to Madras. Five years later, as it moves into more complex work, OfficeTiger, with $18 million from British investors, plans to increase the number of its employees in India this year from 1,500 to 2,500 and more than triple its U.S. work force, from 30 to 100.

## • GETTING LEFT BEHIND

BILLY JOHNSON OF ALTAMONTE SPRINGS, Fla., is convinced that one of the tens of thousands of new jobs in India should be his. Johnson, 41, was a programmer for WorldCom when the company imploded in the wake of a massive accounting scandal. After six months of looking for a programming job, Johnson realized that the work he knows is exactly what outsourcing companies do best. "I spent $5,000 of my own money to become an Oracle [enterprise software] developer," he says. "Nobody's hiring Oracle developers." For a while, he believed it was just the economy. A lifelong Republican, he believed that when the Bush tax cuts kicked in, the jobs would follow. "I feel like I've been betrayed," he says. "I keep hearing about jobs being created, but I don't see them."

Vince Kosmac of Orlando, Fla., has lived both sad chapters of outsourcing—the blue-collar and white-collar versions. He was a trucker in the 1970s and '80s, delivering steel to plants in Johnstown, Pa. When steel melted down to lower-cost competitors in Brazil and China, he used the G.I. Bill to get a degree in computer science. "The conventional wisdom was, 'Nobody can take your education away from you,'" he says bitterly. "Guess what? They took my education away." For nearly 20 years, he worked as a programmer and saved enough for a comfortable life. But programming jobs went missing two years ago, and he is impatient with anyone who suggests that he "retrain" again. "Here I am, 47 years old. I've got a house. I've got a child with cerebral palsy. I've got two cars. What do I do—push the pause button on my life? I'm not a statistic."

Neither is Scott Kirwin, 37, of Wilmington, Del., who represents another trend. A career contract worker, he is under constant threat from outsourcing. He is the breadwinner in his family—his wife is a medical student, and they have a 7-year-old son—and he has twice lost his job to outsourcing. In both cases, he had been hired as a contractor, and he sees little opportunity for anything else. "It's really nasty if you're looking for stability," he says. During unemployment spells, his family accumulates debt and reverts to making minimum credit-card payments. Vague talk about retraining leaves Kirwin cold. "Tell me which other industry I should train for," he says. A few people have suggested his father's trade, plumbing. His father had an eighth-grade education and expected better options for his college-educated son. "My father would be outraged," Kirwin says.

## • WHOM WILL OUTSOURCING AFFECT NEXT?

AS IT PROVES ITS VALUE TO MORE COMPANIES, outsourcing will change the way they hire. San Francisco-based DFS Group, a division of luxury-goods maker LVMH that runs duty-free shops in airports around the world, reduced operating expenses about 40% after hiring the outsourcing firm Cognizant, based in Teaneck, N.J., to take over most of its 265-person internal IT operations in 2002. Today those jobs are being done in India. DFS reinvested the savings primarily in better software. "They can add more stores efficiently. They know more about the products in the store," says Ron Glickman, DFS's former chief information officer. DFS continues to hire in the U.S. but only for certain key functions. When it needs more IT support at peak times or for special projects, DFS is more likely to turn to Cognizant. "We're going to go to them first," Glickman says.

That shift marks another fundamental change in the way companies do business. "Intrinsic to outsourcing is the replacement of the employer-employee function with a third party," says Gregg Kirchhoefer, a partner with the law firm Kirkland & Ellis in Chicago. Kirchhoefer, who has been handling outsourcing transactions with Indian companies since the early 1990s, sees outsourcing as the logical extension of the evolutionary process that began with contract manufacturing and continued into corporate services. Thanks to technology, more kinds of work can now be spun off into contracts rather than tied to employees. Once a person's labor can be reduced to a contract, it matters little whether the contract is filled in India or Indiana; the only relevant issue is cost. And the speed of technological change accelerates the process. As soon as a job becomes routine enough to describe in a spec sheet, it becomes vulnerable to outsourcing. Jobs like data entry, which are routine by nature, were the first among obvious candidates for outsourcing. But with today's advanced engineering, design and financial-analysis skills can, with time, become well-enough understood to be spelled out in a contract and signed away.

Without a "social contract" binding employer and employee, long-term jobs are an illusion. For the past two years, the Department of Labor has reported that household employment is much stronger than payroll numbers—indicating that workers are getting by with freelance or contract work, whether or not they want to. In January, for example, there were 2.8 million more people employed than in January 2002, according to the household survey, while the payroll numbers were almost flat at 130 million.

## • CAN AMERICANS LEARN TO LOVE OUTSOURCING?

WHILE IT'S SMALL CONSOLATION TO WORKERS who lose their jobs, outsourcing has become an essential element of corporate strategy, even for small companies. "Any start-up today, particularly a software company, that does not have an outsourcing strategy is at a competitive disadvantage," says Robin Vasan, managing director of Mayfield, a venture-capital firm based in Menlo Park, Calif. He felt so strongly about "global sourcing" that Mayfield organized a daylong session for the firms it invests in to meet with outsourcing companies and experts. About 60% of them now have an outsourcing plan. "That's a good start," Vasan says.

The move to outsourcing forces a company to use its resources where they count most, like product development. "For some of them, it's almost a question of survival. If they don't develop new products, they'll fail," says Laxmi Narayanan, CEO of Cognizant. Nielsen Media Research, which rates television shows, used Cognizant's programmers in India to develop NetRatings for websites. That new line of business allowed the company to hire sales staff and analysts in the U.S. to interpret the ratings for clients and eventually to start selling the product in Asia. Lightpointe, an optical-networking firm based in San Diego, will add about 10 people to its 75-person staff this year thanks to an arrangement with a company in China. That firm will handle Lightpointe's sales and marketing there as the company expands into a huge new market. Without the local help, says Lightpointe CEO John Griffin, he could not have entered the

Chinese market and would have been limited to the flailing U.S. telecom market. "Some of my competitors were not as flexible," Griffin says. "They're dead. All those employees are gone."

## • SHOULD OUTSOURCING BE CONTROLLED?

AS THE RHETORIC OF THE CAMPAIGN HEATS up, so does populist sentiment that there ought to be a law against outsourcing—or at least something to slow it down. Various schemes have been proposed, such as tax initiatives or trade barriers to keep jobs from moving. Some companies may feel political pressure. Dell has moved some call-center support for business-enterprise customers back to the U.S., but the company cited poor service as the reason.

Analysts doubt that any protectionist strategy will slow what appears to be a permanent shift in the way the U.S. does business. As Mankiw tried to explain before he was shouted down by fellow Republicans, structural change like this is inevitable and recurring. It's just that the transition can be ugly. New England was a textile center until that business went south, to the Carolinas, then east, to China. Software supplanted steel in Pittsburgh, Pa. In both places, high-tech companies later occupied some of the old mill buildings. Now some of those companies' programmers have gone the way of loom operators and steel rollers.

The Economic Policy Institute's Bernstein says businesses ought to find a way to "share some winnings with those who lose" by creating funds for wage insurance or retraining. Otherwise there is a risk that the benefits of outsourcing will widen the gap between the rich and everyone else. The McKinsey Global Institute, a think tank run by McKinsey & Co., recommends that companies sending jobs abroad contribute about 5% of their savings to an insurance fund that would compensate displaced workers for part of the difference in wages paid by their old and new jobs. During the 1980s and '90s, most workers displaced by trade found only lower-paying jobs. Those displaced by outsourcing are likely to share the same fate.

As demand for Indian workers increases, their prices are rising, just like anything else. Wipro's Paul says that even though his sales soared 50% last fall, his margins are shrinking, mostly because of rising labor costs. "India has been discovered," he says. "It's something that is as susceptible to global competition as anything else." Wipro, in an effort to rein in expenses, is pushing workers to be more productive. But at some point in the future, the trend that is pulling jobs out of America will catch up with India. Somewhere a lower-wage alternative will develop—Central Asia, the Philippines or Thailand—and Indian politicians and workers will be clamoring about foreigners taking their jobs. It's not pretty wherever it happens, but it's just the way the business world turns.

# VIEWPOINTS: HOW TO CREATE JOBS

## GET SERIOUS ABOUT JOB POLICY

"In theory, we all benefit when we can get services more cheaply abroad. But as a practical matter, there are huge costs of dislocated workers and job insecurity. The answer is not to try to stop outsourcing, but we do have to get serious about job retrainings, lifetime learning, extended unemployment insurance and wage insurance. We may also want to not permit companies to deduct the expense of outsourcing from their income taxes, and use the saving to help workers who lost jobs."

—**ROBERT REICH**, former Secretary of Labor,
and professor or economic policy at Brandeis University

## LEARN FROM HISTORY

"In the 1990s, some IT hardware production was offshored, taking jobs abroad. But when the components—disc drives, modems— came back to the U.S., they were 10% to 30% cheaper. That meant that many more U.S. businesses could afford to buy computers and use them to produce more of their products better, leading to more jobs in the U.S., especially for workers with IT skills who knew how to use the computers."

—**CATHERINE MANN**, senior fellow,
Institute for International Economics

## YOU HAVE TO KEEP UP WITH THE FIELD

"If you're the CEO of a large company, your responsibility is to your shareholders and to have your company have the lowest costs possible. So if your competition is sending jobs overseas, you're almost forced to do the same. Otherwise you're not going to be able to sell your product."

—**WAYNE HUIZENGA**, chairman of
Huizenga Holdings on CNNfn last week

## ADAPT OR LOSE OUT

"Our system has had obvious strains…We need to be forward-looking to adapt our educational system to the evolving needs of the economy. Protectionism will do little to create jobs, and if foreigners retaliate, we will surely lose jobs. We need to discover the means to enhance the skills of our work force and to further open markets here and abroad."

—**ALAN GREENSPAN,** chairman of the Federal
Reserve Board, speaking in Omaha, Neb., last week

## WE NEED TO LEARN HOW TO WIN AGAIN

"Let's compete—by training the best workers. Investing in R. and D., erecting the best infrastructure and building an education system that graduates students who rank with the world's best. Our goal is to be competitive with the best so we both win and create jobs."

—**CRAIG BARRETT,**
CEO Intel Corp.

# A broken heartland

*Nothing manifest about the destiny
of small towns on the Great Plains*

BY JEFF GLASSER

Larson, N.D.—The white steeple of St. John's German Lutheran Church lists from the weight of its rusted, half-ton church bell. The 93-year-old church's pews, pulpit, baptismal font, and, most important, congregants have vanished. At the end of a deserted Main Street, tumbleweeds obscure the Great Northern Railroad tracks where trains once routinely carried the world's finest durum wheat to the trade centers of the Midwest.

Across from the tracks stands the Larson Hotel, its paint peeling, its roof about to be patched with discarded aluminum newspaper printing plates. It is now home to a disabled construction worker and his family who moved here from Pennsylvania last fall, saying they could only afford to live in the middle of nowhere. An empty lot away sits the X-treme North Bar and Barely South Restaurant, a last-chance saloon with a rich history of bourbon and burlesque.

Welcome to Larson, population 17, the least populated place in one of the nation's fastest-declining counties. Burke County, N.D., lost 25.3 percent of its population in the past 10 years, falling from 3,002 to 2,242, according to 2000 census figures released this spring. Its neighbor, Divide County, shrank by 21 percent, from 2,899 to 2,283, during the same period. The two counties are littered with dozens of Larsons, Northgates, and Alkabos—virtual ghost towns that grew up as stops for steam trains and died along with the railroads. Larson has withered to the point where none of its residents—including the candidate—bothered to vote in last June's election for alderman. Four miles down state Highway 5 in Columbus, all that remains of the 74-year-old brick high school are 700 commemorative letter openers hand carved by the town elder out of its maple floors and given away as mementos. To the north, dozens of Canadian oil rigs, coal mines, and a SaskPower plant loom in the distance, a mirage of economic activity 25 miles away but a country apart. To the west, past forgotten little houses on the prairie, Crosby's cemeteries have so many fresh mounds that it looks like badgers have dug there all winter. "We're going to have to start importing pallbearers," jokes Crosby farmer Ole Svangstu, 55, noting there were 48 more deaths than births last year.

**Ghost towns.** Up and down the Great Plains, the country's spine, from the Sandhills of western Nebraska to the sea of prairie grass in eastern Montana, small towns are decaying, and in some cases, literally dying out. The remarkable prosperity of the last decade never reached this far. Nearly 60 percent (250 of 429) of the counties on the Great Plains lost population in the 1990s, according to a *U.S. News* analysis of the new census data.

The emptying out of the nation's rural breadbasket was all the more surprising considering the population resurgence in cities and suburbs. The nation as a whole grew at a robust 13 percent. The 10 states of the Plains, too, expanded by 10 percent overall, a 672,554-person increase fueled by the growth of cities like Billings, Mont., and the tremendous urban sprawl that swallowed the countryside adjacent to Denver, Austin, and San Antonio. Some larger rural areas in the Plains also blossomed from their natural beauty as recreation areas, but the picture was bleak in counties with fewer than 15,000 people, where 228 of 334 (nearly 70 percent) of the counties regressed. "It's like the parting of the Red Sea," says Fannie Mae demographer Robert Lang, a census expert. "There are rivers of people flowing out of the [rural] Plains."

The degeneration of a large swath of this country's midsection—covering a

317,320-square-mile area spread over parts of the 10 states—has not seeped into the conscience of urban America. City dwellers might still perceive small towns as refuges from society's maddening stew of gridlock, smog, and crime. Where else can a visitor leave a car unlocked, not to mention *running*, on a quick trip to the post office? Farmers in small towns are considered the ultimate entrepreneurs, "our national icon of autonomy," as Yale Prof. Kathryn Marie Dudley writes in *Debt and Dispossession: Farm Loss in America's Heartland*. But, as Dudley points out, the contemporary ideal collides with a harsh economic reality.

The problem is seemingly intractable. Once thriving mining and railroad commerce are distant memories. The farm economy has been in a state of contraction for at least 30 years. Forty-two percent of Midwestern farmers, the dominant economic group, earn less than $20,000 annually. A lack of Plains industry limits other opportunities for professionals. Jeff Peterson, 53, Burke County's sole lawyer, sighs wistfully as he explains why he's packing it in after 26 years. "There just aren't so many people for clients now," says Peterson. There aren't even enough people to justify having county judges. Nearly everyone else has already left Burke County, bailing out when their farming and oil and gas jobs dried up in the late 1980s and early 1990s. Peterson says he will have to write off his $120,000 office building. So far, he has found no takers for his $135,000 house. "This wasn't a smart place to invest in," he says.

**Manifest destiny.** That wasn't always the case. From Thomas Jefferson's stewardship of the Louisiana Purchase, which included present day Burke and Divide counties, sprang forth the concept of America's "Manifest Destiny" to inhabit all the nation's land. In 1862, Congress passed the Homestead Act, giving immigrants free 160-acre parcels called "quarters." Northwestern North Dakota was one of the final places homesteaded. At the turn of the 20th century, the region filled with Norwegians, Swedes, Danes, Belgians, and a few Germans. The territory was so forbidding that it had no trees, so the pioneers built sod homes on a virgin landscape described by novelist Willa Cather as "nothing but land, not a country at all, but the material out of which countries are made."

Postmaster Columbus Larson's settlement on the western tip of Burke County split in two with the coming of the railroads. Half set up in front of the Great Northern tracks at "Larson," half 4 miles to the northeast next to the Soo Line at "Columbus." By 1930, every quarter in Burke and Divide was inhabited, with what would be a peak 19,634 people on the land. Crowds gathered on Saturday nights at the Opera House in Larson to dance the polka and listen to traditional Norwegian yodeling. Colorful vaudeville troops headlined the marquee at Columbus Theater. Lawrence Welk and his dance band played his signature "champagne music" there. Bootleggers peddled liquor during Prohibition, and the Larson Opera House was the place for bawdy pantomime. Occasionally the townspeople gathered on Main Street and fearfully watched local young men test their strength against that of bears for cash prizes (provided they won).

In the "dirty Thirties," pioneer women placed wet bedsheets over windows to keep out dust. The perseverance and courage of the settlers—lionized by Cather in her novel *O Pioneers!*—were tested as the soil crumbled in a series of crop disasters. Most of Larson's 114 residents left the Dust Bowl behind in search of an easier life. Columbus continued to boom in the immediate post-World War II period, though, with coal miners, power-plant workers, farmers, and a few oil roughnecks keeping the place full. The town peaked with nearly 700 people in the early 1950s. Then the coal mines closed, and the local power plant shut down. Advances in technology improved crop yields, so far fewer people were needed to farm the land. A series of government conservation programs prompted hundreds of local farmers to retire to Arizona, exacerbating the exodus.

In 1972, Columbus still had 20 businesses. Larson was hanging on with six shops, including Witty's grocery store and Ole Johnson's gas station. Virtually all are gone today. Columbus, with just 151 residents, has one cafe and a farm tool supplier, both set to close later this year. The only eatery left in Larson is the X-treme North Bar and Barely South Restaurant, which may also close. "The handwriting's on the wall," says Harold Pasche, 80, a retired farmer from Larson who now lives in Columbus. "Every little town in this whole area here is going down." The collapse of the retail trade in Columbus and Larson mirrors a national decline. From 1977 to 1997, the number of American grocery stores fell by 61.2 percent, men's clothing stores dropped by 46.6 percent, and hardware stores slipped by 40.6 percent, according to the Census of Retail Trade. Ken Stone, an Iowa State University economist specializing in rural development, says small-town Main Streets are going the way of the railroads. "There's very little way to bring [them] back," he says.

On the farm, net income is projected to decline 20 percent in the next two years because of a worldwide depression in commodity prices and higher energy costs. Without government intervention, 10 percent of farmers could not survive one year, says former Agriculture Secretary Dan Glickman. He calls federal farm subsidies "rural support" programs and fears "economic devastation in large parts of rural America" if the government nixes them. Yet President Bush's budget package does not allocate any disaster money for farmers, who in the past three years received $25 billion in extra federal relief. Despite Glickman's warnings, there is little room in today's debate for Jeffersonian programs to resettle the Plains. People simply do not want to deal with harsh winters and broiling summers. "It's still a loser in [Plains] politics to say, 'Let them die,'" says Frank Popper, a Rutgers University land-use expert. "You've got an ongoing aversion, a denial of what's going on. But every year there are fewer farmers and ranchers. Every year they are losing their kids." In 1988, Popper and his wife, Deborah, also a professor, dreamed up a radical alternative for the rural Plains: a vast "Buffalo Commons," in which the federal government would return the territory to its pristine state before white settlement, when the buffalo roamed and the prairie grasses grew undisturbed.

**Where the buffalo roam?** Farmers hated the idea. But in the decade that followed, thousands of miles on the Northern Plains have reverted to "wilderness" areas with buffalo herds and fewer than two people per square mile. "I actually think this is the last American frontier," says Larson's town treasurer, Debra Watterud, 53.

That leaves places like Larson and Columbus with even fewer totems of their town histories. The latter held its final Columbus Day Parade in 1992, when Pasche drove his treasured 1932 Chevrolet Roadster down Main one last time. At the last major civic gathering in 1994, residents scooped up bricks and floor planks from the soon-to-be-demolished high school. Doug Graupe, 56, a Divide County farmer, argues that the remaining residents have an obligation to their ancestors to persevere.

"Economics shouldn't drive every decision," he says. "Do you have to have money to have a good quality of life?... People in small towns are always there to help others, to raise kids. You have a sense of community." Graupe and others in the region are excited about a $2.5 million pasta processing plant that they're planning to build in nearby Crosby, but not everyone's confident it will succeed, given the perilous demographics and the area's previous failed attempts at renewal.

In Larson, Debra Watterud proposed shutting down the town after the no-show election because the level of interest was so low. Her father-in-law, retired farmer Myron Watterud, 76, opposed the idea. If Larson deincorporated, he said, who would pay for the lights (which consumes half the $3,000 town budget)? The town would disappear from maps. No one would ever bring it back, a possibility that's hard to fathom for a man who has spent his life here. His daughter-in-law agreed to table her suggestion, but Myron Watterud says he's "scared" to watch the town in the approaching darkness of its final demise. "If the leaders of this town saw what happened," he says, "they'd turn over in their graves."

A survey of migration

# The longest journey

Freeing migration could enrich humanity even more than freeing trade. But only if the social and political costs are contained, says Frances Cairncross

"WITH two friends I started a journey to Greece, the most horrendous of all journeys. It had all the details of a nightmare: barefoot walking in rough roads, risking death in the dark, police dogs hunting us, drinking water from the rain pools in the road and a rude awakening at gunpoint from the police under a bridge. My parents were terrified and decided that it would be better to pay someone to hide me in the back of a car."

This 16-year-old Albanian high-school drop-out, desperate to leave his impoverished country for the nirvana of clearing tables in an Athens restaurant, might equally well have been a Mexican heading for Texas or an Algerian youngster sneaking into France. He had the misfortune to be born on the wrong side of a line that now divides the world: the line between those whose passports allow them to move and settle reasonably freely across the richer world's borders, and those who can do so only hidden in the back of a truck, and with forged papers.

Tearing down that divide would be one of the fastest ways to boost global economic growth. The gap between labour's rewards in the poor world and the rich, even for something as menial as clearing tables, dwarfs the gap between the prices of traded goods from different parts of the world. The potential gains from liberalising migration therefore dwarf those from removing barriers to world trade. But those gains can be made only at great political cost. Countries rarely welcome strangers into their midst.

Everywhere, international migration has shot up the list of political concerns. The horror of September 11th has toughened America's approach to immigrants, especially students from Muslim countries, and blocked the agreement being negotiated with Mexico. In Europe, the far right has flourished in elections in Austria, Denmark and the Netherlands. In Australia, the plight of the *Tampa* and its human cargo made asylum a top issue last year.

Although many more immigrants arrive legally than hidden in trucks or boats, voters fret that governments have lost control of who enters their country. The result has been a string of measures to try to tighten and enforce immigration rules. But however much governments clamp down, both immigration and immigrants are here to stay. Powerful economic forces are at work. It is impossible to separate the globalisation of trade and capital from the global movement of people. Borders will leak; companies will want to be able to move staff; and liberal democracies will balk at introducing the draconian measures required to make controls truly watertight. If the European Union admits ten new members, it will eventually need to accept not just their goods but their workers too.

Technology also aids migration. The fall in transport costs has made it cheaper to risk a trip, and cheap international telephone calls allow Bulgarians in Spain to tip off their cousins back home that there are fruit-picking jobs available. The United States shares a long border with a developing country; Europe is a bus-ride from the former Soviet block and a boat-ride across the Mediterranean from the world's poorest continent. The rich economies create millions of jobs that the underemployed young in the poor world willingly fill. So demand and supply will constantly conspire to undermine even the most determined restrictions on immigration.

For would-be immigrants, the prize is huge. It may include a life free of danger and an escape from ubiquitous corruption, or the hope of a chance for their children. But mainly it comes in the form of an immense boost to earnings potential. James Smith of Rand, a Californian think-tank, is undertaking a longitudinal survey of recent immigrants to America. Those who get the famous green card, allowing them to work and stay indefinitely, are being asked what they earned before and after. "They gain on average $20,000 a year, or $300,000 over a lifetime in net-present-value terms," he reports. "Not many things you do in your life have such an effect."

Such a prize explains not only why the potential gains from liberalising immigration are so great. It explains, too, why so many people try so hard to come—and why immigration is so difficult to control. The rewards to the successful immigrant are often so large, and the penalties for failure so devastating, that they create a huge temptation to take risks, to bend the rules and to lie. That, inevitably, adds to the hostility felt by many rich-world voters.

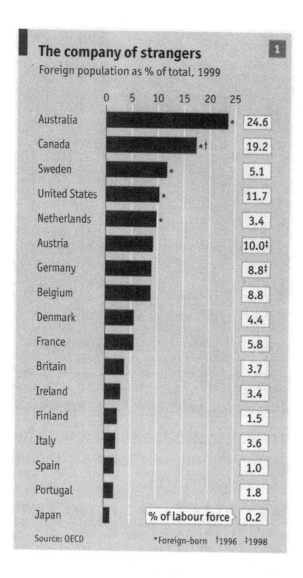

**The company of strangers** ☐ 1
Foreign population as % of total, 1999

|  |  |
|---|---|
| Australia | 24.6 * |
| Canada | 19.2 *† |
| Sweden | 5.1 * |
| United States | 11.7 * |
| Netherlands | 3.4 * |
| Austria | 10.0‡ |
| Germany | 8.8‡ |
| Belgium | 8.8 |
| Denmark | 4.4 |
| France | 5.8 |
| Britain | 3.7 |
| Ireland | 3.4 |
| Finland | 1.5 |
| Italy | 3.6 |
| Spain | 1.0 |
| Portugal | 1.8 |
| Japan | % of labour force ▷ 0.2 |

Source: OECD    *Foreign-born  †1996  ‡1998

This hostility is milder in the four countries—the United States, Canada, Australia and New Zealand—that are built on immigration. On the whole, their people accept that a well-managed flow of eager newcomers adds to economic strength and cultural interest. When your ancestors arrived penniless to better themselves, it is hard to object when others want to follow. In Europe and Japan, immigration is new, or feels new, and societies are older and less receptive to change.

Even so, a growing number of European governments now accept that there is an economic case for immigration. This striking change is apparent even in Germany, which has recently been receiving more foreigners, relative to the size of its population, than has America. Last year, a commission headed by a leading politician, Rita Süssmuth, began its report with the revolutionary words: "Germany needs immigrants." Recent legislation based on the report (and hotly attacked by the opposition) streamlines entry procedures.

But there is a gulf between merely accepting the economic case and delighting in the social transformation that immigrants create. Immigrants bring new customs, new foods, new ideas, new ways of doing things. Does that make towns more interesting or more threatening? They enhance baseball and football teams, give a new twang to popular music and open new businesses. Some immigrants transform drifting institutions, as Mexicans have done with American Catholicism, according to Gregory Rodriguez, a Latino journalist in Los Angeles. And some commit disproportionate numbers of crimes.

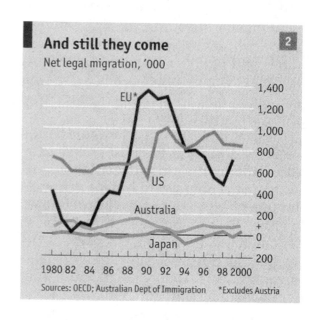

**And still they come** ☐ 2
Net legal migration, '000

Sources: OECD; Australian Dept of Immigration    *Excludes Austria

They also profoundly test a country's sense of itself, forcing people to define what they value. That is especially true in Europe, where many incomers are Muslims. America's 1.2m–1.5m or so Muslim immigrants tend to be better educated and wealthier than Americans in general. Many are Iranians, who fled extremist Islam. By contrast, some of the children of Germany's Turks, Britain's Pakistanis and France's North Africans seem more attracted to fundamentalism than their parents are. If Muslims take their austere religion seriously, is that deplorable or admirable? If Islam constrains women and attacks homosexuality, what are the boundaries to freedom of speech and religion? Even societies that feel at ease with change will find such questions hard.

## No but, maybe yes

Immigration poses two main challenges for the rich world's governments. One is how to manage the inflow of migrants; the other, how to integrate those who are already there.

Whom, for example, to allow in? Already, many governments have realised that the market for top talent is global and competitive. Led by Canada and Australia, they are redesigning migration policies not just to admit, but actively to attract highly skilled immigrants. Germany, for instance, tentatively introduced a green card of its own two years ago for information-technology staff— only to find that a mere 12,000 of the available 20,000 visas were taken up. "Given the higher wages and warmer welcome, no Indians in their right minds would rather go to Germany than to the United States," scoffs Susan Martin, an immigration expert at Georgetown University in Washington, D.C.

Whereas the case for attracting the highly skilled is fast becoming conventional wisdom, a thornier issue is what to do about the unskilled. Because the difference in earnings is greatest in this sector, migration of the unskilled delivers the largest global economic gains. Moreover, wealthy, well-educated, ageing economies create lots of jobs for which their own workers have little appetite.

So immigrants tend to cluster at the upper and lower ends of the skill spectrum. Immigrants either have university degrees or no high-school education. Mr Smith's survey makes the point: among immigrants to America, the proportion with a postgraduate education, at 21%, is almost three times as high as in the native population; equally, the proportion with less than nine years of schooling, at 20%, is more than three times as high as that of the native-born (and probably higher still among illegal Mexican immigrants).

All this means that some immigrants do far better than others. The unskilled are the problem. Research by George Borjas, a Harvard University professor whose parents were unskilled Cuban immigrants, has drawn attention to the fact that the unskilled account for a growing proportion of America's foreign-born. (The same is probably true of Europe's.) Newcomers without high-school education not only drag down the wages of the poorest Americans (some of whom are themselves recent immigrants); their children are also disproportionately likely to fail at school.

These youngsters are there to stay. "The toothpaste is out of the tube," says Mark Krikorian, executive director of the Centre for Immigration Studies, a think-tank in Washington, D.C. And their numbers will grow. Because the rich world's women spurn motherhood, immigrants give birth to many of the rich world's babies. Foreign mothers account for one birth in five in Switzerland and one in eight in Germany and Britain. If these children grow up underprivileged and undereducated, they will create a new underclass that may take many years to emerge from poverty.

For Europe, immigration creates particular problems. Europe needs it even more than the United States because the continent is ageing faster than any other region. Immigration is not a permanent cure (immigrants grow old too), but it will buy time. And migration can "grease the wheels" of Europe's sclerotic labour markets, argues Tito Boeri in a report for the Fondazione Rodolfo Debenedetti, published in July. However, thanks to the generosity of Europe's welfare states, migration is also a sort of tax on immobile labour. And the more immobile Europeans are—the older, the less educated—the more xenophobic they are too.

The barriers need to be dismantled with honesty and care. It is no accident that they began to go up when universal suffrage was introduced. Poor voters know that immigration threatens their living standards. And as long as voters believe that immigration is out of control, they will oppose it. Governments must persuade them that it is being managed in their interests. This survey will suggest some ways in which that might be done.

# Irresistible attraction

## Who moves, and why

LEAVING one's home to settle in a foreign land requires courage or desperation. No wonder only a tiny fraction of humanity does so. Most migration takes place within countries, not between them, part of the great procession of people from country to town and from agriculture to industry. International migrants, defined as people who have lived outside their homeland for a year or more, account for under 3% of the world's population: a total, in 2000, of maybe 150m people, or rather less than the population of Brazil. Many more people—a much faster-growing group—move temporarily: to study, as tourists, or to work abroad under some special scheme for a while. However, the 1990s saw rapid growth in immigration almost everywhere, and because population growth is slowing sharply in many countries, immigrants and their children account for a rising share of it.

Counting migrants is horrendously difficult, even when they are legal. Definitions vary. Some countries keep population registers, others do not. The visitor who comes for a holiday may stay (legally or illegally) to work. Counting those who come is hard, and only Australia and New Zealand rigorously try to count those who leave. So nobody knows whether the rejected asylum-seeker or the illegal who has been told to leave has gone or stayed. But the overall picture is one of continuing growth in the late 1990s.

Between 1989 and 1998, gross flows of immigrants into America and into Europe (from outside the EU) were similar, relative to population size. About 1m people a year enter America legally, and some 500,000 illegally; about 1.2m a year enter the EU legally, and perhaps 500,000 illegally. In both America and Europe, immigration has become the main driver of population growth. In some places, the effects are dramatic. Some 36% of New York's present population is foreign-born, says Andrew Beveridge, a sociology professor at Queens College, New York: "It hasn't been that high since 1910," the last peak.

America at least thinks of itself as an immigrant land. But for many European countries the surge of arrivals in the 1990s came as a shock. For example, the Greek census of 2001 found that, of the 1m rise in the population in the previous decade (to 11m), only 40,000 was due to natural increase. "In a decade, Greece has jumped from being one of the world's least immigrant-dense countries to being nearly as immigrant-dense as the United States," notes Demetrios Papademetriou, co-director of the newly created Migration Policy Institute in Washington, D.C.

Asia too saw a burst of immigration in the 1990s, propelled initially by the region's economic boom. Foreign workers accounted for an increasing share of the growth in the labour supply in the decade to the mid-1990s. Chris Manning, an economist at the Australian National University in Canberra, reckons that foreign workers made up more than half the growth in the less-skilled labour force in Malaysia, perhaps one-third of the growth in Thailand and 15–20% of the growth in Japan, South Korea and Taiwan.

What makes all these people move? In the past, governments often imported them. In Europe, migration in the 1950s and 1960s was by invitation: Britain's West Indians and Asians, for example, first came at the government's request. Britain's worst racial problems descend from the planned import of textile and industrial workers to northern England. Now the market lures the incomers, which may produce less disastrous results.

Three forces often combine to drive people abroad. The most powerful is the hope of economic gain. Alone, though, that may not be enough: a failing state, as in Somalia, Sri Lanka, Iraq or Afghanistan, also creates a powerful incentive to leave. Lastly, a network of friends and relatives lowers the barriers to migrating. Britain has many Bangladeshi immigrants, but most come from the single rural district of Sylhet. Many host countries "specialise" in importing people from particular areas: in Portugal, Brazilians account for 11% of foreigners settling there; in France, Moroccans and Algerians together make up 30% of incomers; and in Canada, the Chinese share of immigrants is more than 15%.

Most very poor countries send few people abroad. Immigration seems to start in earnest with the onset of industrialisation. It costs money to travel, and factory jobs provide it. That pattern emerges strikingly from a study by Frank Pieke of the Oxford University of emigration from China's Fujian province. He describes how internal and overseas migration are intertwined. Typically, a woman from a family will go to work in a factory in a nearby province, supporting a man who then goes abroad and probably needs a few months to find himself a job.

## Incentives to go, incentives to stay

Net immigration flows continue as long as there is a wide gap in income per head between sending and receiving countries. Calculations by the OECD for 1997 looked at GDP per head, adjusted for purchasing power, in the countries that sent immigrants to its rich members, and compared that figure with GDP per head in the host country. In all but one of its seven largest members, average annual income per person in the sending countries was less than half that of the host country.

Migrant flows peter out as incomes in sending and host country converge. Philip Martin, an economist from the University of California at Davis, talks of a "migration hump": emigration first rises in line with GDP per head and then begins to fall. Migration patterns in southern Europe in the 1980s suggested that the turning point at that time came at just under $4,000 a head. In a study for the European Commission last year of the prospective labour-market effect of EU enlargement, Herbert Brücker, of Berlin's German Institute for Economic Research (DIW), estimated that initially 335,000 people from the new members might move west each year, but that after ten years the flow would drop below 150,000 as incomes converged and the most footloose had gone. Net labour migration usually ends long before wages equalise in sending and host countries.

Migrants do not necessarily come to stay. They may want to work or study for a few months or years and then go home. But perversely, they are more likely to remain if they think that it will be hard to get back once they have left. "If you are very strict, you have more illegals," observes Germany's Ms. Süssmuth.

There has always been a return flow of migrants, even when going home meant a perilous return crossing of the Atlantic. According to Dan Griswold of the Cato Institute, a right-of-centre American think-tank, even in the first decade of the 20th century 20–30% of migrants eventually went home. And where migrants are free to come and go, many do not come in the first place. There is no significant net migration between the United States and Puerto Rico, despite free movement of labour. "It's expensive to be underemployed in America," explains Mr. Griswold. But in Europe, with its safety net of welfare benefits, the incentives to have a go are greater.

Tougher border controls deter immigrants from returning home. A book co-authored by Douglas Massey of the University of Pennsylvania, "Beyond Smoke and Mirrors", describes how in the early 1960s the end of a programme to allow Mexicans to work temporarily in America led to a sharp rise in illegal immigrants. Another recent study, published in *Population and Development Re-*

## The going rate

Payments to traffickers for selected migration routes, $ per person

| | | | |
|---|---|---|---|
| Kurdistan-Germany | 3,000 | North Africa-Spain | 2,000-3,500 |
| China-Europe | 10,000-15,000 | Iraq-Europe | 4,100-5,000 |
| China-New York | 35,000 | Middle East-US | 1,000-15,000 |
| Pakistan/India-US | 25,000 | Mexico-Los Angeles | 200-400 |
| Arab states-UAE | 2,000-3,000 | Philippines-Malaysia/Indonesia | 3,500 |

Source: "Migrant Trafficking and Human Smuggling in Europe", International Organisation for Migration, 2000

*view*, also links tighter enforcement to a switch from temporary to permanent migration. Its author, Wayne Cornelius, says the fees paid to *coyotes*, people who smuggle migrants, have risen sharply. He found that, when the median cost of a *coyote*'s services was $237, 50% of male Mexican migrants went home after two years in the United States; but when it had risen to $711, only 38% went back. And, whereas the cost of getting in has risen (as have the numbers who die in the attempt), the cost of staying put has declined, because workplace inspections to catch illegals have almost ceased. The chance of being caught once in the country is a mere 1–2% a year, Mr. Cornelius reckons. So "The current strategy of border enforcement is keeping more unauthorised migrants *in* the US than it is keeping *out*."

Tighter controls in Europe are probably creating similar incentives to stay rather than to commute or return. A complex, bureaucratic system designed to keep many willing workers away from eager employers is bound to breed corruption and distortion. And the way that rich countries select immigrants makes matters worse.

# UNIT 3

# Problems of Poverty and Inequality

## Unit Selections

13. **For Richer: How the Permissive Capitalism of the Boom Destroyed American Equality**, Paul Krugman
14. **The Real Face of Homelessness**, Joel Stein
15. **Requiem for Welfare**, Evelyn Z. Brodkin
16. **What's At Stake**, Barbara Kantrowitz and Pat Wingert
17. **Why We Hate**, Margo Monteith and Jeffrey Winters
18. **Human Rights, Sex Trafficking, and Prostitution**, Alice Leuchtag
19. **The Battle Over Gay Marriage**, John Cloud
20. **Reversing the "Gender Gap"**, Joel Wendland

## Key Points to Consider

- Why has inequality increased over the past two decades? How might increased inequality have adverse impacts on American society?

- How would you compare the lives of people on the bottom with people at the top?

- How would you compare the welfare for the corporations and the wealthy with welfare for the needy?

- How extensive is discrimination between racial and ethnic groups in the U.S. today?

- How different are the worlds of men and women in American society today? Compare the treatment of women in America with their treatment around the world.

- Americans believe in tolerance, but what should be tolerated and what should not be tolerated? Explain.

- What is your view of gay marriage? Should it be legalized?

 **Links: www.dushkin.com/online/**
These sites are annotated in the World Wide Web pages.

**grass-roots.org**
*http://www.grass-roots.org*

**Immigration Facts**
*http://www.immigrationforum.org*

**Joint Center for Poverty Research**
*http://www.jcpr.org*

**SocioSite**
*http://www.pscw.uva.nl/sociosite/TOPICS/Women.html*

**William Davidson Institute**
*http://www.wdi.bus.umich.edu*

**WWW Virtual Library: Demography & Population Studies**
*http://demography.anu.edu.au/VirtualLibrary/*

America is famous as the land of opportunity, and people from around the world have come to these shores in pursuit of the American dream. But how is America living up to this dream today? It is still a place for people to get rich? But it is also a place where people are trapped in poverty. This unit tells a number of stories of Americans dealing with advantages and disadvantages, opportunities and barriers, power and powerlessness.

The first subsection of this unit deals with income inequality and the hardship of the poor. In his article, "For Richer," Paul Krugman describes the great increase in the inequality of income in the past three decades and explains its causes. He also discusses some rather unpleasant political and social consequences of these inequalities. In the next article, Joel Stein shows some of the underside of the inequality that Krugman describes. He discusses homelessness but not the homelessness that is imaged in our minds by the drunk sleeping on the park bench. Increasingly the homeless are mothers with children and Joel Stein tells some of their stories. He also points out why this is the case.

The American welfare system is addressed in the second subsection of unit 4. The truth about all types of welfare is shocking especially because of the grave injustices in the system. The article by Evelyn Brodkin evaluates the results of the 1996 welfare reform. It begins by providing facts that show it was not as bad as it was made out to be. For example, it was not very costly, being less than 5 percent of the costs of social security. Nevertheless, it needed to be reformed and the reform lowered caseloads 57 percent through 2001, and the majority of leavers are working (much of this change was due to the good economy). On the negative side, the jobs generally are bad jobs that pay little and are unsteady. Finally, on several counts the new welfare system is more punitive.

The next subsection examines racial and ethnic inequality and conflict issues. The most poignant inequality in America is the gap between blacks and whites. Recently there has been considerable good news that the gap has been closing and many indicators that quality of life has improved for blacks. In the next article Barbara Kantrowitz and Pat Wingert clarify where affirmative action is today. It had a glorious history in the past when it pushed the nation toward fairness. However, what is its proper role today? Is it needed now and is it unfair now? This article clarifies what affirmative action is, where it stands legally today, and how universities should handle the issue. In the next article in this section, the authors demonstrate the prevalence of prejudice and hatred in America and how quickly hatred toward a group can evolve. Since September 11, 2001, hatred toward Muslims has erupted despite calls for tolerance from President George W. Bush

and other public leaders. One explanation of hatred and prejudice against entire groups is social identity theory. People have a powerful drive to classify people into groups, identify with one group, and develop negative views of some of the out groups. Fortunately, "people who are concerned about their prejudices have the power to correct them."

The next subsection focuses on gender inequality and issues. In its first article, Alice Leuchtag describes one of the great evils that is haunting the world today which is sex slavery. The sex trade system grows out of poverty and profits. Extreme poverty forces parents to sell their girls into servitude often not knowing that they will become sex slaves and considerable profits drive the system. The exploitation involved is horrendous so this is a worldwide human rights issue. In the next article, John Cloud provides an overview of the current hot topic of gay marriage. The Massachusetts Supreme Court ruled that it is unconstitutional to deny gay couples marriage licenses. This has spurred President Bush to sponsor a constitutional amendment defining marriage as limited to heterosexual couples and has spurred eleven states to pass resolutions to this effect. Cloud presents the history of this issue and various views on it. In the last article of the unit, Joel Wendland reacts to the spate of articles in the media about the new gender gap favoring females. She acknowledges that girls do better than boys in school and have higher graduation rates but she shows that this has not yet closed the true gender gap that still considerably disadvantages women. For example, according to the AFL-CIO the average woman will lose $523,000 in lifetime earnings because of unequal pay.

# For Richer

How the permissive capitalism of the boom destroyed American equality.

**By Paul Krugman**

## I. The Disappearing Middle

When I was a teenager growing up on Long Island, one of my favorite excursions was a trip to see the great Gilded Age mansions of the North Shore. Those mansions weren't just pieces of architectural history. They were monuments to a bygone social era, one in which the rich could afford the armies of servants needed to maintain a house the size of a European palace. By the time I saw them, of course, that era was long past. Almost none of the Long Island mansions were still private residences. Those that hadn't been turned into museums were occupied by nursing homes or private schools.

For the America I grew up in—the America of the 1950's and 1960's—was a middle-class society, both in reality and in feel. The vast income and wealth inequalities of the Gilded Age had disappeared. Yes, of course, there was the poverty of the underclass—but the conventional wisdom of the time viewed that as a social rather than an economic problem. Yes, of course, some wealthy businessmen and heirs to large fortunes lived far better than the average American. But they weren't rich the way the robber barons who built the mansions had been rich, and there weren't that many of them. The days when plutocrats were a force to be reckoned with in American society, economically or politically, seemed long past.

Daily experience confirmed the sense of a fairly equal society. The economic disparities you were conscious of were quite muted. Highly educated professionals—middle managers, college teachers, even lawyers—often claimed that they earned less than unionized blue-collar workers. Those considered very well off lived in split-levels, had a housecleaner come in once a week and took summer vacations in Europe. But they sent their kids to public schools and drove themselves to work, just like everyone else.

But that was long ago. The middle-class America of my youth was another country.

We are now living in a new Gilded Age, as extravagant as the original. Mansions have made a comeback. Back in 1999 this magazine profiled Thierry Despont, the "eminence of excess," an architect who specializes in designing houses for the super-rich. His creations typically range from 20,000 to 60,000 square feet; houses at the upper end of his range are not much smaller than the White House. Needless to say, the armies of servants are back, too. So are the yachts. Still, even J.P. Morgan didn't have a Gulfstream.

As the story about Despont suggests, it's not fair to say that the fact of widening inequality in America has gone unreported. Yet glimpses of the lifestyles of the rich and tasteless don't necessarily add up in people's minds to a clear picture of the tectonic shifts that have taken place in the distribution of income and wealth in this country. My sense is that few people are aware of just how much the gap between the very rich and the rest has widened over a relatively short period of time. In fact, even bringing up the subject exposes you to charges of "class warfare," the "politics of envy" and so on. And very few people indeed are willing to talk about the profound effects—economic, social and political—of that widening gap.

Yet you can't understand what's happening in America today without understanding the extent, causes and consequences of the vast increase in inequality that has taken place over the last three decades, and in particular the astonishing concentration of income and wealth in just a few hands. To make sense of the current wave of corporate scandal, you need to understand how the man in the gray flannel suit has been replaced by the imperial C.E.O. The concentration of income at the top is a key reason that the United States, for all its economic achievements, has more poverty and lower life expectancy than any other major advanced nation. Above all, the growing concentration of wealth has reshaped our political system: it is at the root both of a general shift to the right and of an extreme polarization of our politics.

But before we get to all that, let's take a look at who gets what.

## II. The New Gilded Age

The Securities and Exchange Commission hath no fury like a woman scorned. The messy divorce proceedings of Jack Welch, the legendary former C.E.O. of General Electric, have had one unintended benefit: they have given us a peek at the perks of the corporate elite, which are normally hidden from public view. For it turns out that when Welch retired, he was granted for life the use of a Manhattan apartment (including food, wine and laundry), access to corporate jets and a variety of other in-kind benefits, worth at least $2 million a year. The perks were revealing: they illustrated the extent to which corporate leaders now expect to be treated like *ancien régime* royalty. In monetary terms, however, the perks must have meant little to Welch. In 2000, his last full year running G.E., Welch was paid $123 million, mainly in stock and stock options.

> The 13,000 richest families in America now have almost as much income as the 20 million poorest. And those 13,000 families have incomes 300 times that of average families.

Is it news that C.E.O.'s of large American corporations make a lot of money? Actually, it is. They were always well paid compared with the average worker, but there is simply no comparison between what executives got a generation ago and what they are paid today.

Over the past 30 years most people have seen only modest salary increases: the average annual salary in America, expressed in 1998 dollars (that is, adjusted for inflation), rose from $32,522 in 1970 to $35,864 in 1999. That's about a 10 percent increase over 29 years—progress, but not much. Over the same period, however, according to Fortune magazine, the average real annual compensation of the top 100 C.E.O.'s went from $1.3 million—39 times the pay of an average worker—to $37.5 million, more than 1,000 times the pay of ordinary workers.

The explosion in C.E.O. pay over the past 30 years is an amazing story in its own right, and an important one. But it is only the most spectacular indicator of a broader story, the reconcentration of income and wealth in the U.S. The rich have always been different from you and me, but they are far more different now than they were not long ago—indeed, they are as different now as they were when F. Scott Fitzgerald made his famous remark.

That's a controversial statement, though it shouldn't be. For at least the past 15 years it has been hard to deny the evidence for growing inequality in the United States. Census data clearly show a rising share of income going to the top 20 percent of families, and within that top 20 percent to the top 5 percent, with a declining share going to families in the middle. Nonetheless, denial of that evidence is a sizable, well-financed industry. Conservative think tanks have produced scores of studies that try to discredit the data, the methodology and, not least, the motives of those who report the obvious. Studies that appear to refute claims of increasing inequality receive prominent endorsements on editorial pages and are eagerly cited by right-leaning government officials. Four years ago Alan Greenspan (why did anyone ever think that he was nonpartisan?) gave a keynote speech at the Federal Reserve's annual Jackson Hole conference that amounted to an attempt to deny that there has been any real increase in inequality in America.

The concerted effort to deny that inequality is increasing is itself a symptom of the growing influence of our emerging plutocracy (more on this later). So is the fierce defense of the backup position, that inequality doesn't matter—or maybe even that, to use Martha Stewart's signature phrase, it's a good thing. Meanwhile, politically motivated smoke screens aside, the reality of increasing inequality is not in doubt. In fact, the census data understate the case, because for technical reasons those data tend to undercount very high incomes—for example, it's unlikely that they reflect the explosion in C.E.O. compensation. And other evidence makes it clear not only that inequality is increasing but that the action gets bigger the closer you get to the top. That is, it's not simply that the top 20 percent of families have had bigger percentage gains than families near the middle: the top 5 percent have done better than the next 15, the top 1 percent better than the next 4, and so on up to Bill Gates.

Studies that try to do a better job of tracking high incomes have found startling results. For example, a recent study by the nonpartisan Congressional Budget Office used income tax data and other sources to improve on the census estimates. The C.B.O. study found that between 1979 and 1997, the after-tax incomes of the top 1 percent of families rose 157 percent, compared with only a 10 percent gain for families near the middle of the income distribution. Even more startling results come from a new study by Thomas Piketty, at the French research institute Cepremap, and Emmanuel Saez, who is now at the University of California at Berkeley. Using income tax data, Piketty and Saez have produced estimates of the incomes of the well-to-do, the rich and the very rich back to 1913.

The first point you learn from these new estimates is that the middle-class America of my youth is best thought of not as the normal state of our society, but as an interregnum between Gilded Ages. America before 1930 was a society in which a small number of very rich people controlled a large share of the nation's wealth. We became a middle-class society only after the concentration of income at the top dropped sharply during the New Deal, and especially during World War II. The economic historians Claudia Goldin and Robert Margo have dubbed the narrowing of income gaps during those years the Great Compression. Incomes then stayed fairly equally distributed until the 1970's: the rapid rise in incomes during the first postwar generation was very evenly spread across the population.

Since the 1970's, however, income gaps have been rapidly widening. Piketty and Saez confirm what I suspected: by most measures we are, in fact, back to the days of "The Great Gatsby." After 30 years in which the income shares of the top 10 percent of taxpayers, the top 1 percent and so on were far below their levels in the 1920's, all are very nearly back where they were.

And the big winners are the very, very rich. One ploy often used to play down growing inequality is to rely on rather coarse statistical breakdowns—dividing the population into five "quintiles," each containing 20 percent of families, or at most 10 "deciles." Indeed, Greenspan's speech at Jackson Hole relied mainly on decile data. From there it's a short step to denying that we're really talking about the rich at all. For example, a conservative commentator might concede, grudgingly, that there has been some increase in the share of national income going to the top 10 percent of taxpayers, but then point out that anyone with an income over $81,000 is in that top 10 percent. So we're just talking about shifts within the middle class, right?

Wrong: the top 10 percent contains a lot of people whom we would still consider middle class, but they weren't the big winners. Most of the gains in the share of the top 10 percent of taxpayers over the past 30 years were actually gains to the top 1 percent, rather than the next 9 percent. In 1998 the top 1 percent started at $230,000. In turn, 60 percent of the gains of that top 1 percent went to the top 0.1 percent, those with incomes of more than $790,000. And almost half of those gains went to a mere 13,000 taxpayers, the top 0.01 percent, who had an income of at least $3.6 million and an average income of $17 million.

A stickler for detail might point out that the Piketty-Saez estimates end in 1998 and that the C.B.O. numbers end a year earlier. Have the trends shown in the data reversed? Almost surely not. In fact, all indications are that the explosion of incomes at the top continued through 2000. Since then the plunge in stock prices must have put some crimp in high incomes—but census data show inequality continuing to increase in 2001, mainly because of the severe effects of the recession on the working poor and near poor. When the recession ends, we can be sure that we will find ourselves a society in which income inequality is even higher than it was in the late 90's.

So claims that we've entered a second Gilded Age aren't exaggerated. In America's middle-class era, the mansion-building, yacht-owning classes had pretty much disappeared. According to Piketty and Saez, in 1970 the top 0.01 percent of taxpayers had 0.7 percent of total income—that is, they earned "only" 70 times as much as the average, not enough to buy or maintain a mega-residence. But in 1998 the top 0.01 percent received more than 3 percent of all income. That meant that the 13,000 richest families in America had almost as much income as the 20 million poorest households; those 13,000 families had incomes 300 times that of average families.

And let me repeat: this transformation has happened very quickly, and it is still going on. You might think that 1987, the year Tom Wolfe published his novel "The Bonfire of the Vani-

ties" and Oliver Stone released his movie "Wall Street," marked the high tide of America's new money culture. But in 1987 the top 0.01 percent earned only about 40 percent of what they do today, and top executives less than a fifth as much. The America of "Wall Street" and "The Bonfire of the Vanities" was positively egalitarian compared with the country we live in today.

### III. Undoing the New Deal

In the middle of the 1980's, as economists became aware that something important was happening to the distribution of income in America, they formulated three main hypotheses about its causes.

The "globalization" hypothesis tied America's changing income distribution to the growth of world trade, and especially the growing imports of manufactured goods from the third world. Its basic message was that blue-collar workers—the sort of people who in my youth often made as much money as college-educated middle managers—were losing ground in the face of competition from low-wage workers in Asia. A result was stagnation or decline in the wages of ordinary people, with a growing share of national income going to the highly educated.

A second hypothesis, "skill-biased technological change," situated the cause of growing inequality not in foreign trade but in domestic innovation. The torrid pace of progress in information technology, so the story went, had increased the demand for the highly skilled and educated. And so the income distribution increasingly favored brains rather than brawn.

> Some economists think the New Deal imposed norms of relative equality in pay that persisted for more than 30 years, creating a broadly middle-class society. Those norms have unraveled.

Finally, the "superstar" hypothesis—named by the Chicago economist Sherwin Rosen—offered a variant on the technological story. It argued that modern technologies of communication often turn competition into a tournament in which the winner is richly rewarded, while the runners-up get far less. The classic example—which gives the theory its name—is the entertainment business. As Rosen pointed out, in bygone days there were hundreds of comedians making a modest living at live shows in the borscht belt and other places. Now they are mostly gone; what is left is a handful of superstar TV comedians.

The debates among these hypotheses—particularly the debate between those who attributed growing inequality to globalization and those who attributed it to technology—were many and bitter. I was a participant in those debates myself. But I won't dwell on them, because in the last few years there has been a growing sense among economists that none of these hypotheses work.

I don't mean to say that there was nothing to these stories. Yet as more evidence has accumulated, each of the hypotheses has seemed increasingly inadequate. Globalization can explain part of the relative decline in blue-collar wages, but it can't explain the 2,500 percent rise in C.E.O. incomes. Technology may explain why the salary premium associated with a college education has risen, but it's hard to match up with the huge increase in inequality among the college-educated, with little progress for many but gigantic gains at the top. The superstar theory works for Jay Leno, but not for the thousands of people who have become awesomely rich without going on TV.

The Great Compression—the substantial reduction in inequality during the New Deal and the Second World War—also seems hard to understand in terms of the usual theories. During World War II Franklin Roosevelt used government control over wages to compress wage gaps. But if the middle-class society that emerged from the war was an artificial creation, why did it persist for another 30 years?

Some—by no means all—economists trying to understand growing inequality have begun to take seriously a hypothesis that would have been considered irredeemably fuzzy-minded not long ago. This view stresses the role of social norms in setting limits to inequality. According to this view, the New Deal had a more profound impact on American society than even its most ardent admirers have suggested: it imposed norms of relative equality in pay that persisted for more than 30 years, creating the broadly middle-class society we came to take for granted. But those norms began to unravel in the 1970's and have done so at an accelerating pace.

Exhibit A for this view is the story of executive compensation. In the 1960's, America's great corporations behaved more like socialist republics than like cutthroat capitalist enterprises, and top executives behaved more like public-spirited bureaucrats than like captains of industry. I'm not exaggerating. Consider the description of executive behavior offered by John Kenneth Galbraith in his 1967 book, "The New Industrial State": "Management does not go out ruthlessly to reward itself—a sound management is expected to exercise restraint." Managerial self-dealing was a thing of the past: "With the power of decision goes opportunity for making money…. Were everyone to seek to do so… the corporation would be a chaos of competitive avarice. But these are not the sort of thing that a good company man does; a remarkably effective code bans such behavior. Group decision-making insures, moreover, that almost everyone's actions and even thoughts are known to others. This acts to enforce the code and, more than incidentally, a high standard of personal honesty as well."

Thirty-five years on, a cover article in *Fortune* is titled "You Bought. They Sold." "All over corporate America," reads the blurb, "top execs were cashing in stocks even as their companies were tanking. Who was left holding the bag? You." As I said, we've become a different country.

Let's leave actual malfeasance on one side for a moment, and ask how the relatively modest salaries of top executives 30 years ago became the gigantic pay packages of today. There are two main stories, both of which emphasize changing norms rather than pure economics. The more optimistic story draws an

analogy between the explosion of C.E.O. pay and the explosion of baseball salaries with the introduction of free agency. According to this story, highly paid C.E.O.'s really are worth it, because having the right man in that job makes a huge difference. The more pessimistic view—which I find more plausible—is that competition for talent is a minor factor. Yes, a great executive can make a big difference—but those huge pay packages have been going as often as not to executives whose performance is mediocre at best. The key reason executives are paid so much now is that they appoint the members of the corporate board that determines their compensation and control many of the perks that board members count on. So it's not the invisible hand of the market that leads to those monumental executive incomes; it's the invisible handshake in the boardroom.

But then why weren't executives paid lavishly 30 years ago? Again, it's a matter of corporate culture. For a generation after World War II, fear of outrage kept executive salaries in check. Now the outrage is gone. That is, the explosion of executive pay represents a social change rather than the purely economic forces of supply and demand. We should think of it not as a market trend like the rising value of waterfront property, but as something more like the sexual revolution of the 1960's—a relaxation of old strictures, a new permissiveness, but in this case the permissiveness is financial rather than sexual. Sure enough, John Kenneth Galbraith described the honest executive of 1967 as being one who "eschews the lovely, available and even naked woman by whom he is intimately surrounded." By the end of the 1990's, the executive motto might as well have been "If it feels good, do it."

How did this change in corporate culture happen? Economists and management theorists are only beginning to explore that question, but it's easy to suggest a few factors. One was the changing structure of financial markets. In his new book, "Searching for a Corporate Savior," Rakesh Khurana of Harvard Business School suggests that during the 1980's and 1990's, "managerial capitalism"—the world of the man in the gray flannel suit—was replaced by "investor capitalism." Institutional investors weren't willing to let a C.E.O. choose his own successor from inside the corporation; they wanted heroic leaders, often outsiders, and were willing to pay immense sums to get them. The subtitle of Khurana's book, by the way, is "The Irrational Quest for Charismatic C.E.O.'s."

But fashionable management theorists didn't think it was irrational. Since the 1980's there has been ever more emphasis on the importance of "leadership"—meaning personal, charismatic leadership. When Lee Iacocca of Chrysler became a business celebrity in the early 1980's, he was practically alone: Khurana reports that in 1980 only one issue of Business Week featured a C.E.O. on its cover. By 1999 the number was up to 19. And once it was considered normal, even necessary, for a C.E.O. to be famous, it also became easier to make him rich.

Economists also did their bit to legitimize previously unthinkable levels of executive pay. During the 1980's and 1990's a torrent of academic papers—popularized in business magazines and incorporated into consultants' recommendations—argued that Gordon Gekko was right: greed is good; greed works. In order to get the best performance out of executives, these papers argued, it was necessary to align their interests with those of stockholders. And the way to do that was with large grants of stock or stock options.

It's hard to escape the suspicion that these new intellectual justifications for soaring executive pay were as much effect as cause. I'm not suggesting that management theorists and economists were personally corrupt. It would have been a subtle, unconscious process: the ideas that were taken up by business schools, that led to nice speaking and consulting fees, tended to be the ones that ratified an existing trend, and thereby gave it legitimacy.

What economists like Piketty and Saez are now suggesting is that the story of executive compensation is representative of a broader story. Much more than economists and free-market advocates like to imagine, wages—particularly at the top—are determined by social norms. What happened during the 1930's and 1940's was that new norms of equality were established, largely through the political process. What happened in the 1980's and 1990's was that those norms unraveled, replaced by an ethos of "anything goes." And a result was an explosion of income at the top of the scale.

## IV. The Price of Inequality

It was one of those revealing moments. Responding to an e-mail message from a Canadian viewer, Robert Novak of "Crossfire" delivered a little speech: "Marg, like most Canadians, you're ill informed and wrong. The U.S. has the longest standard of living—longest life expectancy of any country in the world, including Canada. That's the truth."

But it was Novak who had his facts wrong. Canadians can expect to live about two years longer than Americans. In fact, life expectancy in the U.S. is well below that in Canada, Japan and every major nation in Western Europe. On average, we can expect lives a bit shorter than those of Greeks, a bit longer than those of Portuguese. Male life expectancy is lower in the U.S. than it is in Costa Rica.

Still, you can understand why Novak assumed that we were No. 1. After all, we really are the richest major nation, with real G.D.P. per capita about 20 percent higher than Canada's. And it has been an article of faith in this country that a rising tide lifts all boats. Doesn't our high and rising national wealth translate into a high standard of living—including good medical care—for all Americans?

Well, no. Although America has higher per capita income than other advanced countries, it turns out that that's mainly because our rich are much richer. And here's a radical thought: if the rich get more, that leaves less for everyone else.

That statement—which is simply a matter of arithmetic—is guaranteed to bring accusations of "class warfare." If the accuser gets more specific, he'll probably offer two reasons that it's foolish to make a fuss over the high incomes of a few people at the top of the income distribution. First, he'll tell you that what the elite get may look like a lot of money, but it's still a small share of the total—that is, when all is said and done the rich aren't getting that big a piece of the pie. Second, he'll tell you that trying to do anything to reduce incomes at the top will hurt, not help, people further down the distribution, because attempts to redistribute income damage incentives.

These arguments for lack of concern are plausible. And they were entirely correct, once upon a time—namely, back when we had a middle-class society. But there's a lot less truth to them now.

First, the share of the rich in total income is no longer trivial. These days 1 percent of families receive about 16 percent of total pretax income, and have about 14 percent of after-tax income. That share has roughly doubled over the past 30 years, and is now about as large as the share of the bottom 40 percent of the population. That's a big shift of income to the top; as a matter of pure arithmetic, it must mean that the incomes of less well off families grew considerably more slowly than average income. And they did. Adjusting for inflation, average family income—total income divided by the number of families—grew 28 percent from 1979 to 1997. But median family income—the income of a family in the middle of the distribution, a better indicator of how typical American families are doing—grew only 10 percent. And the incomes of the bottom fifth of families actually fell slightly.

Let me belabor this point for a bit. We pride ourselves, with considerable justification, on our record of economic growth. But over the last few decades it's remarkable how little of that growth has trickled down to ordinary families. Median family income has risen only about 0.5 percent per year—and as far as we can tell from somewhat unreliable data, just about all of that increase was due to wives working longer hours, with little or no gain in real wages. Furthermore, numbers about income don't reflect the growing riskiness of life for ordinary workers. In the days when General Motors was known in-house as Generous Motors, many workers felt that they had considerable job security—the company wouldn't fire them except in extremis. Many had contracts that guaranteed health insurance, even if they were laid off; they had pension benefits that did not depend on the stock market. Now mass firings from long-established companies are commonplace; losing your job means losing your insurance; and as millions of people have been learning, a 401(k) plan is no guarantee of a comfortable retirement.

Still, many people will say that while the U.S. economic system may generate a lot of inequality, it also generates much higher incomes than any alternative, so that everyone is better off. That was the moral Business Week tried to convey in its recent special issue with "25 Ideas for a Changing World." One of those ideas was "the rich get richer, and that's O.K." High incomes at the top, the conventional wisdom declares, are the result of a free-market system that provides huge incentives for performance. And the system delivers that performance, which means that wealth at the top doesn't come at the expense of the rest of us.

A skeptic might point out that the explosion in executive compensation seems at best loosely related to actual performance. Jack Welch was one of the 10 highest-paid executives in the United States in 2000, and you could argue that he earned it. But did Dennis Kozlowski of Tyco, or Gerald Levin of Time Warner, who were also in the top 10? A skeptic might also point out that even during the economic boom of the late

1990's, U.S. productivity growth was no better than it was during the great postwar expansion, which corresponds to the era when America was truly middle class and C.E.O.'s were modestly paid technocrats.

But can we produce any direct evidence about the effects of inequality? We can't rerun our own history and ask what would have happened if the social norms of middle-class America had continued to limit incomes at the top, and if government policy had leaned against rising inequality instead of reinforcing it, which is what actually happened. But we can compare ourselves with other advanced countries. And the results are somewhat surprising.

Many Americans assume that because we are the richest country in the world, with real G.D.P. per capita higher than that of other major advanced countries, Americans must be better off across the board—that it's not just our rich who are richer than their counterparts abroad, but that the typical American family is much better off than the typical family elsewhere, and that even our poor are well off by foreign standards.

But it's not true. Let me use the example of Sweden, that great conservative *bête noire*.

A few months ago the conservative cyberpundit Glenn Reynolds made a splash when he pointed out that Sweden's G.D.P. per capita is roughly comparable with that of Mississippi—see, those foolish believers in the welfare state have impoverished themselves! Presumably he assumed that this means that the typical Swede is as poor as the typical resident of Mississippi, and therefore much worse off than the typical American.

## As the rich get richer, they can buy a lot besides goods and services. Money buys political influence; used cleverly, it also buys intellectual influence.

But life expectancy in Sweden is about three years higher than that of the U.S. Infant mortality is half the U.S. level, and less than a third the rate in Mississippi. Functional illiteracy is much less common than in the U.S.

How is this possible? One answer is that G.D.P. per capita is in some ways a misleading measure. Swedes take longer vacations than Americans, so they work fewer hours per year. That's a choice, not a failure of economic performance. Real G.D.P. per hour worked is 16 percent lower than in the United States, which makes Swedish productivity about the same as Canada's.

But the main point is that though Sweden may have lower average income than the United States, that's mainly because our rich are so much richer. The median Swedish family has a standard of living roughly comparable with that of the median U.S. family: wages are if anything higher in Sweden, and a higher tax burden is offset by public provision of health care and generally better public services. And as you move further down the income distribution, Swedish living standards are way ahead of those in the U.S. Swedish families with children that are at the 10th percentile—poorer than 90 percent of the population—

have incomes 60 percent higher than their U.S. counterparts. And very few people in Sweden experience the deep poverty that is all too common in the United States. One measure: in 1994 only 6 percent of Swedes lived on less than $11 per day, compared with 14 percent in the U.S.

The moral of this comparison is that even if you think that America's high levels of inequality are the price of our high level of national income, it's not at all clear that this price is worth paying. The reason conservatives engage in bouts of Sweden-bashing is that they want to convince us that there is no tradeoff between economic efficiency and equity—that if you try to take from the rich and give to the poor, you actually make everyone worse off. But the comparison between the U.S. and other advanced countries doesn't support this conclusion at all. Yes, we are the richest major nation. But because so much of our national income is concentrated in relatively few hands, large numbers of Americans are worse off economically than their counterparts in other advanced countries.

And we might even offer a challenge from the other side: inequality in the United States has arguably reached levels where it is counterproductive. That is, you can make a case that our society would be richer if its richest members didn't get quite so much.

I could make this argument on historical grounds. The most impressive economic growth in U.S. history coincided with the middle-class interregnum, the post-World War II generation, when incomes were most evenly distributed. But let's focus on a specific case, the extraordinary pay packages of today's top executives. Are these good for the economy?

Until recently it was almost unchallenged conventional wisdom that, whatever else you might say, the new imperial C.E.O.'s had delivered results that dwarfed the expense of their compensation. But now that the stock bubble has burst, it has become increasingly clear that there was a price to those big pay packages, after all. In fact, the price paid by shareholders and society at large may have been many times larger than the amount actually paid to the executives.

It's easy to get boggled by the details of corporate scandal—insider loans, stock options, special-purpose entities, mark-to-market, round-tripping. But there's a simple reason that the details are so complicated. All of these schemes were designed to benefit corporate insiders—to inflate the pay of the C.E.O. and his inner circle. That is, they were all about the "chaos of competitive avarice" that, according to John Kenneth Galbraith, had been ruled out in the corporation of the 1960's. But while all restraint has vanished within the American corporation, the outside world—including stockholders—is still prudish, and open looting by executives is still not acceptable. So the looting has to be camouflaged, taking place through complicated schemes that can be rationalized to outsiders as clever corporate strategies.

Economists who study crime tell us that crime is inefficient—that is, the costs of crime to the economy are much larger than the amount stolen. Crime, and the fear of crime, divert resources away from productive uses: criminals spend their time stealing rather than producing, and potential victims spend time and money trying to protect their property. Also, the things people do to avoid becoming victims—like avoiding dangerous districts—have a cost even if they succeed in averting an actual crime.

The same holds true of corporate malfeasance, whether or not it actually involves breaking the law. Executives who devote their time to creating innovative ways to divert shareholder money into their own pockets probably aren't running the real business very well (think Enron, WorldCom, Tyco, Global Crossing, Adelphia…). Investments chosen because they create the illusion of profitability while insiders cash in their stock options are a waste of scarce resources. And if the supply of funds from lenders and shareholders dries up because of a lack of trust, the economy as a whole suffers. Just ask Indonesia.

The argument for a system in which some people get very rich has always been that the lure of wealth provides powerful incentives. But the question is, incentives to do what? As we learn more about what has actually been going on in corporate America, it's becoming less and less clear whether those incentives have actually made executives work on behalf of the rest of us.

## V. Inequality and Politics

In September the Senate debated a proposed measure that would impose a one-time capital gains tax on Americans who renounce their citizenship in order to avoid paying U.S. taxes. Senator Phil Gramm was not pleased, declaring that the proposal was "right out of Nazi Germany." Pretty strong language, but no stronger than the metaphor Daniel Mitchell of the Heritage Foundation used, in an op-ed article in The Washington Times, to describe a bill designed to prevent corporations from rechartering abroad for tax purposes: Mitchell described this legislation as the "Dred Scott tax bill," referring to the infamous 1857 Supreme Court ruling that required free states to return escaped slaves.

Twenty years ago, would a prominent senator have likened those who want wealthy people to pay taxes to Nazis? Would a member of a think tank with close ties to the administration have drawn a parallel between corporate taxation and slavery? I don't think so. The remarks by Gramm and Mitchell, while stronger than usual, were indicators of two huge changes in American politics. One is the growing polarization of our politics—our politicians are less and less inclined to offer even the appearance of moderation. The other is the growing tendency of policy and policy makers to cater to the interests of the wealthy. And I mean the wealthy, not the merely well-off: only someone with a net worth of at least several million dollars is likely to find it worthwhile to become a tax exile.

You don't need a political scientist to tell you that modern American politics is bitterly polarized. But wasn't it always thus? No, it wasn't. From World War II until the 1970's—the same era during which income inequality was historically low—political partisanship was much more muted than it is today. That's not just a subjective assessment. My Princeton political science colleagues Nolan McCarty and Howard Rosenthal, together with Keith Poole at the University of Houston, have done a statistical analysis showing that the

voting behavior of a congressman is much better predicted by his party affiliation today than it was twenty-five years ago. In fact, the division between the parties is sharper now than it has been since the 1920's.

What are the parties divided about? The answer is simple: economics. McCarty, Rosenthal and Poole write that "voting in Congress is highly ideological—one-dimensional left/right, liberal versus conservative." It may sound simplistic to describe Democrats as the party that wants to tax the rich and help the poor, and Republicans as the party that wants to keep taxes and social spending as low as possible. And during the era of middle-class America that would indeed have been simplistic: politics wasn't defined by economic issues. But that was a different country; as McCarty, Rosenthal and Poole put it, "If income and wealth are distributed in a fairly equitable way, little is to be gained for politicians to organize politics around nonexistent conflicts." Now the conflicts are real, and our politics is organized around them. In other words, the growing inequality of our incomes probably lies behind the growing divisiveness of our politics.

But the politics of rich and poor hasn't played out the way you might think. Since the incomes of America's wealthy have soared while ordinary families have seen at best small gains, you might have expected politicians to seek votes by proposing to soak the rich. In fact, however, the polarization of politics has occurred because the Republicans have moved to the right, not because the Democrats have moved to the left. And actual economic policy has moved steadily in favor of the wealthy. The major tax cuts of the past twenty-five years, the Reagan cuts in the 1980's and the recent Bush cuts, were both heavily tilted toward the very well off. (Despite obfuscations, it remains true that more than half the Bush tax cut will eventually go to the top 1 percent of families.) The major tax increase over that period, the increase in payroll taxes in the 1980's, fell most heavily on working-class families.

The most remarkable example of how politics has shifted in favor of the wealthy—an example that helps us understand why economic policy has reinforced, not countered, the movement toward greater inequality—is the drive to repeal the estate tax. The estate tax is, overwhelmingly, a tax on the wealthy. In 1999, only the top 2 percent of estates paid any tax at all, and half the estate tax was paid by only 3,300 estates, 0.16 percent of the total, with a minimum value of $5 million and an average value of $17 million. A quarter of the tax was paid by just 467 estates worth more than $20 million. Tales of family farms and businesses broken up to pay the estate tax are basically rural legends; hardly any real examples have been found, despite diligent searching.

You might have thought that a tax that falls on so few people yet yields a significant amount of revenue would be politically popular; you certainly wouldn't expect widespread opposition. Moreover, there has long been an argument that the estate tax promotes democratic values, precisely because it limits the ability of the wealthy to form dynasties. So why has there been a powerful political drive to repeal the estate tax, and why was such a repeal a centerpiece of the Bush tax cut?

There is an economic argument for repealing the estate tax, but it's hard to believe that many people take it seriously. More significant for members of Congress, surely, is the question of who would benefit from repeal: while those who will actually benefit from estate tax repeal are few in number, they have a lot of money and control even more (corporate C.E.O.'s can now count on leaving taxable estates behind). That is, they are the sort of people who command the attention of politicians in search of campaign funds.

But it's not just about campaign contributions: much of the general public has been convinced that the estate tax is a bad thing. If you try talking about the tax to a group of moderately prosperous retirees, you get some interesting reactions. They refer to it as the "death tax"; many of them believe that their estates will face punitive taxation, even though most of them will pay little or nothing; they are convinced that small businesses and family farms bear the brunt of the tax.

These misconceptions don't arise by accident. They have, instead, been deliberately promoted. For example, a Heritage Foundation document titled "Time to Repeal Federal Death Taxes: The Nightmare of the American Dream" emphasizes stories that rarely, if ever, happen in real life: "Small-business owners, particularly minority owners, suffer anxious moments wondering whether the businesses they hope to hand down to their children will be destroyed by the death tax bill,… Women whose children are grown struggle to find ways to re-enter the work force without upsetting the family's estate tax avoidance plan." And who finances the Heritage Foundation? Why, foundations created by wealthy families, of course.

The point is that it is no accident that strongly conservative views, views that militate against taxes on the rich, have spread even as the rich get richer compared with the rest of us: in addition to directly buying influence, money can be used to shape public perceptions. The liberal group People for the American Way's report on how conservative foundations have deployed vast sums to support think tanks, friendly media and other institutions that promote right-wing causes is titled "Buying a Movement."

Not to put too fine a point on it: as the rich get richer, they can buy a lot of things besides goods and services. Money buys political influence; used cleverly, it also buys intellectual influence. A result is that growing income disparities in the United States, far from leading to demands to soak the rich, have been accompanied by a growing movement to let them keep more of their earnings and to pass their wealth on to their children.

This obviously raises the possibility of a self-reinforcing process. As the gap between the rich and the rest of the population grows, economic policy increasingly caters to the interests of the elite, while public services for the population at large—above all, public education—are starved of resources. As policy increasingly favors the interests of the rich and neglects the interests of the general population, income disparities grow even wider.

## VI. Plutocracy?

In 1924, the mansions of Long Island's North Shore were still in their full glory, as was the political power of the class that owned them. When Gov. Al Smith of New York proposed building a system of parks on Long Island, the mansion owners were bitterly opposed. One baron—Horace Havemeyer, the "sultan of sugar"—warned that North Shore towns would be "overrun with rabble from the city." "Rabble?" Smith said. "That's me you're talking about." In the end New Yorkers got their parks, but it was close: the interests of a few hundred wealthy families nearly prevailed over those of New York City's middle class.

America in the 1920's wasn't a feudal society. But it was a nation in which vast privilege—often inherited privilege—stood in contrast to vast misery. It was also a nation in which the government, more often than not, served the interests of the privileged and ignored the aspirations of ordinary people.

Those days are past—or are they? Income inequality in America has now returned to the levels of the 1920's. Inherited wealth doesn't yet play a big part in our society, but given time—and the repeal of the estate tax—we will grow ourselves a hereditary elite just as set apart from the concerns of ordinary Americans as old Horace Havemeyer. And the new elite, like the old, will have enormous political power.

Kevin Phillips concludes his book "Wealth and Democracy" with a grim warning: "Either democracy must be renewed, with politics brought back to life, or wealth is likely to cement a new and less democratic regime—plutocracy by some other name." It's a pretty extreme line, but we live in extreme times. Even if the forms of democracy remain, they may become meaningless. It's all too easy to see how we may become a country in which the big rewards are reserved for people with the right connections; in which ordinary people see little hope of advancement; in which political involvement seems pointless, because in the end the interests of the elite always get served.

Am I being too pessimistic? Even my liberal friends tell me not to worry, that our system has great resilience, that the center will hold. I hope they're right, but they may be looking in the rearview mirror. Our optimism about America, our belief that in the end our nation always finds its way, comes from the past—a past in which we were a middle-class society. But that was another country.

---

*Paul Krugman is a Times columnist and a professor at Princeton.*

# THE REAL FACE OF Homelessness

**More than ever, it is mothers with kids who are ending up on the streets. Bush has a plan, but will it help?**

## By JOEL STEIN

THE LIBERALS TRIED. THEY gave money. They watched boring news specials. They held hands all the way across America. They even pretended to laugh at sketches with Robin Williams, Billy Crystal and Whoopi Goldberg. But at some point in every one-way relationship, pity turns to resentment, and now even the liberals are turning on the homeless: San Francisco has voted to reduce their benefits 85%; Santa Monica, Calif., passed laws preventing them from sleeping in the doors of shops or receiving food from unlicensed providers; Madison, Wis., is handing them a record number of tickets; Seattle banned the sale of malt liquor and Thunderbird in Pioneer Square as its initiative to shoo away the alcoholics.

## THE YOUNG MOM

**LOCATION Falls Church, Va.**

**NAMES Jessica Lampman, 22; Destinee, 2**

**HOW THEY BECAME HOMELESS**

After dropping out of ninth grade, Jessica fled her mom's home because her brother was using drugs. Looking for stability for her daughter, she pitched a tent at a campground. She got into a shelter and found a job, but a low salary and bad credit kept her from getting an apartment

Sensing an opening, the Bush Administration has decided to make the homeless problem a target of compassionate conservatism, which got pushed back after Sept. 11, when conservatism was everywhere but compassion was available only for the attack victims. And it's putting its central domestic doctrine to the test on an issue on which the Democrats have been unable to show much progress. It's a good choice, not only because the expectations are so low after decades of failure but also because it is unassailable in its immediate need.

With a freak-show economy in which unemployment has reached 60%—a 50% increase since November 2000—but housing prices have stayed at or near historic highs, the number of homeless appears to be at its highest in at least a decade in a wide range of places across the U.S., according to Bush's own homelessness czar. "It's embarrassing to say that they're up," says czar Philip Mangano of the number, "but it's better to face the truth than to try to obfuscate."

## THE PRICED-OUT

**LOCATION Harlem, N.Y.**

**NAMES Kim Berrios, 26; Julius Cabrera, 22; Jonathan, 8; Sunsarei, 5; Jerimiah, 2**

**HOW THEY BECAME HOMELESS**

Kim and Julius had to leave their Staten Island apartment when the landlord renovated and raised the rent. Kim's family is in Florida, and Julius' mother has five other kids in a three-bedroom apartment. "We couldn't go stay with anybody," says Kim, who is pregnant. After moving to a Harlem shelter, she quit work to take care of Jonathan, who has attention-deficit disorder; Julius had to quit a nighttime supermarket job owing to the shelter's curfew. They are waiting for an apartment in the projects

You don't see homeless people as much as you did in the '80s because the one great policy initiative of the past 20 years has been to move them from grates into the newest form of the poorhouse, the shelter. Even though cities are building shelters as fast as they can, the homeless are pouring out of them again, returning to the grates. Homeless numbers are notoriously unreliable (many people may be counted twice or not at all, and some homeless advocates include people who move in with family members), but a TIME survey of the eight jurisdictions that have good statistics shows that this population has grown significantly and that its fastest-growing segment is composed of families. Homeless parents and their kids made up roughly 15% of the case load in 1999—or, if you count every head, about 35% of all homeless people, according to the Urban Institute, a liberal D.C. think tank. The TIME survey suggests that population has since increased—registering year-over-year jumps in either 2001 or 2002 (*see graphic for individual cities*). These families mainly consist of single women with kids, whose greater housing needs, compared with those of single people, make them more vulnerable to rental increases than are single people.

Even as the problem worsens, there's little appetite in Washington for the large-scale solutions the Democrats have been advocating for 40 years: creating affordable housing and strengthening programs that attack the causes of poverty by finding people jobs, teaching them skills, giving them transportation to jobs, getting them off drugs, providing medical care—essentially trying to fix entire lives. Some homeless experts are beginning to wonder whether building shelters only exaggerates the numbers: they argue that poor people who wouldn't otherwise be homeless are attracted to shelters as a way of quickly tapping into government assistance. "It didn't take long for people to figure out that this was a way to scam the system," admits Andrew Cuomo, the Secretary of Housing and Urban Development (HUD) under President Bill Clinton. Given all this failure and disgust, Republicans could deal with this problem however they wanted.

The first G.O.P. member to pick up on this was Susan Baker, who had the ability to get the White House's attention because she's the wife of James Baker, chief of staff to Ronald Reagan, Secretary of State to Bush's father and, more important, the guy who ran W.'s election-after-the-election campaign in Florida. Baker is co-chairwoman of the National Alliance to End Homelessness, a cause in which she became interested in the early '80s, when she got involved in organizing D.C. food banks.

Baker read a 1998 study by University of Pennsylvania professor of social work Dennis Culhane that suggested that the most efficient solution to homelessness was to provide permanent housing to the "chronic homeless"—those helpless cases, usually the mentally ill, substance abusers or very sick—who will probably be homeless for life. The study found the chronic homeless make temporary shelters their long-term home; they take up 50% of the beds each year, even though they make up 10% of the homeless population. Culhane's idea appeals to conservatives: it has had proved results in 20-year-old projects across the country; it gets the really hard-to-look-at people off the street; and it saves money, because administrative costs make it more expensive to put up people at a shelter than to give them their own apartment (sheltering a homeless person on a cot in a New York City shelter, for example, costs on average $1,800 a month). It's similar to the problem faced by hospitals, where the uninsured use ambulances and emergency rooms as a very expensive version of primary care. Culhane's finding is also attractive in its simple if unspoken logic: because the mentally ill were put out into the street after the public discovered the abuses in mental hospitals and J.F.K. passed the 1963 Community Health Center Act, which deinsitutionalized 430,000 people, the plan really amounts to building much nicer, voluntary mental hospitals.

Three weeks after Bush named Mel Martinez his HUD Secretary, Baker landed a meeting with him. She sold him Culhane's research, arguing that with just 200,000 apartments, the Administration could end chronic homelessness in 10 years. The meeting went so well that the plan became Bush's official stance on homelessness: the 2003 budget has four paragraphs promising to end chronic homelessness in a decade.

## THE LARGE FAMILY

**LOCATION Dallas**

**NAMES Gina Christian, 36; David, 34; Alex, 14; Martin, 11; Thalia, 6; Tatiana, 4**

**HOW THEY BECAME HOMELESS**

David worked as a mechanic in Austin, Texas, for a company that fixed Hertz cars. When the business went under, Gina's income as a nursing-home temp wasn't enough to cover rent and food for six. They hocked their belongings, and Gina resorted to begging. David still wasn't able to find work, so they moved to Dallas' Interfaith House, a private shelter for needy families. "We went from doing fine to one day being homeless," says Gina

Bush reinstated last spring the office of homeless czar, a position that had been dormant for six years, tapping Mangano to be head of the Interagency Council on Homelessness. He is liked by members of both parties and fits Bush's theme of faith-based compassion. A former rock manager who represented members of Buffalo Springfield and Peter, Paul and Mary, Mangano says his life changed in 1972 when he saw Franco Zeffirelli's *Brother Sun, Sister Moon,* a movie about the life of St. Francis. For Mangano, who calls himself a homeless abolitionist, ending chronic homeless is a moral call. "Is there any manifestation of homelessness more tragic or more visible than chronic homelessness experienced by those who are suffering from mental illness, addiction or physical disability?" he asks.

Building permanent housing for the chronically ill is in fact a long-standing Democratic initiative. In 1990 New York Governor Mario Cuomo began building "supportive housing" projects with attached mental-health services; there are now more than 60,000 such units across the country, funded by a combination of government and private organizations. While the buildings are not licensed like mental hospitals, nurses, social workers and psychologists keep office hours. In midtown Manhattan's Prince George Hotel, which has a ballroom, a restored lobby and salon, former street dwellers bake cookies, use the computer lab and take Pilates and yoga classes. Director Nancy Porcaro says the surroundings give the homeless enough help and pride to better themselves. "People do rise to the occasion, despite what the mainstream may think. They want more," she says.

That's the compassionate part. Here's the conservatives side: Bush isn't spending any money on this. While HUD already spends 30% of its homeless dollars on permanent housing, all the administration has added so far for its new push is $35 million, scraped together from within the existing budgets of three departments. To give a sense of how much that means in Washington budgetary terms, $35 million is equal to the money set aside to help keep insects from crossing the border. Although last month HUD touted the $1.1 billion in the budget for homeless services as the largest amount of homeless assistance in history, it's about the same as the amount set aside before Newt Gingrich's Congress made major cuts. And the Administration, more quietly, also announced a 30% cut in operating funds for public housing last week.

Congressman Barney Frank, ranking Democrat on the House Financial Services Committee (which oversees government housing agencies), is not kind about the Bush Administration's intentions. "They are just lying when they say they have a housing program," he says. And of the additional $35 million pledged to end chronic homelessness, Frank says, "it's not only peanuts; it's taking the peanuts from one dish and putting them in another." In fact, in October the House Appropriations Committee approved a bill that, if it becomes law, will cut $938 million from the President's budget for rental vouchers, one of the government's main methods of paying to house the homeless.

## THE WANDERER

**LOCATION Los Angeles**

**NAMES Debra Rollins, 35; two daughters, 11 and 16**

**HOW THEY BECAME HOMELESS**

Having lived in 19 places in the past 30 years, including a stint as a teen-age runaway, Rollins spent the past five years in a one-bedroom flat with her two daughters, two friends and one of their kids. She moved to a hotel after falling out with her roommates. "I didn't have family or any friends around, so I didn't have anybody to help," she says. When her money ran out, she landed in a shelter. A high school dropout, Rollins is trying to obtain a GED and is working part time as a cashier so she can get a place of her own.

The old-school Democrats are also upset at the philosophy behind Bush's plan, which they argue is more interested in getting the homeless out of view than in solving their problems. "The largest-growing sector is actually women and children," says Donald Whitehead, the executive director of the National Coalition for the Homeless, the oldest and largest advocacy group on this issue. "A true strategy needs to include the entire population."

Andrew Cuomo, founder of HELP USA, a national, non-profit shelter provider, says the Administration is merely redefining the issue so as to appear to be doing something. "What makes you say that a guy who has been on the street for five years and is a heroin addict is any more needy than a woman who is being beaten nightly in front of her children?" he asks. For his part, Senator John Kerry, a Democrat running for President, has proposed legislation that would add 1.5 million units of affordable housing to address the fact that America's population has grown 11% in the past decade while rental stock has shrunk. According to the National Low Income Housing Coalition, which lobbies for government housing, for the fourth year in a row there isn't a single jurisdiction in the U.S., with the exception of places in Puerto Rico, where a person working full time for minimum wage can afford to rent a one-bedroom home at fair-market value.

Without a federal plan that has worked, cities have lost patience, concentrating on getting the homeless out of sight. In New York City, where shelter space can't be created fast enough, Mayor Mike Bloomberg has proposed using old cruise ships for housing. New Orleans removed park benches in Jackson Square to discourage the homeless; Philadelphia launched an ad campaign asking people not to give to panhandlers; and in Orlando, Fla., a new law makes it a jailable offense to lie down on the sidewalk.

## THE LAID-OFF WORKER

**LOCATION Dallas**

**NAME Gary Jones, 36**

**HOW HE BECAME HOMELESS**

Jones was pulling in $12 an hour as a welder who often dangled from skyscrapers. Then he got laid off and started drinking heavily and doing drugs. "My self-esteem kind of left me," he says. "I've thought about trying to get back out there and find work, get myself off these here mean streets, but you have to be in the right frame of mind to do that."

Polls in San Francisco, where the streets are clogged with the homeless who lose the nightly lottery for limited shelter beds, indicate that homelessness is a major concern. Billboards show resident holding cardboard signs that read, I DON'T WANT TO HOLD MY BREATH PAST EVERY ALLEY. Voters last November overwhelmingly passed Proposition N, which cuts handouts from $395 a month to $59, providing food and shelter instead. The proposition was proposed by Gavin Newsom, 35, a member of the city's Board of Supervisors who describes himself as a liberal. Newsom's proposal was supported by a $1 million campaign and was so controversial that Newsom felt compelled to travel with police protection as Election Day approached. To his critics who contend that Proposition N doesn't do much to help the people whose assistance he's taking away, Newsom says, "We never said N is going to solve homelessness." Two weeks after the proposal became law, Newsom announced a mayoral bid.

Even in Miami, where homelessness has been reduced because of a 1997 court settlement that forced the city to decriminalize it and develop an elaborate system for dealing with it, citizens are demanding that the streets be cleared. New laws prevent sleeping on the beach and building shelters too close to one another. "They want to hide us with all kind of zoning tricks and such," says Steve Silva, 50, who makes $7 and a 5% commission selling Miami Heat tickets and lives in a shelter. "But it's a Band-Aid on a sucking chest wound, man."

Likewise in Dallas, where the problem continues to worsen, the homeless complain of cops delivering wake-up calls from their car loudspeakers by blaring "Wake up, crackheads!" and handing out vagrancy tickets. "It doesn't make you want to go and rejoin society," says Gary Jones, 36, a laid-off welder. "What's lower than writing a man a ticket for sleeping on the street? If he had somewhere else to go, don't you think he'd be there?"

Neither cracking down on vagrancy nor Bush's plan to end chronic homelessness is going to help the growing number of families without housing. David and Gina Christian and their four children have avoided the streets by staying in a 600-sq.-ft. apartment

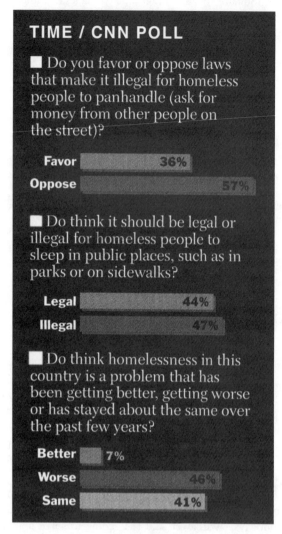

## TIME / CNN POLL

■ Do you favor or oppose laws that make it illegal for homeless people to panhandle (ask for money from other people on the street)?

| | |
|---|---|
| Favor | 36% |
| Oppose | 57% |

■ Do think it should be legal or illegal for homeless people to sleep in public places, such as in parks or on sidewalks?

| | |
|---|---|
| Legal | 44% |
| Illegal | 47% |

■ Do think homelessness in this country is a problem that has been getting better, getting worse or has stayed about the same over the past few years?

| | |
|---|---|
| Better | 7% |
| Worse | 46% |
| Same | 41% |

From a telephone poll of 1,006 adult Americans taken for TIME/ CNN on Nov. 13-14 by Harris Interactive. Margin of error is ±3.1%. "Not sures" omitted

at the Interfaith House in Dallas, which provides three months' housing to 100 needy families each year. David, 34, lost his job fixing rental cars in Austin after Sept. 11 when the tourism industry fell apart. Gina, 36, wasn't making enough as a nursing-home temp to cover the family's expenses. The Christians hocked everything they owned—their TV, the kids' PlayStation, Dad's tools—to follow David's old boss to a new job in Dallas. When that business fell apart too, David sold the tires from their two cars to pay for their nightly meals of rice and beans. "I was reduced to begging. I felt degraded, like I was less than human," Gina says. "When I was a child growing up in Watts, there was a 10-month period where we were homeless. I didn't want that for my family." Interfaith has

found David an $8-an-hour job as a mechanic at a Texaco station, and now that the Christians are not paying rent, they are able to save a little money. But time at Interfaith is running out. The program already broke its own rule by letting the family back for a second stay.

Given that so many are without a home but have temporary shelter, the real policy debate is no longer about whether society is responsible for keeping people out of the cold—we have agreed it is—but whether it is obligated to give them somewhere permanent to live. By fighting to end chronic homelessness, the Bush Administration argues that we need to give houses to those who are incapable of providing for themselves. The others will have to weather the storm in a shelter, if it can be built fast enough.

**RHODE ISLAND**
Number of families, 700, topped singles for the first time, up 17% over '01

**COLUMBUS, OHIO**
Families jumped 11% in '02 to 340. The number has grown 20% in two years

**ANCHORAGE**
Families accounted for 1,700 people seeking shelter, up 17% from '00 to '01

**PHILADELPHIA**
After a decline in '01, the number of families rose 5% last year to 400

**SPOKANE, WASH.**
It sheltered 1,500 families in '01, up 35%, and numbers still grow

**BOSTON**
A city report in '01 found 1,692 family members, up 9%, as singles rose just 1%

**KANSAS CITY, MO.**
It counted 960 families in '01 in the area, up 18% from '00

**NEW YORK CITY**
Its system now harbors 9,000 families, up 40% in the past year

*—Reported by Simon Crittle and Jyoti Thottam/New York, Laura A. Locke/San Francisco, Deborah Edler Brown and Margot Roosevelt/Los Angeles, Tim Padgett/Miami, Melissa August/Washington, Adam Pitluk/Dallas, Greg Land/Atlanta and Matt Baron/Chicago*

# Requiem for Welfare

## Evelyn Z. Brodkin

THERE WERE few mourners at welfare's funeral. In fact, its demise was widely celebrated when congressional Republicans teamed up with a majority of their Democratic colleagues and then-president Bill Clinton to enact a new welfare law in 1996. The law ended the sixty-one-year old federal commitment to aid poor families and ushered in a commitment to lower welfare rolls and put recipients to work.

To many politicians and the public, anything seemed preferable to the widely discredited program known as Aid to Families with Dependent Children (AFDC). Conservatives were sure that the new welfare would pull up the poor by their bootstraps and redeem them through the virtues of work. Liberals set aside their misgivings, hoping that work would redeem the poor politically and open opportunities to advance economic equality.

More than six years later, the demise of the old welfare remains largely unlamented. But what to make of the changes that have occurred in the name of reform? Often, laws produce more smoke than fire, intimating big change, but producing little. Not this time. In ways both apparent and not fully appreciated, welfare reform has reconfigured both the policy and political landscape. Some of these changes can evoke nostalgia for the bad old days of welfare unreformed.

## Reconsidering Welfare's Fate

An immediate consequence of the new law was to defuse welfare as a hot political issue. There's little attention to it these days—apart from some five million parents and children who rely on welfare to alleviate their poverty (and the policy analysts who pore over mountains of data to calculate how it "works"). Legislators have shown no appetite for restarting the welfare wars of prior years. And is it any wonder? The news about welfare has looked good—at least, superficially. Caseloads have plummeted since implementation of the new welfare, dropping 57 percent between 1997 and 2001. Some smaller states essentially cleared their caseloads, with Wyoming and Idaho proudly announcing reductions of 88.9 percent and 85.1 percent, respectively. Even states with large, urban populations have cut caseloads by one-half to three-quarters.

As an issue, welfare ranked among the top five items of interest to the public in 1995 and 1996. But in recent years, it has almost dropped off the Gallup charts. Other polls show that, among respondents who are aware of welfare reform, more than 60 percent think it's working well. Meanwhile, the nation has moved on to other concerns: terrorism, Iraq, the economy. Why reopen the welfare issue now?

In part, the 1996 law itself spurred reassessment. The law was designed to expire in 2002 unless reauthorized by Congress. With Congress unable to reach agreement before the 2002 election, welfare's reauthorization became one of the many measures to get a temporary extension and a handoff to the 108th Congress.

Beyond reauthorization, welfare merits a close look because battles over welfare policy have often been a bellwether of broader political developments. Welfare policy was near the forefront of sixties social activism, one of the banners under which the urban poor, minorities, and other disaffected groups successfully pressed for greater government intervention on behalf of social and economic equality. For the national Democratic Party, the politics of poverty fit an electoral strategy aimed at mobilizing urban and minority voters. Although the expansion of welfare proved to be temporary and limited, the politics of poverty produced federal initiatives that had broad and lasting impact, among them Medicaid, food stamps, earned income tax credits, and programs to aid schools in poor communities.

Attacks on welfare marked the beginning of a conservative mobilization against the welfare state in the late 1970s. Lurid accounts in George Gilder's *Wealth and Poverty* and Mickey Kaus's *The End of Equality* portrayed welfare and the poor as enemies of the democratic marketplace. President Ronald Reagan picked up these themes and contributed his own colorful anecdotes about welfare cheats and fraud, as he pushed forward cuts in taxes and social welfare programs. These forays into the politics of personal piety fit a Republican electoral strategy aimed at mobilizing the religious right and bringing the white working class into the party fold.

# Out with the "Old" Welfare

Reforming welfare assumed new urgency in the 1990s, an urgency grounded less in policy realities than in electoral politics. Alarms were sounded about a crisis of cost, although for three decades, spending on AFDC amounted to less than 2 percent of the federal budget. The $16 billion the federal government allocated to AFDC was dwarfed by spending on Social Security and defense, each costing more than $300 billion per year. Public opinion polls, however, indicated a different perception. Forty percent of respondents believed that welfare was one of the most expensive national programs, even larger than Social Security or defense.

Polls also indicated that much of the public believed welfare recipients had it too easy, although few knew what welfare really provided. In fact, AFDC gave only meager support to poor families. In 1996, the median monthly benefit for a family of three was $366. Even when combined with food stamps, welfare lifted few poor families above the federal poverty line. Even the much-touted crisis of dependency ("dependent" being a term loosely applied to anyone receiving welfare) was not reflected in the evidence. The share of families receiving welfare for extended periods declined between 1970 and 1985 and leveled off after that. Families that received welfare for more than six years constituted only a small minority of the welfare caseload at any point in time.

Although the hue and cry over a supposed welfare crisis was greatly overblown, Bill Clinton clearly appreciated welfare's potent political symbolism. As a presidential candidate, he famously pledged to "end welfare as we know it," a turn of phrase useful in demonstrating that he was a "new Democrat" unburdened by the liberalism of his predecessors. His proposals for reform emphasized neoliberal themes of work and individual responsibility, but coupled demands for work with provision of social services intended to improve individual employment prospects. The Clinton administration's plans also assumed the enactment of universal health insurance that would help underwrite the well-being of the working poor. But that did not happen.

After the Republicans took over Congress in 1994, and Clinton began his fateful descent into personal irresponsibility, the initiative shifted decidedly toward the right. House Majority Leader Newt Gingrich seized the opportunity to turn Clinton's pledge against him, sending the president two welfare measures then thought to be so harsh that they almost begged for a veto. The measures ended the federal guarantee of income support, imposed strict work rules, and set time limits on the provision of benefits. Clinton vetoed them.

But on the eve of his renomination at the 1996 Democratic convention, Clinton signed a measure much like those he had vetoed. There followed a few highly public resignations among indignant staff and a rebuke from the Congressional Black Caucus. But Clinton's decision (advocated by strategist Dick Morris and running mate Al Gore, among others) effectively took the welfare issue away from the Republicans and highlighted Clinton's "new Democratic" appeal to critical swing suburban and blue-collar, crossover voters.

Clinton became the first elected Democratic President since Franklin Roosevelt to win a second term. But Clinton was no Roosevelt. In fact, he redeemed his pledge to "end welfare" by presiding over the destruction of a pillar of the New Deal welfare state.

# Enter the "New" Welfare

The Personal Responsibility and Work Opportunity Reconciliation Act of 1996 replaced AFDC with a program aptly named Temporary Assistance to Needy Families (TANF). AFDC had provided an open-ended entitlement of federal funds to states based on the amount of benefits they distributed to poor families. TANF ended that entitlement, establishing a five-year block grant fixed at $16.5 billion annually (based on the amount allocated to AFDC in its last year) that states could draw down to subsidize welfare and related expenditures.

Mistrusting the states' willingness to be tough enough on work, Congress incorporated detailed and coercive provisions. First, it set time limits for assistance, restricting federal aid to a lifetime maximum of sixty months. If states wanted to exceed those limits, they would have to pay for most of it themselves. Second, parents were required to work or participate in so-called work activities after a maximum of two years of welfare receipt. Third, TANF established escalating work quotas. States that wanted to collect their full portion of federal dollars would have to show, by 2002, that 50 percent of adults heading single-parent households were working thirty hours per week. Fourth, it meticulously specified those work "activities" that would enable states to meet their quotas, among them paid work, job search, and unpaid workfare (in which recipients "worked off" their welfare benefits at minimum wage or provided child care for other welfare recipients). It limited the use of education and vocational training as countable activities.

Although the "work" side of TANF was clearly pre-eminent, there were some modest provisions on the "opportunity" side, with Congress providing $2.3 billion to help subsidize child care for working mothers and $3 billion in a block grant for welfare-to-work programs.

Beyond these prominent features, the new welfare also packed some hidden punches. It rewarded states for cutting welfare caseloads, largely without regard to how they did it. States that reduced their caseloads (whether those losing welfare found work or not) received credit against officially mandated quotas. If Congress was worried about states' slacking off from its tough work demands, the law indicated no concern that they might go too far in restricting access to benefits or pushing people off the welfare rolls. Only caseload reductions counted.

Under the banner of devolution, the law also gave states new authority to design their own welfare programs. While the welfare debate highlighted the professed virtues of innovation, less obvious was the license it gave states to craft policies even tougher and more restrictive than those allowed by federal law.

Pushing welfare decision making to the state and local level has never been good for the poor. In many states, poor families and their allies have little political influence. Moreover, constitutional balanced-budget requirements make states structurally unsuited to the task of protecting vulnerable residents against economic slumps. When unemployment goes up and state tax revenue goes down, the downward pressure on social spending intensifies.

The secret triumph of devolution lay, not in the opportunities for innovation, but in the opportunity for a quiet unraveling of the safety net.

# The Unfolding Story of Welfare Transformed[1]

What has happened since 1996? For one thing, the new welfare changed a national program of income assistance to an array of state programs, each with its own assortment of benefits, services, restrictions, and requirements. There has always been wide variation in the amount of cash aid states provided, and federal waivers allowed states to deviate from some national rules. But devolution spurred far greater policy inconsistency by allowing states, essentially, to make their own rules. Consequently, what you get (or whether you get anything at all) depends on where you live.

In addition, devolution set off a state "race to the bottom," not by reducing benefit levels as some had predicted, but by imposing new restrictions that limited access to benefits. States across the nation have taken advantage of devolution to impose restrictions tougher than those required by federal law.

For example, although federal law required recipients to work within two years, most states require work within one year, some require immediate work, and others demand a month of job search before they even begin to process an application for assistance. No longer required to exempt mothers with children under three years old from work requirements, most states permit an exemption only for mothers with babies under one year old, and some have eliminated exemptions altogether. In nineteen states, lifetime limits for welfare receipt are set below the federal maximum of sixty months. Other states have imposed so-called family caps that preclude benefits for babies born to mothers already receiving welfare. If federal policymakers secretly hoped that states would do part of the dirty work of cutting welfare for them, they must be pleased with these results.

However, the picture from the states is anything but consistent or uniformly punitive. Many help those recipients accepting low-wage jobs by subsidizing the costs of transportation, child care, and medical insurance (although often only for one year). Twenty-two states try to keep low-wage workers afloat by using welfare benefits to supplement their incomes, "stopping the clock" on time limits for working parents. Significantly, the federal clock keeps ticking, and states adopting this strategy must use their own funds to support working families reaching the five-year lifetime limit. With state budgets increasingly squeezed by recession, it is hard to predict how strong the state commitment to preserve these supports will be.

Many state and local agencies have already cut back work preparation and placement programs funded under a $3 billion federal welfare-to-work block grant. Those funds spurred a short-term boom in contracting to private agencies. But the block grant expired leaving little evidence that states were able to build new systems for supporting work over the long term. In fact, no one knows exactly what all of this contracting produced, as state and local agencies kept limited records and conducted few careful evaluations. A close look at contracting in Illinois, for example, revealed the creation of a diffuse array of short-term programs operating under contract requirements that left many agencies unable to build anything of lasting value.

There is another strange twist to the convoluted welfare story: in their zest for services over support, states actually shifted government funds from the pockets of poor families to the pockets of private service providers. They distributed 76 percent of their AFDC funds in cash aid to the poor in 1996, but gave poor families only 41 percent of their TANF funds in 2000. Substantial portions of the TANF budget were consumed by child care costs, although it is difficult to say exactly how all the TANF funds were used. The General Accounting Office suggests that there is a fair amount of "supplantation" of services previously funded from other budget lines but now paid for by TANF.

# Beyond the Caseload Count

The picture becomes still more complicated when one attempts to peer behind the head count in order to assess what actually happened in the purge of welfare caseloads. Exactly how did states push those caseloads down? What has happened to poor families that no longer have recourse to welfare? What kind of opportunities does the lower wage labor market really offer? Research has only begun to illuminate these crucial questions, but the evidence is disheartening.

**Finding Good Jobs:** There are three ways to lower welfare caseloads. One is by successfully moving recipients into good jobs with stable employment where they can earn enough to maintain their families above poverty (or, at least, above what they could get on welfare). Recipients may find jobs on their own, which many do, or with connections facilitated by welfare agencies and service providers.

Financial supports provided by TANF have allowed some recipients to take jobs where they earn too little to make ends meet on their own. Child-care and transportation subsidies make a difference for those workers. They also benefit from federally funded food stamps that stretch the grocery budget. But food stamp use fell off 40 percent after 1994, although fewer families were receiving welfare and more had joined the ranks of the working poor. Absent external pressures, most states made no effort to assure access to food stamps for those losing welfare. In fact, government studies indicate that administrative hassles and misinformation discouraged low-income families from obtaining benefits.

**Taking Bad Jobs:** A second way to lower welfare caseloads is to pressure recipients into taking bad jobs. Not all lower wage jobs are bad, but many of those most readily available to former recipients undermine their best efforts to make it as working parents. These jobs are characterized by unstable schedules, limited access to health insurance or pensions, no sick leave, and job insecurity. Because high turnover is a feature of these jobs, at any given moment, many are apt to be available. Indeed, employers seeking to fill these undesirable "high-velocity" jobs, where there is continuous churning of the workforce, are all too eager to use welfare agencies as a hiring hall.

This may partially explain why more than a fifth of those leaving welfare for work return within a year or two. Proponents of the new welfare conveniently blame individual work behavior or attitudes for job churning, but ignore the role of employers who structure jobs in ways that make job loss inevitable. What's a supermarket clerk to do when her manager makes frequent schedule changes, periodically shortens her hours, or asks her to work in a store across town? What happens is that carefully constructed child care arrangements break down, lost pay days break the family budget, and the hours it takes to commute on public transportation become unmanageable. The family-friendly workplace that more sought-after workers demand couldn't be farther from the hard reality of lower wage jobs.

One of the little appreciated virtues of the old welfare is that it served as a sort of unemployment insurance for these lower wage workers excluded from regular unemployment insurance by their irregular jobs. Welfare cushioned the layoffs, turnover, and contingencies that go with the territory. Under the new welfare, these workers face a hard landing because welfare is more difficult to get and offers little leeway to acquire either the time or skills that might yield a job with a future. Over the longer term, low-wage workers may find their access to welfare blocked by time limits. Although the five-year lifetime limit ostensibly targets sustained reliance on welfare, this limit could come back to bite those who cycle in and out of the lower wage labor force. At this point, no one knows how this will play out.

**Creating Barriers to Access:** A third way to reduce welfare caseloads is by reducing access—making benefits harder to acquire and keep. Some states explicitly try to divert applicants by imposing advance job-search requirements, demanding multiple trips to the welfare office in order to complete the application process, or informally advising applicants that it may not be worth the hassle. In some welfare offices, caseworkers routinely encourage applicants to forgo cash aid and apply only for Medicaid and food stamps.

Benefits are also harder to keep, as caseworkers require recipients to attend frequent meetings either to discuss seemingly endless demands for documentation or to press them on issues involving work. Everyday life in an urban welfare office is difficult to describe and, for many, even harder to believe. There are the hours of waiting in rows of plastic chairs, the repeated requests for paperwork, the ritualized weekly job club lectures about how to smile, shake hands, and show a good attitude to employers. As inspiration, caseworkers leading job club ses-

sions often tell stories from their own lives of rising from poverty to become welfare workers (positions likely to be cut back as caseloads decline). When clients tell their own tales of cycling from bad jobs to worse and ask for help getting a good job, caseworkers are apt to admonish them for indulging in a "pity party."

Access to welfare may also be constrained through a profoundly mundane array of administrative barriers that simply make benefits harder to keep. A missed appointment, misplaced documents (often lost by the agency), delayed entry of personal data—these common and otherwise trivial mishaps can result in a loss of benefits for "non-cooperation."

The Public Benefits Hotline, a call-in center that provides both advice and intervention for Chicago residents, received some ten thousand calls in the four years after welfare reform, most of them involving hassles of this sort.[2] In other parts of the country, these types of problems show up in administrative hearing records and court cases, where judges have criticized welfare agencies for making "excessive" demands for verification documents, conducting "sham assessments" leading to inappropriate imposition of work requirements, and sanctioning clients for missing appointments when they should have helped them deal with child care or medical difficulties.

## Is There a Bottom Line?

The new welfare has produced neither the immediate cataclysm its opponents threatened nor the economic and social redemption its proponents anticipated. Opponents had warned that welfare reform would plunge one million children into poverty. In the midst of an unprecedented economic boom, that didn't happen. But, even in the best of times, prospects were not auspicious for those leaving welfare.

According to the Urban Institute, about half of those leaving welfare for work between 1997 and 1999 obtained jobs where they earned a median hourly wage of only $7.15. If the jobs offered a steady forty hours of work a week (which lower wage jobs usually don't), that would provide a gross annual income of $14,872. That places a mother with two children a precarious $1,000 above the formal poverty line for the year 2000 and a two-parent family with two children nearly $3,000 *below* that line. But more than one-fifth of those leaving welfare for work didn't make it through the year—either because they lost their jobs, got sick, or just couldn't make ends meet. The only thing surprising about these figures is that the numbers weren't higher. Others left or lost welfare, but did not find work, with one in seven adults losing welfare reporting no alternative means of support. Their specific fate is unknown, but most big cities have been reporting worrisome increases in homelessness and hunger.

If there is any bottom line, it is that caseloads have been purged. But neither the market for lower wage workers nor the policies put into practice in the name of welfare reform have purged poverty from the lives of the poor. Even in the last years of the economic boom, between 1996 and 1998, the Urban Institute found that three hundred thousand more individuals in single-parent families slipped into extreme poverty. Although they qualified for food stamps that might have stretched their resources a bit further, many did not get them. Government figures indicate that families leaving welfare for work often lose access to other benefits, which states do not automatically continue irrespective of eligibility.

More recently, census figures have begun to show the effects of recession coupled with an eroded safety net. The nation's poverty rate rose to 11.7 percent in 2001, up from 11.3 percent the prior year. More troubling still, inequality is growing and poverty is deepening. In 2001, the "poverty gap," the gap between the official poverty line and the income of poor individuals, reached its highest level since measurements were first taken in 1979. In California, often a harbinger of larger social trends, a startling two in three poor children now live in families where at least one adult is employed. Can the families of lower wage workers live without access to welfare and other government supports? Apparently, they can live, but not very well.

## Slouching Toward Reauthorization

"We have to remember that the goal of the reform program was not to get people out of poverty, but to achieve financial independence, to get off welfare." This statement by a senior Connecticut welfare official quoted in the *New York Times* is more candid than most. But it illustrates the kind of political rationale that policymakers use to inoculate themselves against factual evidence of the new welfare's failure to relieve poverty.

With TANF facing reauthorization in the fall of 2002, it was clear that reconsideration of welfare policy would take place on a new playing field. Tough work rules, time limits, and devolution were just the starting point. The Bush administration advanced a reauthorization plan that increased work requirements, cut opportunities for education and training, added new doses of moralism, and extended devolution.

The Republican-controlled House passed a TANF reauthorization bill (later deferred by the Senate) requiring recipients to work forty hours a week and demanding that states enforce these requirements for 70 percent of families receiving welfare by 2007. The bill also created incentives for states to require work within a month of granting welfare benefits and continued to credit states for caseload reductions, regardless of whether families losing welfare had jobs that could sustain them.

Families would face harsh new penalties, simply for running afoul of administrative rules. The House-passed measure required states to impose full family sanctions if caseworkers find a recipient in violation of those rules for sixty days. This makes entire families vulnerable to losing aid if a parent misses a couple of appointments or gets tangled in demands to supply documents verifying eligibility, just the type of problem that crops up routinely in states with complicated rules and outdated record-keeping systems.

One of the least mentioned but most dangerous features of the House bill was a "superwaiver" that would allow the executive branch to release states from social welfare obligations contained in more than a dozen federal poverty programs, in-

cluding not only TANF, but also food stamps and Medicaid. This stealth provision would allow the Bush administration to override existing legislation by fiat. The nominal justification for the superwaiver is that it would ease the path of state innovation and experimentation. It would also ease the path for state cuts in social programs beyond all previous experience.

A more visibly contentious feature of the House bill was a provision to spend $300 million dollars per year on programs to induce welfare recipients to marry. This provision is one of the favorites of the religious right, along with the administration's funding for faith-based social services. These moral redemption provisions may be more important for what they signify to the Republican Party's conservative base than for what they do, as many states have resisted these types of things in the past. However, on this point, it is irresistible to quote America's favorite president, the fictional President Josiah Bartlet of the television series *West Wing*, who quipped: "When did the government get into the yenta business?"

## Of Poverty, Democracy, and Welfare

The demise of the old welfare marked more than an end to a policy that many believed had outlived its usefulness. It also marked the end of welfare *politics* as we knew it. In the tepid debate over reauthorization in the fall of 2002, the bitter conflicts of earlier years over government's role in addressing poverty were replaced by half-hearted tinkering. Even provisions with the potential to induce hand-to-hand combat—such as those on marriage or the superwaiver—elicited relatively low-intensity challenges.

Is this because the new welfare yielded the benefits that liberals had hoped for, removing a contentious issue from the table and conferring legitimation on the poor, not as recipients, but as workers? Did it satisfy conservatives by clearing caseloads and demanding work? That does not seem to be the case.

If the poor have benefited from a new legitimacy, it is hard to see the rewards. Congress has not rushed to offer extensive new work supports. In fact, the House bill contained $8 to $10 billion less for work supports than the Congressional Budget Office estimated would be needed. In 2002, Congress couldn't even agree to extend unemployment insurance for those outside the welfare system who were felled by recession, corporate collapses, and the high-tech slide. While conservatives celebrated the caseload count, they also savored the opportunity to raise the ante with more onerous work requirements and marriage inducements, and even made a bid to eliminate other social protections through the superwaiver.

In the aftermath of the November 2002 election, a conservative consolidation of power was in the air. In a televised interview with Jim Lehrer, Republican spokesman Grover Norquist dared Democrats to take on the welfare issue. "If the Democrats want to stand up against welfare reform, let them! Two years from now, they'll be in even worse shape in the Senate elections."

Some congressional Democrats did take tentative steps against the tide, suggesting provisions that would fund new welfare-to-work services, provide additional job subsidies, increase the child care allotment, provide alternatives to work for recipients categorized as having work "barriers," and restore benefits to legal immigrants who were cut from welfare in 1996. Maryland Representative Benjamin Cardin was chief sponsor of a bill suggesting that states should be held accountable, not only for caseload reduction, but for poverty reduction. This notion had little traction in the 107th Congress and is likely to have even less in the next. Without the foundation of a politics of poverty to build on, such laudable ideas seem strangely irrelevant, even to the Democrats' agenda.

If welfare is a bellwether of broader political developments, there's little mistaking which way the wind is blowing. It has a decidedly Dickensian chill. The politics of poverty that gave birth to the old welfare has been supplanted by the politics of personal piety that gave birth to the new. This reflects a convergence between a neoliberal agenda of market dominance and a neoconservative agenda of middle-class moralism. In this reconfigured politics, personal responsibility is code for enforcement of the market. The new Calvinism advanced by welfare policy treats inequality as a natural consequence of personal behavior and attitude in an impartial marketplace. It is consistent with a shift in the role of the state from defender of the vulnerable and buffer against the market to one of protector-in-chief of both market and morals. This shift does not favor a small state, but a different state, one capable of enforcing market demands on workers, responding to corporate demands for capital (through public subsidies, bailouts, and tax breaks), and, perhaps more symbolically, regulating morality.

Welfare policy neither created, nor could prevent, these developments. Nor is it a foregone conclusion that government will shirk its social responsibilities. After all, America's growing economic inequality is fundamentally at odds with its commitment to political equality.

In contrast to the United States, the policies of Western European countries suggest that there need not be an absolute conflict between the welfare state and the market. Despite their allegiance to the latter, other nations continue to offer greater social protection to their citizens and worry about the democratic consequences of excluding the disadvantaged from the economy and the polity. U.S. policymakers need to move past stale debates pitting work against welfare and the poor against the nonpoor, if they are to advance policies that promote both social inclusion and economic opportunity.

Welfare, though small in scope, is large in relevance because it is a place where economic, social, and political issues converge. The old welfare acknowledged, in principle, a political commitment to relieve poverty and lessen inequality, even if, in practice, that commitment was limited, benefits were ungenerous, and access uneven. The new welfare dramatically changed the terms of the relationship between disadvantaged citizens and their state. It devolved choices about social protection from the State to the states, and it placed the value of work over the values of family well-being and social equity. As bad as the old welfare may have been, there is reason to lament its demise after all.

# Notes

1. The discussion in this section draws, in part, on research conducted for the Project on the Public Economy of Work at the University of Chicago, supported by the Ford Foundation, the National Science Foundation, and the Open Society Institute. The author and Susan Lambert are co-directors.

2. The Hotline is a collaborative effort of the Legal Assistance Foundation of Chicago and community antipoverty advocates.

**EVELYN Z. BRODKIN** is associate professor at the School of Social Service Administration and lecturer in the Law School of the University of Chicago. She writes widely on poverty and politics.

From *Dissent*, Winter 2003 pp. 29–36. © 2003 by Dissent Magazine. Reprinted by permission. www.dissentmagazine.com

# What's At Stake

In the competitive world of college admissions, 'fairness' is often in the eye of the beholder. Here are the facts about affirmative action.

**BY BARBARA KANTROWITZ AND PAT WINGERT**

IN 1978, THE SUPREME COURT opened the doors of America's elite campuses to a generation of minority students when it ruled that universities' admissions policies could take applicants' race into account. But the decision, by a narrowly divided court drawing a hairsplitting distinction between race as a "plus factor" (allowed) and numerical quotas (forbidden), did not end an often bitter and emotional debate. A quarter of a century after the ruling in *Regents of the University of California v. Bakke,* affirmative action is still being challenged by disappointed applicants to selective colleges and graduate schools, and still hotly defended by civil-rights groups. Now that two such cases, both involving the University of Michigan, have reached the Supreme Court, the issue can no longer be evaded: when, if ever, should schools give preferential treatment to minorities, based solely on their race?

---

## 4.3%
**THE PERCENTAGE OF BLACK PLAYERS ON THE UNIVERSITY OF MICHIGAN FOOTBALL TEAM, 1941**

## 45%
**THE PERCENTAGE OF BLACK PLAYERS ON THE UNIVERSITY OF MICHIGAN FOOTBALL TEAM, 2002**

## 7%
**THE PERCENTAGE OF YALE UNIVERSITY STUDENTS WHOM ARE BLACK**

---

It's a measure of how far we've come that the desirability of improving opportunities for black and Hispanic students is a given in the debate. But the fundamental question of where "fairness" lies hasn't changed, and the competition keeps growing. Each year, more students apply to the top universities, which by and large have not increased the sizes of their classes in the past 50 years. The court will have to decide who deserves first crack at those scarce resources. (Right now, about one sixth of blacks get college degrees, compared with 30 percent of whites and 40 percent of Asians.) And if the court allows affirmative action to continue in some form, it will only set the stage for future debate over even more perplexing questions. Do all minorities deserve an edge or just those from disadvantaged backgrounds? What about white students from poor families? And how do you balance the academic records of students from the suburbs and the inner cities? As the controversy heats up, here's a 10-step guide to sorting out the issues at stake:

## 1 What is affirmative action?

When President Kennedy first used the term in the early 1960s, "affirmative action" simply meant taking extra measures to ensure integration in federally funded jobs. Forty years later, a wide range of programs fall under this rubric, although all are meant to encourage enrollment of underrepresented minorities—generally blacks, Hispanics and Native Americans. Schools vary in how much weight they assign to the student's race. For some, it's a decisive consideration; for others, it's jut one among a number of factors such as test scores, grades, family background, talents and extracurricular activities. After the *Bakke* decision emphasized the importance of campus diversity as a "compelling" benefit to society, colleges quickly responded with efforts not just to attract minorities but to create a broader geographic and socioeconomic mix, along with a range of academic, athletic or artistic talent.

In 2003, the debate over the merits of affirmative action essentially boils down to questions of fairness for both black and white applicants. Critics say it results in "reverse discrimination" against white applicants who are passed over in favor of less well-qualified black students, some of whom suffer when they attend schools they're not prepared for. But Gary Orfield, director of Harvard University's Civil Rights Project, argues that emphasizing diversity has not meant admitting unqualified students. "I have been on the admissions committees of five different

# Diversity Is Essential...

**He knew he was in for a fight. But it's a battle the former University of Michigan president believes must be won.**

BY LEE C. BOLLINGER

When I became president of the University of Michigan in 1997, affirmative action in higher education was under siege from the right. Buoyed by a successful lawsuit against the University of Texas Law School's admissions policy and by ballot initiatives such as California's Proposition 209, which outlawed race as a factor in college admissions, the opponents set their sights on affirmative-action programs at colleges across the country.

The rumor that Michigan would be the next target in this campaign turned out to be correct. I believed strongly that we had no choice but to mount the best legal defense ever for diversity in higher education and take special efforts to explain this complex issue, in simple and direct language, to the American public. There are many misperceptions about how race and ethnicity are considered in college admissions. Competitive colleges and universities are always looking for a mix of students with different experiences and backgrounds—academic, geographic, international, socioeconomic, athletic, public-service oriented and, yes, racial and ethnic.

It is true that in sorting the initial rush of applications, large universities will give "points" for various factors in the selection process in order to ensure fairness as various officers review applicants. Opponents of Michigan's undergraduate system complain that an applicant is assigned more points for being black, Hispanic or Native American than for having a perfect SAT score. This is true, but it trivializes the real issue: whether, in principle, race and ethnicity are appropriate considerations.

The simple fact about the Michigan undergraduate policy is that it gives overwhelming weight to traditional academic factors—some 110 out of a total of 150 points. After that, there are some 40 points left for other factors, of which 20 can be allocated for race or socioeconomic status.

Race has been a defining element of the American experience. The historic *Brown v. Board of Education* decision is almost 50 years old, yet metropolitan Detroit is more segregated now than it was in 1960. The majority of students who each year arrive on a campus like Michigan's graduated from virtually all-white or all-black high schools. The campus is their first experience living in an integrated environment.

This is vital. Diversity is not merely a desirable addition to a well-rounded education. It is as essential as the study of the Middle Ages, of international politics and of Shakespeare. For our students to better understand the diverse country and world they inhabit, they must be immersed in a campus culture that allows them to study with, argue with and become friends with students who may be different from them. It broadens the mind, and the intellect—essential goals of education.

Reasonable people can disagree about affirmative action. But it is important that we do not lose the sense of history, the compassion and the largeness of vision that defined the best of the civil-rights era, which has given rise to so much of what is good about America today.

BOLLINGER is president of Columbia University.

# ... But Not at This Cost

**Admissions policies like Michigan's focus not on who, but what, you are—perpetuating a culture of victimhood**

BY ARMSTRONG WILLIAMS

Back in 1977, when I was a senior in high school, I received scholarship offers to attend prestigious colleges. The schools wanted me in part because of my good academic record—but also because affirmative action mandates required them to encourage more black students to enroll. My father wouldn't let me take any of the enticements. His reasoning was straightforward: scholarship money should go to the economically deprived. And since he could pay for my schooling, he would. In the end, I chose a historically black college—South Carolina State.

What I think my father meant, but was perhaps too stern to say, was that one should always rely on hard work and personal achievement to carry the day—every day. Sadly, this rousing point seems lost on the admissions board at the University of Michigan, which wrongly and unapologetically discriminates on the basis of skin color. The university ranks applicants on a scale that awards points for SAT scores, high school grades and race. For example, a perfect SAT score is worth 12 points. Being black gets you 20 points. Is there anyone who can look at those two numbers and think they are fair?

Supporters maintain that the quota system is essential to creating a diverse student body. And, indeed, there is some validity to this sort of thinking. A shared history of slavery and discrimination has ingrained racial hierarchies into our national identity, divisions that need to be erased. There is, however, a very real danger that we are merely reinforcing the idea that minorities are first and foremost victims. Because of this victim status, the logic goes, they are owed special treatment. But that isn't progress, it's inertia.

If the goal of affirmative action is to create a more equitable society, it should be need-based. Instead, affirmative action is defined by its tendency to reduce people to fixed categories: at many universities, it seems, admissions officers look less at who you are than *what* you are. As a result, affirmative-action programs rarely help the least among us. Instead, they often benefit the children of middle- and upper-class black Americans who have been conditioned to feel they are owed something.

This is alarming. We have finally, after far too long, reached a point where black Americans have pushed into the mainstream—and not just in entertainment and sports. From politics to corporate finance, blacks succeed. Yet many of us still feel entitled to special benefits—in school, in jobs, in government contracts.

It is time to stop. We must reach a point where we expect to rise or fall on our own merits. We just can't continue to base opportunities on race while the needs of the poor fall by the wayside. As a child growing up on a farm, I was taught that personal responsibility was the lever that moved the world. That is why it pains me to see my peers rest their heads upon the warm pillow of victim status.

WILLIAMS is a syndicated columnist.

universities," he says, "and I have never seen a student admitted just on the basis of race. [Committees] think about what the class will be like, what kind of educational experience the class will provide." Opponents also say that with the expansion of the black middle class in the past 20 years, these programs should be refocused on kids from low-income homes. "It just doesn't make sense to give preference to the children of a wealthy black businessman, but not to the child of a Vietnamese boat person or an Arab-American who is suffering discrimination," says Curt Levey, director of legal affairs at the Center for Individual Rights, which is representing the white applicants who were turned down by the University of Michigan.

Despite the public perception that affirmative action is rampant on campuses, these programs really only affect a very small number of minority students. It's a legal issue mainly on highly selective public campuses, such as Michigan, Berkeley or Texas. Even at these schools, the actual numbers of minority students are still small—which is why supporters of affirmative action say race should still matter. Blacks account for 11 percent of undergraduates nationally; at the most elite schools the percentage is often smaller. For example, fewer than 7 percent of Harvard's current freshman class is black, compared with 12.9 percent of the overall population.

## 2 How did the University of Michigan become the test case?

Both sides say it was really a matter of chance more than anything else. "It's not like we studied 1,000 schools and picked them out," says Levey. To have the makings of a test case, the suit had to involve a public university whose admissions information could be obtained under the Freedom of Information Act. It also had to be a very large school that relied on some kind of numerical admissions formula—unlike the more individualized approach generally used by private colleges with large admissions staffs.

In fact, Michigan is just one of a number of public universities that have faced legal challenges in recent years. In 1996, the U.S. Court of Appeals for the Fifth Circuit banned the use of race in admissions at the University of Texas Law School. The Supreme Court declined to hear the law school's appeal, but by that time, the university had changed its admissions procedures anyway. The University of Georgia dropped race as a factor after a similar suit. But when Michigan's admissions policy came under challenge in the mid-1990s, university officials decided to fight back—all the way to the Supreme Court.

## 3 How does the Michigan system work?

Although President George W. Bush reduced Michigan's complex admissions process to a single sound bite—comparing the relative values given to SAT scores and race—a student's academic record is actually the most important factor. For undergraduate applicants, decisions are made on a point system. Out of a total of 150 possible points, a student can get up to 110 for academics. That includes a possible 80 points for grades and 12 points for standardized test scores. Admissions counselors then add or subtract points for the rigor of the high school (up to 10) and the difficulty of the curriculum (up to 8 for students who take the toughest courses). Applicants can get up to 40 more points for such factors as residency in underrepresented states (2 points) or Michigan residency (10 points, with a 6-point bonus for living in an underrepresented county). Being from an underrepresented minority group or from a predominantly minority high school is worth 20 points. So is being from a low-income family—even for white students. The same 20 points are awarded to athletes. Students also earn points for being related to an alumnus (up to 4 points), writing a good personal essay (up to 3 points) and participating in extracurricular activities (up to 5 points). Admissions officials say the scale is only a guide; there's no target number that automatically determines whether a student is admitted or rejected. Michigan also has a "rolling" admissions policy, which means that students hear a few months after they apply. The number of spaces available depends on when in this cycle a student applies.

At the law school, there's no point system, but the admissions officers say higher grades and standardized test scores do increase an applicant's chances. Those factors are considered along with the rigor of an applicant's courses, recommendations and essays. The school also says that race "sometimes makes the difference in whether or not a student is admitted."

## 4 Does the Michigan system create quotas?

This is an issue the court will probably have to decide. Awarding points could amount to a quota if it resulted in routinely filling a fixed number of places. Levey claims that the fact that the number of minority students admitted is relatively stable from year to year proves there is a target Michigan tries to hit. Michigan's president, Mary Sue Coleman, is adamant that that's not the case. "We do not have, and never have had, quotas or numerical targets in either the undergraduate or Law School admissions programs," she said in a statement issued after Bush's speech last week. At the law school, the most recent entering class of 352 students included 21 African-Americans, 24 Latinos and 8 Native Americans. The year before, there were 26 African-Americans, 16 Latinos and 3 Native Americans. The university says that over the past nine years, the number of blacks in the entering class has ranged from 21 to 37. On the undergraduate level, the university says that blacks generally make up between 7 and 9 percent of the entering class.

In general, few outright quota systems exist anymore. "The only legal way to have quotas today is to address a proven constitutional violation," says Orfield. "For instance, if you can prove that a police or fire department intentionally did not hire any blacks for 25 years, and you can prove discrimination, a judge can rule that there can be a quota for the next five years."

# Affirmative Action, 25 Years Later

Lawsuits are prompting the Supreme Court to revisit a landmark 1978 decision in favor of race-based college admissions. Affirmative action's legacy, and its uncertain future.

## SAT Scores

| SAT1: 2002 NAT'L AVERAGE | |
|---|---|
| White | 1060 |
| Black | 857 |
| Hispanic | 910 |
| Asian/Pac. Islander | 1070 |
| Native American | 962 |
| **SAT1: 2002 UNIV. AVERAGE** | |
| UC Berkeley | 1180–1440* |
| Univ. of Florida (2001) | 1229 |
| Univ. of Michigan | 1180–1390* |
| UT Austin | 1222 |

## The Case Against Michigan

Plaintiff Barbara Grutter claims she lost her spot at Michigan Law School to less qualified minorities; 100% of blacks with Grutter's ranking were accepted the year she applied, but only 9% of whites.

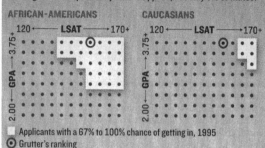

☐ Applicants with a 67% to 100% chance of getting in, 1995
◉ Grutter's ranking

## Univ. of Mich. Point System

The university uses a point scale to rate prospective students. Its policy of awarding minorities an extra 20 has stirred protest. Here's how a fictional applicant would score a promising 130:

| GPA Score | Points |
|---|---|
| 2.0 | 40 |
| 2.1 | 42 |
| 2.2 | 44 |
| 2.3 | 46 |
| 2.4 | 48 |
| 2.5 | 50 |
| 2.6 | 52 |
| 2.7 | 54 |
| 2.8 | 56 |
| 2.9 | 58 |
| 3.0 | 60 |
| 3.1 | 62 |
| 3.2 | 64 |
| 3.3 | 66 |
| 3.4 | 68 |
| 3.5 | (70) |
| 3.6 | 72 |
| 3.7 | 74 |
| 3.8 | 76 |
| 3.9 | 78 |
| 4.0 | 80 |

**HIGH-SCHOOL QUALITY**

| Score | Points |
|---|---|
| 0 | 0 |
| 1 | 2 |
| 2 | 4 |
| 3 | (6) |
| 4 | 8 |
| 5 | 10 |

**DIFFICULTY OF CURRICULUM**

| Score | Points |
|---|---|
| -2 | -4 |
| -1 | -2 |
| 0 | 0 |
| 1 | 2 |
| 2 | (4) |
| 3 | 6 |
| 4 | 8 |

**TEST SCORES**

| ACT | SAT1 | Points |
|---|---|---|
| 1–19 | 400–920 | 0 |
| 20–21 | 930–1000 | 6 |
| 22–26 | 1010–1190 | (10) |
| 27–30 | 1200–1350 | 11 |
| 31–36 | 1360–1600 | 12 |

**Points** (maximum of 40)

**GEOGRAPHY**
- (10) Michigan resident
- 6 Underrepresented Michigan county
- 2 Underrepresented state

**ALUMNI**
- 4 Legacy (parents, stepparents)
- 1 Other (grandparents, siblings)

**ESSAY**
- 1 Very good
- (2) Excellent
- 3 Outstanding

**PERSONAL ACHIEVEMENT**
- 1 State
- (3) Regional
- 5 National

**LEADERSHIP AND SERVICE**
- 1 State
- 2 Regional
- (5) National

**MISCELLANEOUS** (choose one)
- 20 Socioeconomic disadvantage
- (20) Underrepresented racial/ethnic minority identification or education
- 5 Men in nursing
- 20 Scholarship athlete
- 20 Provost's discretion

## Race and Higher Education

The number of minorities attending four-year colleges has risen about 85% since the Supreme Court OK'd affirmative action in admissions.

Race/ethnicity
- ▨ White
- ■ Black
- ■ Hispanic
- ■ Asian/Pac. Islander
- ■ Native American
- ☐ Other/Did not answer

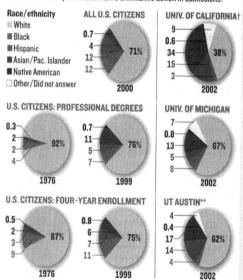

ALL RACES ARE NON-HISPANIC EXCEPT "HISPANIC." NUMBERS DO NOT ADD TO 100 DUE TO ROUNDING. "25TH TO 75TH PERCENTILES. †FRESHMAN ADMITS ONLY. **UNDERGRADUATES. SOURCES: U.S. CENSUS BUREAU, UC BERKELEY, UNIV. OF MICHIGAN, UT AUSTIN, UNIV. OF FLORIDA, THE CENTER FOR INDIVIDUAL RIGHTS, THE COLLEGE BOARD. RESEARCH AND TEXT BY JOSH ULICK. GRAPHIC BY BONNIE SCRANTON.

## New Options for Diversity?

Several states have enacted the alternatives to affirmative action that Bush favors. But do they reach an equal number of minorities?

- **CALIFORNIA**: Voters passed Proposition 209 in **1996**. It bans affirmative action in university admissions. The plan promises a state-university spot for the top **4%** of students from every high school, including the most disadvantaged ones. Other factors may be involved, but Berkeley's black undergraduate enrollment has dropped **33%** from **1996** to **2001**.
- **TEXAS**: A **1997** plan ended affirmative action in admissions. High-school students in the top **10%** of their class are guaranteed slots at state schools. Since then, black enrollment has remained relatively stable at UT Austin.
- **FLORIDA**: As of **2000**, state universities no longer consider race in admissions, but promise slots for students in the top **20%** of classes.

## AFFIRMATIVE ACCESS

# Making the Grade
### Bush wants admissions policies to look like his home state's. But in Texas, his plan gets middling marks.

BY LEIF STRICKLAND

Natalie Fogiel, an 18-year-old high-school senior in Dallas, has SAT scores higher than the Ivy League's collective average—she scored 1490 out of 1600. She's a National Merit Scholar semifinalist, and she's active in Student Congress. Fogiel doesn't want to go to Harvard or Yale. She wants to go to the business school at her state university's flagship campus, the University of Texas at Austin. But under Texas's five-year-old "affirmative access" policy—which guarantees admission to any state university for all seniors graduating in the top 10 percent of their classes—Fogiel isn't sure she'll get in. Because she goes to Highland Park High School in Dallas—one of the most competitive public schools in the country—she's only in the top 15 percent.

As the Supreme Court prepares to review the constitutionality of affirmative-action programs, President Bush has been championing programs such as Texas's, which passed when he was governor. But at some of the state's best schools, the policy has been attacked with the same words—"unfair" and "divisive"—that Bush uses to describe affirmative action. "If I had gone anywhere else, I probably would be in the top 1 percent," Fogiel says. While Texas's program prohibits using race as a factor, Texas's many segregated high schools mean the result is much the same. Since the 10 percent plan was implemented, minority enrollment at UT Austin has returned to roughly the same levels as when affirmative action was in effect.

The problem with the 10 percent policy, some Highland Park students say, is that it assumes all high schools are alike. And Highland Park High—with its 97 percent white student population—is clearly unique. Even a student who scores all A's in regular classes for four straight years wouldn't be guaranteed a place in the top quarter of his class. (You'd need to add honors classes to the mix.)

But elsewhere, the policy is playing well. Israel Hernandez is in the top 10 percent of W. H. Adamson High School, which is overwhelmingly Hispanic. He's the first member of his family to go to college; he'll be attending Texas A&M in the fall. "It's like everyone has their hopes and dreams on me," he says. Texas A&M has been to Adamson (average SAT score: 838) more than a dozen times this year touting its Century Scholars program, which specifically targets promising inner-city students like Hernandez.

Texas's plan doesn't just help traditional minorities. "The 10 percent diversifies economically," says Harvard Law professor Lani Guinier. "It benefits rural west Texas, which is primarily white but also very poor."

The policy isn't causing Highland Park students too much hardship—98 percent of its graduates went to college last year. Most of those who applied to UT and didn't get into their preferred programs were admitted to the university nonetheless—either into another school or to a provisional program. For her part, Fogiel says she probably won't go to UT if she isn't accepted to Austin's business program. She'll opt for one of her safeties: Georgetown or Boston College.

With MARK MILLER in Dallas

---

On campuses, some education experts say that what appear to be quotas may actually just reflect a relatively steady number of minority applicants within a certain state. "I don't know of a public or private institution that uses quotas," says Alexander Astin, director of the Higher Education Research Institute at UCLA. "That's a red herring. There is always a consideration of merit given." Nonetheless, admissions officers at public and private universities admit that they are always very conscious of demography—and work hard to make sure that the number of minority students does not decline precipitously from one year to the next.

## 5 How can the court rule?

The short answer is: the Supreme Court can do whatever it wants. The options range from leaving the *Bakke* decision intact to barring any use of race in college admissions. Or the court could issue a narrowly tailored opinion, one that would affect only Michigan's point system and perhaps only the number of points the university assigns to race. "I think it's a good guess that they may say that they cannot give minorities a specific number of points, or say points are fine, but they can only award 10," says Levey.

The experts agree that the key vote will belong to Justice Sandra Day O'Connor. Some court watchers predict that she will try to find a very specific solution that will leave affirmative action largely intact. "She probably won't buy anything that's open-ended," says Sheldon Steinbach, general counsel of the American Council on Education, a consortium of the nation's leading research universities. "Maybe she will say that it can be done in some narrowly defined way." Steinbach doesn't think the court will order schools to disregard everything but the supposedly objective criteria of grades and test scores. Such a ruling "would tie the hands of admissions officers from shaping the kind of class they want to fulfill the academic mission of the institution," Steinbach says. Another possibility is that the court will order schools to give preference to students who are economically disadvantaged, which would cover many minority applicants.

## 6 Will the decision affect private universities and colleges?

The answer really depends on what the justices rule, but legal experts generally agree that private institutions would have to follow the court's guidelines because virtually all receive some federal funding. However, the ruling would have a noticeable impact only at elite institutions since most colleges in this country accept the vast majority of applicants. And the elite schools—no more than several dozen around the country—generally employ multistep admissions procedures that leave plenty of room for subjective judgments. Unlike the numerical formulas used by large public universities, these would be difficult to challenge in court.

Already, several landmark state cases have pushed private schools to make changes. In the wake of the Texas decision, officials at highly selective Rice University in Houston, on the advice of the state attorney general, banned the use of race in all admissions decisions. Clerks were told to strip any reference to a student's race or ethnicity from admissions and financial-aid applications before they were forwarded to the admission committee. Although the proportion of minorities dropped right after the change, it's now back up to the levels before the ruling, officials say—about 7 percent black and 10.5 percent Hispanic. That was accomplished through "significant" recruiting, a Rice spokesman said.

## 7 How would an anti-affirmative-action ruling affect other preferences for legacies and athletes?

Some educators think legacies (the children or grandchildren of alumni) could become unintended victims of an anti-affirmative-action ruling. On the face of it, providing preferential treatment to these applicants does not violate the Constitution, but as a matter of fairness—and politics—legacies would be hard to defend, since they are usually white and middle class. However, many colleges would probably resist the change because legacies bring a sense of tradition and continuity to the school. (They also are a powerful inducement to alumni donations.) Athletic preferences are a different story. They don't disproportionately favor whites so they're probably not as vulnerable.

## 8 Whom does affirmative action hurt and whom does it help?

Opponents of affirmative action claim it actually hurts some minority students, particularly those who end up struggling to compete in schools they're not prepared for. And, they say, it unfairly tars well-qualified minority students with the suspicion that they were admitted because of their race. Supporters say that's a spurious argument because race may sometimes be the deciding factor between qualified applicants, but it is never the only reason a student is admitted.

The more obvious potential victims, of course, are white students who have been denied admission—like the plaintiffs in the Michigan suit. But there's no guarantee that these students would have been admitted even if there were no black applicants. In their 1998 book "The Shape of the River," William Bowen and Derek Bok (former presidents of Princeton and Harvard, respectively) analyzed the records of 45,000 students at elite uni-

versities and found that without race-sensitive admissions, white applicants' chances of being admitted to selective universities would have increased only slightly, from 25 to 26.2 percent. But Bowen and Bok also found that black applicants' chances were greatly enhanced by affirmative action, and the vast majority of black students went on to graduate within six years—even at the most selective institutions. The black graduates were more likely to go to graduate or professional school than their white counterparts and more likely to be leaders of community, social service or professional organizations after college.

Supporters of affirmative action say both white and black students benefit from living in a diverse academic environment, one that closely resembles the increasingly diverse workplace. Opponents say schools don't need affirmative action to create a diverse campus; instead they say that other admissions strategies, such as "affirmative access," can accomplish the same goals.

## 9 What is "affirmative access"?

In the wake of lawsuits, several states have adopted alternative ways to bring minority students to campus. Modern political marketing seems to require a label for everything, and "affirmative access" has emerged as the label for these plans. Each operates differently. In California, the top 4 percent of students at each in-state high school is guaranteed admission to the University of California (although not necessarily to the most prestigious campuses, Berkeley and UCLA). For the University of Texas, it's the top 10 percent, and in Florida, the top 20 percent. The success of these new initiatives varies. California's plan was enacted after the passage of Proposition 209, which forbids using race in admissions. In 1997, the last year before the use of race was banned, 18.8 percent of the class consisted of underrepresented minorities. Last year that number was 19.1 percent systemwide. But some individual campuses, like Berkeley and UCLA, have not returned to pre-1997 levels. At the University of Texas, the percentage of black and Hispanic entering freshmen has remained fairly steady, but officials say the 10 percent law alone isn't enough. "You have to add some targeted procedures that work in tandem with the law," says University of Texas president Larry Faulkner. "And for us that's been pretty aggressive recruiting programs aimed at top 10 percent students in areas where minority students live, and carefully tailored scholarship programs aimed at students in areas or schools that have not historically attended UT."

Opponents of affirmative access like lawyer Martin Michaelson, who specializes in higher-education cases, say these programs rest on the dubious premise that "residential segregation patterns are a better method for choosing a college class than the judgment of educators" and create, in effect, a built-in constituency for continued segregation. Critics also worry that a program that mixes schools of widely different qualities may reward less-

# What Merit Really Means

JONATHAN ALTER

ANYONE WITH HALF A BRAIN KNOWS THAT GRADES AND TEST scores aren't the only way to define "merit" in college admissions. Sometimes a good jump shot or batting average is "merit." Or a commitment to a soup kitchen. Or the ability to overcome an obstacle in life. Conscientious admissions officers take a wide variety of factors into account and make rounded, subtle judgments about the composition of the incoming class. The debate over affirmative action in education boils down to whether universities should be free to make that judgment or be told by the government how to choose.

The problem with affirmative action is not, as some conservatives suggest, that it has eroded standards and dumbed down elite institutions. The level of academic achievement among freshmen at, say, Yale is far higher than it was when George W. Bush entered in 1964. With his highschool record, he probably wouldn't be admitted today, even if he were black. No, what's wrong with affirmative action is that it has too often been routinized and mechanized, and has thus begun to resemble the very thinking it was supposed to replace.

Conservatives, trying to stand on principle, argue that affirmative action is simply reverse discrimination. In certain realms, like the awarding of federal contracts, that may be true. But college is different. The college experience is partly about preparing students for adult life, which increasingly means learning to deal with people of many different backgrounds. To hear the Bill Bennetts of the world, whites and Asian-Americans rejected by the colleges of their choice are like blacks rejected by the lunch counters of their choice in the Jim Crow South. It's a lame analogy. Lunch counters (and other public facilities) have no right to discriminate; neither do nonselective colleges, about 80 percent of the total. But exclusive institutions, by definition, must exclude.

The basis on which they do so should at least be consistent. You either favor weighing immutable nonacademic "preferences" or you don't. Some conservatives want to continue preferences for alumni children and end those for minorities. Some liberals want the reverse—to keep affirmative action but end legacies. Both sides ace their hypocrisy boards. Personally, I go for preferences, within limits, because I want the smart alumni kid from Pacific Palisades to sit in the dining hall and get to know the smart poor kid from Camden. Neither the University of Michigan policy nor the Bush administration challenge to it are likely to take us closer to that end.

The larger problem is that exclusive colleges too often use that worn-out crutch of a word—"diversity"—to cover for their lack of genuine integration (in dorms, for instance), and a lack of progress on socioeconomic affirmative action. Only 3 percent of students in top universities come from the poorest quarter of the American population. A Harvard study last year found that colleges are too often "recyclers of privilege" instead of "engines of upward mobility." Harvard itself falls short on this score, with fewer than 9 percent of its students coming from families eligible for Pell grants (i.e., the modest means). Princeton and Notre Dame are among those that don't do discernibly better.

Ironically, colleges like these with nice-sounding "needs-blind admission" policies consistently admit fewer poorer kids because, as a James Irvine Foundation report discovered, "they feel like they're off the hook." They're so proud of themselves for not calculating students' ability to pay in making admissions decisions that they do less than they could to recruit poorer students—and thus fail to take enough "affirmative action" (in its original, beating-the-bushes sense) to redress socioeconomic disparities. It's easier to go with familiar, relatively affluent high schools they know will produce kids more likely to succeed.

Recently, Berkeley, UCLA and USC have done twice or three times better than every other elite school in enrolling economically disadvantaged students. Why? Because California has abolished racial preferences, which forced these schools to adopt economic affirmative action. Richard Kahlenberg of The Century Foundation says that's the only way to get more poor kids admitted. A forthcoming study from that foundation will show that substituting economic preferences for race at the top 146 schools would lessen the black and Hispanic representation only two percentage points (from 12 percent currently to 10 percent).

But I still think it makes sense to allow both class and race to be considered—and to let 1,000 other factors bloom, as good colleges do. Just don't make it mechanical. The anti-affirmative-action forces have to abandon the notion that GPAs and SATs add up to some numerical right to admission; the advocates for the status quo have to give up the numerical awarding of points for things like race, because sometimes being African American or Hispanic or Native American should be a big plus, and sometimes it shouldn't. It depends on the kid. All of which means that no matter what happens in the Supreme Court, the University of Michigan and other large schools should spend the money needed for a more subtle and subjective quest for true merit.

qualified students than more-traditional programs. At the University of Texas, Faulkner says no; he believes that class rank is a better predictor of collegiate success than test scores, even at high schools with large numbers of disadvantaged students. But Orfield, who is in the final stages of completing a formal study of these programs, disagrees; he says that less-qualified students are being admitted under the percentage programs. Often, Orfield says, 60 percent of kids at suburban high schools have better credentials than the top 10 percent of kids at inner-city schools (sidebar). The affirmative-access approach would also be hard to apply in nonstate colleges and graduate schools that draw students from all over the country.

Another approach would be to target students from low-income homes, regardless of race. That would eliminate the problem of giving middle-class blacks an edge. But Orfield says that being middle class does not protect black students from the effects of racism, and they are still often at a disadvantage in the admissions process. "Race still matters," he says. "It's fine with me if we apply affirmative action to poor people, but I think we need it for middle-class blacks as well."

## 10 So what is the most equitable way to select the best-qualified applicants?

In judging admissions policies, it's important to remember that schools aren't just looking to reward past achievement. They want to attract students who will create the richest academic and social communities, and who have the best odds of success in college and later life. As a result, admissions officers say, what they really look for are signs of intellectual energy and personal enthusiasm—qualities that can show up in grades, scores, essays, recommendations, extracurricular activities, or a mix of all these. "Merit" has become particularly difficult to define in an era when elite colleges are getting many more well-qualified applicants than they can possibly accept, and when distrust of standardized admissions tests is growing. And making hard and fast distinctions based on race isn't going to get any easier as the growing trend toward racial mixing increases over the next century and people choose to identify with more than one group. The only thing educators who have struggled with these issues agree on is that there is no magic formula, not even for the Supreme Court.

With VANESSA JUAREZ
and ANA FIGUEROA

# WHY WE HATE

**We may not admit it, but we are plagued with xenophobic tendencies. Our hidden prejudices run so deep, we are quick to judge, fear and even hate the unknown.**

By Margo Monteith, Ph.D. and Jeffrey Winters

**BALBIR SINGH SODHI WAS SHOT TO DEATH ON** September 15 in Mesa, Arizona. His killer claimed to be exacting revenge for the terrorist attacks of September 11. Upon his arrest, the murderer shouted, "I stand for America all the way." Though Sodhi wore a turban and could trace his ancestry to South Asia, he shared neither ethnicity nor religion with the suicide hijackers. Sodhi—who was killed at the gas station where he worked—died just for being different in a nation gripped with fear.

For Arab and Muslim Americans, the months after the terrorist attacks have been trying. They have been harassed at work and their property has been vandalized. An Arab San Francisco shop owner recalled with anger that his five-year-old daughter was taunted by name-callers. Classmates would yell "terrorist" as she walked by.

Public leaders from President George W. Bush on down have called for tolerance. But the Center for American-Islamic Relations in Washington, D.C., has tallied some 1,700 incidents of abuse against Muslims in the five months following September 11. Despite our better nature, it seems, fear of foreigners or other strange-seeming people comes out when we are under stress. That fear, known as xenophobia, seems almost hardwired into the human psyche.

Researchers are discovering the extent to which xenophobia can be easily—even arbitrarily—turned on. In just hours, we can be conditioned to fear or discriminate against those who differ from ourselves by characteristics as superficial as eye color. Even ideas we believe are just common sense can have deep xenophobic underpinnings. Research conducted this winter at Harvard reveals that even among people who claim to have no bias, the more strongly one supports the ethnic profiling of Arabs

at airport-security checkpoints, the more hidden prejudice one has against Muslims.

But other research shows that when it comes to whom we fear and how we react, we do have a choice. We can, it seems, choose not to give in to our xenophobic tendencies.

## THE MELTING POT

America prides itself on being a melting pot of cultures, but how we react to newcomers is often at odds with that self-image. A few years ago, psychologist Markus Kemmelmeier, Ph.D., now at the University of Nevada at Reno, stuck stamped letters under the windshield wipers of parked cars in a suburb of Detroit. Half were addressed to a fictitious Christian organization, half to a made-up Muslim group. Of all the letters, half had little stickers of the American flag.

Would the addresses and stickers affect the rate at which the letters would be mailed? Kemmelmeier wondered. Without the flag stickers, both sets of letters were mailed at the same rate, about 75 percent of the time. With the stickers, however, the rates changed: Almost all the Christian letters were forwarded, but only half of the Muslim letters were mailed. "The flag is seen as a sacred object," Kemmelmeier says. "And it made people think about what it means to be a good American."

In short, the Muslims didn't make the cut.

Not mailing a letter seems like a small slight. Yet in the last century, there have been shocking examples of xenophobia in our own back yard. Perhaps the most famous in American history was the fear of the Japanese during World War II. This particular wave of hysteria lead to the rise of slurs and bigoted depictions in the media, and more alarmingly, the mass internment of 120,000 people of Japanese ancestry beginning in 1942. The internments have become a national embarrassment: Most of the Japanese held were American citizens, and there is little evidence that the imprisonments had any real strategic impact.

Today the targets of xenophobia—derived from the Greek word for *stranger*—aren't the Japanese. Instead, they are Muslim immigrants. Or Mexicans. Or Chinese. Or whichever group we have come to fear.

Just how arbitrary are these xenophobic feelings? Two famous public-school experiments show how easy it is to turn one "group" against another. In the late 1960s, California high school history teacher Ron Jones recruited students to participate in an exclusive new cultural program called "the Wave." Within weeks, these students were separating themselves from others and aggressively intimidating critics. Eventually, Jones confronted the students with the reality that they were unwitting participants in an experiment demonstrating the power of nationalist movements.

## Sonam Wangmo:
"Am I fearful of Arab men in turbans? No, I am not. I was born and raised in India, and I am familiar with other races. I have learned to be attuned to different cultures. I find that there are always new, positive things to be learned from other people; it brings out the best in us."

A few years later, a teacher in Iowa discovered how quickly group distinctions are made. The teacher, Jane Elliott, divided her class into two groups—those with blue eyes and those with brown or green eyes. The brown-eyed group received privileges and treats, while the blue-eyed students were denied rewards and told they were inferior. Within hours, the once-harmonious classroom became two camps, full of mutual fear and resentment. Yet, what is especially shocking is that the students were only in the third grade.

## SOCIAL IDENTITY

The drive to completely and quickly divide the world into "us" and "them" is so powerful that it must surely come from some deep-seated need. The exact identity of that need, however, has been subject to debate. In the 1970s, the late Henri Tajfel, Ph.D., of the University of Bristol in England, and John Turner, Ph.D., now of the Australian National University, devised a theory to explain the psy-

chology behind a range of prejudices and biases, not just xenophobia. Their theory was based, in part, on the desire to think highly of oneself. One way to lift your self-esteem is to be part of a distinctive group, like a winning team; another is to play up the qualities of your own group and denigrate the attributes of others so that you feel your group is better.

## Terry Kalish:
"I am planning a trip to Florida, and I'm nervous about flying with my kids; I'm scared. If an Arab man sat next to me, I would feel nervous. I would wonder, 'Does he have explosives?' But then I feel ashamed to think this way. These poor people must get so scrutinized. It's wrong."

Tajfel and Turner called their insight "social identity theory," which has proved valuable for understanding how prejudices develop. Given even the slenderest of criteria, we naturally split people into two groups—an "in-group" and an "out-group." The categories can be of geopolitical importance—nationality, religion, race, language—or they can be as seemingly inconsequential as handedness, hair color or even height.

Once the division is made, the inferences and projections begin to occur. For one, we tend to think more highly of people in the in-group than those in the out-group, a belief based only on group identity. Also, a person tends to feel that others in the in-group are similar to one's self in ways that—although stereotypical—may have little to do with the original criteria used to split the groups. Someone with glasses may believe that other people who wear glasses are more voracious readers—even more intelligent—than those who don't, in spite of the fact that all he really knows is that they don't see very well. On the other hand, people in the out-group are believed to be less distinct and less complex than are cohorts in the in-group.

Although Tajfel and Turner found that identity and categorization were the root cause of social bias, other researchers have tried to find evolutionary explanations for discrimination. After all, in the distant past, people who shared cultural similarities were found to be more genetically related than those who did not. Therefore, favoring the in-group was a way of helping perpetuate one's genes. Evolutionary explanations seem appealing, since they rely on the simplest biological urges to drive complicated behavior. But this fact also makes them hard to prove. Ironically, there is ample evidence backing up the "softer" science behind social identity theory.

## HIDDEN BIAS

Not many of us will admit to having strong racist or xenophobic biases. Even in cases where bias becomes public debate—such as the profiling of Arab Muslims at airport-security screenings—proponents of prejudice claim that they are merely promoting common sense. That reluctance to admit to bias makes the issue tricky to study.

To get around this problem, psychologists Anthony Greenwald, Ph.D., of the University of Washington in Seattle, and Mahzarin Banaji, Ph.D., of Harvard, developed the Implicit Association Test. The IAT is a simple test that measures reaction time: The subject sees various words or images projected on a screen, then classifies the images into one of two groups by pressing buttons. The words and images need not be racial or ethnic in nature—one group of researchers tested attitudes toward presidential candidates. The string of images is interspersed with words having either pleasant or unpleasant connotations, then the participant must group the words and images in various ways—Democrats are placed with unpleasant words, for instance.

# Rangr:
## "For the months following 9/11, I had to endure my daily walk to work along New York City's Sixth Avenue. It seemed that half the people stared at me with accusation. It became unbearable. Yet others showed tremendous empathy. Friends, co-workers and neighbors, even people I had never met, stopped to say, 'I hope your turban has not caused you any trouble.' At heart, this is a great country."

The differences in reaction time are small but telling. Again and again, researchers found that subjects readily tie in-group images with pleasant words and out-group images with unpleasant words. One study compares such groups as whites and blacks, Jews and Christians, and young people and old people. And researchers found that if you identify yourself in one group, it's easier to pair images of that group with pleasant words—and easier to pair the opposite group with unpleasant imagery. This reveals the underlying biases and enables us to study how quickly they can form.

Really though, we need to know very little about a person to discriminate against him. One of the authors of this story, psychologist Margo Monteith, Ph.D., performed an IAT experiment comparing attitudes toward two sets of made-up names; one set was supposedly "American,"

the other from the fictitious country of Marisat. Even though the subjects knew nothing about Marisat, they showed a consistent bias against it.

While this type of research may seem out in left field, other work may have more "real-world" applications. The Southern Poverty Law Center runs a Web version of the IAT that measures biases based on race, age and gender. Its survey has, for instance, found that respondents are far more likely to associate European faces, rather than Asian faces, with so-called American images. The implication being that Asians are seen as less "American" than Caucasians.

Similarly, Harvard's Banaji has studied the attitudes of people who favor the racial profiling of Arab Muslims to deter terrorism, and her results run contrary to the belief that such profiling is not driven by xenophobic fears. "We show that those who endorse racial profiling also score high on both explicit and implicit measures of prejudice toward Arab Muslims," Banaji says. "Endorsement of profiling is an indicator of level of prejudice."

## BEYOND XENOPHOBIA

If categorization and bias come so easily, are people doomed to xenophobia and racism? It's pretty clear that we are susceptible to prejudice and that there is an unconscious desire to divide the world into "us" and "them." Fortunately, however, new research also shows that prejudices are fluid and that when we become conscious of our biases we can take active—and successful—steps to combat them.

Researchers have long known that when observing racially mixed groups, people are more likely to confuse the identity of two black individuals or two white ones, rather than a white with a black. But Leda Cosmides, Ph.D., and John Tooby, Ph.D., of the Center for Evolutionary Psychology at the University of California at Santa Barbara, and anthropologist Robert Kurzban, Ph.D., of the University of California at Los Angeles, wanted to test whether this was innate or whether it was just an artifact of how society groups individuals by race.

To do this, Cosmides and her colleagues made a video of two racially integrated basketball teams locked in conversation, then they showed it to study participants. As reported in the *Proceedings of the National Academy of Sciences*, the researchers discovered that subjects were more likely to confuse two players on the same team, regardless of race, rather than two players of the same race on opposite teams.

Cosmides says that this points to one way of attacking racism and xenophobia: changing the way society imposes group labels. American society divides people by race and by ethnicity; that's how lines of prejudice form. But simple steps, such as integrating the basketball teams, can reset mental divisions, rendering race and ethnicity less important.

This finding supports earlier research by psychologists Samuel Gaertner, Ph.D., of the University of Delaware in Newark, and John Dovidio, Ph.D., of Colgate University in Hamilton, New York. Gaertner and Dovidio have studied how bias changes when members of racially mixed groups must cooperate to accomplish shared goals. In situations where team members had to work together, bias could be reduced by significant amounts.

Monteith has also found that people who are concerned about their prejudices have the power to correct them. In experiments, she told subjects that they had performed poorly on tests that measured belief in stereotypes. She discovered that the worse a subject felt about her performance, the better she scored on subsequent tests. The guilt behind learning about their own prejudices made the subjects try harder not to be biased.

This suggests that the guilt of mistaking individuals for their group stereotype—such as falsely believing an Arab is a terrorist—can lead to the breakdown of the belief in that stereotype. Unfortunately, such stereotypes are reinforced so often that they can become ingrained. It is difficult to escape conventional wisdom and treat all people as individuals, rather than members of a group. But that seems to be the best way to avoid the trap of dividing the world in two—and discriminating against one part of humanity.

## READ MORE ABOUT IT:

*Nobody Left to Hate: Teaching Compassion After Columbine,* Elliot Aronson (W.H. Freeman and Company, 2000)
*The Racist Mind: Portraits of American Neo-Nazis and Klansmen,* Madonna Kolbenschlag (Penguin Books, 1996)

---

*Margo Monteith, Ph.D., is an associate professor of psychology at the University of Kentucky. Jeffrey Winters is a New York-based science writer.*

# Human Rights, Sex Trafficking, and Prostitution

by Alice Leuchtag

Despite laws against slavery in practically every country, an estimated twenty-seven million people live as slaves. Kevin Bales, in his book *Disposable People: New Slavery in the Global Economy* (University of California Press, Berkeley, 1999), describes those who endure modern forms of slavery. These include indentured servants, persons held in hereditary bondage, child slaves who pick plantation crops, child soldiers, and adults and children trafficked and sold into sex slavery.

## A Life Narrative

Of all forms of slavery, sex slavery is one of the most exploitative and lucrative with some 200,000 sex slaves worldwide bringing their slaveholders an annual profit of $10.5 billion. Although the great preponderance of sex slaves are women and girls, a smaller but significant number of males—both adult and children—are enslaved for homosexual prostitution.

The life narrative of a Thai girl named Siri, as told to Bales, illustrates how sex slavery happens to vulnerable girls and women. Siri is born in northeastern Thailand to a poor family that farms a small plot of land, barely eking out a living. Economic policies of structural adjustment pursued by the Thai government under the aegis of the World Bank and the International Monetary Fund have taken former government subsidies away from rice farmers, leaving them to compete against imported, subsidized rice that keeps the market price artificially depressed.

Siri attends four years of school, then is kept at home to help care for her three younger siblings. When Siri is fourteen, a well-dressed woman visits her village. She offers to find Siri a "good job," advancing her parents $2,000 against future earnings. This represents at least a year's income for the family. In a town in another province the woman, a trafficker, "sells" Siri to a brothel for $4,000. Owned by an "investment club" whose members are business and professional men—government bureaucrats and local politicians—the brothel is extremely profitable. In a typical thirty-day period it nets its investors $88,000.

To maintain the appearance that their hands are clean, members of the club's board of directors leave the management of the brothel to a pimp and a bookkeeper. Siri is initiated into prostitution by the pimp who rapes her. After being abused by her first "customer," Siri escapes, but a policeman—who gets a percentage of the brothel profits—brings her back, whereupon the pimp beats her up. As further punishment, her "debt" is doubled from $4,000 to $8,000. She must now repay this, along with her monthly rent and food, all from her earnings of $4 per customer. She will have to have sex with three hundred men a month just to pay her rent. Realizing she will never be able to get out of debt, Siri tries to build a relationship with the pimp simply in order to survive.

The pimp uses culture and religion to reinforce his control over Siri. He tells her she must have committed terrible sins in a past life to have been born a female; she must have accumulated a karmic debt to deserve the enslavement and abuse to which she must reconcile herself. Gradually Siri begins to see herself from the point of view of the slaveholder—as someone unworthy and deserving of punishment. By age fifteen she no longer protests or runs away. Her physical enslavement has become psychological as well, a common occurrence in chronic abuse.

Siri is administered regular injections of the contraceptive drug Depo-Provera for which she is charged. As the same needle is used for all the girls, there is a high risk of HIV and other sexual diseases from the injections. Siri knows that a serious illness threatens her and she prays to Buddha at the little shrine in her room, hoping to earn merit so he will protect her from dreaded disease. Once a month she and the others, at their own expense, are tested for HIV. So far Siri's tests have been negative. When Siri tries to get the male customers to wear condoms—distributed free to brothels by the Thai Ministry of Health—some resist wearing them and she can't make them do so.

As one of an estimated 35,000 women working as brothel slaves in Thailand—a country where 500,000 to one million prostituted women and girls work in conditions of degradation and exploitation short of brothel slavery—Siri faces at least a 40 percent chance of contracting the HIV virus. If she is lucky, she can look forward to live more years before she becomes too ill to work and is pushed out into the street.

## Thailand's Sex Tourism

Though the Thai government denies it, the World Health Organization finds that HIV is epidemic in Thailand, with the largest segment of new cases among wives and girlfriends of men who buy prostitute sex. Viewing its women as a cash crop to be exploited, and depending on sex tourism for foreign exchange dollars to help pay interest on the foreign debt, the Thai government can't acknowledge the epidemic without contradicting the continued promotion of sex tourism and prostitution.

By encouraging investment in the sex industry, sex tourism creates a business climate conducive to the trafficking and enslavement of vulnerable girls such as Siri. In 1996 nearly five million sex tourists from the United States, Western Europe, Australia, and Japan visited Thailand. These transactions brought in about $26.2 billion—thirteen times more than Thailand earned by building and exporting computers.

In her 1999 report *Pimps and Predators on the Internet: Globalizing the Sexual Exploitation of Women and Children*, published by the Coalition Against Trafficking in Women (CATW), Donna Hughes quotes from postings on an Internet site where sex tourists share experiences and advise one another. The following is one man's description of having sex with a fourteen-year-old prostituted girl in Bangkok:

> "Even though I've had a lot of better massages... after fifteen minutes, I was much more relaxed... Then I asked for a condom and I fucked her for another thirty minutes. Her face looked like she was feeling a lot of pain.... She blocked my way when I wanted to leave the room and she asked for a tip. I gave her 600 bath. Altogether, not a good experience."

Hughes says, "To the men who buy sex, a 'bad experience' evidently means not getting his money's worth, or that the prostituted woman or girl didn't keep up the act of enjoying

what she had to do... one glimpses the humiliation and physical pain most girls and women in prostitution endure."

Nor are the men oblivious to the existence of sexual slavery. One customer states, "Girls in Bangkok virtually get sold by their families into the industry; they work against their will." His knowledge of their sexual slavery and lack of sensitivity thereof is evident in that he then names the hotels in which girls are kept and describes how much they cost!

As Hughes observes, sex tourists apparently feel they have a right to prostitute sex, perceiving prostitution only from a self-interested perspective in which they commodify and objectify women of other cultures, nationalities, and ethnic groups. Their awareness of racism, colonialism, global economic inequalities, and sexism seems limited to the way these realities benefit them as sex consumers.

## Sex Traffickers Cast Their Nets

According to the *Guide to the New UN Trafficking Protocol* by Janice Raymond, published by the CATW in 2001, the United Nations estimates that sex trafficking in human beings is a $5 billion to $7 billion operation annually. Four million persons are moved illegally from one country to another and within countries each year, a large proportion of them women and girls being trafficked into prostitution. The United Nations International Children's Emergency Fund (UNICEF) estimates that some 30 percent of women being trafficked are minors, many under age thirteen. The International Organization on Migration estimates that some 500,000 women per year are trafficked into Western Europe from poorer regions of the world. According to *Sex Trafficking of Women in the United States: International and Domestic Trends*, also published by the CATW in 2001, some 50,000 women and children are trafficked into the United States each year, mainly from Asia and Latin America.

Because prostitution as a system of organized sexual exploitation depends on a continuous supply of new "recruits," trafficking is essential to its continued existence. When the pool of available women and girls dries up, new women must be procured. Traffickers cast their nets ever wide and become ever more sophisticated. The Italian Camorra, Chinese Triads, Russian Mafia, and Japanese Yakuza are powerful criminal syndicates consisting of traffickers, pimps, brothel keepers, forced labor lords, and gangs which operate globally.

After the breakdown of the Soviet Union, an estimated five thousand criminal groups formed the Russian Mafia, which operates in thirty countries. The Russian Mafia traffics women from African countries, the Ukraine, the Russian Federation, and Eastern Europe into Western Europe, the United States, and Israel. The Triads traffic women from China, Korea, Thailand, and other Southeast Asian countries into the United States and Europe. The Camorra traffics women from Latin America into Europe. The Yakuza traffics women from the Philipines, Thailand, Burma, Cambodia, Korea, Nepal, and Laos into Japan.

# A Global Problem Meets a Global Response

Despite these appalling facts, until recently no generally agreed upon definition of trafficking in human beings was written into international law. In Vienna, Austria, during 1999 and 2000, 120 countries participated in debates over a definition of trafficking. A few nongovernmental organizations (NGOs) and a minority of governments—including Australia, Canada, Denmark, Germany, Ireland, Japan, the Netherlands, Spain, Switzerland, Thailand, and the United Kingdom—wanted to separate issues of trafficking from issues of prostitution. They argued that persons being trafficked should be divided into those who are forced and those who give their consent, with the burden of proof being placed on persons being trafficked. They also urged that the less explicit means of control over trafficked persons—such as abuse of a victim's vulnerability—not be included in the definition of trafficking and that the word *exploitation* not be used. Generally supporters of this position were wealthier countries where large numbers of women were being trafficked and countries in which prostitution was legalized or sex tourism encouraged.

## People being trafficked shouldn't be divided into those who are forced and those who give their consent because trafficked persons are in no position to give meaningful consent.

The CATW—140 other NGOs that make up the International Human Rights Network plus many governments (including those of Algeria, Bangladesh, Belgium, China, Columbia, Cuba, Egypt, Finland, France, India, Mexico, Norway, Pakistan, the Philippines, Sweden, Syria, Venezuela, and Vietnam)—maintains that trafficking can't be separated from prostitution. Persons being trafficked shouldn't be divided into those who are forced and those who give their consent because trafficked persons are in no position to give meaningful consent. The subtler methods used by traffickers, such as abuse of a victim's vulnerability, should be included in the definition of trafficking and the word *exploitation* be an essential part of the definition. Generally supporters of this majority view were poorer countries from which large numbers of women were being trafficked or countries in which strong feminist, anti-colonialist, or socialist influences existed. The United States, though initially critical of the majority position, agreed to support a definition of trafficking that would be agreed upon by consensus.

The struggle—led by the CATW to create a definition of trafficking that would penalize traffickers while ensuring that all victims of trafficking would be protected—succeeded when a compromise proposal by Sweden was agreed to. A strongly worded and inclusive *UN Protocol to Prevent, Suppress, and Punish Trafficking in Persons*—especially women and children—was drafted by an ad hoc committee of the UN as a supplement to the Convention Against Transnational Organized Crime. The UN protocol specifically addresses the trade in human beings for purposes of prostitution and other forms of sexual exploitation, forced labor or services, slavery or practices similar to slavery, servitude, and the removal of organs. The protocol defines trafficking as:

> The recruitment, transportation, transfer, harboring or receipt of persons, by means of the threat or use of force or other forms of coercion, of abduction, of fraud, of deception, of the abuse of power or of a position of vulnerability or of the giving or receiving of payments or benefits to achieve the consent of a person having control over another person, for the purpose of exploitation.

While recognizing that the largest amount of trafficking involves women and children, the wording of the UN protocol clearly is gender and age neutral, inclusive of trafficking in both males and females, adults and children.

In 2000 the UN General Assembly adopted this convention and its supplementary protocol; 121 countries signed the convention and eighty countries signed the protocol. For the convention and protocol to become international law, forty countries must ratify them.

## Highlights

Some highlights of the new convention and protocol are:

For the first time there is an accepted international definition of trafficking and an agreed-upon set of prosecution, protection, and prevention mechanisms on which countries can base their national legislation.

- The various criminal means by which trafficking takes place, including indirect and subtle forms of coercion, are covered.
- Trafficked persons, especially women in prostitution and child laborers, are no longer viewed as illegal migrants but as victims of a crime.

## For the first time there is an accepted international definition of trafficking and an agreed-upon set of prosecution, protection, and prevention mechanisms on which countries can base their national legislation.

- The convention doesn't limit its scope to criminal syndicates but defines an organized criminal group as "any structured group of three or more persons which engages in criminal activities such as trafficking and pimping."

- All victims of trafficking in persons are protected, not just those who can prove that force was used against them.
- The consent of a victim of trafficking is meaningless and irrelevant.
- Victims of trafficking won't have to bear the burden of proof.
- Trafficking and sexual exploitation are intrinsically connected and not to be separated.
- Because women trafficked domestically into local sex industries suffer harmful effects similar to those experienced by women trafficked transnationally, these women also come under the protections of the protocol.
- The key element in trafficking is the exploitative purpose rather than the movement across a border.

The protocol is the first UN instrument to address the demand for prostitution sex, a demand that results in the human rights abuses of women and children being trafficked. The protocol recognizes an urgent need for governments to put the buyers of prostitution sex on their policy and legislative agendas, and it calls upon countries to take or strengthen legislative or other measures to discourage demand, which fosters all the forms of sexual exploitation of women and children.

As Raymond says in the *Guide to the New UN Trafficking Protocol*:

> "The least discussed part of the prostitution and trafficking chain has been the men who buy women for sexual exploitation in prostitution.... If we are to find a permanent path to ending these human rights abuses, then we cannot just shrug our shoulders and say, "men are like this," or "boys will be boys," or "prostitution has always been around." Or tell women and girls in prostitution that they must continue to do what they do because prostitution is inevitable. Rather, our responsibility is to make men change their behavior, by all means available—educational, cultural and legal."

Two U.S. feminist, human rights organizations—Captive Daughters and Equality Now—have been working toward that goal. Surita Sandosham of Equality Now says that when her organization asked women's groups in Thailand and the Philippines how it could assist them, the answer came back, "Do something about the demand." Since then the two organizations have legally challenged sex tours originating in the United States and have succeeded in closing down at least one operation.

## Refugees, Not Illegal Aliens

In October 2000 the U.S. Congress passed a bill, the Victims of Trafficking and Violence Protection Act of 2000, introduced by New Jersey republican representative Chris Smith. Under this law penalties for traffickers are raised and protections for victims increased. Reasoning that desperate women are unable to give meaningful consent to their own sexual exploitation, the law adopts a broad definition of sex trafficking so as not to exclude so-called consensual prostitution or trafficking that occurs solely within the United States. In these respects the new federal law conforms to the UN protocol.

Two features of the law are particularly noteworthy:

- In order to pressure other countries to end sex trafficking, the U.S. State Department is to make a yearly assessment of other countries' anti-trafficking efforts and to rank them according to how well they discourage trafficking. After two years of failing to meet even minimal standards, countries are subject to sanctions, although not sanctions on humanitarian aid. "Tier 3" countries—those failing to meet even minimal standards—include Greece, Indonesia, Israel, Pakistan, Russia, Saudi Arabia, South Korea, and Thailand.
- Among persons being trafficked into the United States, special T-visas will be provided to those who meet the criteria for having suffered the most serious trafficking abuses. These visas will protect them from deportation so they can testify against their traffickers. T-non immigrant status allows eligible aliens to remain in the United States temporarily and grants specific non-immigrant benefits. Those acquiring T-1 non-immigrant status will be able to remain for a period of three years and will be eligible to receive certain kinds of public assistance—to the same extent as refugees. They will also be issued employment authorization to "assist them in finding safe, legal employment while they attempt to retake control of their lives."

## A Debate Rages

A worldwide debate rages about legalization of prostitution fueled by a 1998 International Labor Organization (ILO) report entitled *The Sex Sector: The Economic and Social Bases of Prostitution in Southeast Asia*. The report follows years of lobbying by the sex industry for recognition of prostitution as "sex work." Citing the sex industry's unrecognized contribution to the gross domestic product of four countries in Southeast Asia, the ILO urges governments to officially recognize the "sex sector" and "extend taxation nets to cover many of the lucrative activities connected with it." Though the ILO report says it stops short of calling for legalization of prostitution, official recognition of the sex industry would be impossible without it.

Raymond points out that the ILO's push to redefine prostitution as sex work ignores legislation demonstrating that countries can reduce organized sexual exploitation rather than capitulate to it. For example, Sweden prohibits the purchase of sexual services with punishments of still fines or imprisonment, thus declaring that prostitution isn't a desirable economic and labor sector. The government also helps women getting out of prostitution to rebuild their lives. Venezuela's Ministry of Labor has ruled that prostitution can't be considered work because it lacks the basic elements of dignity and social justice. The Socialist Republic of Vietnam punishes pimps, traffickers, brothel owners, and buyers—sometimes publishing buyer's names in the mass media. For women in prostitution, the government finances medical, educational, and economic rehabilitation.

# Instead of transforming the male buyer into a legitmate customer, the ILO should give thought to innovative programs that make the buyer accountable for his sexual exploitation.

Raymond suggests that instead of transforming the male buyer into a legitimate customer, the ILO should give thought to innovative programs that make the buyer accountable for his sexual exploitation. She cites the Sage Project, Inc. (SAGE) program in San Francisco, California, which educates men arrested for soliciting women in prostitution about the risks and impacts of their behavior.

Legalization advocates argue that the violence, exploitation, and health effects suffered by women in prostitution aren't inherent to prostitution but simply result from the random behaviors of bad pimps or buyers, and that if prostitution were regulated by the state these harms would diminish. But examples show these arguments to be false.

# Prostituted women are even more marginalized and tightly locked into the system of organized sexual exploitation while the state, now an official party to the exploitation, has become the biggest pimp of all.

In the pamphlet entitled *Legalizing Prostitution Is Not the Answer: The Example of Victoria, Australia,* published by the CATW in 2001, Mary Sullivan and Sheila Jeffreys describe the way legalization in Australia has perpetuated and strengthened the culture of violence and exploitation inherent in prostitution. Under legalization, legal and illegal brothels have proliferated, and trafficking in women has accelerated to meet the increased demand. Pimps, having even more power, continue threatening and brutalizing the women they control. Buyers continue to abuse women, refuse to wear condoms, and spread the HIV virus—and other sexually transmitted diseases—to their wives and girlfriends. Stigmatized by identity cards and medial inspections, prostituted women are even more marginalized and tightly locked into the system of organized sexual exploitation while the state, now an official party to the exploitation, has become the biggest pimp of all.

The government of the Netherlands has legalized prostitution, doesn't enforce laws against pimping, and virtually lives off taxes from the earnings of prostituted women. In the book *Making the Harm Visible* (published by the CATW in 1999), Marie-Victoire Louis describes the effects on prostituted women of municipal regulation of brothels in Amsterdam and other Dutch cities. Her article entitled "Legalizing Pimping, Dutch Style" explains the way immigration policies in the Netherlands are shaped to fit the needs of the prostitution industry so that traffickers are seldom prosecuted and a continuous supply of women is guaranteed. In Amsterdam's 250 officially listed brothels, 80 percent of the prostitutes have been trafficked in from other countries and 70 percent possess no legal papers. Without money, papers, or contact with the outside world, these immigrant women live in terror instead of being protected by the regulations governing brothels, prostituted women are frequently beaten up and raped by pimps. These "prostitution managers" have practically been given a free hand by the state and by buyers who, as "consumers of prostitution," feel themselves entitled to abuse the women they buy. Sadly and ironically the "Amsterdam model" of legalization and regulation is touted by the Netherlands and Germany as "self-determination and empowerment for women." In reality it simply legitimizes the "right" to buy, sexually use, and profit from the sexual exploitation of someone else's body.

# A Human Rights Approach

As part of a system of organized sexual exploitation, prostitution can be visualized along a continuum of abuse with brothel slavery at the furthest extreme. All along the continuum, fine lines divide the degrees of harm done to those caught up in the system. At the core lies a great social injustice no cosmetic reforms can right: the setting aside of a segment of people whose bodies can be purchased for sexual use by others. When this basic injustice is legitimized and regulated by the state and when the state profits from it, that injustice is compounded.

In her book *The Prostitution of Sexuality* (New York University Press, 1995), Kathleen Barry details a feminist human rights approach to prostitution that points the way to the future. Ethically it recognizes prostitution, sex trafficking, and the globalized industrialization of sex as massive violations of women's human rights. Sociologically it considers how and to what extent prostitution promotes sex discrimination against individual women, against different racial categories of women, and against women as a group. Politically it calls for decriminalizing prostitutes while penalizing pimps, traffickers, brothel owners, and buyers.

Understanding that human rights and restorative justice go hand in hand, the feminist human rights approach to prostitution addresses the harm and the need to repair the damage. As Barry says:

"Legal proposals to criminalize customers, based on the recognition that prostitution violates and harms women, must... include social-service, health and counseling and job retraining programs. Where states would be closing down brothels if customers were criminalized, the economic resources poured into the former prostitution areas could be turned toward producing gainful employment for women."

With the help of women's projects in many countries—such as Buklod in the Philippines and the Council for Prostitution Alternatives in the United States—some women have begun to confront their condition by leaving prostitution, speaking out against it, revealing their experiences, and helping other women leave the sex industry.

Ending the sexual exploitation of trafficking and prostitution will mean the beginning of a new chapter in building, a humanist future—a more peaceful and just future in which men and women can join together in love and respect, recognizing one another's essential dignity and humanity. Humanity's sexuality then will no longer be hijacked and distorted.

_Freelance writer Alice Leuchtag has worked as a social worker, counselor, college instructor, and researcher. Active in the civil rights, peace, socialist, feminist, and humanist movements, she has helped organize women in Houston to oppose sex trafficking._

# THE BATTLE OVER GAY MARRIAGE

**IT'S OFFICIAL: GAYS CAN MARRY IN MASSACHUSETTS COME MAY.
A TIME REPORT ON HOW IT HAPPENED, WHAT IT MEANS—
AND HOW IT MAY PLAY OUT IN THE RACE FOR THE WHITE HOUSE**

## By John Cloud

OUR MARRIAGES OFTEN PROVOKE US to throw the china and utter the unforgivables. The context is usually personal, not political, but either way, passions run high. In May, barring some unforeseen procedural hindrance, gay couples will wed for the first time ever in the U.S. They will have that opportunity by order of the Massachusetts Supreme Judicial Court, which ruled last week that it is unconstitutional to deny them marriage licenses. Gays and lesbians across the country celebrated. Hundreds of gay people have already called or e-mailed town clerk Doug Johnstone in Provincetown, Mass., to ask when they can marry. One of the licenses Johnstone's office will issue will be his own. After 25 years together, he and his partner will finally have the chance to say their vows before the commonwealth.

Many other Americans are worried that even though a freedom has been granted, an institution has been threatened. "If we have homosexual marriage mainstream, I can't even describe to you what our culture will be like," warns Sandy Rios, president of Concerned Women for America, one of the leading anti-gay-marriage organizations. Many conservatives object that such a monumental social change was sanctioned by

such a small group—four of seven judges on the Massachusetts court. "We're hearing from people throughout the country," says a hoarse Glenn Stanton, spokesman for Focus on the Family, a conservative group in Colorado Springs, Colo. "They don't know which to be more outraged at—the death of marriage or the death of democracy."

Marriage may or may not be dead, but democracy is doing fine. The court decision has intensified efforts to pass a U.S. constitutional amendment banning gay marriage. One version of the amendment already has more than 100 cosponsors in Congress. (Two-thirds of both houses will be required to pass the amendment, which will then have to be ratified by at least three-quarters—38—of the states.) Conservative activists will make sure that voters hear a lot about gay marriage between now and November since the likely Democratic nominee for President, Senator John Kerry, comes from Massachusetts. By unhappy coincidence, the Democrats will also hold their convention in Boston this summer. "It could be like Chicago 1968," says gay-marriage foe Ray Flynn, a former Democratic mayor of Boston and ambassador to the Vatican, who is now president of Your Catholic Voice.

"The country will see the party as taken over by the radical left."

Last Thursday, at various campaign stops, Kerry was forced to say—over and over, to the point of understandable exasperation—that he opposes gay marriage and disagrees with his state's court ruling. But he also favors civil unions for gay couples and would vote against a U.S. constitutional amendment. You can find a consistent line here: Kerry thinks the matter should be left to states. But in a debate as raw as the one over same-sex unions, President Bush's simple position—marriage should be between a man and a woman—will be easier to explain, not least because a clear majority of Americans also hold it. In a TIME/CNN poll conducted last week, 62% of respondents said they oppose the legalization of same-sex marriage; less than a third favor it.

But the President remembers the lessons of 1992, when moderate voters punished his father for a G.O.P. convention loaded with extremist declarations on the culture wars. Bush the son is careful to avoid coarse language about gays and lesbians. As Air Force One flew to South Carolina last week, the President made clear his opposition to gay marriage but added, "I'm not

# Gay Marriage: A History

**1901** Murray Hall, a prominent Tammany Hall politician, masquerades as a man over a 30-year period and twice marries a woman. Not until death comes, in 1901, is it discovered that Hall is a woman.

**1969** The Rev. Troy Perry of the Metropolitan Community Church, a Los Angeles–based church founded for gay, bisexual and transgender people, begins conducting same-sex marriage ceremonies that he calls holy unions.

**1971** Jack Baker and his partner, James McConnell, both 28, unsuccessfully sue for a marriage license in Minnesota. A judge lets them acquire a legal relationship by allowing McConnell to adopt Baker.

**1989** Denmark becomes the first country to recognize same-sex unions, allowing couples to register as partners.

**1991** Three same-sex couples in Hawaii sue the state for the right to get married. Before the courts can issue a final ruling, the voters in 1998 amend the state constitution to ensure marriage is limited to couples of the opposite sex.

**1994** IKEA airs a groundbreaking television commercial in the U.S. that features a gay male couple shopping together for furniture.

**1994** Two characters on the TV show *Northern Exposure,* innkeepers Ron and Erick, are married. But prime time is not ready for everything: the two men do not kiss as the ceremony ends.

**1996** Two characters on NBC's *Friends,* Ross's ex-wife and her girlfriend, get married. Newt Gingrich's sister Candace performs the TV ceremony.

**1996** President Clinton signs the Defense of Marriage Act, denying federal recognition of same-sex marriage.

**1998** In response to a court case brought by a male couple seeking to marry, Alaska amends its constitution to ban same-sex marriage.

**2000** Governor Howard Dean of Vermont signs a law permitting civil unions between same-sex partners. Vermont is the first state to legally recognize same-sex unions.

**2000** The Netherlands is the first country to allow same-sex couples the right to marry, providing the benefits that come with a civil marriage. The first couples marry in April 2001.

**2002** The first same-sex union is announced in the *New York Times.* The partners are Daniel Andrew Gross and Steven Goldstein, and their civil-union ceremony takes place in Vermont.

**2003** Belgium joins the Netherlands in recognizing marriage between same-sex couples.

**2003** Two Canadian provinces, Ontario and British Columbia, permit same-sex marriage.

**2003** *Bride's* magazine runs a one-page article on same-sex weddings. This is the first time that a major bridal magazine has published a piece on the subject.

**2003** The Supreme Judicial Court of Massachusetts rules that the commonwealth's constitution protects the right of homosexual couples to marry.

**2004** The Massachusetts court rules that mere civil unions are discriminatory, thereby paving the way for same-sex marriages to start taking place in May.

against anybody," according to Jim DeMint, a Republican Congressman who was aboard. "If some people want to have a contract, that's O.K., but marriage is the foundation of society."

Though it was an offhand comment, the idea that Bush might favor some kind of "contract" for gay couples—presumably a type of state recognition—is astonishing when you look back at the brief history of the gay-marriage debate. As recently as 1993, when the Hawaii Supreme Court issued the first appellate-court ruling in favor of gay marriage (a ruling that never took effect because Hawaiians voted to amend their constitution), even domestic partnerships were still considered radical. Only a few liberal municipalities offered them—Berkeley and West Hollywood in California, for example—and they didn't cover much. You could get a certificate suitable for framing and the assurance that a hospital within city limits would let you visit a sick partner. That was about it. FORTUNE 500 companies were only beginning to allow partners of gay and lesbian employees to buy into health insurance plans. Most big cities didn't offer their employees such arrangements; in 1993 plans to extend health benefits to same-sex partners of city employees in Atlanta and Seattle caused great public consternation.

Today municipalities routinely invite partners of gay employees to join health plans. Kansas City, Kans., became the latest to do so just last week. The website of the Human Rights Campaign, the nation's largest gay political group, now lists 7,414 U.S. employers that offer domestic-partner benefits. And New Jersey, Hawaii, California and Vermont have established statewide registries for gay couples. Until last week, Vermont's law was the most famous (thanks to former Governor Howard Dean) as well as the most sweeping. That state's civil unions go well beyond the limited package of benefits usually associated with domestic partnerships and offer everything except the word marriage—inherit-ance rights, joint state-tax filings, joint adoptions, the whole show. But not the word marriage.

Which is where things stood until last week. The Massachusetts decision laid out the case for why, in the majority's opinion, everything but marriage is not enough. The state senate had asked the court if it could establish civil unions to meet the constitutional requirement of equality for gay couples set forth in an earlier ruling. "The answer," the court replied, "is 'No.'" Why not? "Because the proposed law [establishing civil unions] by its express terms forbids same-sex couples entry into civil marriage [and therefore] continues to relegate same-sex couples to a different status ... The history of our nation has demonstrated that separate is seldom, if ever, equal."

But in her dissent, Justice Martha Sosman pointed out that even if Massachusetts allowed gay marriages, those marriages would still not be fully equal since "differences in Federal law and the law of other States will frustrate the goal of complete equality." What she meant is that even after Zach and Brad marry in Massachusetts, the couple will not be married in, say, Alaska, which has a constitutional amendment prohibiting same-sex marriages. (In all, 39 states have laws or amendments restricting marriage to straight couples.) What's more, the couple will not be married in the eyes of the Federal Government, which enacted a law in 1996—supporters called it the Defense of Marriage Act—defining marriage as "only a legal union between one man and one woman." Zach will not be able to take advantage of the Family and Medical Leave Act to care for Brad when he is ill, nor will he be eligible for the surviving-spouse benefit offered by the Social Security Administration if Brad dies. In fact, Zach and Brad will not enjoy any of the 1,049 benefits and protections afforded to married couples by federal statutes.

Sosman wrote that "once the euphoria of [the case] subsides, the reality of the still less than truly equal status of same-sex couples will emerge." With all the practical differences between straight and gay unions, she argued, "it is eminently reasonable to give a different name to the legal status being conferred on same-sex couples by the proposed bill." But the majority dismissed that reasoning. It countered that federal and other states' laws were "irrelevant … Courts define what is constitutionally permissible, and the Massachusetts Constitution does not permit this type of labeling."

For gay-rights lawyers, the language was gratifying. They have tried to persuade Americans for years that they were not arguing for a "special right" called *gay* marriage but rather for simple equality. Exclusion from marriage was discrimination, they argued—even if it was a cushy, Vermont-syrup discrimination. For those attorneys, civil unions were, as the court itself said, a "type of labeling." The Massachusetts lawyers wanted no half measures: "It was always about marriage," says lead attorney Mary Bonauto of Gay and Lesbian Advocates and Defenders.

But it wasn't always about marriage. As recently as the early '90s, bringing marriage cases was considered foolish in gay legal circles. At least six court cases

arguing that gays should have the right to marry were filed in the 1970s, and all had promptly failed. None were filed in the 1980s, and by the early 1990s only a few gay intellectuals, like Andrew Sullivan, then editor of the *New Republic*, a center-left magazine of policy and politics based in Washington, were arguing for marriage. In the rest of the gay community, there was division, uncertainty, even among the attorneys at Lambda Legal, the leading gay legal group. Gay radicals felt that marriage was a patriarchal, retro institution that gays should avoid altogether. Others felt that pressing for gay marriage was a strategic mistake—"too much, too soon," in the words of a gay lawyer familiar with the battles.

It was in this environment that Lambda declined to represent three couples who in 1991 sued Hawaii for the right to marry. By 1993 that case had quietly made its way to the state supreme court, and in May of that year the court startled the gay-rights movement—and drew international attention—when it ruled that barring gay people from getting married amounted to discrimination based on sex. (The court sent the case back to trial, but by 1998 the state constitutional amendment had passed, and no gay couples ever wed in the Aloha State.)

After the Hawaii ruling, Lambda reversed course. One of its top attorneys, Evan Wolfson, began traveling the country to speak on gay marriage. Both gay and straight audiences needed convincing that it wasn't a distant fantasy. "I spoke in churches, gay organizations, the Federalist Society. I spoke in almost every state in the country. This went on for years. And the real thing that started to make the big difference is when we started to believe it could happen," says Wolfson, 47, who now runs his own project called Freedom to Marry. "And once that happened—after Hawaii, after this was being debated in California and Vermont—we saw a surge of people who had not been particularly active in the movement now come into it." High-profile losses in California and other states were eventually followed by a halfway win in Vermont and then, of course, a full victory last week in Massachusetts.

AS WOLFSON WAS TRYING TO PROMOTE same-sex marriage, Matt Daniels was becoming convinced that it would damage the institution of the family. Daniels, 40, runs the Alliance for Marriage, which wrote the Federal Marriage Amendment now before Congress. Daniels comes to the issues of marriage and family breakdown from a very personal place. His father walked out when he was 2, leaving his mom to work as a secretary. One night when Daniels was in third grade, she was assaulted on her way home. "She ends up with a broken back, disabled, on welfare, depressed," says Daniels, trailing off. "So I was basically raised on welfare."

Daniels got a scholarship to Dartmouth, but after college he had to return home to care for his mother, who was dying of congestive heart failure. (She passed away in 1990.) During that period, he began volunteering in homeless shelters, where he says he saw the consequences of family breakdown, including welfare dependency and youth crime. "And it's about that time that we began to see the court activity in Vermont," he recalls. "Already we had seen it in Hawaii." Daniels was deeply troubled by the prospect of gay marriage, he says, "because of the unique combination of gifts that the two genders bring to the raising of children. The family—defined as built on the union of male and female—from my perspective is the foundation of society. The United States could survive without ideologies on left and right, without the Democratic Party or the Republican Party, but if you look at social-science data, we cannot thrive if we continue to see the disintegration of the unit of the family."

By the late '90s, Daniels was working for the Boston-based Massachusetts Family Institute, an independent conservative group loosely affiliated with Focus on the Family. In Boston, he became friendly with the Rev. Dr. Ray Hammond, a physician turned pastor who had won national plaudits for helping inner-city youths in Boston. Eventually Daniels—with the help of Hammond and several other minority ministers—founded the Alliance for Marriage.

Although the alliance has a modest budget of $900,000 a year, compared

## MAINLINE CHURCHES
# Not Quite as Liberal as They Look

Readers of newspaper "Vows" columns, which have lately blossomed to include gay and lesbian ceremonies, may think that although the Catholic and evangelical churches regard same-sex wedlock as ungodly, *somebody* must be churning out gay marriages wholesale. In fact, no major church offers a ritual for full-fledged gay marriage. True, the old liberal Protestant mainline churches have over decades, bestow on thousands of couples alternative sanctions called union ceremonies or same-sex blessings. But even these are ferociously debated. Controversy over them—along with a new argument about whether to enter the national fight over marriage in its civil form—may soon rival the gay-ordination issue as liberal Protestantism's worst headache.

Mainline churches are sometimes more liberal regarding society at large than they are about themselves. Last November, for instance, Bishop Susan Hassinger, the top United Methodist Church official in New England, sent out a pastoral letter about the Massachusetts Supreme Judicial Court's initial ruling allowing gay civil marriages. She made two points. One was that the Methodists' Social Principles explicitly promote "basic human rights and civil liberties ... for homosexual persons" and so should "imply support" for the civil decision. The other was that since the Principles define marriage *within the church* as being between a man and a women, "at this point in our denomination's common life, the covenant of marriage is reserved for heterosexual couples."

Many fellow Methodists may not even concede her first assertion. Among mainline churches, theirs have proved the least tolerant of any sort of gay commitment. Four years ago at a bitter denominational meeting, delegates emphatically sustained a ban on gay union ceremonies by Methodist ministers, one of whom had been defrocked when he went ahead anyway. At the Methodists' next conference in April, emboldened conservatives hope to pass some statement that not just Methodist marriages but all marriages should be hetero-only. "It's a timely, front-burner issue," says James Heidinger, publisher of the traditionalist magazine *Good News*.

In June the precise opposite may occur at the convention of the Presbyterian Church (U.S.A.). Unlike the Methodists, the Presbyterians upheld holy-union ceremonies back in 2001, and this June the denomination's pro-gay-rights faction will press for a liberal stance regarding the world at large.

The meetings of both churches will be heated, yet the combative mood may be tempered by the recent history of the Episcopal Church USA, where the gay-blessings fracas proved costly. The rites were commonly practiced in the church, and Episcopal bishops voted last August to designate communities that celebrate them as "within the bounds of our common life." That approval, along with the enthronement of openly gay bishop Gene Robinson, sparked a movement by conservatives to disassociate their dioceses from the main church leadership, which may result in something, like a schism. If they can, the other mainline denominations will try to avoid letting things go quite that far.

—By David Van Biema.
**With reporting by Jill Underwood/Los Angeles**

with $120 million for Focus on the Family, it has influence beyond its means. Just as Wolfson was promoting gay marriage when gays wouldn't listen, Daniels was suggesting a constitutional amendment to ban gay marriage when conservatives wouldn't listen. When the alliance held a press conference to announce the idea in the summer of 2001, Daniels says, "there wasn't any debate going on about a marriage amendment." But by the following May, the alliance had lined up a Congressman—a Democrat, actually—to introduce the Federal Marriage Amendment. Today it has 109 co-sponsors in the House and five in the Senate.

The amendment would limit marriage to opposite-sex couples, but it would not outlaw civil unions, which Daniels believes should be available to states. His moderation on that point is considered

apostasy on the right, and Daniels has had to battle more powerful groups that want the amendment to go further, explicitly banning not only gay marriages but any state's recognition of gay relationships. For the past few months, about 20 serious movement conservatives—stalwarts like former presidential candidate Gary Bauer, Louis Sheldon of the Traditional Values Coalition and Don Wildmon of the American Family Association—have strategized on how to toughen the language. Daniels, who says one conservative leader told him his multicultural alliance "looks like the bar scene from *Star Wars*," has not been invited.

Calling themselves the Arlington group because they first met last summer in that Washington suburb, these conservatives feel that "ideally," as Bauer said last week, "we would like an amendment that would make it unconstitutional to

have gay marriage or fake marriage, the civil unions." Realistically, however, they have concluded that such a sweeping amendment probably won't pass. It's very early in the process, but the White House seems to be leaning toward the more flexible language.

THE PROPOSED AMENDMENT GOT A BIG PUSH last week, and it is likely to get another in May, when pictures of lesbians kissing their brides will be broadcast round the world. (One caveat: there is still a slim chance that gay-marriage opponents in the Bay State—including G.O.P. Governor Mitt Romney—will find a way to stop the marriages before May. But the state's highest court is not likely to approve any delays, so stopping gay weddings would probably mean outright defiance of the court. Most observers don't think Romney would risk his future on an Orval Faubus ploy.)

By May the Bush machine will be in high gear. You can expect that if Kerry is the nominee, plenty of television commercials accusing Kerry of being a Massachusetts liberal will air during breaks from newscasts about the latest gay wedding. Another problem for Kerry may lie across the continent in California, a state any Democrat must carry to win the White House. This week assemblyman Mark Leno is expected to introduce a bill in the California legislature that would legalize gay marriage. Gay activists plan an all-out battle. "Our goal is to be the first state in the nation to [legalize gay marriage] through the democratic process as opposed to the courts," says Toni Broaddus of Equality California, the state's leading gay-advocacy group. The last thing the Democrats want in California is a conservative base energized by a bloody gay-marriage fight over the summer.

But it gets worse. Because of Massachusetts, other states will be considering constitutional amendments to ban same-sex marriage. In fact, some 20 states have already introduced (or are expected to introduce) such amendments, according to the Human Rights Campaign. "I fear all this will create a backlash so much more powerful than our community is prepared to handle," says Matt Foreman of the National Gay and Lesbian Task Force.

For now, Kerry's advisers say they aren't worried their candidate will be mauled in the showdown. "The court has decided one thing, and Kerry has said he disagrees," says a senior Kerry adviser. Every time the Republicans bring up the issue, they give Kerry "the opportunity to highlight that his view isn't the traditional Massachusetts-liberal view." Kerry himself snapped last week, "I have the same position that Vice President Dick Cheney has. [The Republicans] ought to talk to Dick Cheney … before they start playing games with this. And we'll find out just how political and how craven they are." Kerry was referring to Cheney's statement during the 2000 campaign that he believes the issue of rights for gay couples "is regulated by the states. I think different states are likely to come to different conclusions, and that's appropriate." Cheney's daughter is a lesbian, and many gays hoped he would openly support same-sex marriage. But last month Cheney told the Denver *Post* that he will support whatever position the President takes, even if that means backing a ban on gay marriages.

The gay-marriage debate, because it touches the emotional and social fabric that makes up family, can be brutal. Last March in Nebraska, the attorney general issued an opinion saying that under the state's constitution, gay people do not have the right to make burial arrangements for their partners. The generally civil members of the Massachusetts court were barely civil to one another by the time they issued their second opinion. In her ruling, Chief Justice Margaret Marshall said Justice Sosman, who had dissented, "so clearly misses the point that further discussion appears to be useless." It is a small sign that tempers are likely to flare when the national debate begins.

# REVERSING *The* "GENDER GAP"

By Joel Wendland

"**B**oys are becoming the second sex" proclaimed *Business Week* last May in a cover story titled "The New Gender Gap." *Business Week's* article appeared as part of a spate of articles and television news segments on the subject of increased educational opportunities for women. The basics of the story are that in the education system, teachers have become so conscious of catering to the needs of girls and young women that boys are being left behind. Boys, they say, are being punished for "boyish" behavior. They are being put more often into special education programs or disciplinary classes, and the outcome is that boys have a negative educational experience. This trend translates into poorer high school performances and perhaps college as well.

According to statistics offered by *Business Week*, 57 percent of all new bachelor's degrees and 58 percent of master's degrees are awarded to women. This "education grab," according to the article, was the source of the "new gender gap." Though, the article did hint that even with the new trend in the numbers, women still had some ways to go in order to catch up after 350 years of being almost entirely excluded from the university.

Most observers of this situation will find such an article perplexing. Certainly most women will likely be skeptical of its major argument. That this "reverse gender gap" argument exists, however, is not surprising. Like its cousins in other areas of social life (reverse discrimina-

tion or reverse class warfare), it is being generated primarily by the ultra-right. The purpose is to stifle the struggle for equality by implying (or stating directly) that the gains made by women through struggle over the last 40 years have gone too far and have detrimentally affected society.

Some in this camp go so far as to suggest that women who demand equality are out to hurt men. At worst, it demonstrates that the right wants to twist the outcome of social progress to divide us. They say that a struggle between men and women for social goods is the fundamental source of social conflict and that women are winning—a situation that, for some, means reversed gender inequality and for others goes against natural laws of male supremacy invoked by God.

Any way you look at it, however, this picture is a distortion of reality. So what does the real gender gap look like?

Barbara Gault, director of research at the Institute for Women's Policy Research, recently told *Women's Wall-Street.com* that there are several explanations for and holes in the current data on the educational experiences of men and women. First, high-paying occupations that do not require college degrees, such as skilled trades, are still male dominated. Second, women need a college degree in order to earn roughly hat men do with only high school diplomas, giving them stronger motives to make a special effort to obtain financial security. Third, among African Ameri-

cans, where the difference between women and men earning college degrees is the widest among all racial or ethnic groups, it is clear that institutional racism directed at African American men plays a large role in keeping them out of college. Fourth, in the crucial field of information technology, women continue to earn only about one-third of the degrees awarded and get only about one-third of the jobs available. Finally, men continue to outpace women in completing doctoral and professional degrees (81 women for every 100 men), resulting in continued male dominance in corporate board rooms, the seats of political power, the highest positions in universities, etc.

The average **woman**, according to the AFL-CIO, **will lose $523,000** in her lifetime due to **unequal pay**.

The successes of the women's equality movement, progressive changes in attitudes about roles women can have and the implementation of affirmative action policies (which benefited women as a whole most) have had a tremendous positive impact on the access women have had in education. Just 30 years ago, women earned advanced or professional degrees at a rate of only 23 women per 100 men. In other arenas, such as the workforce or the political field, the gender gap, in sheer numbers, has largely narrowed. But the numbers still don't paint the whole picture.

While higher education is a major factor in gaining financial security, it is something that is only available to about one-fifth of the adult population. So for the vast majority of women, this supposed "new gender gap" means absolutely nothing. Other data on the condition of women's economic security paint another picture altogether. About eight of ten retired women are not eligible for pension benefits. When retired women do get a pension, it is typically far less than retired men get. Fifty percent of women who receive pension benefits get only about 60 cents for every dollar of male pensioners. On the average, retired women depend on Social Security for 71 percent of their income, and about 25 percent of retired women rely solely on Social Security for their income.

In the work force, women's pay averages only 76 percent of men's pay (at a cost of about $200 billion for working families annually). A report produced by the General Accounting Office last October shows that since 1983, the wage differential has actually increased. 60 percent of all women earn less than $25,000 annually. Women are one-third more likely to live below the poverty level. Black women and Latinas are between two and three times more likely to live below the poverty line than men are.

For women of color, facing the double oppression of racism and sexism, pay losses are even greater: 64 cents on the dollar at a loss of about $210 a week. The average woman, according to the AFL-CIO, will lose $523,000 in her lifetime due to unequal pay.

Even more costly to women, is the "price of motherhood," as journalist Ann Crittenden argues in her recent book of that title. In almost every case, women lose income, jobs, job experience and retirement income (while work hours increase) when they decide to have children. With some slight improvements, women remain the primary caregiver in nearly every family. For many mothers, single or married, the economic inequalities described above are exacerbated. For married women, dependence on men is heightened and the threat of economic hardship enforces interpersonal inequality and conflict. Divorced mothers and their children have among the highest rates of poverty of any demographic.

Crittenden argues that unless other sources of financial support for motherhood are made available institutionalized inequality will persist. She suggests retirement benefits for mothers, public funding for day care and health care for children and their caregivers, salaries for primary caregivers, expanded public education for pre-school children, equalized social security for spouses, increased financial contri-

butions from husbands and fathers, increased educational and support resources for parents and equalization of living standards for divorced parents.

As for the fallacy of female supremacy, the gains made by women through struggle and implementation of policies such as affirmative action point to the necessity of broader systematic change. But if female supremacy is a fallacy, does this mean that men go unhurt by gender inequalities? No. Men and boys are hurt when their families suffer because pay inequity causes their mothers, grandmothers, sisters and aunts to lose income, get fired, face hiring discrimination, are refused pensions, don't have equal Social Security benefits, lose out on promotions or have limited access to higher education. Additionally, if the average woman loses $523,000 in income in her life, does this mean that the average man is enriched by $523,000 in his lifetime? If pay inequity costs women $200 billion yearly, does this mean that men are enriched by $200 billion? The answer is no. These billions are savings in labor costs to employers. Employers enjoy the profits of male supremacy and gendered divisions among working people. So it makes sense that the right tries to portray the benefits of progressive social change toward equality as bad. It cuts into their bottom line.

From *Political Affairs*, March 2004, pp. 24-25, 43. Copyright © 2004 by Political Affairs. Reprinted by permission.

# UNIT 4

# Institutional Problems

## Unit Selections

21. **The American Family**, Stephanie Coontz
22. **Living Better: Get Wed**, Amy M. Braverman
23. **We're Not in the Mood**, Kathleen Deveny
24. **Against School: How Public Education Cripples Our Kids, and Why**, John Taylor Gatto
25. **How I Joined Teach for America—and Got Sued for $20 Million**, Joshua Kaplowitz
26. **Whose Hospital Is It?**, Arthur Allen
27. **Death Stalks a Continent**, Johanna McGeary

## Key Points to Consider

• What changes in the family in the past half century do you think are good and what changes do you think are bad? What can be done about the bad changes?

• What are the forces behind the high divorce rates? Will these forces decline or increase? Defend your answer.

• What is wrong with America's education system and how can it be improved?

• What are some major health issues today and why did they become so troublesome?

 **Links: www.dushkin.com/online/**
These sites are annotated in the World Wide Web pages.

**The Center for Education Reform**
*http://edreform.com/school_choice/*

**Go Ask Alice!**
*http://www.goaskalice.columbia.edu*

**The National Academy for Child Development (NACD)**
*http://www.nacd.org*

**National Council on Family Relations (NCFR)**
*http://www.ncfr.com*

**National Institute on Aging (NIA)**
*http://www.nih.gov/nia/*

**National Institute on Drug Abuse (NIDA)**
*http://165.112.78.61*

**National Institutes of Health (NIH)**
*http://www.nih.gov*

**Parenting and Families**
*http://www.cyfc.umn.edu/features/index.html*

**A Sociological Tour Through Cyberspace**
*http://www.trinity.edu/~mkearl/index.html*

**World Health Organization (WHO)**
*http://www.who.int/home-page/*

T his unit looks at the problems in three institutional areas: the family, education, and health care. The first subsection deals with the problems of the family. The family is important. Politicians and preachers are earnestly preaching this message today as though most people need to be converted. Of course, since everyone already agrees, the preaching is mostly ritual. Nevertheless, families are having real problems. The causes of the problems are not due to a lack of commitment as much as to numerous changes in society that have had an impact on the family. For example, women have to work because many men do not make enough income to support a family adequately. Women are working not only to enjoy a career but also out of necessity. With women working, they are less dependent on their husbands. As a result, divorce becomes more of an option and psychologically more likely. Since there are many other forces that make divorce more likely, the issue of strong families is complex and the articles in this section shed some helpful light on the problems. In the first article, Stephanie Coontz corrects many common misunderstandings about the family. She takes issue with the data presented for the decline of marriage and the family thesis and offers evidence that marriage is strong today even though divorce is common. In fact, she argues that today's families are better than families a century ago in many ways. According to Coontz "the biggest problem facing most families … is not that our families have changed too much but that our institutions have changed too little." In the second article, Amy M. Braverman reviews the recent research on the benefits of marriage which are many. The title summarizes the findings in one sentence: if you want a better life you should get married. Marrieds have better sex lives, better physical and mental health, better material conditions and finances, and of course the children are better off. In the next article Kathleen Deveny discusses the problem of modern couples often overworking or having so many activities that they do not have enough energy in the evening for much of a sex life. Many couples, however, make special efforts to overcome this problem.

The second subsection deals with education, a perennial problem area. John Taylor Gatto attacks the American school system for slowing the maturation of students and for being boring. He suspects that this result is exactly what those who control the school system want schools to do. In arguing his radical thesis he presents a very provocative history of the evolution of the American school system. The next article is included because the worst problems afflicting school systems are found in inner-city schools. One way to understand these problems is to accompany

a dedicated teacher to one of these schools. Joshua Kaplowitz's experience teaching at Emery Elementary School in Washington DC gets to the heart of the matter. His major problem was just maintaining order in class. Among his many other problems was the problem of fraudulent harassment lawsuits that ruined his and others' careers at Emery.

The last subsection deals with health care issues and this sphere is also in turmoil and plagued with problems. The particular problem discussed in the next article is the closing of many badly needed hospitals by for-profit hospital chains for lower than acceptable profit rates. Arthur Allen tells the story of the closing of the Medical College of Pennsylvania Hospital in Philadelphia as an example of "more that 560 hospitals [that] have closed since 1990–clobbered by stagnant reimbursement rates from government and the insurance industry, rising malpractice rates, skyrocketing prices for drugs and medical equipment, and increasing numbers of uninsured patients who can't pay their bills." The next article is full of pain and death for it deals with the worldwide epidemic of AIDS, with its focus on sub-Saharan Africa where 70 percent of those infected with HIV/AIDS reside. Of course, we would expect the various governments to do everything in their power to stop the epidemic and help the victims, and for the friends and relatives of the victims to have compassion on them. Unfortunately the true story is quite ugly. The shocking failure of many societies in the AIDS crisis reveals the fragility of these societies. The unbelievable brutality of the treatment of the AIDS victims by relatives and others reveals the depths of the evil that many people are capable of when they are afraid.

# THE AMERICAN FAMILY

## New research about an old institution challenges the conventional wisdom that the family today is worse off than in the past. Essay by Stephanie Coontz

As the century comes to an end, many observers fear for the future of America's families. Our divorce rate is the highest in the world, and the percentage of unmarried women is significantly higher than in 1960. Educated women are having fewer babies, while immigrant children flood the schools, demanding to be taught in their native language. Harvard University reports that only 4 percent of its applicants can write a proper sentence.

## Things were worse at the turn of the last century than they are today. Most workers labored 10 hours a day, six days a week, leaving little time for family life.

There's an epidemic of sexually transmitted diseases among men. Many streets in urban neighborhoods are littered with cocaine vials. Youths call heroin "happy dust." Even in small towns, people have easy access to addictive drugs, and drug abuse by middle-class wives is skyrocketing. Police see 16-year-old killers, 12-year-old prostitutes, and gang members as young as 11.

America at the end of the 1990s? No, America at the end of the 1890s.

The litany of complaints may sound familiar, but the truth is that many things were worse at the start of this century than they are today. Then, thousands of children worked full-time in mines, mills and sweatshops. Most workers labored 10 hours a day, often six days a week, which left them little time or energy for family life. Race riots were more frequent and more deadly than those experienced by recent generations. Women couldn't vote, and their wages were so low that many turned to prostitution.

Photograph courtesy of Thomas L. Gavin.

© 1900 A Couple and their eight children sit for a family portrait. Wth smaller families today, mothers are able to spend twice as much time with each child.

In 1900 a white child had one chance in three of losing a brother or sister before age 15, and a black child had a fifty-fifty chance of seeing a sibling die. Children's-aid groups reported widespread abuse and neglect by parents. Men who deserted or divorced their wives rarely paid child support. And only 6 percent of the children graduated from high school, compared with 88 percent today.

Photograph courtesy of Kathryn M. Gavin.

On the 1940s family farm, fathers out working the fields had less time to spend with their families.

Why do so many people think American families are facing worse problems now than in the past? Partly it's because we compare the complex and diverse families of the 1990s with the seemingly more standard-issue ones of the 1950s, a unique decade when every long-term trend of the 20th century was temporarily reversed. In the 1950s, for the first time in 100 years, the divorce rate fell while marriage and fertility rates soared, crating a boom in nuclear-family living. The percentage of foreign-born individuals in the country decreased. And the debates over social and cultural issues that had divided Americans for 150 years were silenced, suggesting a national consensus on family values and norms.

Some nostalgia for the 1950s is understandable: Life looked pretty good in comparison with the hardship of the Great Depression and World War II. The GI Bill gave a generation of young fathers a college education and a subsidized mortgage on a new house. For the first time, a majority of men could support a family and buy a home without pooling their earnings with those of other family members. Many Americans built a stable family life on these foundations.

But much nostalgia for the 1950s is a result of selective amnesia—the same process that makes childhood memories of summer vacations grow sunnier with each passing year. The superficial sameness of 1950s family life was achieved through censorship, coercion and discrimination. People with unconventional beliefs faced governmental investigation and arbitrary firings. African Americans and Mexican Americans were prevented from voting in some states by literacy tests that were not administered to whites. Individuals who didn't follow the rigid gender and sexual rules of the day were ostracized.

*Leave It to Beaver* did not reflect the real-life experience of most American families. While many moved into the middle class during the 1950s, poverty remained more widespread than in the worst of our last three recessions. More children went hungry, and poverty rates for the elderly were more than twice as high as today's.

Even in the white middle class, not every woman was as serenely happy with her lot as June Cleaver was on TV. Housewives of the 1950s may have been less rushed than today's working mothers, but they were more likely to suffer anxiety and depression. In many states, women couldn't serve on juries or get loans or credit cards in their own names.

And not every kid was as wholesome as Beaver Cleaver, whose mischievous antics could be handled by Dad at the dinner table. In 1955 alone, Congress discussed 200 bills aimed at curbing juvenile delinquency. Three years later, LIFE reported that urban teachers were being terrorized by their students. The drugs that were so freely available in 1900 had been outlawed, but many children grew up in families ravaged by alcohol and barbiturate abuse.

Rates of unwed childbearing tripled between 1940 and 1958, but most Americans didn't notice because unwed mothers generally left town, gave their babies up for adoption and returned home as if nothing had happened. Troubled youths were encouraged to drop out of high school. Mentally handicapped children were warehoused in institutions like the Home for Idiotic and Imbecilic Children in Kansas, where a woman whose sister had lived there for most of the 1950s once took me. Wives routinely told pollsters that being disparaged or ignored by their husbands was a normal part of a happier than-average marriage.

## Many of our worries today reflect how much better we want to be, not how much better we used to be.

Denial extended to other areas of life as well. In the early 1900s, doctors refused to believe that the cases of gonorrhea and syphilis they saw in young girls could have been caused by sexual abuse. Instead, they reasoned, girls could get these diseases from toilet seats, a myth that terrified generations of mothers and daughters. In the 1950s, psychiatrists dismissed incest reports as Oedipal fantasies on the part of children.

Spousal rape was legal throughout the period and wife beating was not taken seriously by authorities. Much of what we now label child abuse was accepted as a normal part of parental discipline. Physicians saw no reason to question parents who claimed that their child's broken bones had been caused by a fall from a tree.

---

# American Mirror

Muncie, Ind. (pop. 67,476), calls itself America's Hometown. But to generations of sociologists it is better known as America's Middletown—the most studied place in the 20th century American landscape. "Muncie has nothing extraordinary about it," says University of Virginia professor Theodore Caplow, which is why, for the past 75 years, researchers have gone there to observe the typical American family. Muncie's averageness first drew sociologists Robert and Helen Lynd in 1924. They returned in 1935 (their follow-up study was featured in a LIFE photo essay by Margaret Bourke-White). And in 1976, armed with the Lynds' original questionnaires, Caplow launched yet another survey of the town's citizens.

Caplow discovered that family life in Muncie was much healthier in the 1970s than in the 1920s. No only were husbands and wives communicating more, but unlike married couples in the 1920s, they were also shopping, eating out, exercising and going to movies and concerts together. More than 90 percent of Muncie's couples characterized their marriages as "happy" or "very happy." In 1929 the Lynds had described partnerships of a drearier kind, "marked by sober accommodation of each partner to his share in the joint undertaking of children, paying off the mortgage and generally 'getting on.'"

Caplow's five-year study, which inspired a six-part PBS series, found that even though more moms were working outside the home, two thirds of them spent at least two hours a day with their children; in 1924 fewer than half did. In 1924 most children expected their mothers to be good cooks and housekeepers, and wanted their fathers to spend time with them and respect their opinions. Fifty years later, expectations of fathers were unchanged, but children wanted the same—time and respect—from their mothers.

This year, Caplow went back to survey the town again. The results (and another TV documentary) won't be released until December 2000.

—*Sora Song*

---

There are plenty of stresses in modern family life, but one reason they seem worse is that we no longer sweep them under the rug. Another is that we have higher expectations of parenting and marriage. That's a good thing. We're right to be concerned about inattentive parents, conflicted marriages, antisocial values, teen violence and child abuse. But we need to realize that many of our worries reflect how much better we *want* to be, not how much better we *used* to be.

Fathers in intact families are spending more time with their children than at any other point in the past 100 years. Although the number of hours the average woman spends at home with her children has declined since the early 1900s, there has been a decrease in the number of children per family and an increase in individual attention to each child. As a result, mothers today, including working moms, spend almost twice as much time with each child as mothers did in the 1920s. People who raised children in the 1940s and 1950s typically report that their own adult children and grandchildren communicate far better with their kids and spend more time helping with homework than they did—even as they complain that other parents today are doing a worse job than in the past.

Despite the rise in youth violence from the 1960s to the early 1990s, America's children are also safer now than they've ever been. An infant was four times more likely to die in the 1950s than today. A parent then was three times more likely than a modern one to preside at the funeral of a child under the age of 15, and 27 percent more likely to lose an older teen to death.

If we look back over the last millennium, we can see that families have always been diverse and in flux. In each period, families have solved one set of problems only to face a new array of challenges. What works for a family in one economic and cultural setting doesn't work for a family in another. What's helpful at one stage of a family's life may be destructive at the next stage. If there is one lesson to be drawn from the last millennium of family history, it's that families are always having to play catch-up with a changing world.

Take the issue of working mothers. Families in which mothers spend as much time earning a living as they do raising children are nothing new. They were the norm throughout most of the last two millennia. In the 19th century, married women in the United States began a withdrawal from the workforce, but for most families this was made possible only by sending their children out to work instead. When child labor was abolished, married women began reentering the workforce in ever large numbers.

For a few decades, the decline in child labor was greater than the growth of women's employment. The result was an aberration: the male-breadwinner family. In the 1920s, for the first time, a bare majority of American children grew up in families where the husband provided all the income, the wife stayed home full-time, and they and their siblings went to school instead of work. During the 1950s, almost two thirds of children grew up in such families, an all-time high. Yet that same decade saw an acceleration of workforce participation by wives and mothers that soon made the dual-earner family the norm, a trend not likely to be reversed in the next century.

What's new is not that women make half their families' living, but that for the first time they have substantial control over their own income, along with the social freedom

© Getty Images/Index Stock

In the 1950s, life looked pretty good in comparison with the hardships of the Great Depression and World War II.

to remain single or to leave an unsatisfactory marriage. Also new is the declining proportion of their lives that people devote to rearing children, both because they have fewer kids and because they are living longer. Until about 1940, the typical marriage was broken by the death of one partner within a few years after the last child left home. Today, couples can look forward to spending more than two decades together after the children leave.

The growing length of time partners spend with only each other for company has made many individuals less willing to put up with an unhappy marriage, while women's economic independence makes it less essential for them to do so. It is no wonder that divorce has risen steadily since 1900. Disregarding a spurt in 1946, a dip in the 1950s and another peak around 1980, the divorce rate is just where you'd expect to find it, based on the rate of increase from 1900 to 1950. Today, 40 percent of all marriages will end in divorce before a couple's 40th anniversary. Yet despite this high divorce rate, expanded life expectancies mean that more couples are reaching that anniversary than ever before.

Families and individuals in contemporary America have more life choices than in the past. That makes it easier for some to consider dangerous or unpopular options. But it also makes success easier for many families that never would have had a chance before—interracial, gay or lesbian, and single-mother families, for example. And it expands horizons for most families.

Women's new options are good not just for themselves but for their children. While some people say that women who choose to work are selfish, it turns out that maternal self-sacrifice is not good for children. Kids do better when their mothers are happy with their lives, whether their satisfaction comes from being a full-time homemaker or from having a job.

Largely because of women's new roles at work, men are doing more at home. Although most men still do less housework than their wives, the gap has been halved since the 1960s. Today, 49 percent of couples say they share childcare equally, compared with 25 percent of 1985.

Men's greater involvement at home is good for their relationships with their parents, and also good for their children. Hands-on fathers make better parents than men who let their wives do all the nurturing and childcare: They raise sons who are more expressive and daughters who are more likely to do well in school, especially in math and science.

**The biggest problem is not that our families have changed too much but that our institutions have changed too little.**

113

In 1900, life expectancy was 47 years, and only 4 percent of the population was 65 or older. Today, life expectancy is 76 years, and by 2025, about 20 percent of Americans will be 65 or older. For the first time, a generation of adults must plan for the needs of both their parents and their children. Most Americans are responding with remarkable grace. One in four households gives the equivalent of a full day a week or more in unpaid care to an aging relative, and more than half say they expect to do so in the next 10 years. Older people are less likely to be impoverished or incapacitated by illness than in the past, and they have more opportunity to develop a relationship with their grandchildren.

Even some of the choices that worry us the most are turning out to be manageable. Divorce rates are likely to remain high, but more non-custodial parents are staying in touch with their children. Child-support receipts are up. And a lower proportion of kids from divorced families are exhibiting problems than in earlier decades. Stepfamilies are learning to maximize children's access to supportive adults rather than cutting them off from one side of the family.

Out-of-wedlock births are also high, however, and this will probably continue because the age of first marriage for women has risen to an all-time high of 25, almost five years above what it was in the 1950s. Women who marry at an older age are less likely to divorce, but they have more years when they are at risk—or at choice—for a nonmarital birth.

Nevertheless, births to teenagers have fallen from 50 percent of all nonmarital births in the late 1970s to just 30 percent today. A growing proportion of women who have a nonmarital birth are in their twenties and thirties and usually have more economic and educational resources than unwed mothers of the past. While two involved parents are generally better than one, a mother's personal maturity, along with her educational and economic status, is a better predictor of how well her child will turn out than her marital status. We should no longer assume that children raised by single parents face debilitating disadvantages.

As we begin to understand the range of sizes, shapes and colors that today's families come in, we find that the differences *within* family types are more important than the differences *between* them. No particular family form guarantees success, and no particular form is doomed to fail. How a family functions on the inside is more important than how it looks from the outside.

The biggest problem facing most families as this century draws to a close is not that our families have changed too much but that our institutions have changed too little. America's work policies are 50 years out of date, designed for a time when most moms weren't in the workforce and most dads didn't understand the joys of being involved in childcare. Our school schedules are 150 years out of date, designed for a time when kids needed to be home to help with the milking and haying. And many political leaders feel they have to decide whether to help parents stay home longer with their kids or invest in better childcare, preschool and afterschool programs, when most industrialized nations have long since learned it's possible to do both.

So America's social institutions have some Y2K bugs to iron out. But for the most part, our families are ready for the next millennium.

# *LIVING BETTER GET WED*

*AMY M. BRAVERMAN*

While pundits, politicians, and moralists weigh the pros and cons of gay marriage, Linda Waite is still focused on traditional American couples, countering messages from the "antimarriage" culture and championing marriage's benefits: specifically, that marriage itself is good for your physical and mental health, good for your financial stability, good for your sex life, good for your kids—good for almost every aspect of what many Americans consider a happy life.

And Waite, the Lucy Flower professor in Sociology, is spreading the word. Her book, *The Case for Marriage: Why Married People Are Happier, Healthier, and Better Off Financially* (Doubleday, 2000), cowritten by Maggie Gallagher of the Institute of American Values, has sold 25,000 copies. Although its title sounds like a socially conservative missive, its coauthor is a conservative columnist, and its message helped to inform President George W. Bush's marriage initiative for welfare recipients, the book is not, Waite says, a right-wing tract. Waite, in fact, describes herself as a liberal Democrat. "I come at this from a researcher's perspective." What the slim, 55-year-old with a short, no-nonsense haircut means is, she didn't create the facts, she's just reporting them.

Those facts refute much conventional wisdom. They show that married men, rather than trading their libidos for lawnmowers, have more sex than single men. And married women are less depressed than single women, contrary to feminist sociologist Jessie Bernard's explosive 1972 book arguing that wives were more phobic, depressed, dependent, and passive—findings that have shaped cultural conceptions, ever since. More recently, Waite has shown that divorce docs not make unhappily married people any happier. In a study released in July 2002, she and five colleagues analyzed data from the University of Wisconsin's National Survey of Family and Households. When the adults who said they were unhappily married in the late 1980s were interviewed again five years later, those who had divorced were on average still unhappy or even *less* happy, while those who stayed in their marriages on average had moved past the bad times and were at a happier stage. After controlling for race, age, gender, and income, Waite's group found that divorce usually did not reduce symptoms of depression, raise self esteem, or. increase a sense of mastery over one's life.

"The general pattern," Waite says, "is that people who stay in an unhappy marriage are at least as well off as those who divorce, so there's no benefit to leaving a marriage you're unhappy with." That argument—that people who at some point are unhappy with their marriage later become happy in the same marriage—is the subject of Waite and Gallagher's forthcoming book, *The Case for Staying Married*, under contract with Oxford University Press.

Not that Waite's exchanging her sociological expertise for a counseling certificate. "I don't give advice," she says. "All we can say is, the suggestion is that a lot of things that make people unhappy don't stay." She may not counsel couples, but she actively promotes her findings, organizing several conferences on marriage, sitting on the research board for the National Marriage Project, whose mission is to "strengthen the institution of marriage" through research and education, and advising the University's Religion, Culture, and Family Project. *The Case for Marriage*, Waite says, is more than anything else a public health argument. "It's like exercise," she says. "Studies show that, on average, people who exercise experience health benefits. The next step is to say that you should exercise." Similarly, "a consistent body of work suggests to me that an OK marriage, one that isn't terrible, causes improvements" in general well-being. And those studies, she notes, point to marriage not only as a sign of a longer, healthier life, higher income, and better sex, but also as a cause.

A 1990 study, for example, showed that unmarried women have a 50 percent higher mortality rate than married women; single men 250 percent higher than married men. Husbands' greater health benefit, Waite and Gallagher write, "appears to flow from the fact that single men behave in particularly unhealthy, risky ways that single women typically do not," such as drinking, smoking, and reckless driving—"stupid bachelor tricks" that, Waite notes, divorced and widowed men often return to. Wives tend to track their husbands' health, scheduling doctor's appointments and providing direct care. And husbands benefit from wives' emotional support, making them more likely than single men to recover from a serious illness or to manage a chronic illness.

Wives also experience health gains, including their mental health, It's true that married women with young children generally report feeling more "overburdened" than single, childless women, but studies have found that married women—and men—have better mental health than singles. Although women are more prone to depression than men, marriage doesn't account for the gap.

## FINANCIAL BENEFITS

For women the biggest marriage benefit, however, is not health but finances. With the higher incomes men often contribute to a relationship, married women can access better housing, safer neighborhoods, and often the security of owning their own homes. They're more likely to have private health insurance—only half of divorced, widowed, and never-married women do, according to one study. Married men benefit financially as well—they make at least 10 percent more than single men do, Waite and Gallagher write, and perhaps as much as 40 percent more. Economic theory suggests that husbands earn more money because they are freer to specialize in money-making—while wives typically specialize in housework and child care. (But it does not necessarily follow, Waite and Gallagher note, that men make more money because they do less housework. "While time spent on housework does affect the earnings of wives, some evidence suggests that husbands who spend more hours on household tasks do not earn less money as a result."

Skeptics may wonder if it's really marriage that makes the difference. Perhaps people who are happier and healthier to begin with are more likely to get married. Perhaps the divorced are sicker and die younger because marriages are more likely to break up from the stress of an illness. Perhaps men who make more money are more likely to attract (and keep) a wife. Certain "selection mechanisms," Waite and Gallagher admit, do play a role in explaining married people's better health and higher incomes. But in addition, they believe, marriage itself creates better lives. Accounting for initial health status, the married live longer. "Even sick people who marry live longer than their counterparts who don't," they write. And selection alone doesn't explain married men's higher earnings; "their wages actually rise faster while they are married" than single men's wages do—even when occupation, industry, hours and weeks worked, and tenure are factored in.

Meanwhile, living together, or cohabiting, "does not confer the same protection as being married," they write. "The big health difference is between married people and the nonmarried, not between people who live alone and those who don't," Waite's own research of people in their 50s and 60s showed that single adults, "whether living alone, with children, or with others, described their emotional health more negatively than did the married people." Those who divorce or are widowed regain many of marriage's benefits if they remarry, and cohabitation provides some of marriage's emotional benefits, but for a shorter term. Breakups are more likely with live-in couples than with married ones, and cohabitors, Waite and Gallagher write, are generally less happy and less satisfied with their sex lives than the wed. In fact, the National Sex Survey led by Chicago professors Edward Laumann and Robert Michael and another large sex study by University of Denver psychologists showed that married people have more sex than single people do, and they enjoy it more, both physically and emotionally.

Of course, not all marriages are happy, and Waite isn't suggesting that victims of domestic violence or chronic infidelity should stay married. Rather, she's targeting the relatively quick, no-fault divorces—people unhappy because one spouse works long hours, because they're taking care of a sick child, because they have money problems, those who wonder if something better is out there, if they could be more satisfied, if the thrill from their newly married days could be rekindled with a new partner. Those are the kinds of issues, Waite and Gallagher learned in focus groups they held to complement Waite's statistical analysis, that couples can move past if they decide to work on their marriages.

"Maybe by demanding perfection we're setting our standards too high," Waite says. "The very intense emotion people feel when they fall in love is physiologically by definition, fleeting. To think that another relationship will make you feel that way forever dooms you because it's not possible."

## ANTIMARRIAGE CULTURE

The proclivity to leave results from the antimarriage culture. Waite believes, perpetuated by television and movies, athletes and other media stars, friends and relatives. If a struggling spouse heard "Hang in there, you're doing the right thing" more often than "You don't need to put up with this," Waite says, "at the margin somebody's going to listen." But instead friends encourage each other to leave, "and then it's easier for other people to leave because they have a role model."

## NO-FAULT DIVORCE

No-fault divorce, which California instituted in 1969 and all slates have in some form today, has made it easier to leave a marriage for less-than-dire reasons, In a no-fault divorce a spouse does not have to prove the other's wrongdoing, such as adultery, but only that there is no reasonable prospect of reconciliation. A spouse can receive a no-fault divorce even if the other spouse doesn't want it, and the couple may divorce out of court. Advocates see the process as a boon for women who want to leave abusive marriages without paying court fees, while critics such as Waite views no-fault as another cause of society's carefree attitude toward divorce. Then there's Barbara Dafoe Whitehead, AM'71, PhD'76, who codirects the National Marriage Project and writes extensively on family and child welfare. Although no-fault divorce "has unintentionally led to a legal system of divorce on demand," Whitehead wrote in the August/September 1997 *First Things: The Journal of Religion and Public Life*, a point/counterpoint piece in which she squared off with Waite coauthor Gallagher, she does not believe it should be eliminated as legislators in some states have attempted. Restoring a fault requirement, rather than forcing couples to work harder on their marriages, Whitehead wrote, would among other consequences deter "socially isolated and timorous women, often battered wives, from seeking divorce."

But no-fault, Whitehead concedes, has contributed to a culture more comfortable with divorce than it used to be. A 1998 *American Economic Review* study, Waite and Gallagher note in their book, showed that no-fault raised divorce rates by about 6.5 percent, accounting for 17 percent of the increase between 1968 and 1988. Today the chance that a marriage will end after 15 years—the figure widely cited as the "divorce rate"—is 43 percent, according to the National Center for Health Statistics' provisional 2001 numbers. While legislators in states such as Iowa and New Mexico have introduced measures to eliminate no-fault, in 1997 Louisiana became the first state to institute optional "covenant marriages," more binding unions that require premarital counseling, forgo the no-fault divorce option, and mandate up to a two-year cooling-off period before a divorce. That waiting period is something Waite advocates. Rather than running to divorce lawyers, she suggests, couples should first try counseling, or—because many men in her focus groups didn't like the idea of paying someone they weren't sure was committed to saving their marriage—seek out a religious leader or a marriage class.

After arguing so heavily for marriage and against divorce, it's more than a bit surprising to learn that—years before she began research on the subject Waite was divorced herself. Married as Michigan State undergraduates, she and her first husband split after four years. "We realized we wanted to live different kinds of lives," she says. Which may sound like one of those flippant reasons to divorce, but for people married a short time who have no children, she argues, "it's very different. You're not leaving somebody who's financially dependent, you haven't built years of friendships, you don't have kids, you're not as much a working single unit as people who are married for a long time." It's what demographer Pamela Paul would call a "starter marriage," which she defines in *The Starter Marriage and the Future of Matrimony* (Villard, 2002) as a union lasting live years or less and producing no children. Census Bureau statistics show that in 1998 more than 3 million 18- to 29-year-olds were divorced. In 1962, Paul notes, there were 253,000 divorced 25- to 29-year-olds, In fact, a 2001 Center for Disease Control and Prevention report shows, 20 percent of first-marriage divorces now occur within five years.

## PARENTAL CONFLICT

Many of those marriages, like Waite's first, are childless. But once spouses have children, the divorce outlook changes. Researchers disagree whether children of unhappily married couples are better off if the parents stay together or divorce. After analyzing the studies, Waite and Gallagher conclude that children are usually *not* better off when unhappy spouses divorce. Marital dissatisfaction, they write, "is probably not in and of itself psychologically damaging for children: what count, is whether, how often, and how intensely parents fight in front of their children both before and after divorce." And while divorce may end marital conflict for adults, it doesn't stop "what really

bothers kids: parental conflict," they write. Children of divorce also have less money, live in poorer neighborhoods, go to poorer schools, and do worse in school than children of married parents—even if those marriages have a high degree of conflict. Divorce-for-the-children advocates point to a 1991 study showing that kids with mental health problems, such as anxiety or depression, are usually affected more by home conflict before the divorce than after it. But study author Andrew Cherlin, of Johns Hopkins University, re-examined the issue in two later studies and concluded, Waite and Gallagher write, that "the divorce itself does have additional long-term negative effects on children's psychological well-being." Twenty-three-year-olds whose parents divorced before they turned 16, Cherlin found, had poorer mental health than children from intact families.

Waite has two children with her second husband of 30 years, Chicago sociology professor Ross Stolzenberg, who does research on the effects of work, and is the editor of *Sociological Methodology*, the research methods journal of the American Sociological Association. Their 24-year-old daughter is married, lives in Israel, and has a two-year-old child. Their 18-year-old daughter lives at home and has cerebral palsy, which has strained the family at times. "When it was terrible we all had emotional responses," Waite says, "but everybody has times like that."

Waite didn't begin promoting marriage because of an underlying ideology. She actually stumbled upon the topic. In the early 1990s she and a colleague studied the relationship between marital status and mortality for the National Institutes of health. Controlling for age, they found that when both men and women became divorced or widowed, they were more likely to die than if they were married. Before writing up the study for a scientific journal Waite reviewed existing literature to see "what it might be about marriage that increases chances for living." She found a lot of material on physical and emotional health related to marriage. Then in 1995 Waite was elected president of the Population Association of America, a society of professionals using population data, and was asked to give a "big picture" address to the group. By then she was researching sexual behavior in different kinds of unions—couples dating, cohabiting, married. At the same time a colleague from the RAND Corporation, whose Population Research Center Waite had directed, was studying marriage and health issues, and Waite read additional studies showing that married men had higher earnings than other men. "I put all this stuff together and realized that the people working on wages don't know anything about the sex stuff and so on," she says. "There's a general pattern here that nobody's noticed. All of the big things in life—good outcomes for children, health, long life—depend on marriage." So marriage's many rewards became her talk, which was published in *Demography*, the association's journal. A Harvard University Press editor proposed she turn it into a book called *The Case for Marriage*.

## AN APOLITICAL BOOK

A colleague suggested Gallagher as a cowriter, someone to help make the research accessible to lay readers. Waite had read

Gallagher's work and was "impressed by how carefully and accurately she represented the social-science research." During the writing, Gallagher "always deferred to me on the facts," Waite says, and because of their differing politics they kept certain topics, such as gay marriage, out of the book altogether. "In some sense I was naive to think others would just listen to the arguments and evidence," Waite says. "But some people inferred from [Gallagher's] other life"—that is, as a conservative writer and activist—"that the book was political. But I wrote it, and I'm [professionally] apolitical."

Then Wade Horn, assistant secretary for children and families in the U.S. Department of Health and Human Services, read the book. Horn, a Ph.D. in clinical psychology and past president of the National Fatherhood Initiative, which promotes responsibility and marriage, says Waite's empirical research helped to provide a nonideological basis for Bush's "healthy marriage" initiative for welfare recipients. "Linda's research made the case that marriage matters for the community and for children." Horn says. "Now we have to figure out what we're going to do about it." Bush's measure, part of the welfare-reform package approved by the House and still winding through Senate committees in mid-September, would provide money to slate or community governments or organizations for marriage-strengthening projects, such as conflict-management or marriage courses. Although it's been portrayed as an effort to impose marriage on welfare recipients to solve their problems, the initiative, Horn says, would actually target people already considering marriage. More than two-thirds of unmarried urban couples with children are "actively considering marriage," says Horn, "but we never ask them" about it and point them to resources that might help them get there. Funding different approaches in different places, Horn hopes some ideas prove successful and in time a good model might emerge.

So how does Waite feel about providing conservatives with more fuel for their traditional-family arguments? To Waite, it just so happens that a specific political movement has found in her a researcher whose message they like. As Horn puts it. "Marriage is not an institution that's the sole purview of any aspect of the political spectrum. As a real empiricist [Waite] didn't set out to prove an ideological point. She looked at the evidence and made a conclusion."

## LOOKING FORWARD

Those pro-family conclusions have taken her far. Besides *The Case for Marriage* and its forthcoming sequel, she and fellow Chicago sociologist Barbara Schneider will soon publish a book on the Sloan 500 Family Study, which examined 500 American families—married and working parents with either adolescents or kindergartners. "Doing things with the family made parents more cheerful, friendly, and cooperative," Waite told the *Chicago Tribune*. "Parents who spend less time with the kids and spouse are stressed, anxious, and angry."

Again, the message seems plain. The benefits of family life, like those of marriage, are significant but require work. It's a lesson Waite hopes, through her research, that couples will hear.

---

*Ms. Braverman is an associate editor of the University of Chicago Magazine. From "Healthy, Wealthy, & Wed," by Amy M. Braverman,* University of Chicago Magazine, *October 2003, pages 32–39.*

---

# WE'RE NOT IN THE MOOD

**For married couples with kids and busy jobs, sex just isn't what it used to be. How stress causes strife in the bedroom—and beyond.**

**BY KATHLEEN DEVENY**

FOR MADDIE WEINREICH, SEX HAD ALWAYS BEEN A JOY. IT helped her recharge her batteries and reconnect with her husband, Roger. But teaching yoga, raising two kids and starting up a business—not to mention cooking, cleaning and renovating the house—left her exhausted. She often went to bed before her husband, and was asleep by the time he joined her. Their once steamy love life slowly cooled. When Roger wanted to have sex, she would say she was too beat. He tried to be romantic; to set the mood he'd light a candle in their bedroom. "I would see it and say, 'Oh, God, not that candle'," Maddie recalls. "It was just the feeling that I had to give something I didn't have."

Lately, it seems, we're just not in the mood. We're overworked, anxious about the economy—and we have to drive our kids to way too many T-Ball games. Or maybe it's all those libido-dimming antidepressants we're taking. We resent spouses who never pick up the groceries or their dirty socks. And if we actually find we have 20 minutes at the end of the day—after bath time and story time and juice-box time and e-mail time—who wouldn't rather zone out to Leno than have sex? Sure, passion ebbs and flows in even the healthiest of relationships, but judging from the conversation of the young moms at the next table at Starbucks, it sounds like we're in the midst of a long dry spell.

It's difficult to say exactly how many of the 113 million married Americans are too exhausted or too grumpy to get it on, but some psychologists estimate that 15 to 20 percent of couples have sex no more than 10 times a year, which is how the experts define sexless marriage. And even couples who don't meet that definition still feel like they're not having sex as often as they used to. Despite the stereotype that women are more likely to dodge sex, it's often the men who decline. The number of sexless marriages is "a grossly underreported statistic," says therapist Michele Weiner Davis, author of "The Sex-Starved Marriage."

IF SO, THE PROBLEM MUST BE HUGE, GIVEN HOW MUCH WE already hear about it. Books like "The Sex-Starved Marriage," "Rekindling Desire: A Step-by-Step Program to Help Low-Sex and No-Sex Marriages" and "Resurrecting Sex" have become talk-show fodder. Dr. Phil has weighed in on the crisis; his Web site proclaims "the epidemic is undeniable." Avlimil, an herbal concoction that promises to help women put sex back into sexless marriage, had sales of 200,000 packages in January, its first month on the market. The company says it's swamped with as many as 3,000 calls a day from women who are desperately seeking desire. Not that the problem is confined to New Agers: former U.S. Labor secretary Robert Reich jokes about the pressure couples are under in speeches he gives on overworked Americans. Have you heard of DINS? he asks his audience. It stands for dual income, no sex.

# Sex and the Century: A History

Over the past 100 years, our understanding of sexual behavior has changed dramatically—and it's still evolving. From Sigmund to Sarah Jessica and Lucy to Lorena, here are some of the highlights:

**1905** Sigmund Freud's 'Three Essays on Sexuality' misinform generations about the nature of the female orgasm.

**1934** Henry Miller's 'Tropic of Cancer,' a semifictional memoir, debuts in Paris. But the expatiriate's libidinous adventures get banned in the United States.

**1952** Lucille Ball is the first pregnant woman to play a mother-to-be in a sitcom—but she isn't allowed to say the word 'pregnancy' on TV.

**1953** Alred Kinsey publishes 'Sexual Behavior in the Human Female,' the first major U.S. survey on women's sexual habits. He finds that Americans' attitudes don't match their behavior—50 percent have had premarital sex.

**December 1953** Marilyn Monroe takes it all off in the first issue of Playboy. Hugh Hefner's open love letter to bachelorhood.

**1960** The Food and Drug Administration OKs the birth-control pill, fueling the sexual revolution.

**1962** Helen Gurley Brown publishes her best-selling book 'Sex and the Single Girl.'

**1965** In *Griswold v. Connecticut*, the Supreme Court rules that the government cannot regulate a married couple's use of birth control.

**1966** William Masters and Virginia Johnson's 'Human Sexual Response' finds that half of all U.S. Marriages are plagued by some kind of sexual inadequacy.

**1970** Female college students nationwide adopt 'Our Bodies, Ourselves' as their bible on health and sexuality.

**1973** In *Roe v. Wade*, the Supreme Court decides that a woman's right to privacy encompasses her decision to terminate a pregnancy.

**1981** State Supreme Court cases in Massachusetts and New Jersey rule that husbands can be prosecuted for raping their wives—overturning the centuries-old marital-rape exception.

**1984** Researchers isolate the virus responsible for causing AIDS.

**1987** In 'Fatal Attraction,' Michael Douglas and Glenn Close share a one-night stand that turns mighty ugly. Mmm, rabbit.

**1993** Lorena Bobbit cuts off her husband's penis with a kitchen knife. Men nationwide cross their legs a little tighter.

**June 2003** HBO's 'Sex and the City,' which candidly chronicles the love lives of four professional, single women in New York City, kicks off its final season.

—MELISSA BREWSTER

## LOOKING FOR LOVE: New Yorkers Rosemary Breslin and her husband, Tony Dunne, joke that they've shelved sex till 2004.

Marriage counselors can't tell you how much sex you should be having, but most agree that you should be having *some*. Sex is only a small part of a good union, but happy marriages usually include it. Frequency of sex may be a measure of a marriage's long-term health; if it suddenly starts to decline, it can be a leading indicator of deeper problems, just like "those delicate green frogs that let us know when we're destroying the environment," says psychologist John Gottman, who runs the Family Research Lab (dubbed the Love Lab) at the University of Washington. Marriage pros say intimacy is often the glue that holds a couple together over time. If either member of a couple is miserable with the amount of sex in a marriage, it can cause devastating problems—and, in some cases, divorce. It can affect moods and spill over into all aspects of life—relationships with other family members, even performance in the office.

Best-selling novels and prime-time sit-coms only reinforce the idea that we're not having sex. In the opening pages of Allison Pearson's portrait of a frazzled working mom, "I Don't Know How She Does It," the novel's heroine, Kate Reddy, carefully brushes each of her molars 20 times. She's not fighting cavities. She's stalling in the hopes that her husband will fall asleep and won't try to have sex with her. (That way, she can skip a shower the next morning.) And what would Ray Romano joke about on his hit series "Everybody Loves Raymond" if he didn't have to wheedle sex out of his TV wife? Romano, who has four kids, including 10-year-old twins, says his comedy is

120

inspired by real life. "After kids, everything changes," he told NEWSWEEK. "We're having sex about every three months. If I have sex, I know my quarterly estimated taxes must be due. And if it's oral sex, I know it's time to renew my driver's license."

# "It wasn't that I didn't love him. It had nothing to do with him. What it boiled down to was being exhausted."

### —TARA PATERSON

Yet some couples seem to accept that sexless marriage is as much a part of modern life as traffic and e-mail. It's a given for Ann, a 39-year-old lawyer with two kids who lives in Brooklyn. When she and her husband were first married, they had sex almost every day. Now their 5-year-old daughter comes into their bedroom every night. Pretty soon, the dog starts whining to get on the bed, too. "At 3 or 4 a.m., I kick my husband out for snoring and he ends up sleeping in my daughter's princess twin bed with the Tinkerbell night light blinking in his face," she says. "So how are we supposed to have sex?"

The statistical evidence would seem to show everything is fine. Married couples say they have sex 68.5 times a year, or slightly more than once a week, according to a 2002 study by the highly respected National Opinion Research Center at the University of Chicago, and the NORC numbers haven't changed much over the past 10 years. At least according to what people tell researchers, DINS are most likely an urban myth: working women appear to have sex just as often as their stay-at-home counterparts. And for what it's worth, married people have 6.9 more sexual encounters a year than people who have never been married. After all, you can't underestimate the value of having an (occasionally) willing partner conveniently located in bed next to you.

But any efforts to quantify our love lives must be taken with a shaker of salt. The problem, not surprisingly, is that people aren't very candid about how often they have sex. Who wants to sound like a loser when he's trying to make a contribution to social science? When pressed, nearly everyone defaults to a respectable "once or twice a week," a benchmark that probably seeped into our collective consciousness with the 1953 Kinsey Report, a study that's considered flawed because of its unrepresentative, volunteer sample.

"As a result, we have no idea what's 'normal'," says Pepper Schwartz, a sociologist and author of "Everything You Know About Love and Sex Is Wrong." Her best guess: three times a week during the first year of marriage, much less over time. When people believe they have permission to complain, she says, they often admit to having sex less than once a month: "And these are couples who like each other!"

In fact, the problem may be just as much perception as reality. Because we have the 100-times-a-year myth in our minds, and because there are so many movies and TV shows out there with characters who frequently have better-than-you-get sex, it's easy to think that everybody else is having more fun. Forget the four hotties on HBO's "Sex and the City." Even Ruth Fisher, the frumpy, middle-aged widow on the network's "Six Feet Under," gets lucky week after week. Armed with birth-control pills and dog-eared copies of "The Sensuous Woman," boomers were the front line of the sexual revolution. They practically invented guilt-free, premarital sex, and they know what they're missing better than any previous generation in history. "Boomers are the first generation to imagine that they can have exciting monogamous sex through old age," says Marty Klein, a marriage and sex therapist in Palo Alto, Calif. "The collision between that expectation and reality is pretty upsetting for most people."

And sexlessness has a long and rich tradition. In Aristophanes' bawdy play "Lysistrata," written in 411 B.C., Spartan and Athenian women agree to withhold sex from their husbands until the two warring city-states make peace. Virginia Woolf's Mrs. Dalloway was in a sexless marriage; it's likely Dorothea Brooke and Edward Casaubon, characters in George Eliot's "Middlemarch," were, too. And what about the "frigid" housewives of the 1950s?

Marriage experts say there's no single reason we're suddenly so unhappy with our sex lives. Many of us are depressed; last year Americans filled more than 200 million prescriptions for antidepressants. The sexual landscape may have been transformed in the last 40 years by birth control, legalized abortion and a better understanding of women's sexuality. But women have changed, too. Since they surged into the workplace in the 1970s, their economic power has grown steadily. Women now make up 47 percent of the work force; they're awarded 57 percent of all bachelor's degrees. About 30 percent of working women now earn more than their husbands.

Like never before, women have the financial clout to leave their husbands if they choose. In his new book, "Mismatch: The Growing Gulf Between Women and Men," sociologist Andrew Hacker says women are less and less inclined to stay married when they're not emotionally satisfied. Wives say they were the driving force in 56.2 percent of divorces, according to Hacker, while men say they were the ones who wanted out only 23.3 percent of the time. When women have those kinds of choices, marital "duties" become options and the debate over how much, or how little, sex to have is fundamentally altered.

MEANWHILE, FAMILIES HAVE CHANGED. THE YEAR AFTER the first child is born has always been a hazardous time for marriages—more divorces happen during those sleepless months than at any other time in a marriage, except for the very first year. But some researchers say parents are now obsessed with their children in a way that can be unhealthy. Kids used to go to dance class or take piano lessons once a week; now parents organize an array of activities—French classes, cello lessons and three different sports—that would make an air-traffic controller dizzy. And do you remember being a child at a restaurant with your parents and having every adult at the table focus on your happiness? No? That's probably because you weren't taken along.

Working parents who wish they could spend more time with their kids often compensate by dragging their brood everywhere with them. That means couples are sacrificing sleep and companionship. Parents of infants sometimes stop thinking of themselves as sexual beings altogether. Gottman recalls treating a couple with a 4-month-old; the wife was nursing. One morning the husband reached over and caressed his wife's breast. The woman sat bolt upright in bed and said, "Those are for *Jonathan*." "They laugh about it now," Gottman says. "But you can understand why a guy might withdraw in that kind of situation."

## "We say, 'Meet me in the bedroom at noon.' We put on music and light candles and take some time to enjoy each other."

REGENA THOMASHAUER

There's another theme winding through popular culture and private conversations. Because let's face it: no one is *really* too tired to have sex. Arguing over whether you should have sex can easily take longer than the act itself. For many couples, consciously or not, sex has become a weapon. A lot of women out there are mad. Working mothers, stay-at-home moms, even women without kids. They're mad that their husband couldn't find the babysitter's home number if his life depended on it. Mad that he would never think to pick up diapers or milk on his way home. Mad that he doesn't have to sing all the verses of "The Wheels on the Bus" while trying to blow-dry his hair. Those of us who were weaned on "Fear of Flying" or "Our Bodies, Ourselves" understand that we're responsible for our own orgasms. But then couldn't somebody else take responsibility for the laundry once in a while?

Researchers say women have some legitimate gripes. Most two-income couples without children divide up the household chores pretty evenly. After the kids come, however, men may be happy to play with Junior, but they actually do *less* around the house. Men's contributions to household chores increased dramatically in the '70s and '80s, but haven't changed much since then, according to Andrew Cherlin, a sociologist at Johns Hopkins. And it isn't just that Dad isn't doing the dishes. Researchers say many new fathers—55 percent—actually start spending *more time* at work after a child is born. Experts can only

speculate on why: fathers may suddenly take their role as breadwinner more seriously. Others may feel slighted by how much attention their wives lavish on the new baby.

But men are mad, too. "The big loser between job, kids and the dogs is me," says Alex, a 35-year-old financial executive from Manhattan. "I need more sex, but that's not the whole story. I want more time alone with my wife and I want more attention." They may not be perfect, but most husbands today do far more around the house than their fathers would have ever dreamed of doing. They're also more involved than ever in their children's lives. And they want points for it, points they're not getting.

Experts say very few women openly withhold sex. More often, lingering resentments slowly drive a wedge between partners. After two kids and 10 years of marriage, Bill, an actor in his 50s, loves his wife, Laurie (not their real names), though he'd like to have sex more often than the once or twice a month they average now. Laurie, a graphic designer in her 40s, agreed to hire a babysitter and make a standing Saturday-night date. But when Saturday rolled around, she was too tired to go out. They missed the next week's appointment, too. She's tired, she says, but resentful, too. "I get angry because he doesn't help around the house enough or with the kids. He sees the groceries sitting on the counter. Why doesn't he take them out of the bag and put them away? How can I get sexy when I'm ticked off all the time?"

Advice on how to stay connected, however, varies widely. Traditionally, marriage counselors have focused on bridging emotional gaps between husbands and wives, with the idea that better sex flows out of better communication. More important than a fancy meal at a restaurant (where you can still have a rip-roaring fight, of course) is to just make time to sit down and talk. The Weinreichs managed to rekindle romance after their sons, now 18 and 21, got a little older. All it really took, Maddie says, was being more committed to intimacy.

But a new breed of marriage therapists take a more action-oriented approach. Regena Thomashauer, a relationship counselor and author of "Mama Gena's Owner's and Operator's Guide to Men," agrees that scheduling time together is essential. Use the time to have sex, she urges. Michele and Marcelo Sandoval, 40 and 42, respectively, sought help from Thomashauer when they were expecting their first child; now they make two "dates" a week. "We call them dates," says Marcelo, "but we know it means sex, and we make it a priority."

Author Weiner Davis has a similar strategy: just do it. Don't wait until you're in the mood. And view thoughtful gestures, such as letting your spouse sleep in, as foreplay. Chris Paterson, 31, and his wife, Tara, 29, say Weiner Davis has helped them. Early in their marriage, they had sex nearly every night. But after she gave birth to their first child, Tara lost interest. Their nightly sessions became infrequent events. In addition to raising the kids, now 6 and 2, both Tara and Chris run their own businesses—she has a Web site called justformom.com and he's a general contractor. Tara says she's just exhausted. Chris also shoulders part of the blame. "I haven't always been the most romantic, getting-her-in-the-mood kind of individual," he says. Since talking to Weiner Davis and reading her book, Chris and Tara say they now have sex almost once a week, when they "try really hard."

## "When you have young children and you're working, your husband goes from the top of the food chain to the bottom."

**MADDIE WEINREICH**

Most therapists do agree on one thing. You can't force a sexy situation. There's nothing wrong with dressing up like a cowgirl or answering the front door in "black mesh stockings, and an apron—that's all," a la Marabel Morgan's 1973 classic, "Total Woman." But if it feels silly, it won't work. Rosemary Breslin, 45, a writer and filmmaker in New York, says she still has a great relationship with her husband, Tony Dunne. "But one of the things I ask him is, 'Are we going to have sex in 2003 or are we shelving it to 2004?' I asked him what he would do if I put on a black negligee, and he said he would laugh." Maybe she should persuade him to help out a little more around the house. After all, we know there's nothing sexier these days than a man who takes out the trash without being asked.

With HOLLY PETERSON, PAT WINGERT, KAREN SPRINGEN, JULIE SCELFO, MELISSA BREWSTER, TARA WEINGARTEN and JOAN RAYMOND

# AGAINST SCHOOL

## How public education cripples our kids, and why

*By John Taylor Gatto*

**I** taught for thirty years in some of the worst schools in Manhattan, and in some of the best, and during that time I became an expert in boredom. Boredom was everywhere in my world, and if you asked the kids, as I often did, *why* they felt so bored, they always gave the same answers: They said the work was stupid, that it made no sense, that they already knew it. They said they wanted to be doing something real, not just sitting around. They said teachers didn't seem to know much about their subjects and clearly weren't interested in learning more. And the kids were right: their teachers were every bit as bored as they were.

Boredom is the common condition of schoolteachers, and anyone who has spent time in a teachers' lounge can vouch for the low energy, the whining, the dispirited attitudes, to be found there. When asked why *they* feel bored, the teachers tend to blame the kids, as you might expect. Who wouldn't get bored teaching students who are rude and interested only in grades? If even that. Of course, teachers are themselves products of the same twelve-year compulsory school programs that so thoroughly bore their students, and as school personnel they are trapped inside structures even more rigid than those imposed upon the children. Who, then, is to blame?

We all are. My grandfather taught me that. One afternoon when I was seven I complained to him of boredom, and he batted me hard on the head. He told me that I was never to use that term in his presence again, that if I was bored it was my fault and no one else's. The obligation to amuse and instruct myself was entirely my own, and peo-

ple who didn't know that were childish people, to be avoided if possible. Certainly not to be trusted. That episode cured me of boredom forever, and here and there over the years I was able to pass on the lesson to some remarkable student. For the most part, however, I found it futile to challenge the official notion that boredom and childishness were the natural state of affairs in the classroom. Often I had to defy custom, and even bend the law, to help kids break out of this trap.

## DO WE REALLY NEED SCHOOL? SIX CLASSES A DAY, FIVE DAYS A WEEK, NINE MONTHS A YEAR, FOR TWELVE YEARS? IS THIS DEADLY ROUTINE REALLY NECESSARY?

The empire struck back, of course; childish adults regularly conflate opposition with disloyalty. I once returned from a medical leave to discover that all evidence of my having been granted the leave had been purposely destroyed, that my job had been terminated, and that I no longer possessed even a teaching license. After nine months of tormented effort I was able to retrieve the license when a school secretary testified to witnessing the plot unfold. In the meantime my family suffered more than I care to remember. By the time I finally retired in 1991, I had more than enough reason to think of our schools—with their long-term, cell-block-style, forced confinement of both students and teachers—as virtual factories of childishness. Yet I honestly could not see *why* they had to be that way. My own experience had revealed to me what many other teachers must learn along the way, too, yet keep to themselves for fear of reprisal: if we wanted to we could easily and inexpensively jettison the old, stupid structures and help kids *take* an education rather than merely *receive* a schooling. We could encourage the best qualities of youthfulness—curiosity, adventure, resilience, the capacity for surprising insight—simply by being more flexible about time, texts, and tests, by introducing kids to truly competent adults, and by giving each student what autonomy he or she needs in order to take a risk every now and then.

But we don't do that. And the more I asked why not, and persisted in thinking about the "problem" of schooling as an engineer might, the more I missed the point: What if there is no "problem" with our schools? What if they are the way they are, so expensively flying in the face of common sense and long experience in how children learn things, not because they are doing something wrong but because they are doing something right? Is it possible that George W. Bush accidentally spoke the truth when he said we would "leave no child behind"? Could it be that our schools are designed to make sure not one of them ever really grows up?

**D**o we really need school? I don't mean education, just forced schooling: six classes a day, five days a week, nine months a year, for twelve years. Is this deadly routine really necessary? And if so, for what? Don't hide behind reading, writing, and arithmetic as a rationale, because 2 million happy homeschoolers have surely put that banal justification to rest. Even if they hadn't, a considerable number of well-known Americans never went through the twelve-year wringer our kids currently go through, and they turned out all right. George Washington, Benjamin Franklin, Thomas Jefferson, Abraham Lincoln? Someone taught them, to be sure, but they were not products of a school *system*, and not one of them was ever "graduated" from a secondary school. Throughout most of American history, kids generally didn't go to high school, yet the unschooled rose to be admirals, like Farragut; inventors, like Edison; captains of industry like Carnegie and Rockefeller; writers, like Melville and Twain and Conrad; and even scholars, like Margaret Mead. In fact, until pretty recently people who reached the age of thirteen weren't looked upon as children at all. Ariel Durant, who co-wrote an enormous, and very good, multivolume history of the world with her husband, Will, was happily married at fifteen, and who could reasonably claim that Ariel Durant was an uneducated person? Unschooled, perhaps, but not uneducated.

We have been taught (that is, schooled) in this country to think of "success" as synonymous with, or at least dependent upon, "schooling," but historically that isn't true in either an intellectual or a financial sense. And plenty of people throughout the world today find a way to educate themselves without resorting to a system of compulsory secondary schools that all too often resemble prisons. Why, then, do Americans confuse education with just such a system? What exactly is the purpose of our public schools?

## IN 1843, HORACE MANN WROTE A PAEAN TO THE LAND OF FREDERICK THE GREAT AND CALLED FOR ITS SCHOOLING TO BE BROUGHT HERE.

Mass schooling of a compulsory nature really got its teeth into the United States between 1905 and 1915, though it was conceived of much earlier and pushed for throughout most of the nineteenth century. The reason given for this enormous upheaval of family life and cultural traditions was, roughly speaking, threefold:

1) To make good people.
2) To make good citizens.
3) To make each person his or her personal best.

These goals are still trotted out today on a regular basis, and most of us accept them in one form or another as a decent definition of public education's mission, however short schools actually fall in achieving them. But we are dead wrong. Compounding our error is the fact that the national literature holds numerous and surprisingly consistent statements of compulsory schooling's true purpose. We have, for example, the great H. L. Mencken, who wrote in *The American Mercury* for April 1924 that the aim of public education is not

> to fill the young of the species with knowledge and awaken their intelligence.... Nothing could be further from the truth. The aim… is simply to reduce as many individuals as possible to the same safe level, to breed and train a standardized citizenry, to put down dissent and originality. That is its aim in the United States… and that is its aim everywhere else.

Because of Mencken's reputation as a satirist, we might be tempted to dismiss this passage as a bit of hyperbolic sarcasm. His article, however, goes on to trace the template for our own educational system back to the now vanished, though never to be forgotten, military state of Prussia. And although he was certainly aware of the irony that we had recently been at war with Germany, the heir to Prussian thought and culture, Mencken was being perfectly serious here. Our educational system really is Prussian in origin, and that really is cause for concern.

The odd fact of a Prussian provenance for our schools pops up again and again once you know to look for it. William James alluded to it many times at the turn of the century. Orestes Brownson, the hero of Christopher Lasch's 1991 book, *The True and Only Heaven*, was publicly denouncing the Prussianization of American schools back in the 1840s. Horace Mann's "Seventh Annual Report" to the Massachusetts State Board of Education in 1843 is essentially a paean to the land of Frederick the Great and a call for its schooling to be brought here. That Prussian culture loomed large in America is hardly surprising, given our early association with that utopian state. A Prussian served as Washington's aide during the Revolutionary War, and so many German-speaking people had settled here by 1795 that Congress considered publishing a German-language edition of the federal laws. But what shocks is that we should so eagerly have adopted one of the very worst aspects of Prussian culture: an educational system deliberately designed to produce mediocre intellects, to hamstring the inner life, to deny students appreciable leadership skills, and to ensure docile and incomplete citizens—in order to render the populace "manageable."

## MODERN, INDUSTRIALIZED, COMPULSORY SCHOOLING WAS TO MAKE A SURGICAL INCISION INTO THE PROSPECTIVE UNITY OF THE UNDERCLASSES.

It was from James Bryant Conant—president of Harvard for twenty years, WWI poison-gas specialist, WWII executive on the atomic-bomb project, high commissioner of the American zone in Germany after WWII, and truly one of the most influential figures of the twentieth century—that I first got wind of the real purposes of American schooling. Without Conant, we would probably not have the same style and degree of standardized testing that we enjoy today, nor would we be blessed with gargantuan high schools that warehouse 2,000 to 4,000 students at a time, like the famous Columbine High in Littleton, Colorado. Shortly after I retired from teaching I picked up Conant's 1959 book-length essay, *The Child the Parent and the State*, and was more than a little intrigued to see him mention in passing that the modern schools we attend were the result of a "revolution" engineered between 1905 and 1930. A revolution? He declines to elaborate, but he does direct the curious and the uninformed to Alexander Inglis's 1918 book, *Principles of Secondary Education*, in which "one saw this revolution through the eyes of a revolutionary."

Inglis, for whom a lecture in education at Harvard is named, makes it perfectly clear that compulsory schooling on this continent was intended to be just what it had been for Prussia in the 1820s: a fifth column into the burgeoning democratic movement that threatened to give the peasants and the proletarians a voice at the bargaining table. Modern, industrialized, compulsory schooling was to make a sort of surgical incision into the prospective unity of these underclasses. Divide children by subject, by age-grading, by constant rankings on tests, and by

many other more subtle means, and it was unlikely that the ignorant mass of mankind, separated in childhood, would ever re-integrate into a dangerous whole.

Inglis breaks down the purpose—the *actual* purpose—of modern schooling into six basic functions, any one of which is enough to curl the hair of those innocent enough to believe the three traditional goals listed earlier:

1) The *adjustive* or *adaptive* function. Schools are to establish fixed habits of reaction to authority. This, of course, precludes critical judgment completely. It also pretty much destroys the idea that useful or interesting material should be taught, because you can't test for *reflexive* obedience until you know whether you can make kids learn, and do, foolish and boring things.

2) The *integrating* function. This might well be called "the conformity function," because its intention is to make children as alike as possible. People who conform are predictable, and this is of great use to those who wish to harness and manipulate a large labor force.

3) The *diagnostic* and *directive* function. School is meant to determine each student's proper social role. This is done by logging evidence mathematically and anecdotally on cumulative records. As in "your permanent record." Yes, you do have one.

4) The *differentiating* function. Once their social role has been "diagnosed," children are to be sorted by role and trained only so far as their destination in the social machine merits—and not one step further. So much for making kids their personal best.

## SCHOOL DIDN'T HAVE TO TRAIN KIDS TO THINK THEY SHOULD CONSUME NONSTOP; IT SIMPLY TAUGHT THEM NOT TO THINK AT ALL.

5) The *selective* function. This refers not to human choice at all but to Darwin's theory of natural selection as applied to what he called "the favored races." In short, the idea is to help things along by consciously attempting to improve the breeding stock. Schools are meant to tag the unfit—with poor grades, remedial placement, and other punishments—clearly enough that their peers will accept them as inferior and effectively bar them from the reproductive sweepstakes. That's what all those little humiliations from first grade onward were intended to do: wash the dirt down the drain.

6) The *propaedeutic* function. The societal system implied by these rules will require an elite group of caretakers. To that end, a small fraction of the kids will quietly be taught how to manage this continuing project, how to watch over and control a population deliberately dumbed down and declawed in order that government might proceed unchallenged and corporations might never want for obedient labor.

That, unfortunately, is the purpose of mandatory public education in this country. And lest you take Inglis for an isolated crank with a rather too cynical take on the educational enterprise, you should know that he was hardly alone in championing these ideas. Conant himself, building on the ideas of Horace Mann and others, campaigned tirelessly for an American school system designed along the same lines. Men like George Peabody, who funded the cause of mandatory schooling throughout the South, surely understood that the Prussian system was useful in creating not only a harmless electorate and a servile labor force but also a virtual herd of mindless consumers. In time a great number of industrial titans came to recognize the enormous profits to be had by cultivating and tending just such a herd via public education, among them Andrew Carnegie and John D. Rockefeller.

There you have it. Now you know. We don't need Karl Marx's conception of a grand warfare between the classes to see that it is in the interest of complex management, economic or political, to dumb people down, to demoralize them, to divide them from one another, and to discard them if they don't conform. Class may frame the proposition, as when Woodrow Wilson, then president of Princeton University, said the following to the New York City School Teachers Association in 1909: " We want one class of persons to have a liberal education, and we want another class of persons, a very much larger class, of necessity, in every society, to forgo the privileges of a liberal education and fit themselves to perform specific difficult manual tasks." But the motives behind the disgusting decisions that bring about these ends need not be class-based at all. They can stem purely from fear, or from the by now familiar belief that "efficiency" is the paramount virtue, rather than love, liberty, laughter, or hope. Above all, they can stem from simple greed.

There were vast fortunes to be made, after all, in an economy based on mass production and organized to favor the large corporation rather than the small business or the family farm. But mass production required mass consumption, and at the turn of the twentieth century most Americans considered it both unnatural and unwise to buy things they didn't actually need. Mandatory schooling was a godsend on that count. School didn't have to train kids in any direct sense to think they should consume nonstop, because it did something even better: it encouraged them not to think at all. And that left them sitting ducks for another great invention of the modern era—marketing.

Now, you needn't have studied marketing to know that there are two groups of people who can always be convinced to consume more than they need to: addicts and children. School has done a pretty good job of turning our children into addicts, but it has done a spectacular job of turning our children into children. Again, this is no accident. Theorists from Plato to Rousseau to our own Dr. Inglis knew that if children could be cloistered with other children, stripped of responsibility and independence,

encouraged to develop only the trivializing emotions of greed, envy, jealousy, and fear, they would grow older but never truly grow up. In the 1934 edition of his once well-known book *Public Education in the United States*, Ellwood P. Cubberley detailed and praised the way the strategy of successive school enlargements had extended childhood by two to six years, and forced schooling was at that point still quite new. This same Cubberley—who was dean of Stanford's School of Education, a textbook editor at Houghton Mifflin, and Conant's friend and correspondent at Harvard—had written the following in the 1922 edition of his book *Public School Administration*: "Our schools are… factories in which the raw products (children) are to be shaped and fashioned…. And it is the business of the school to build its pupils according to the specifications laid down."

## MANDATORY SCHOOLING'S PURPOSE IS TO TURN KIDS INTO SERVANTS. DON'T LET YOUR OWN HAVE THEIR CHILDHOODS EXTENDED, NOT EVEN FOR A DAY.

It's perfectly obvious from our society today what those specifications were. Maturity has by now been banished from nearly every aspect of our lives. Easy divorce laws have removed the need to work at relationships; easy credit has removed the need for fiscal self-control; easy entertainment has removed the need to learn to entertain oneself; easy answers have removed the need to ask questions. We have become a nation of children, happy to surrender our judgments and our wills to political exhortations and commercial blandishments that would insult actual adults. We buy televisions, and then we buy the things we see on the television. We buy computers, and then we buy the things we see on the computer. We buy $150 sneakers whether we need them or not, and when they fall apart too soon we buy another pair. We drive SUVs and believe the lie that they constitute a kind of life insurance, even when we're upside-down in them. And, worst of all, we don't bat an eye when Ari Fleischer tells us to "be careful what you say," even if we remember having been told somewhere back in school that America is the land of the free. We simply buy that one too. Our schooling, as intended, has seen to it.

Now for the good news. Once you understand the logic behind modern schooling, its tricks and traps are fairly easy to avoid. School trains children to be employees and consumers; teach your own to be leaders and adventurers. School trains children to obey reflexively; teach your own to think critically and independently. Well-schooled kids have a low threshold for boredom; help your own to develop an inner life so that they'll never be bored. Urge them to take on the serious material, the *grown-up* material, in history, literature, philosophy, music, art, economics, theology—all the stuff schoolteachers know well enough to avoid. Challenge your kids with plenty of solitude so that they can learn to enjoy their own company, to conduct inner dialogues. Well-schooled people are conditioned to dread being alone, and they seek constant companionship through the TV, the computer, the cell phone, and through shallow friendships quickly acquired and quickly abandoned. Your children should have a more meaningful life, and they can.

First, though, we must wake up to what our schools really are: laboratories of experimentation on young minds, drill centers for the habits and attitudes that corporate society demands. Mandatory education serves children only incidentally; its real purpose is to turn them into servants. Don't let your own have their childhoods extended, not even for a day. If David Farragut could take command of a captured British warship as a pre-teen, if Thomas Edison could publish a broadsheet at the age of twelve, if Ben Franklin could apprentice himself to a printer at the same age (then put himself through a course of study that would choke a Yale senior today), there's no telling what your own kids could do. After a long life, and thirty years in the public school trenches, I've concluded that genius is as common as dirt. We suppress our genius only because we haven't yet figured out how to manage a population of educated men and women. The solution, I think, is simple and glorious. Let them manage themselves.

---

*John Taylor Gatto is a former New York State and New York City Teacher of the Year and the author, most recently, of* The Underground History of American Education. *He was a participant in the* Harper's Magazine *forum "School on a Hill," which appeared in the September 2001 issue.*

---

# How I Joined Teach for America—and Got Sued for $20 Million

## Joshua Kaplowitz

It was May 2000, and the guy at Al Gore's polling firm seemed baffled. A Yale political-science major, I'd already walked away from a high-paying consulting job a few weeks earlier, and now I was walking away from a job working on a presidential campaign to do … *what*?

Well, when push came to shove, I didn't want to devote my life to helping the rich get richer or crunching numbers to see what views were most popular for the vice president to adopt. This wasn't what my 17 years of education were for.

My doctor parents had drummed into me that education was the key to every door, the one thing they couldn't take away from my ancestors during pogroms and persecutions. They had also filled me with a strong sense of social justice. I couldn't help feeling guilty dismay when I thought of the millions of kids who'd never even tasted the great teaching—not to mention the supportive family—I'd enjoyed for my entire life.

I told the Al Gore guy, "Thanks, but no thanks." Weird as he might have thought it, I had decided to teach in an inner-city school.

Five weeks later, I found myself steering my parents' old Volvo off R Street and into a one-block cul-de-sac. There it was: Emery Elementary School, a 1950s-ugly building tucked behind a dead-end street—an apt metaphor, I thought, for the lives of many of the children in this almost all-black neighborhood a mile north of the U.S. Capitol in Washington. I had seen signs of inner-city blight all over the neighborhood, from the grown men who skulked in the afternoon streets to the bulletproof glass that sealed off the cashier at the local Kentucky Fried Chicken. This was the "other half" of Washington, the part of the city I had missed during my grade-school field trips to the Smithsonian and my two summers as a Capitol Hill intern.

I parked the car and bounded into the main office to say hi to Mr. Bledsoe, the interim principal who had hired

me a few weeks before. As he showed me around the clean but bare halls, my head filled with visions of my students happily painting imaginative murals under my artistic direction. I peered through windows into classrooms, where students were bent over their desks, quietly filling out worksheets. I smiled to myself as I imagined the creative lessons I would give to these children, who had never had a dynamic young teacher to get them excited about scholarship the way I knew I could. Their minds were like kindling, I reflected; all they needed was a spark to ignite a love of learning that would lift them above the drugs, violence, and poverty. The spark, I hoped, would be me.

As the tour ended and I was about to leave, Mr. Bledsoe pulled me aside. "The one thing you need to do above all else is to have your children under control. Once you have done that, you'll be fine."

Fine. But as I learned to my great cost, that was easier said than done.

I was supposed to pick up that skill over the summer from Teach for America (TFA), an organization, affiliated with AmeriCorps, that places young people with no ed-school background, and usually just out of college, in disadvantaged school districts suffering from teacher shortages. Applicants request placement in one of over a dozen rural and urban school districts around the country that contract with TFA, and I got my first choice, in the city I hoped to live in for the rest of my life.

Teach for America conducts an intensive five-week training program for its inductees during the summer before they start teaching. My year, this "teacher boot camp" took place in Houston. It was there that I quickly figured out that enthusiasm and creativity alone wouldn't suffice in an inner-city classroom. I was part of a tag team of four recruits teaching a summer-school class of low-income fourth-graders. Even in one- to two-hour blocks of teaching, I quickly realized that my best-planned, most imaginative lessons fell apart if I didn't have control of my students.

In the seminars we attended when we weren't teaching, I learned the basics of lesson planning and teaching theory. I also internalized the TFA philosophy of high expectations, the idea that if you set a rigorous academic course, all students will rise to meet the challenge.

But the training program skimped on actual teaching and classroom-management techniques, instead overwhelming us with sensitivity training. My group spent hours on an activity where everyone stood in a line and then took steps forward or backward based on whether we were the oppressor or the oppressed in the categories of race, income, and religion. The program had a college bull session, rather than professional, atmosphere. And it had a college-style party line: I heard of two or three trainees being threatened with expulsion for expressing in their discussion groups politically incorrect views about inner-city poverty—for example, that families and culture, not economics, may be the root cause of the achievement gap.

Nothing in the program simulated what I soon learned to be the life of a teacher. Though I didn't know it, I was completely ill equipped when I stepped into my own fifth-grade classroom at Emery Elementary in September 2000.

The year before I taught, a popular veteran principal had been dismissed without explanation. Mr. Bledsoe finished out the rest of the year on an interim basis, hired me and four other Teach for America teachers, and then turned over the reins to a woman named V. Lisa Savoy. Ms. Savoy had been an assistant principal at the District's infamous Anacostia High School, in Washington's equivalent of the South Bronx. Before the start of school, she met with her four first-year TFA teachers to assure us that we would be well supported, and that if we needed anything we should just ask. Most of my veteran colleagues, 90 percent of them black, also seemed helpful, though a few showed flickers of disdain for us eager, young white teachers. By the time school opened, I was thrilled to start molding the brains of my children.

My optimism and naiveté evaporated within hours. I tried my best to be strict and set limits with my new students; but I wore my inexperience on my sleeve, and several of the kids jumped at the opportunity to misbehave. I could see clearly enough that the vast majority of my fifth-graders genuinely wanted to learn—but all it took to subvert the whole enterprise were a few cutups.

On a typical day, DeAngelo (a pseudonym, as are the other children's names in this and the next paragraph) would throw a wad of paper in the middle of a lesson. Whether I disciplined him or ignored him, his actions would cause Kanisha to scream like an air-raid siren. In response, Lamond would get up, walk across the room, and try to slap Kanisha. Within one minute, the whole

class was lost in a sea of noise and fists. I felt profoundly sorry for the majority of my students, whose education was being hijacked. Their plaintive cries punctuated the din: "Quiet everyone! Mr. Kaplowitz is trying to teach!"

Ayisha was my most gifted student. The daughter of Senegalese immigrants, she would tolerantly roll her eyes as Darnetta cut up for the ninth time in one hour, patiently waiting for the day when my class would settle down. Joseph was a brilliant writer who struggled mightily in math. When he needed help with a division problem, I tried to give him as much attention as I could, before three students wandering around the room inevitably distracted me. Eventually, I settled on tutoring him after school. Twenty more students' educations were sabotaged, each kid with specific needs that I couldn't attend to, because I was too busy putting out fires. Though I poured my heart into inventive lessons and activities throughout the entire year, they almost always fell apart in the face of my students' disrespect and indifference.

To gain control, I tried imposing the kinds of consequences that the classroom-management handbooks recommend. None worked. My classroom was too small to give my students "time out." I tried to take away their recess, but depriving them of their one sanctioned time to blow off steam just increased their penchant to use my classroom as a playground. When I called parents, they were often mistrustful and tended to question or even disbelieve outright what I told them about their children. It was sometimes worse when they believed me, though; the tenth time I heard a mother swear that her child was going to "get a beating for this one," I almost decided not to call parents. By contrast, I saw immediate behavioral and academic improvement in students whose parents had come to trust me.

I quickly learned from such experiences how essential parental support is in determining whether a school succeeds in educating a child. And of course, parental support not just of the teachers but of the kids: as I came to know my students better, I saw that those who had seen violence, neglect, or drug abuse at home were usually the uncontrollable ones, while my best-behaved, hardest-working kids were typically those with the most nurturing home environments.

Being a white teacher in a mostly black school unquestionably hindered my ability to teach. Certain students hurled racial slurs with impunity; several of their parents intimated to my colleagues that they didn't think a white teacher had any business teaching their children-and a number of my colleagues agreed. One parent who was also a teacher's aide threatened to "kick my white ass" in front of my class and received no punishment from the principal, beyond being told to stay out of my classroom. The failure of the principal, parents, and teachers to react more decisively to racist disrespect emboldened students to behave worse. Such poisonous bigotry directed at a black teacher at a mostly white school would of course have created a federal case.

Still, other colleagues, friendly and supportive, helped me with my discipline problems. They let me send unruly students to their classrooms for brief periods of time to cool off, allowing me to teach the rest of my class effectively. But when I turned to my school administration for similar help, I was much less fortunate.

I had read that successful schools have chief executives who immerse themselves in the everyday operations of the institution, set clear expectations for the student body, recognize and support energetic and creative teachers, and foster constructive relationships with parents. Successful principals usually are mavericks, too, who skirt stupid bureaucracy to do what is best for the children. Emery's Principal Savoy sure didn't fit this model.

To start with, from all that I could see, she seemed mostly to stay in her office, instead of mingling with students and observing classes, most of which were up at least one flight of stairs, perhaps a disincentive for so heavy a woman. Furthermore, I saw from the first month that she generally gave delinquents no more than a stern talking-to, followed by a pat on the back, rather than suspensions, detentions, or any other meaningful punishment. The threat of sending a student to the office was thus rendered toothless.

Worse, Ms. Savoy effectively undermined my classroom-management efforts. She forbade me from sending students to other teachers—the one tactic that had any noticeable effect. Exiling my four worst students had produced a vast improvement in the conduct of the remainder of my class. But Ms. Savoy was adamant, insisting that the school district required me to teach all my children, all the time, in the "least restrictive" environment. This was just the first instance of Ms. Savoy blocking me with a litany of D.C. Public Schools regulations, as she regularly frustrated my colleagues on disciplinary issues.

Some of Ms. Savoy's actions defied explanation. She more than once called me to her office in the middle of my lessons to lecture me on how bad a teacher I was—well before her single visit to observe me in my classroom. She filled my personnel file with lengthy memos articulating her criticisms. I eventually concluded that Ms. Savoy tended similarly to trouble any teacher, experienced or novice, who rocked the boat.

And in November I really rocked it. By then, despite mounting tension with Ms. Savoy, and despite the pandemonium that continued to ravage my teaching efforts, I had managed—painstakingly—to build a rapport with my fifth-graders. I felt I was turning a corner. I thought that my students (and their parents) would completely shape up once they saw their abysmal first report cards. D.C. Public Schools grade kids on a highly subjective 1 to 4 scale, 4 being the highest. Most of my students entered fifth grade with grave academic deficiencies, yet their cumulative records revealed fair to excellent grades, making clear that social promotion was standard practice at Emery. I wasn't playing along. I had given regular tests and quizzes that first semester, and most of my students had earned straight 1s by any rational measure. True to the credo of high expectations, I would give them the grades they earned.

I submitted my report cards to Ms. Savoy, who insisted that my grades were "too low" and demanded that I raise them immediately. I offered to show her all of my students' work portfolios; but she demurred, informing me that the law obliged me to pass a certain percentage of my students. I paid no attention, gave my students the grades they deserved, and patiently explained to every parent that their child's grades would improve once he or she started behaving in class and doing the assigned lessons. For this, Ms. Savoy cited me for insubordination.

Just after the New Year, Ms. Savoy informed me that she was switching me from fifth grade to second grade; the veteran second-grade teacher would then take over my fifth-graders. Her justification was that I would be able to control younger students more effectively—though I assumed she thought that I could wreak less disruption with the younger kids, who were relatively flunk-proof.

From the start, I tried my best to combat understandable parental resentment that their experienced teacher was being yanked out and replaced by me, a first-year teacher with notoriously poor classroom-management skills. I wrote letters home describing my ambitious plans, called parents with enthusiastic words about their children, and walked my students home after school to increase my visibility in the neighborhood.

Unfortunately, I never got a chance to show that I was in control. Unbelievable as it sounds, my second-graders were even wilder than my fifth-graders. Just as before, a majority of kids genuinely wanted to learn, but the antics of a few spun my entire class into chaos. This time, though, my troublemakers were even more immature and disruptive, ranging from a boy who roamed around the room punching his classmates and threatening to kill himself to a borderline-mentally retarded student, who would throw crumpled wads of paper all day. I was so busy trying to quell anarchy that I never had the chance to get to know my new students, let alone teach them anything.

Ms. Savoy had abandoned all pretense of administrative support by this point. Nearly every student I sent to the office returned within minutes.

This lack of consequences encouraged a level of violence I never could have imagined among any students, let alone second-graders. Fights broke out daily—not just during recess or bathroom breaks but also in the middle of lessons. And this wasn't just playful shoving: we're talking fists flying, hair yanked, heads slammed against lockers.

When I asked other teachers to come help me stop a fight, they shook their heads and reminded me that D.C. Public Schools banned teachers from laying hands on students for any reason, even to protect other children. When a fight brewed, I was faced with a Catch-22. I could call the office and wait ten minutes for the security guard to arrive, by which point blood could have been shed and students injured. Or I could intervene physically, in violation of school policy.

Believe me, you have to be made of iron, or something other than flesh and blood, to stand by passively while some enraged child is trying to inflict real harm on another eight-year-old. I couldn't do it. And each time I let normal human instinct get the best of me and broke up a fight, one of the combatants would go home and fabricate a story about how I had hurt him or her. The parent, already suspicious of me, would report this accusation to Ms. Savoy, who would in turn call in a private investigative firm employed by D.C. Public Schools. Investigators would come to Emery and interview me, as well as several students whom the security guard thought might tell the truth about the alleged incident of corporal punishment.

I had previously heard of three other teachers at Emery that year who were being investigated for corporal punishment. When I talked to them—they were all experienced male teachers—they heatedly protested their innocence and bitterly complained about Ms. Savoy's handling of the situation. Now that I had joined the club, I began to understand their fears and frustrations.

To define as "corporal punishment" the mere physical separation of two combatants not only puts students at risk but also gives children unconscionable power over teachers who choose to intervene. False allegations against me and other teachers snowballed, as certain students realized that they had the perfect tool for getting their teacher in deep trouble. As I began to be investigated on almost a weekly basis, parents came to school to berate and threaten me—naturally, without reprisals from the administration. One day, a rather large father came up to me after school and told me he was going to "get me" if he heard that I put my hands on his daughter one more time. Forget the fact that I had pulled her off of a boy whom she was clobbering at the time.

With such a weak disciplinary tone set by the administration, by late February the whole school atmosphere had devolved into chaos. Gangs of students roamed the halls at will. You could hear screaming from every classroom—from students and teachers alike. Including me, four teachers (or 20 percent of the faculty) were under investigation on bogus corporal-punishment charges, including a fourth-grade instructor whose skills I greatly respected. The veteran teachers constantly lamented that things were better the previous year, when the principal ran a tight disciplinary ship, and the many good instructors were able to do their job.

It was nearly March, and the Stanford-9 standardized tests, the results of which determine a principal's success in D.C. Public Schools, were imminent. Ms. Savoy unexpectedly instituted a policy allowing teachers to ship their two or three most disruptive students to the computer lab to be warehoused and supervised by teachers' aides. My classroom's behavior and attentiveness improved dramatically for two weeks. Unfortunately, Ms. Savoy abandoned this plan the instant the standardized tests had passed.

After that, my classroom became more of a gladiatorial venue than a place of learning. Fights erupted hourly; no student was immune. The last three months were a blur of violence, but several incidents particularly stand out. One week, two of my emotionally disturbed boys went on a binge of sexual harassment, making lewd gestures and grabbing girls' buttocks—yes, seven- and eight-year-olds. On another occasion, three students piled on top of one of their peers and were punching him with their fists before I intervened. My students were not even afraid to try to hurt me: two boys spent a month throwing pencils at me in the middle of lessons; another child slugged me in the gut.

But for Ms. Savoy, apparently I was the problem. It seemed to me that she was readier to launch investigations when a student or parent made an accusation against me than to help me out when my students were acting up.

Faced with a series of corporal-punishment charges, no administrative support, and no hope of controlling my second-grade class in the foreseeable future, I should have packed up and left midyear. Surely there were other schools, even inner-city ones, where I could have developed and succeeded as a teacher.

Why did I stay on? Part of the answer lay in my own desperate desire not to fail. I felt that if I just worked harder, I could turn my children around and get them to learn. Another part of the answer was Teach for America's having instilled in each corps member the idea that you have made a commitment to the children and that you must stick with them at all costs, no matter how much your school is falling apart. Because of this mentality, my TFA friends and I put up with nonsense from our schools and our students that few regular teachers would have tolerated.

The three-person TFA-D.C. staff was stretched too thin to support any of us. When I told them about the debacle at Emery, the D.C. program directors told me to keep my chin up and work harder. They wouldn't transfer me to another TFA-affiliated elementary school, and pooh-poohed the idea that I had it worse than anyone else in the program. So I was stuck at Emery, unwilling to incur the disgrace that came with quitting.

**F**ate made the decision for me.

Four days before the end of my first year, I was still planning to return to Emery in the fall. The rumor was that Ms. Savoy would be replaced. With her gone, I thought, I could start fresh and use my hard-won battlefield experience to make a positive difference in underprivileged children's lives.

The afternoon of June 13 started with the usual mixture of disorder and disrespect. This time, a boy named Raynard, a particularly difficult child, whom I had seen punch other students and throw things in the past, was repeating over and over, "I got to go to the bathroom. I need some water." The rest of the class tittered as I told him in my sternest teacher voice that we would be having a class bathroom break once everyone was quiet and in his seat.

"I got to go to the bathroom. I need some water."

Frustrated, I led him to the classroom door with my hand on the small of his back. I nudged him into the hall and closed the door. He would probably spend the remainder of the day roaming the halls with the rest of the troublemakers at Emery, but at least he would be out of sight, so I could get the rest of my class under control. I had given up on teaching for the rest of the day; my class was slated to watch a movie with Ms. Perkins's first-graders across the hall.

Once Raynard left, I guided my students through a characteristically raucous bathroom break and filed them into Ms. Perkins's room, where they lapsed into a rare TV-induced calm.

After 15 minutes, the school security guard appeared at the door and beckoned for me. My stomach hit the floor, as I guessed what this meant: yet another corporal-punishment charge. But this time was different. Chaos reigned in the main entranceway as police officers swarmed into the building. Raynard's mother, I was told, had been in school for a meeting to place her son in a class for emotionally disturbed children. Raynard had told her that I had violently shoved him in the chest out the door of my classroom, injuring his head and back. His mother had dialed 911 and summoned the cops and the fire department. The police hustled me into the principal's office, where I sat in bewilderment and desperately denied I had hurt Raynard in any way.

**I**n the blink of an afternoon, my search for the perfect lesson plan gave way to my search for the perfect lawyer. I was lucky that my parents could afford Hank Asbill, a highly regarded Washington defense attorney.

Two months later, Raynard's mother filed a $20 million lawsuit against the school district, Ms. Savoy, and myself—and the D.C. police charged me with a misdemeanor count of simple assault against my former student. Thus ended my first and last year as a public school teacher.

After I was charged, Hank Asbill chose a day in early September for me to turn myself in at the District 5 police station near Emery and receive a trial date. The whole ordeal was supposed to take about six hours—but five minutes after I was admitted into custody, the two planes hit the World Trade Center. After the third plane crashed into the Pentagon, the D.C. courts shut down. It was only after 33 hours in jail that I saw daylight again, on September 12.

**M**y criminal trial spanned six days in early March of 2002. It was agonizing watching several former students testifying against me, not to mention facing the very real prospect of spending time in the D.C. jail. The children's stories as to what happened on June 13 were wildly inconsistent—not surprising, considering that the layout of my classroom precluded them from witnessing anything Raynard had alleged. Hank Asbill countered with a string of character witnesses, friends who attested to my peaceful nature and law-abiding ways, as well as other teachers at Emery who reported on the brutal atmosphere of the school. Hank then brought me to the stand to explain what had actually happened, and he also brought to light Raynard's medical records from June 13, which showed that the emergency-room doctors had found no evidence of any injury. Fortunately, we drew a rational, deliberative judge, unswayed by the case's racially charged nature: a poor black kid against a rich white Ivy Leaguer. He found me not guilty, touching off an outpouring of relief from my friends and former colleagues and—not least—me.

My elation was short-lived. As I had surmised, this whole case finally came down to money. Even after my acquittal, even after the accuracy of Raynard's story had been seriously undermined, his mother and her big-firm lawyers aggressively pursued multi-million-dollar damage claims on the civil side. Yet even as the lawsuit dragged on and the legal cloud over me caused me to lose a job opportunity I really wanted, I refused to entertain Raynard's mother's offers to settle the case by my paying her $200,000—a demand that ultimately diminished to $40,000. The school system had no such scruples; it settled the mother's tort claim in October 2002 for $75,000 (plus $15,000 from the teachers' union's insurance company-chump change compared with the cost of defending the litigation). It wasn't $20 million, but it was still more money than I imagine this woman had seen in her life—a pretty good payout and hardly deterrence to other parents in the neighborhood who felt entitled to shanghai the system.

I stayed in touch with several of my more supportive colleagues and parents, who have told me that Emery, although it has a new principal, is just as out of control two years after I taught there. Veteran teachers with nowhere else to go, they say, are giving up all pretense of teaching; their goal is to make it through the end of each year. Young teachers like my TFA colleagues are staying for a year or two and moving on to private, charter, or suburban schools, or to new careers.

In all the reading and talking I've done to try to make sense out of what happened to me, I've learned that Emery is hardly unique. Numerous new friends and acquaintances who have taught in D.C.'s inner-city schools—some from Teach for America, some not—report the same outrageous discipline problems that turned them from educators into U.N. peacekeepers.

I've learned that an epidemic of violence is raging in elementary schools nationwide, not just in D.C. A recent *Philadelphia Inquirer* article details a familiar pattern—kindergartners punching pregnant teachers, third-graders hitting their instructors with rulers. Pennsylvania and New Jersey have reported nearly 30 percent increases in elementary school violence since 1999, and many school districts have established special disciplinary K-6 schools. In New York City, according to the *New York Post*, some 60 teachers recently demonstrated against out-of-control pupil mayhem, chanting, "Hey, hey, ho, ho; violent students must go." Kids who stab each other, use teachers as shields in fights, bang on doors to disrupt classes, and threaten to "kick out that baby" from a pregnant teacher have created a "climate of terror," the *Post* reports.

Several of my new acquaintances in the Washington schools told me of facing completely fabricated corporal-punishment allegations, as I did. Some even faced criminal charges. Washington teachers' union officials won't give me hard numbers, but they intimate that each year they are flooded with corporal-punishment or related charges against teachers, most of which get settled without the media ever learning of this disturbing new trend. It is a state of affairs that Philip K. Howard vividly describes in his recent *The Collapse of the Common Good*: parents sue teachers and principals for suspending their children, for allegedly meting out corporal punishment,

and for giving failing marks. As a result, educators are afraid to penalize misbehaving students or give students grades that reflect the work they do. The real victims are the majority of children whose education is being commandeered by their out-of-control classmates.

I've come to believe that the most unruly and violent children should go to alternative schools designed to handle students with chronic behavior problems. A school with a more military structure can do no worse for those children than a permissive mainstream school, and it spares the majority of kids the injustice of having their education fall victim to the chaos wreaked by a small minority.

I know for sure that inner-city schools don't have to be hellholes like Emery and its District of Columbia brethren, with their poor administration and lack of parental support, their misguided focus on children's rights, their anti-white racism, and their lawsuit-crazed culture. Some of my closest TFA friends, thrilled to be liberated from the D.C. system, went on to teach at D.C. charter schools, where they really can make a difference in underprivileged children's lives. For example, at Paul Junior High School, which serves students with the same economic and cultural background as those at Emery, the principal's tough approach to discipline fosters a serious atmosphere of scholarship, and parents are held accountable, because the principal can kick their children back to the public school system if they refuse to cooperate. A friend who works at the Hyde School, which emphasizes character education (and sits directly across a field from Emery), tells me that this charter school is quiet and orderly, the teachers are happy, and the children are achieving at a much higher level—so much higher that several of the best students at Emery who transferred to Hyde nearly flunked out of their new school.

It should come as no surprise that students are leaving Emery in droves, in hopes of enrolling in this and other alternative schools. Enrollment, 411 when I was there, now is about 350. If things don't change, it will soon be—and should be—zero.

---

# whose hospital is it?

MCP Hospital didn't have any celebrity doctors or slick ad campaigns All it had was a 150-year history serving its Philadelphia neighborhood—and in today's cutthroat health care industry that's no longer enough.

## By Arthur Allen

GREGORY GAY WAS BORN 21 years ago at the Medical College of Pennsylvania Hospital (MCP), a venerable community hospital in Philadelphia's East Falls neighborhood. He was shot six blocks away on January 24, not long after Tenet Healthcare Corp. decided to close the hospital. Tenet, the second-largest for-profit hospital chain in the United States, was in the process of shuttering or selling a quarter of its more than 100 hospitals nationwide. As it waited for a judge's permission to shut down MCP, the company was slowly withdrawing services, closing floors, and letting the staff fade away through attrition.

When police and paramedics arrived moments after four bullets pierced Gay's body that icy Friday night, he was fighting for his life and lucid enough to give the names of two men who had shot him. But instead of zipping up Henry Avenue to MCP, the ambulance raced to Temple University Hospital, some 20 minutes away. MCP'S struggling emergency room was on "diversion"—temporarily closed to new patients—that night, as it had been for much of that month. Gay died less than an hour later.

Gay's death, one of many in the violent North Philadelphia streets whose sick and wounded feed the hospital, has become part of a lawsuit seeking to keep MCP open while charging that Tenet neglected its obligations to the city. (Tenet management refused to comment for this story.) Of course, it is uncertain whether Gay would have survived even had the hospital been fully operational. But the closing of MCP, a community hospital in every sense of the word, would clearly mean more hardship for thousands of its neighbors. Symbolically, in the minds of the hospital's defenders, Gay's death has come to stand for the deaths to come—not only the gunshot wounds, but the asthma attacks, the strokes and embolisms and diabetic comas that are likely to be aggravated by new delays and complications.

Not that MCP's fate is unusual. Tenet has closed three hospitals during its five years in Philadelphia; over the past decade, four other North Philadelphia hospitals have shut down their inpatient units. Nationwide, according to data compiled by the federal government and *Modern Healthcare* magazine, more than 560 hospitals have closed since 1990—clobbered by stagnant reimbursement rates from government and the insurance industry, rising malpractice rates, skyrocketing prices for drugs and medical equipment, and increasing numbers of uninsured patients who can't pay their bills.

Still, when Tenet tried to shut MCP, it hit a particular nerve. The hospital, whose 70,000 potential clients ranged from homeless crack addicts to the governor of Pennsylvania, has become a local cause célèbre. This is partly because Tenet has blossomed into the Enron of the hospital business, notorious for creative accounting and out-size payouts to its executives. It is a corporate behemoth whose entry into Philadelphia in the late 1990s was subsidized with generous tax breaks because of the city's desperate need to save hospitals then on the verge of bankruptcy. The struggle to keep MCP open, in other words, embodies a frightening larger story about the decline of health care in the United States.

BY A STRANGE PARADOX, we live in a time in which scientific breakthroughs are revolutionizing American medicine, while the system for caring for the majority of the population seems to be breaking down. "As a microdelivery system, medicine provides increasingly exquisite molecular elegance," says Eliot Sorel, a professor of psychiatry at George Washington University School of Medicine and the former president of the D.C. Medical Society. "As a macrodelivery system, it is falling apart."

All across the nation, doctors and other health care providers are battling thick layers of bureaucracy and crushing financial burdens to deliver care. "We're watching the meltdown of the medical system," says Dr. Donald Palmisano, the president of the American Medical Association. "We have a broken medical liability system, price-fixing on Medicare and Medicaid, and managed care has such monopoly power in many states that the physician has no power to negotiate a contract." Nurses have also been leaving their field, creating serious shortages that imperil care. "I advise all my patients before they go into the hospital," Palmisano's predecessor at the AMA, Dr. Yank Coble, recently told *Medical Economics*, "to take somebody with them. A friend or relative will increase safety more than anything else, especially in these days of nursing shortage." According to a 1999 Institute of Medicine report, as many as 98,000 people die in hospitals each year as the result of medical mistakes, making such errors—often caused by staff shortages and overwork—the eighth leading cause of death in this country.

A growing number of hospitals are facing an even more fundamental crisis: They simply cannot make ends meet. The price of a pint of blood went up 30 percent in just one year; a CAT scan machine costs $1 million. Malpractice insurance rates have been rising at vertiginous rates—20 to 30 percent nationally, and 40 to 50 percent in some areas, including Pennsylvania. The MCP emergency room has seen its malpractice rates increase from $18,000 to $40,000 for each doctor in five years.

And even as the cost of caring for patients has increased, a decade of payment cuts from insurers as well as the government—especially Medicare and Medicaid, the public programs designed to provide coverage for the elderly and the poor—has pushed hospital finances into the red. In Philadelphia, Medicaid now pays only 75 percent of the cost of patient care, leaving hospitals and doctors to absorb the rest. In his fiscal year 2005 budget, President Bush has proposed another $2 billion cut in federal funding for Medicaid, and Medicare reimbursements are failing to keep up with costs. "Hospitals," concluded a recent report by the American Hospital Association, "are bearing the cumulative impact of a series of forces that are beginning to erode the foundation of the essential public service they provide."

Nowhere are those forces more apparent than in the community hospitals that serve as the nation's health care system of last resort. A shortage of primary care doctors in urban neighborhoods is driving more and more patients to crowded hospital emergency rooms: ER visits in community hospitals rose from 92 million in 1990 to 106 million in 2001, according to the American Hospital Association. The ERs at 3 out of 4 urban hospitals are "at" or "over" capacity, and more than half of all urban hospitals sometimes turn ambulances away. Last year, 25,000 MCP patients—60 percent of the hospital's total—came in through the ER.

Many of those patients can't pay their bills. Nationally, the number of uninsured people is on the rise after declining through the 1990s; in 2003 it stood at 42.3 million, 3.6 million more than in 1999, according to the National Center for Health Statistics. In Philadelphia, surveys by the Philadelphia Health Management Corp. show that the number of uninsured people in the city of 1.4 million has increased by nearly one-third, rising from 94,000 to 136,000 in only two years; that's 42,000 people who lost health benefits. And given that a single intensive-care visit can cost hundreds of thousands of dollars—and that hospitals by law cannot turn away patients who need treatment—any increase in the number of uninsured people is disastrous for a hospital's bottom line. In 2003, according to Richard Centafont of the Delaware Valley Healthcare Council, a hospital trade group, Philadelphia hospitals saw 22 percent more uninsured patients than they did the previous year, resulting in half a billion dollars' worth of uncompensated care.

Traditionally, hospitals subsidized their "charity" care for uninsured patients by collecting a substantial margin on private insurance reimbursements. But insurers, under pressure from employers, have pushed hard to trim those payments over the past decade. In the Philadelphia area, where a single private insurer—Independent Blue Cross and its health management organization, Keystone—dominates the market, this squeeze has become painful. Nationally, insurance payments cover 115 percent of hospitals' actual costs for patient care; in Philadelphia they cover an average of 104 percent. "It used to be that the rich subsidized health care for the poor," says Dr. Philip S. Mead, medical director of MCP's Emergency Department. "It ain't that way in Pennsylvania anymore."

Not that MCP is a poverty hospital. Though it never attracted the jet-set clientele you'd find at the best university medical centers, its patient base has always been diverse. The hospital traces its roots to the Female Medical College of Pennsylvania, founded in 1850 as the first school in the world established to provide full medical training to women. It outlasted other women-only institutions, admitting men for the first time in 1969. By 1990, at least 10 African American women had been trained at the school, including Dr. Eliza Grier, who was born a slave. Today, MCP retains an almost old-fashioned aura of collegiality. Most of its doctors, as one physician notes, are "not major egos or out to make money," but rather salaried academic medicine types in the traditional mold.

While many of MCP's patients have been the impoverished and working-class people of neighborhoods like Strawberry Mansion, to its north the hospital borders East Falls, a well-to-do district where Governor Ed Rendell, U.S. Senator Arlen Specter, and Rep. Chaka Fattah live. These high-profile neighbors have proved crucial in the fight to keep MCP open. But as patients, East Falls residents increasingly patronize upscale Center City hospitals.

# More than 560 hospitals have closed in the past 14 years—

clobbered by stagnant reimbursement rates, high
malpractice costs, rising drug prices, and increasing numbers of
uninsured patients who can't pay their bills.

Partly, this is due to the failure of MCP Hospital's academic overseers, most recently Drexel University College of Medicine, to cultivate relationships with private physicians that could bring in well-insured clients. To be a moneymaking hospital in today's market, it helps to do the sort of complex procedures well reimbursed by insurers or the federal government. For example, a wrinkle in the Medicare system explains why so many companies have opened "heart centers" in the past few years—surgery on the heart is among the most lavishly reimbursed by Medicare. Unless a community hospital like MCP can attract the well insured, it's at risk.

As more such hospitals close, cities like Philadelphia are moving to a two-tiered health system. "If you have good insurance and want a hip replacement, there are plenty of nice hospitals that will schedule you at your convenience," says Dr. Steven Peitzman, a longtime MCP physician who has written a history of the Woman's Medical College and its successor. "Whereas if you're wheezing with the worst asthma attack of your life, there isn't likely to be a hospital nearby."

AROUND THE TIME Tenet was negotiating to run MCP, Thomas Morgan, a community activist who has lived his entire life on the same quiet block in the Germantown neighborhood where Grace Kelly's family lived, was diagnosed with a thyroid disorder and kidney failure. On September 4, 1999—his 44th birthday—Morgan, who has four children and works nights as a toll collector, went on dialysis for the first time. The procedure required at least 15 hours in the hospital each week, but there was a silver lining. It turns out that universal health care already exists for one kind of patient in America—the dialysis patient.

Under a 1972 law, passed after an end-stage kidney disease patient testified before the House Ways and Means Committee while undergoing dialysis in the committee room, Congress expanded Medicare to fully fund the medical costs of kidney patients, whether or not they have private insurance. When it comes to dialysis, the American health care system actually lives up to its promise, says Dr. Walter Tsou, a former Philadelphia health commissioner. "The solution to the crisis at MCP and every health care facility in Philadelphia and the nation," he says, "is a properly financed, single-payer, national health-insurance program like this."

For reasons that are not entirely clear, blacks are four times more likely than whites to suffer kidney failure in America, and nearly all of the 130 or so dialysis patients at MCP are African Americans. Dialysis is an exhausting, at times painful, procedure, but for Morgan, who is dialyzed from 6:00 a.m. to 10:30 a.m. three times a week after he gets off work, it's almost something to look forward to. "It's my community," he says of the 25 or so patients who share his shift. "We talk for a while—politics, sports, whatever—then you drift off to sleep. And you care for the other patients. We look out for each other. We have a Christmas party. We've had bus trips to Atlantic City." The dialysis unit is attached to the hospital, which means that emergency or inpatient care is available for kidney patients when they need it.

Morgan's life's rhythms—work, sleep, taking his six-year-old daughter to school—are all linked to the dialysis center. If it closes, he will find another dialysis center, but many such centers are not located at hospitals. Morgan may have to wait months to find a rotation in a dialysis center with the care available at MCP. A warm, soft-spoken man with closely cropped salt-and-pepper hair and beard, Morgan, a Democratic Party committeeman for the city's 12th Ward, says his political activism has always come from a sense of duty to others in his neighborhood. But MCP's struggle, to him, is also profoundly personal. "If the hospital closes," he says, "it throws my whole life into turmoil."

FOR A WHILE IT SEEMED as though Tenet Healthcare had figured out a way around the hospital-financing conundrum, a way to game the system; gaming the system, in fact, turns out to have been one of the company's principal assets. The Santa Barbara, California-based company arose from the ashes of Santa Monica-based National Medical Enterprises, a firm that flamed out in the early 1990s after being targeted by the federal government for confining psychiatric patients over long periods to collect more money from their insurers. In 1993, Jeffrey Barbakow, a financial wizard who had been an investment banker and chairman of MGM, was brought in to remake the company.

For several years in the late 1990s, Tenet seemed to produce miraculous results in Philadelphia. MCP and Hahnemann hospitals, which had been losing millions, were suddenly in the black. At MCP, Tenet says it spent more than $43 million for capital improvements; it spruced up hallways, bed units, and operating rooms, and purchased a high-tech Gamma Knife to perform brain surgery.

The first inkling of trouble for MCP filtered east from California in 2002. Dr. Chae Hyun Moon, the chief cardiologist at Tenet's Redding Medical Center, and Dr. Fidel Realyvasquez, a cardiac surgeon, were accused that year of running a macabre for-profit fraud upon Medicare—conducting hundreds of unnecessary heart catheterizations and bypass surgeries for which they billed the federal government. Tenet later agreed to pay the government $54 million to resolve federal fraud charges, although civil suits against the hospital and the doctors are still pending.

---

# "If you have good insurance and want a hip replacement,
there are plenty of nice hospitals that will schedule you," says one
longtime MCP doctor. "Whereas if you're wheezing with the worst asthma
attack of your life, there isn't likely to be a hospital nearby."

As it turns out, there was more to the scam than a couple of zealous cardiologists. In the 12 months ending in December 2002, Redding Medical Center reported $92 million in pretax income. Its similarly sized neighbor down the street in Redding, Mercy Medical Center, brought in only $4 million. There wasn't $88 million worth of difference in the services they offered. Moon's procedures were part of the explanation, but the hospital was also using a more general practice to squeeze millions out of Medicare. This involved a complex billing category known as "outlier payments." Intending to support the care of particularly sick, or "outlier," patients, Medicare essentially allowed hospitals with very high patient costs—which were determined by whatever amounts the hospital chose to put in its bills—to charge the government—higher fees.

It boiled down to a remarkably simple scheme: To qualify for more outlier payments, Tenet hiked its prices. By 2002, when Medicare began to crack down on the practice, the company was earning more than $800 million a year on outlier payments. That year, Barbakow cashed in a whopping $111 million in stock options, a few months before resigning from his position as chairman and CEO.

At the MCP emergency room, Dr. Mead remembers one moment that tipped him off to the outlier system. An uninsured college student had come to the ER with a bad cut that required 27 stitches. About a month later, the student appeared in Mead's office, crying, in her hand a bill for $600 for the removal of the sutures, a procedure that had taken Mead all of 20 seconds using a pair of cheap scissors. Mead called administrators to complain but was told that was how things were done. What had happened, Mead would later realize, was that he had stumbled upon the iceberg of Tenet's inflated billings. "If Blue Cross had gotten the bill they would have said, 'Yeah, right,' and paid $30," he explains. "But since this was an uninsured person, they were charged the full price." Tenet had to charge someone the full price to demonstrate its high costs to Medicare.

"It turns out they don't know how to run hospitals," says Mead, who has a degree from Wharton Business School and was a Pepsico executive before going to medical school. "They know financial tricks."

WITH THE OUTLIER PAYMENTS yanked out from under Tenet, MCP suddenly fell deep into the red—the hospital lost more than $30 million in 2003, according to Tenet—and the full consequences of some of the company's management decisions began to hit home. Many of MCP's potentially money-earning fixtures, including its orthopedics department and pathology labs, had been allowed to wither away as doctors left in droves. "Most people who used those services were insured," notes Ginny Holzworth, an intensive-care nurse. "They removed these services, leaving basically services for the poor, which brought in no money. They stabbed MCP and let it bleed to death."

A consultant's report delivered in December concluded that MCP could be turned around, "if given a new clinical direction and a reasonable period of time." Tenet, losing massive amounts of money and heavily exposed to lawsuits and multiple federal and state investigations, couldn't be bothered. Management advised Drexel's medical school of the closing on December 17, 2003, the evening before the news release was faxed out. More than 150 years of history would essentially be erased without so much as a sniff.

In public statements, Tenet officials have said that the company did the best it could under difficult conditions, but that MCP was simply no longer viable. "This hospital was run by competent people and by a competent hospital management company," Philip Schaengold, Tenet's vice president for Pennsylvania, told a testy meeting of the Philadelphia City Council.

After much protest, and an intervention by Governor Rendell, Tenet and the state agreed to keep the hospital open until at least June 30 to give it time to seek a buyer. Temple and Einstein, two large Philadelphia hospital systems, were said to be interested, but as of this writing, neither had made a commitment to either buy MCP or keep its doors open long-term.

Whether or not MCP can survive with a different owner, the critical condition of hospitals around the country shows that it is not an isolated case. One-third of the nation's hospitals are now losing money every year, according to a 2002 report from the American Hospital Association, and many are in such precarious condition, they can't even get loans for badly needed improvements: Only 30 percent of hospitals seeking credit to fix their buildings or buy new equipment, the association reported, were able to get commercial bank financing. "As Wall Street experts have recognized," the report noted, "many of America's hospitals are on the edge of financial viability."

Dragged before the City Council repeatedly to explain their decision, Tenet officials sometimes sounded like Howard Dean. "We need universal health insurance in this country," Thomas Leonard, a Tenet attorney, said at a February 12 hearing. "It's a national problem. You can't solve it. Tenet can't solve it. And beating up Tenet isn't going to solve it."

At the same hearing, Morgan, the activist and dialysis patient, told his story while Tenet's Schaengold sat a few feet away. Morgan described the high-tension juggle of a working life with severe illness—the dozens of pills, the disturbed sleep and odd hours, the effort to be a normal father for his children. He told of his anxiety about finding another dialysis center. Then he began to weep. "I feel like you're playing with my life," he said, looking angrily at Schaengold. "I've got a family just like you. I've got a home, I live right."

Schaengold, a mustachioed man in his 50s, maintained an icy, composure. A week later, Tenet sacked him too.

# DEATH STALKS A CONTINENT

**In the dry timber of African societies, AIDS was a spark. The conflagration it set off continues to kill millions. Here's why**

By Johanna McGeary

IMAGINE YOUR LIFE THIS WAY. You get up in the morning and breakfast with your three kids. One is already doomed to die in infancy. Your husband works 200 miles away, comes home twice a year and sleeps around in between. You risk your life in every act of sexual intercourse. You go to work past a house where a teenager lives alone tending young siblings without any source of income. At another house, the wife was branded a whore when she asked her husband to use a condom, beaten silly and thrown into the streets. Over there lies a man desperately sick without access to a doctor or clinic or medicine or food or blankets or even a kind word. At work you eat with colleagues, and every third one is already fatally ill. You whisper about a friend who admitted she had the plague and whose neighbors stoned her to death. Your leisure is occupied by the funerals you attend every Saturday. You go to bed fearing adults your age will not live into their 40s. You and your neighbors and your political and popular leaders act as if nothing is happening.

Across the southern quadrant of Africa, this nightmare is real. The word not spoken is AIDS, and here at ground zero of humanity's deadliest cataclysm, the ultimate tragedy is that so many people don't know—or don't want to know—what is happening.

As the HIV virus sweeps mercilessly through these lands—the fiercest trial Africa has yet endured—a few try to address the terrible depredation. The rest of society looks away. Flesh and muscle melt from the bones of the sick in packed hospital wards and lonely bush kraals. Corpses stack up in morgues until those on top crush the identity from the faces underneath. Raw earth mounds scar the landscape, grave after grave without name or number. Bereft children grieve for parents lost in their prime, for siblings scattered to the winds.

The victims don't cry out. Doctors and obituaries do not give the killer its name. Families recoil in shame. Leaders shirk responsibility. The stubborn silence heralds victory for the disease: denial cannot keep the virus at bay.

The developed world is largely silent too. AIDS in Africa has never commanded the full-bore response the West has brought to other, sometimes lesser, travails. We pay sporadic attention, turning on the spotlight when an international conference occurs, then turning it off. Good-hearted donors donate; governments acknowledge that more needs to be done. But think how different the effort would be if what is happening here were happening in the West.

By now you've seen pictures of the sick, the dead, the orphans. You've heard appalling numbers: the number of new infections, the number of the dead, the number who are sick without care, the number walking around already fated to die.

But to comprehend the full horror AIDS has visited on Africa, listen to the woman we have dubbed Laetitia Hambahlane in

Durban or the boy Tsepho Phale in Francistown or the woman who calls herself Thandiwe in Bulawayo or Louis Chikoka, a long-distance trucker. You begin to understand how AIDS has struck Africa—with a biblical virulence that will claim tens of millions of lives—when you hear about shame and stigma and ignorance and poverty and sexual violence and migrant labor and promiscuity and political paralysis and the terrible silence that surrounds all this dying. It is a measure of the silence that some asked us not to print their real names to protect their privacy.

## HALF A MILLION AFRICAN CHILDREN WERE INFECTED WITH HIV LAST YEAR

Theirs is a story about what happens when a disease leaps the confines of medicine to invade the body politic, infecting not just individuals but an entire society. As AIDS migrated to man in Africa, it mutated into a complex plague with confounding social, economic and political mechanics that locked together to accelerate the virus' progress. The region's social dynamics colluded to spread the disease and help block effective intervention.

We have come to three countries abutting one another at the bottom of Africa—Botswana, South Africa, Zimbabwe—the heart of the heart of the epidemic. For nearly a decade, these nations suffered a hidden invasion of infection that concealed the dimension of the coming calamity. Now the omnipresent dying reveals the shocking scale of the devastation.

AIDS in Africa bears little resemblance to the American epidemic, limited to specific high-risk groups and brought under control through intensive education, vigorous political action and expensive drug therapy. Here the disease has bred a Darwinian perversion. Society's fittest, not its frailest, are the ones who die—adults spirited away, leaving the old and the children behind. You cannot define risk groups: everyone who is sexually active is at risk. Babies too, unwittingly infected by mothers. Barely a single family remains untouched. Most do not know how or when they caught the virus, many never know they have it, many who do know don't tell anyone as they lie dying. Africa can provide no treatment for those with AIDS.

They will all die, of tuberculosis, pneumonia, meningitis, diarrhea, whatever overcomes their ruined immune systems first. And the statistics, grim as they are, may be too low. There is no broad-scale AIDS testing: infection rates are calculated mainly from the presence of HIV in pregnant women. Death certificates in these countries do not record AIDS as the cause. "Whatever stats we have are not reliable," warns Mary Crewe of the University of Pretoria's Center for the Study of AIDS. "Everybody's guessing."

## THE TB PATIENT

CASE NO. 309 IN THE TUGELA FERRY HOME-CARE PROGRAM shivers violently on the wooden planks someone has knocked into a bed, a frayed blanket pulled right up to his nose. He has the flushed skin, overbright eyes and careful breathing of the tubercular. He is alone, and it is chilly within the crumbling mud walls of his hut at Msinga Top, a windswept outcrop high above the Tugela River in South Africa's KwaZulu-Natal province. The spectacular view of hills and veld would gladden a well man, but the 22-year-old we will call Fundisi Khumalo, though he does not know it, has AIDS, and his eyes seem to focus inward on his simple fear.

Before he can speak, his throat clutches in gasping spasms. Sharp pains rack his chest; his breath comes in shallow gasps. The vomiting is better today. But constipation has doubled up his knees, and he is too weak to go outside to relieve himself. He can't remember when he last ate. He can't remember how long he's been sick—"a long time, maybe since six months ago." Khumalo knows he has TB, and he believes it is just TB. "I am only thinking of that," he answers when we ask why he is so ill.

But the fear never leaves his eyes. He worked in a hair salon in Johannesburg, lived in a men's hostel in one of the cheap townships, had "a few" girlfriends. He knew other young men in the hostel who were on-and-off sick. When they fell too ill to work anymore, like him, they straggled home to rural villages like Msinga Top. But where Khumalo would not go is the hospital. "Why?" he says. "You are sick there, you die there."

"He's right, you know," says Dr. Tony Moll, who has driven us up the dirt track from the 350-bed hospital he heads in Tugela Ferry. "We have no medicines for AIDS. So many hospitals tell them, 'You've got AIDS. We can't help you. Go home and die.'" No one wants to be tested either, he adds, unless treatment is available. "If the choice is to know and get nothing," he says, "they don't want to know."

Here and in scattered homesteads all over rural Africa, the dying people say the sickness afflicting their families and neighbors is just the familiar consequence of their eternal poverty. Or it is the work of witchcraft. You have done something bad and have been bewitched. Your neighbor's jealousy has invaded you. You have not appeased the spirits of your ancestors, and they have cursed you. Some in South Africa believe the disease was introduced by the white population as a way to control black Africans after the end of apartheid.

Ignorance about AIDS remains profound. But because of the funerals, southern Africans can't help seeing that something more systematic and sinister lurks out there. Every Saturday and often Sundays too, neighbors trudge to the cemeteries for costly burial rites for the young and the middle-aged who are suddenly dying so much faster than the old. Families say it was pneumonia, TB, malaria that killed their son, their wife, their baby. "But you starting to hear the truth," says Durban home-care volunteer Busi Magwazi. "In the church, in the graveyard, they saying, 'Yes, she died of AIDS.' Oh, people talking about it even if the families don't admit it." Ignorance is the crucial reason the epidemic has run out of control. Surveys say many Africans here are becoming aware there is a sexually transmitted disease called AIDS that is incurable. But they don't think the risk applies to them. And their vague knowledge does not translate into changes in their sexual behavior. It's easy to see why so many don't yet sense the danger when few talk openly about the disease. And Africans are beset by so plentiful a roster of perils—famine, war, the violence of desperation or ethnic hatred, the regular illnesses of poverty, the dangers inside mines or on the roads—that the delayed risk of AIDS ranks low.

# A CONTINENT IN PERIL

17 million Africans have died since the AIDS epidemic began in the late 1970s, more than 3.7 million of them children. An additional 12 million children have been orphaned by AIDS. An estimated 8.8% of adults in Africa are infected with HIV/AIDS, and in the following seven countries, at least 1 adult in 5 is living with HIV

### 1. Botswana

Though it has the highest per capita GDP, it also has the highest estimated adult infection rate—**36%**. 24,000 die each year. 66,000 children have lost their mother or both parents to the disease.

### 2. Swaziland

More than **25%** of adults have HIV/AIDS in this small country. 12,000 children have been orphaned, and 7,100 adults and children die each year.

### 3. Zimbabwe

**One-quarter** of the adult population is infected here. 160,000 adults and children died in 1999, and 900,000 children have been orphaned. Because of AIDS, life expectancy is 43.

### 4. Lesotho

**24%** of the adults are infected with HIV/AIDS. 35,000 children have been orphaned, and 16,000 adults and children die each year.

### 5. Zambia

**20%** of the adult population is infected, 1 in 4 adults in the cities. 650,000 children have been orphaned, and 99,000 Zambians died in 1999.

### 6. South Africa

This country has the largest number of people living with HIV/AIDS, about **20%** of its adult population, up from 13% in 1997. 420,000 children have been orphaned, and 250,000 people die each year from the disease.

### 7. Namibia

**19.5%** of the adult population is living with HIV. 57% of the infected are women. 67,000 children are AIDS orphans, and 18,000 adults and children die each year.

Source: UNAIDS

# THE OUTCAST

TO ACKNOWLEDGE AIDS IN YOURSELF IS TO BE BRANDED AS monstrous. Laetitia Hambahlane (not her real name) is 51 and sick with AIDS. So is her brother. She admits it; he doesn't. In her mother's broken-down house in the mean streets of Umlazi township, though, Laetitia's mother hovers over her son, nursing him, protecting him, resolutely denying he has anything but TB, though his sister claims the sure symptoms of AIDS mark him. Laetitia is the outcast, first from her family, then from her society.

For years Laetitia worked as a domestic servant in Durban and dutifully sent all her wages home to her mother. She fell in love a number of times and bore four children. "I loved that last man," she recalls. "After he left, I had no one, no sex." That was 1992, but Laetitia already had HIV.

She fell sick in 1996, and her employers sent her to a private doctor who couldn't diagnose an illness. He tested her blood and found she was HIV positive. "I wish I'd died right then," she says, as tears spill down her sunken cheeks. "I asked the doctor, 'Have you got medicine?' He said no. I said, 'Can't you keep me alive?' " The doctor could do nothing and sent her away. "I couldn't face the word," she says. "I couldn't sleep at night. I sat on my bed, thinking, praying. I did not see anyone day or night. I ask God, Why?"

Laetitia's employers fired her without asking her exact diagnosis. For weeks she could not muster the courage to tell anyone. Then she told her children, and they were ashamed and frightened. Then, harder still, she told her mother. Her mother raged about the loss of money if Laetitia could not work again. She was so angry she ordered Laetitia out of the house. When her daughter wouldn't leave, the mother threatened to sell the house to get rid of her daughter. Then she walled off her daughter's room with plywood partitions, leaving the daughter a pariah, alone in a cramped, dark space without windows and only a flimsy door opening into the alley. Laetitia must earn the pennies to feed herself and her children by peddling beer, cigarettes and candy from a shopping cart in her room, when people are brave enough to stop by her door. "Sometimes they buy, sometimes not," she says. "That is how I'm surviving."

Her mother will not talk to her. "If you are not even accepted by your own family," says Magwazi, the volunteer home-care giver from Durban's Sinoziso project who visits Laetitia, "then others will not accept you." When Laetitia ventures outdoors, neighbors snub her, tough boys snatch her purse, children taunt her. Her own kids are tired of the sickness and don't like to help her anymore. "When I can't get up, they don't bring me food," she laments. One day local youths barged into her room, cursed her as a witch and a whore and beat her. When she told the police, the youths returned, threatening to burn down the house.

But it is her mother's rejection that wounds Laetitia most. "She is hiding it about my brother," she cries. "Why will she do nothing for me?" Her hands pick restlessly at the quilt covering her paper-thin frame. "I know my mother will not bury me properly. I know she will not take care of my kids when I am gone."

Jabulani Syabusi would use his real name, but he needs to protect his brother. He teaches school in a red, dusty district of KwaZulu-Natal. People here know the disease is all around them, but no one speaks of it. He eyes the scattered huts that make up his little settlement on an arid bluff. "We can count 20 who died just here as far as we can see. I personally don't remember any family that told it was AIDS," he says. "They hide it if they do know."

Syabusi's own family is no different. His younger brother is also a teacher who has just come home from Durban too sick to work anymore. He says he has tuberculosis, but after six months the tablets he is taking have done nothing to cure him. Syabusi's wife Nomsange, a nurse, is concerned that her 36-year-old brother-in-law may have something worse. Syabusi finally asked the doctor tending his brother what is wrong. The doctor said the information is confidential and will not tell him. Neither will his brother. "My brother is not brave enough to tell me," says Syabusi, as he stares sadly toward the house next door, where his only sibling lies ill. "And I am not brave enough to ask him."

Kennedy Fugewane, a cheerful, elderly volunteer counselor, sits in an empty U.S.-funded clinic that offers fast, pinprick blood tests in Francistown, Botswana, pondering how to break through the silence. This city suffers one of the world's highest infection rates, but people deny the disease because HIV is linked with sex. "We don't reveal anything," he says. "But people are so stigmatized even if they walk in the door." Africans feel they must keep private anything to do with sex. "If a man comes here, people will say he is running around," says Fugewane, though he acknowledges that men never do come. "If a woman comes, people will say she is loose. If anyone says they got HIV, they will be despised."

Pretoria University's Mary Crewe says, "It is presumed if you get AIDS, you have done something wrong." HIV labels you as living an immoral life. Embarrassment about sexuality looms more important than future health risks. "We have no language to talk candidly about sex," she says, "so we have no civil language to talk about AIDS." Volunteers like Fugewane try to reach out with flyers, workshops, youth meetings and free condoms, but they are frustrated by a culture that values its dignity over saving lives. "People here don't have the courage to come forward and say, 'Let me know my HIV status,'" he sighs, much less the courage to do something about it. "Maybe one day…"

Doctors bow to social pressure and legal strictures not to record AIDS on death certificates. "I write TB or meningitis or diarrhea but never AIDS," says South Africa's Dr. Moll. "It's a public document, and families would hate it if anyone knew." Several years ago, doctors were barred even from recording compromised immunity or HIV status on a medical file; now they can record the results of blood tests for AIDS on patient charts to protect other health workers. Doctors like Moll have long agitated to apply the same openness to death certificates.

# THE TRUCK DRIVER

**HERE, MEN HAVE TO MIGRATE TO WORK, INSIDE THEIR COUN**tries or across borders. All that mobility sows HIV far and wide, as Louis Chikoka is the first to recognize. He regularly drives the highway that is Botswana's economic lifeline and its curse. The road runs for 350 miles through desolate bush that is the Texas-size country's sole strip of habitable land, home to a large majority of its 1.5 million people. It once brought prospectors to Botswana's rich diamond reefs. Now it's the link for transcontinental truckers like Chikoka who haul goods from South Africa to markets in the continent's center. And now the road brings AIDS.

Chikoka brakes his dusty, diesel-belching Kabwe Transport 18-wheeler to a stop at the dark roadside rest on the edge of Francistown, where the international trade routes converge and at least 43% of adults are HIV-positive. He is a cheerful man even after 12 hard hours behind the wheel freighting rice from Durban. He's been on the road for two weeks and will reach his destination in Congo next Thursday. At 39, he is married, the father of three and a long-haul trucker for 12 years. He's used to it.

Lighting up a cigarette, the jaunty driver is unusually loquacious about sex as he eyes the dim figures circling the rest stop. Chikoka has parked here for a quickie. See that one over there, he points with his cigarette. "Those local ones we call bitches. They always waiting here for short service." Short service? "It's according to how long it takes you to ejaculate," he explains. "We go to the 'bush bedroom' over there [waving at a clump of trees 100 yds. away] or sometimes in the truck. Short service, that costs you 20 rands [$2.84]. They know we drivers always got money."

Chikoka nods his head toward another woman sitting beside a stack of cardboard cartons. "We like better to go to them," he says. They are the "businesswomen," smugglers with gray-market cases of fruit and toilet paper and toys that they need to transport somewhere up the road. "They come to us, and we negotiate privately about carrying their goods." It's a no-cash deal, he says. "They pay their bodies to us." Chikoka shrugs at a suggestion that the practice may be unhealthy. "I been away two weeks, madam. I'm human. I'm a man. I have to have sex."

What he likes best is dry sex. In parts of sub-Saharan Africa, to please men, women sit in basins of bleach or saltwater or stuff astringent herbs, tobacco or fertilizer inside their vagina. The tissue of the lining swells up and natural lubricants dry out. The resulting dry sex is painful and dangerous for women. The drying agents suppress natural bacteria, and friction easily lacerates the tender walls of the vagina. Dry sex increases the risk of HIV infection for women, already two times as likely as men to contract the virus from a single encounter. The women, adds

Chikoka, can charge more for dry sex, 50 or 60 rands ($6.46 to $7.75), enough to pay a child's school fees or to eat for a week.

# UNVANQUISHED

## A Fighter in a Land of Orphans

Silence and the ignorance it promotes have fed the AIDS epidemic in Africa perhaps more than any other factors. In Malawi, where until the end of dictator Hastings Banda's rule in 1994 women were barred from wearing short skirts and men could be jailed for having long hair, public discussion of AIDS was forbidden. According to the government, AIDS didn't exist inside Malawi. Catherine Phiri, 38, knew otherwise. She tested positive in 1990, after her husband had died of the disease. Forced to quit her job as a nurse when colleagues began to gossip, she sought refuge with relatives in the capital, Lilongwe. But they shunned her and eventually forced her to move, this time to Salima on beautiful Lake Malawi. "Even here people gossiped," says Phiri, whose brave, open face is fringed by a head of closely cropped graying hair.

Determined to educate her countrymen, Phiri set up a group that offers counseling, helps place orphans and takes blood that can then be tested in the local hospital. "The community began to see the problem, but it was very difficult to communicate to the government. They didn't want to know."

They do now. According to a lawmaker, AIDS has killed dozens of members of Parliament in the past decade. And Malawi's government has begun to move. President Bakili Muluzi incorporates AIDS education into every public rally. In 1999 he launched a five-year plan to fight the disease, and last July he ordered a crackdown on prostitution (though the government is now thinking of legalizing it). At the least, his awareness campaign appears to be working: 90% of Malawians know about the dangers of AIDS. But that knowledge comes too late for the estimated 8% of HIV-positive citizens—800,000 people in 1999—or the 276,000 children under 15 orphaned by the disease.

Last October, Phiri picked up an award for her efforts from the U.N. But, she says, "I still have people who look at me like trash…" Her voice trails off. "Sometimes when I go to sleep I fear for the future of my children. But I will not run away now. Talking about it: that's what's brave."
—**By Simon Robinson/Salima**

Chikoka knows his predilection for commercial sex spreads AIDS; he knows his promiscuity could carry the disease home to his wife; he knows people die if they get it. "Yes, HIV is terrible, madam," he says as he crooks a finger toward the business-woman whose favors he will enjoy that night. "But, madam, sex is natural. Sex is not like beer or smoking. You can stop them.

But unless you castrate the men, you can't stop sex—and then we all die anyway."

Millions of men share Chikoka's sexually active lifestyle, fostered by the region's dependence on migrant labor. Men desperate to earn a few dollars leave their women at hardscrabble rural homesteads to go where the work is: the mines, the cities, the road. They're housed together in isolated males-only hostels but have easy access to prostitutes or a "town wife" with whom they soon pick up a second family and an ordinary STD and HIV. Then they go home to wives and girlfriends a few times a year, carrying the virus they do not know they have. The pattern is so dominant that rates of infection in many rural areas across the southern cone match urban numbers.

## IN SOME AFRICAN COUNTRIES, THE INFECTION RATE OF TEEN GIRLS IS FOUR TIMES THAT OF BOYS

If HIV zeros in disproportionately on poor migrants, it does not skip over the educated or the well paid. Soldiers, doctors, policemen, teachers, district administrators are also routinely separated from families by a civil-service system that sends them alone to remote rural posts, where they have money and women have no men. A regular paycheck procures more access to extramarital sex. Result: the vital professions are being devastated.

Schoolmaster Syabusi is afraid there will soon be no more teachers in his rural zone. He has just come home from a memorial for six colleagues who died over the past few months, though no one spoke the word AIDS at the service. "The rate here—they're so many," he says, shaking his head. "They keep on passing it at school." Teachers in southern Africa have one of the highest group infection rates, but they hide their status until the telltale symptoms find them out.

Before then, the men—teachers are mostly men here—can take their pick of sexual partners. Plenty of women in bush villages need extra cash, often to pay school fees, and female students know they can profit from a teacher's favor. So the schoolmasters buy a bit of sex with lonely wives and trade a bit of sex with willing pupils for A's. Some students consider it an honor to sleep with the teacher, a badge of superiority. The girls brag about it to their peers, preening in their ability to snag an older man. "The teachers are the worst," says Jabulani Siwela, an AIDS worker in Zimbabwe who saw frequent teacher-student sex in his Bulawayo high school. They see a girl they like; they ask her to stay after class; they have a nice time. "It's dead easy," he says. "These are men who know better, but they still do it all the time."

## THE PROSTITUTE

THE WORKINGWOMAN WE MEET DIRECTS OUR CAR TO A reedy field fringing the gritty eastern townships of Bulawayo, Zimbabwe. She doesn't want neighbors to see her being interviewed. She is afraid her family will find out she is a prostitute, so we will call her Thandiwe. She looked quite prim and proper in her green calf-length dress as she waited for johns outside 109 Tongogaro Street in the center of downtown. So, for that matter, do the dozens of other women cruising the city's dim street corners: not a mini or bustier or bared navel in sight. Zimbabwe is in many ways a prim and proper society that frowns on commercial sex work and the public display of too much skin.

## FINANCIAL AID

# A Lending Tree

Getting ahead in Africa is tough. Banks lend money only to the middle class and the wealthy. Poor Africans—meaning most Africans—stay poor. It's even harder if you're sick. Without savings to fall back on, many HIV-positive parents pull their kids out of school. They can't afford the fees and end up selling their few possessions to feed the family. When they die, their kids are left with nothing.

Though not directly targeted at people with AIDS, microcredit schemes go some way toward fixing that problem. The schemes work like minibanks, lending small amounts—often as little as $100—to traders or farmers. Because they lack the infrastructure of banks and don't charge fees, most charge an interest rate of as much as 1% a week and repayment rates of over 99%—much better than that for banks in Africa, or in most places.

Many microcredit schemes encourage clients to set aside some of the extra income generated by the loan as savings. This can be used for medical bills or to pay school fees if the parents get sick. "Without the loans I would have had to look for another way to make money," says Florence Muriungi, 40, who sings in a Kampala jazz band and whose husband died of AIDS four years ago. Muriungi, who cares for eight children—five of her own and three her sister left when she too died of AIDS—uses the money to pay school fees in advance and fix her band's equipment. Her singing generates enough money for her to repay the loans and save a bit.

Seventeen of the 21 women at a weekly meeting of regular borrowers in Uganda care for AIDS orphans. Five are AIDS widows. "I used to buy just one or two bunches of bananas to sell. Now I buy 40, 50, 60," says Elizabeth Baluka, 47, the group's secretary. "Every week I put aside a little bit of money to help my children slowly by slowly."

**—By Simon Robinson/Kampala**

That doesn't stop Thandiwe from earning a better living turning tricks than she ever could doing honest work. Desperate for a job, she slipped illegally into South Africa in 1992. She cleaned floors in a Johannesburg restaurant, where she met a cook from back home who was also illegal. They had two

daughters, and they got married; he was gunned down one night at work.

She brought his body home for burial and was sent to her in-laws to be "cleansed." This common practice gives a dead husband's brother the right, even the duty, to sleep with the widow. Thandiwe tested negative for HIV in 1998, but if she were positive, the ritual cleansing would have served only to pass on the disease. Then her in-laws wanted to keep her two daughters because their own children had died, and marry her off to an old uncle who lived far out in the bush. She fled.

Alone, Thandiwe grew desperate. "I couldn't let my babies starve." One day she met a friend from school. "She told me she was a sex worker. She said, 'Why you suffer? Let's go to a place where we can get quick bucks.'" Thandiwe hangs her head. "I went. I was afraid. But now I go every night."

She goes to Tongogaro Street, where the rich clients are, tucking a few condoms in her handbag every evening as the sun sets and returning home strictly by 10 so that she won't have to service a taxi-van driver to get a ride back. Thandiwe tells her family she works an evening shift, just not at what. "I get 200 zim [$5] for sex," she says, more for special services. She uses two condoms per client, sometimes three. "If they say no, I say no." But then sometimes resentful johns hit her. It's pay-and-go until she has pocketed 1,000 or 1,500 Zimbabwe dollars and can go home—with more cash than her impoverished neighbors ever see in their roughneck shantytown, flush enough to buy a TV and fleece jammies for her girls and meat for their supper.

"I am ashamed," she murmurs. She has stopped going to church. "Every day I ask myself, 'When will I stop this business?' The answer is, 'If I could get a job'…" Her voice trails off hopelessly. "At the present moment, I have no option, no other option." As trucker Chikoka bluntly puts it, "They give sex to eat. They got no man; they got no work; but they got kids, and they got to eat." Two of Thandiwe's friends in the sex trade are dying of AIDS, but what can she do? "I just hope I won't get it."

In fact, casual sex of every kind is commonplace here. Prostitutes are just the ones who admit they do it for cash. Everywhere there's premarital sex, sex as recreation. Obligatory sex and its abusive counterpart, coercive sex. Transactional sex: sex as a gift, sugar-daddy sex. Extramarital sex, second families, multiple partners. The nature of AIDS is to feast on promiscuity.

## 79% OF THOSE WHO DIED OF AIDS LAST YEAR WERE AFRICAN

Rare is the man who even knows his HIV status: males widely refuse testing even when they fall ill. And many men who suspect they are HIV positive embrace a flawed logic: if I'm already infected, I can sleep around because I can't get it again. But women are the ones who progress to full-blown AIDS first and die fastest, and the underlying cause is not just sex but power. Wives and girlfriends and even prostitutes in this part of the world can't easily say no to sex on a man's terms. It matters little what comes into play, whether it is culture or tradition or the pathology of violence or issues of male identity or the subservient status of women.

Beneath a translucent scalp, the plates of Gertrude Dhlamini's cranium etch a geography of pain. Her illness is obvious in the thin, stretched skin under which veins throb with the shingles that have blinded her left eye and scarred that side of her face. At 39, she looks 70. The agonizing thrush, a kind of fungus, that paralyzed her throat has ebbed enough to enable her to swallow a spoon or two of warm gruel, but most of the nourishment flows away in constant diarrhea. She struggles to keep her hand from scratching restlessly at the scaly rash flushing her other cheek. She is not ashamed to proclaim her illness to the world. "It must be told," she says.

Gertrude is thrice rejected. At 19 she bore a son to a boyfriend who soon left her, taking away the child. A second boyfriend got her pregnant in 1994 but disappeared in anger when their daughter was born sickly with HIV. A doctor told Gertrude it was her fault, so she blamed herself that little Noluthando was never well in the two years she survived. Gertrude never told the doctor the baby's father had slept with other women. "I was afraid to," she says, "though I sincerely believe he gave the sickness to me." Now, she says, "I have rent him from my heart. And I will never have another man in my life."

Gertrude begged her relatives to take her in, but when she revealed the name of her illness, they berated her. They made her the household drudge, telling her never to touch their food or their cooking pots. They gave her a bowl and a spoon strictly for her own use. After a few months, they threw her out.

Gertrude sits upright on a donated bed in a cardboard shack in a rough Durban township that is now the compass of her world. Perhaps 10 ft. square, the little windowless room contains a bed, one sheet and blanket, a change of clothes and a tiny cooking ring, but she has no money for paraffin to heat the food that a home-care worker brings. She must fetch water and use a toilet down the hill. "Everything I have," she says, "is a gift." Now the school that owns the land under her hut wants to turn it into a playground and she worries about where she will go. Gertrude rubs and rubs at her raw cheek. "I pray and pray to God," she says, "not to take my soul while I am alone in this room."

Women like Gertrude were brought up to be subservient to men. Especially in matters of sex, the man is always in charge. Women feel powerless to change sexual behavior. Even when a woman wants to protect herself, she usually can't: it is not uncommon for men to beat partners who refuse intercourse or request a condom. "Real men" don't use them, so women who want their partners to must fight deeply ingrained taboos. Talk to him about donning a rubber sheath and be prepared for accusations, abuse or abandonment.

A nurse in Durban, coming home from an AIDS training class, suggested that her mate should put on a condom, as a kind of homework exercise. He grabbed a pot and banged loudly on it with a knife, calling all the neighbors into his house. He pointed the knife at his wife and demanded: "Where was she between 4 p.m. and now? Why is she suddenly suggesting this? What has changed after 20 years that she wants a condom?"

Schoolteacher Syabusi is an educated man, fully cognizant of the AIDS threat. Yet even he bristles when asked if he uses a condom. "Humph," he says with a fine snort. "That question is nonnegotiable." So despite extensive distribution of free condoms, they often go unused. Astonishing myths have sprung up. If you don one, your erection can't grow. Free condoms must be too cheap to be safe: they have been stored too long, kept too hot, kept too cold. Condoms fill up with germs, so they spread AIDS. Condoms from overseas bring the disease with them. Foreign governments that donate condoms put holes in them so that Africans will die. Education programs find it hard to compete with the power of the grapevine.

# THE CHILD IN NO. 17

IN CRIB NO. 17 OF THE SPARTAN BUT CROWDED CHILDREN'S ward at the Church of Scotland Hospital in KwaZulu-Natal, a tiny, staring child lies dying. She is three and has hardly known a day of good health. Now her skin wrinkles around her body like an oversize suit, and her twig-size bones can barely hold her vertical as nurses search for a vein to take blood. In the frail arms hooked up to transfusion tubes, her veins have collapsed. The nurses palpate a threadlike vessel on the child's forehead. She mews like a wounded animal as one tightens a rubber band around her head to raise the vein. Tears pour unnoticed from her mother's eyes as she watches the needle tap-tap at her daughter's temple. Each time the whimpering child lifts a wan hand to brush away the pain, her mother gently lowers it. Drop by drop, the nurses manage to collect 1 cc of blood in five minutes.

The child in crib No. 17 has had TB, oral thrush, chronic diarrhea, malnutrition, severe vomiting. The vial of blood reveals her real ailment, AIDS, but the disease is not listed on her chart, and her mother says she has no idea why her child is so ill. She breast-fed her for two years, but once the little girl was weaned, she could not keep solid food down. For a long time, her mother thought something was wrong with the food. Now the child is afflicted with so many symptoms that her mother had to bring her to the hospital, from which sick babies rarely return.

---

**VIRGINITY TESTING IS BACK** The practice of virginity testing used to be part of traditional Zulu rites. It is regaining popularity among anxious mothers who believe that if their daughters remain virgins, they won't get AIDS.

---

She hopes, she prays her child will get better, and like all the mothers who stay with their children at the hospital, she tends her lovingly, constantly changing filthy diapers, smoothing sheets, pressing a little nourishment between listless lips, trying to tease a smile from the vacant, staring face. Her husband works in Johannesburg, where he lives in a men's squatter camp. He comes home twice a year. She is 25. She has heard of

AIDS but does not know it is transmitted by sex, does not know if she or her husband has it. She is afraid this child will die soon, and she is afraid to have more babies. But she is afraid too to raise the subject with her husband. "He would not agree to that," she says shyly. "He would never agree to have no more babies."

Dr. Annick DeBaets, 32, is a volunteer from Belgium. In the two years she has spent here in Tugela Ferry, she has learned all about how hard it is to break the cycle of HIV transmission from mother to infant. The door to this 48-cot ward is literally a revolving one: sick babies come in, receive doses of rudimentary antibiotics, vitamins, food; go home for a week or a month; then come back as ill as ever. Most, she says, die in the first or second year. If she could just follow up with really intensive care, believes Dr. DeBaets, many of the wizened infants crowding three to a crib could live longer, healthier lives. "But it's very discouraging. We simply don't have the time, money or facilities for anything but minimal care."

Much has been written about what South African Judge Edwin Cameron, himself HIV positive, calls his country's "grievous ineptitude" in the face of the burgeoning epidemic. Nowhere has that been more evident than in the government's failure to provide drugs that could prevent pregnant women from passing HIV to their babies. The government has said it can't afford the 300-rand-per-dose, 28-dose regimen of AZT that neighboring nations like Botswana dole out, using funds and drugs from foreign donors. The late South African presidential spokesman Parks Mankahlana even suggested publicly that it was not cost effective to save these children when their mothers were already doomed to die: "We don't want a generation of orphans."

Yet these children—70,000 are born HIV positive in South Africa alone every year—could be protected from the disease for about $4 each with another simple, cheap drug called nevirapine. Until last month, the South African government steadfastly refused to license or finance the use of nevirapine despite the manufacturer's promise to donate the drug for five years, claiming that its "toxic" side effects are not yet known. This spring, however, the drug will finally be distributed to leading public hospitals in the country, though only on a limited basis at first.

The mother at crib No. 17 is not concerned with potential side effects. She sits on the floor cradling her daughter, crooning over and over, "Get well, my child, get well." The baby stares back without blinking. "It's sad, so sad, so sad," the mother says. The child died three days later.

The children who are left when parents die only add another complex dimension to Africa's epidemic. At 17, Tsepho Phale has been head of an indigent household of three young boys in the dusty township of Monarch, outside Francistown, for two years. He never met his father, his mother died of AIDS, and the grieving children possess only a raw concrete shell of a house. The doorways have no doors; the window frames no glass. There is not a stick of furniture. The boys sleep on piled-up blankets, their few clothes dangling from nails. In the room that passes for a kitchen, two paraffin burners sit on the dirt floor alongside the month's food: four cabbages, a bag of oranges and one of potatoes, three sacks of flour, some yeast, two jars of oil

and two cartons of milk. Next to a dirty stack of plastic pans lies the mealy meal and rice that will provide their main sustenance for the month. A couple of bars of soap and two rolls of toilet paper also have to last the month. Tsepho has just brought these rations home from the social-service center where the "orphan grants" are doled out.

Tsepho has been robbed of a childhood that was grim even before his mother fell sick. She supported the family by "buying and selling things," he says, but she never earned more than a pittance. When his middle brother was knocked down by a car and left physically and mentally disabled, Tsepho's mother used the insurance money to build this house, so she would have one thing of value to leave her children. As the walls went up, she fell sick. Tsepho had to nurse her, bathe her, attend to her bodily functions, try to feed her. Her one fear as she lay dying was that her rural relatives would try to steal the house. She wrote a letter bequeathing it to her sons and bade Tsepho hide it.

As her body lay on the concrete floor awaiting burial, the relatives argued openly about how they would divide up the profits when they sold her dwelling. Tsepho gave the district commissioner's office the letter, preventing his mother's family from grabbing the house. Fine, said his relations; if you think you're a man, you look after your brothers. They have contributed nothing to the boys' welfare since. "It's as if we don't exist anymore either," says Tsepho. Now he struggles to keep house for the others, doing the cooking, cleaning, laundry and shopping.

The boys look at the future with despair. "It is very bleak," says Tsepho, kicking aimlessly at a bare wall. He had to quit school, has no job, will probably never get one. "I've given up my dreams. I have no hope."

Orphans have traditionally been cared for the African way: relatives absorb the children of the dead into their extended families. Some still try, but communities like Tsepho's are becoming saturated with orphans, and families can't afford to take on another kid, leaving thousands alone.

Now many must fend for themselves, struggling to survive. The trauma of losing parents is compounded by the burden of becoming a breadwinner. Most orphans sink into penury, drop out of school, suffer malnutrition, ostracism, psychic distress. Their makeshift households scramble to live on pitiful handouts—from overstretched relatives, a kind neighbor, a state grant—or they beg and steal in the streets. The orphans' present desperation forecloses a brighter future. "They hardly ever succeed in having a life," says Siphelile Kaseke, 22, a counselor at an AIDS orphans' camp near Bulawayo. Without education, girls fall into prostitution, and older boys migrate illegally to South Africa, leaving the younger ones to go on the streets.

## 1 IN 4 SOUTH AFRICAN WOMEN AGES 20 TO 29 IS INFECTED WITH HIV

EVERY DAY SPENT IN THIS PART OF AFRICA IS ACUTELY DEPRESSING: there is so little countervailing hope to all the stories of the dead and the doomed. "More than anywhere else in the world, AIDS in Africa was met with apathy," says Suzanne LeClerc-

Madlala, a lecturer at the University of Natal. The consequences of the silence march on: infection soars, stigma hardens, denial hastens death, and the chasm between knowledge and behavior widens. The present disaster could be dwarfed by the woes that loom if Africa's epidemic rages on. The human losses could wreck the region's frail economies, break down civil societies and incite political instability.

In the face of that, every day good people are doing good things. Like Dr. Moll, who uses his after-job time and his own fund raising to run an extensive volunteer home-care program in KwaZulu-Natal. And Busi Magwazi, who, along with dozens of others, tends the sick for nothing in the Durban-based Si-noziso project. And Patricia Bakwinya, who started her Shining Stars orphan-care program in Francistown with her own zeal and no money, to help youngsters like Tsepho Phale. And countless individuals who give their time and devotion to ease southern Africa's plight.

But these efforts can help only thousands; they cannot turn the tide. The region is caught in a double bind. Without treatment, those with HIV will sicken and die; without prevention, the spread of infection cannot be checked. Southern Africa has no other means available to break the vicious cycle, except to change everyone's sexual behavior—and that isn't happening.

The essential missing ingredient is leadership. Neither the countries of the region nor those of the wealthy world have been able or willing to provide it.

South Africa, comparatively well off, comparatively well educated, has blundered tragically for years. AIDS invaded just when apartheid ended, and a government absorbed in massive transition relegated the disease to a back page. An attempt at a national education campaign wasted millions on a farcical musical. The premature release of a local wonder drug ended in scandal when the drug turned out to be made of industrial solvent. Those fiascoes left the government skittish about embracing expensive programs, inspiring a 1998 decision not to provide AZT to HIV-positive pregnant women. Zimbabwe too suffers savagely from feckless leadership. Even in Botswana, where the will to act is gathering strength, the resources to follow through have to come from foreign hands.

AIDS' grip here is so pervasive and so complex that all societies—theirs and ours—must rally round to break it. These countries are too poor to doctor themselves. The drugs that could begin to break the cycle will not be available here until global pharmaceutical companies find ways to provide them inexpensively. The health-care systems required to prescribe and monitor complicated triple-cocktail regimens won't exist unless rich countries help foot the bill. If there is ever to be a vaccine, the West will have to finance its discovery and provide it to the poor. The cure for this epidemic is not national but international.

The deep silence that makes African leaders and societies want to deny the problem, the corruption and incompetence that render them helpless is something the West cannot fix. But the fact that they are poor is not. The wealthy world must help with its zeal and its cash if southern Africa is ever to be freed of the AIDS plague.

---

### A UGANDAN TALE

## Not Afraid to Speak Out

Major Rubaramira Ruranga knows something about fighting. During Idi Amin's reign of terror in Uganda in the 1970s, Ruranga worked as a spy for rebels fighting the dictator. After Amin's ouster, the military man studied political intelligence in Cuba before returning to find a new dictator at the helm and a blood war raging. Hoping for change, Ruranga supplied his old rebel friends with more secrets, this time from within the President's office. When he was discovered, he fled to the bush to "fight the struggle with guns."

The turmoil in Uganda was fueling the spread of another enemy—AIDS. Like many rebel soldiers, Ruranga was on the move constantly to avoid detection. "You never see your wife, and so you get to a new place and meet someone else," he says. "I had sex without protection with a few women." Doctors found he was HIV positive in 1989. "They told me I would die in two to three years, so I started preparing for when I was away. I told my kids, my wife. Worked on finishing the house for them. I gave up hope." But as he learned about AIDS, his attitude changed. After talking to American and European AIDS activists—some had lived with the disease for 15 years or more—"I realized I was not going to die in a few years. I was reborn, determined to live."

He began fighting again. After announcing his HIV status at a rally on World AIDS Day in 1993—an extraordinarily brave act in Africa, where few activists, let alone army officers, ever admit to having HIV—he set up a network for those living with HIV/AIDS in Uganda, "so that people had somewhere to go to talk to friends." And while Uganda has done more to slow the spread of AIDS than any other country—in some places the rate of infection has dropped by half—"we can always do better," says Ruranga. "Why are we able to buy guns and bullets to kill people and we are not able to buy drugs to save people?" The fight continues.

**—By Simon Robinson/Kampala**

---

From *Time*, February 12, 2001, pp. 36-38, 40-42, 44-45. © 2001 by Time, Inc. Magazine Company. Reprinted by permission.

# UNIT 5

# Crime, Violence, and Law Enforcement

## Unit Selections

28. **The Criminal Menace: Shifting Global Trends**, Gene Stephens
29. **The Aggregate Burden of Crime**, David A. Anderson
30. **Reasonable Doubts**, Stephen Pomper
31. **On Patrol**, Eli Lehrer
32. **The Terrorism to Come**, Walter Laqueur
33. **Understanding the Terrorist Mind-Set**, Randy Borum

## Key Points to Consider

- What are some of the reasons why America has a high crime rate? Why has the crime rate dropped recently?

- What are some of the policy options for reducing crime?

- What law enforcement policies are most heavily relied upon today? What do you think are the best policies and why?

- What are the costs of crime to society? What kinds of crimes are the most costly and why?

- Do you think that many innocent people are convicted of murder? How do you explain cases of the miscarriage of justice?

- How much of a threat is terrorism toward the United States? How can the public be protected from it?

 **Links: www.dushkin.com/online/**
These sites are annotated in the World Wide Web pages.

**ACLU Criminal Justice Home Page**
*http://aclu.org/CriminalJustice/CriminalJusticeMain.cfm*
**Terrorism Research Center**
*http://www.terrorism.com*

This unit deals with criminal behavior and its control by the law enforcement system. The first line of defense against crime is the socialization of the young to internalize norms against harmful and illegal behavior. Thus families, schools, religious institutions, and social pressure are the major crime fighters, but they do not do a perfect job. The police have to handle their failures. For the last half century, crime has increased, signaling for some commentators a decline in morality. If the power of norms to control criminal behavior declines, the role of law enforcement must increase, and that is what has happened. The societal response to crime has been threefold: hire more police, build more prisons, and toughen penalties for crimes. These policies by themselves can have only limited success. For example, putting a drug dealer in prison just creates an opportunity for another person to become a drug dealer. Another approach is to give potential criminals alternatives to crime. The key factor in this approach is a healthy economy that provides many job opportunities for unemployed young men. To some extent that has happened, and the crime rate has dropped. Programs that work with inner-city youth might also help, but budget-tight cities are not funding many programs like this. Amid the policy debates there is one thing we can agree upon: Crime has declined significantly in the past decade after rising substantially for a half century.

The first subsection deals with crime; a major concern today because crime and violence seem to be out of control. In the first article in this subsection, Gene Stephens describes crime trends throughout the world but focuses on the United States. Overall crime rates in the United States were the highest in the Western world in 1980 but have fallen in the United States and increased in many other nations so that several Western countries now have higher rates. Nevertheless, the U.S. murder rate is still the highest. Stephens presents three competing explanations for the crime decline in the U.S.: 1) greater success of the justice system in catching and locking up criminals, 2) the lowering of the percent of the population in the high crime ages, 3) the greater prevalence and success of community based approaches. In the second article on crime, David A. Anderson tries to put into monetary terms the impacts of various types of crimes in the United States. The results produce some surprises. First, when he includes many costs that are seldom taken into account such as the costs of law enforcement, security measures, and lost time at work, the total bill is over $1 trillion or over $4000 per person. Another surprise is the relative costs of white collar crime versus street crime. Fraud and cheating on taxes costs Americans over 20 times the costs of theft, burglary, and robbery.

The next subsection deals with law enforcement. In the first article, Stephen Pomper proposes seven major reforms of the criminal justice system. Pomper accepts the critical view that "the guilty are over-protected, the innocent are under-served, too many violent and dangerous felons wind up with Get-Out-of Jail-Free cards and too many non-violent and just-plain-innocent peo-

ple wind up doing time." He proposes the following reforms: (1) reduce the extent to which evidence is excluded in court, (2) create a universal DNA database, (3) truly protect witnesses, (4) police the prosecutors as well as the police, (5) abolish the insanity defense, (6) repeal the mandatory minimum laws, and (7) improve the administration of the courts. Some of the problems that these reforms seek to correct include the many existing severe impediments to the prosecution of criminals and the extreme laws that were passed out of emotional public responses to some outrageous crimes.

Eli Lehrer, in the next article, gives us an up-close and personal picture of police work by following a policewoman on her patrol and observing a policeman who is a Community Policing Coordinator.

The final subsection deals with terrorism. First, Walter Laqueur provides a rich lesson on different types of terrorism from the left-wing revolutionary terrorism of several decades ago to the religiously inspired terrorism of today. He stresses that today's terrorism is not a response to poverty conditions, and therefore, not solved by changing the economic conditions of dissident groups. We must recognize the cultural basis of the current terrorist war. In the final article, Randy Borum probes further into the thinking of today's terrorists. He explains how they think and what are their beliefs, values, and motives. This understanding is essential to dealing appropriately with them.

# THE CRIMINAL MENACE
## SHIFTING GLOBAL TRENDS

### GENE STEPHENS

Crime in the United States is bottoming out after a steep slide downward during the past decade. But crime in many other nations—particularly in eastern and parts of western Europe—has continued to climb. In the United States, street crime overall remains near historic lows, prompting some analysts to declare life in the United States safer than it has ever been. In fact, statistics show that, despite terrorism, the world as a whole seems to be becoming safer. This is in sharp contrast to the perceptions of Americans and others, as polls indicate they believe the world gets more dangerous every day.

## CURRENT CRIME RATES AROUND THE WORLD

Although the United States still has more violent crime than other industrialized nations and still ranks high in overall crime, the nation has nevertheless been experiencing a decline in crime numbers. Meanwhile, a number of European countries are catching up; traditionally low-crime societies, such as Denmark and Finland, are near the top in street crime rates today. Other countries that weren't even on the crime radar—such as Japan—are also experiencing a rise in crime.

Comparing crime rates across countries is difficult. Different definitions of crimes, among other factors, make official crime statistics notoriously unreliable. However, the periodic World Crime Survey, a UN initiative to track global crime rates, may offer the most reliable figures currently available:

• *Overall crime (homicide, rape, major assault, robbery) and property crime.* The United States in 1980 clearly led the Western world in overall crime and ranked particularly high in property crime. A decade later, statistics show a marked decline in U.S. property crime. By 2000, overall crime rates for the U.S.

dropped below those of England and Wales, Denmark, and Finland, while U.S. property-crime rates also continued to decline.

• *Homicide.* The United States had consistently higher homicide rates than most Western nations from 1980 to 2000. In the 1990s, the U.S. rate was cut almost in half, but the 2000 rate of 5.5 homicides per 100,000 people was still higher than all nations except those in political and social turmoil. Colombia, for instance, had 63 homicides per 100,000 people; South Africa, 51.

• *Rape.* In 1980 and 1990, U.S. rape rates were higher than those of any Western nation, but by 2000, Canada took the lead. The lowest reported rape rates were in Asia and the Middle East.

• *Robbery* has been on a steady decline in the United States over the past two decades. As of 2000, countries with more reported robberies than the United States included England and Wales, Portugal, and Spain. Countries with fewer reported robberies include Germany, Italy, and France, as well as Middle Eastern and Asian nations.

• *Burglary,* usually considered the most serious property crime, is lower in the United States today than it was in 1980. As of 2000, the United States had lower burglary rates than Australia, Denmark, Finland, England and Wales, and Canada. It had higher reported burglary rates than Spain, Korea, and Saudi Arabia.

• *Vehicle theft* declined steadily in the United States from 1980 to 2000. The 2000 figures show that Australia, England and Wales, Denmark, Norway, Canada, France, and Italy all have higher rates of vehicle theft.

Overall, the United States has experienced a downward trend in crime while other Western nations, and even industrialized non-Western nations, are witnessing higher numbers. What's behind the U.S. decreases? Some analysts believe that tougher laws, enforcement, and incarceration policies have lowered crime in the United States. They point to "three-strikes" legislation, mandatory incarceration for offenses such as drug possession and domestic violence, and tougher street-level enforcement. The reason many European countries are suffering higher crime rates, analysts argue, is because of their fewer laws and more-lenient enforcement and sentencing.

Other analysts argue that socioeconomic changes—such as fewer youth in the crime-prone 15- to 25-year old age group, a booming economy, and more community care of citizens—led to the drop in U.S. crime. They now point out that the new socioeconomic trends of growing unemployment, stagnation of wages, and the growing numbers in the adolescent male population are at work in today's terror-wary climate and may signal crime increases ahead.

Still other analysts see community-oriented policing (COP) problem-oriented policing (POP), and restorative justice (mediation, arbitration, restitution, and community service instead of criminal courts and incarceration) as the nexus of recent and future crime control successes.

### U.S. CRIME TREND

Just which crime fighting tactics have effected this U.S. crime trend is a matter of debate. Three loose coalitions offer their views:

*Getting tough works.* "There is, in fact, a simple explanation for America's success against crime: The American justice system now does a better job of catching criminals and locking them up," writes Eli Lehrer, senior editor of *The American Enterprise.* Lehrer says local control of policing was probably what made a critical difference between the United States and European countries where regional and national systems predominate. He holds that local control allowed police to use enforcement against loitering and other minor infractions to keep the streets clean of potential lawbreakers. He acknowledges that "positive loitering"—stickers or a pat on the back for well-behaved juveniles—was the other side of the successful effort. In addition, more people have since been imprisoned for longer periods of time, seen by "get-tough" advocates as another factor in safer streets today.

*Demographics rule.* Some criminologists and demographers see the crime decrease as a product of favorable socioeconomic population factors in the mid- through late-1990s. High employment rates, with jobs in some sectors going unfilled for lack of qualified candidates, kept salaries growing. Even the unemployed went back to school to gain job skills. By the end of the decade the older students filled the college classrooms, taking up the slack left by the lower numbers in the traditional student age group. In such times, both violent and property crimes have usually dropped, as economic need decreased and frustration and anger subsided.

"Get-tough" theorists hold that 200 crimes a year could be prevented for each criminal taken off the streets but criminologist Albert Reiss counters that most offenders work in groups and are simply replaced when one leaves.

If demographic advocates are right, then the next few years could see a boom in street crime in the United States due to a combination of growing unemployment, stagnant wages, and

state and local governments so strapped for funds that social programs and even education are facing major cutbacks.

*Community-based approaches succeed.* Whereas the "get-tough" advocates mention community policing as a factor in the crime decrease, this third group sees the service aspects (rather than strict enforcement) of COP combined with the emerging restorative-justice movement as being the catalyst for success in crime prevention and control.

More criminologists believe street crime is a product of socioeconomic conditions interacting on young people, primarily adolescent males. Usually their crimes occur in interaction with others in gangs or groups, especially when law-abiding alternatives (youth athletic programs, tutors, mentors, community centers, social clubs, after-school programs) are not available. Thus, any chance of success in keeping crime rates low on a long-term basis depends on constant assessment of the community and its needs to maintain a nurturing environment.

COP and POP coordinate community cohesion by identifying problems that will likely result in crime and by simply improving the quality of life in the neighborhoods. The key: partnerships among police, citizens, civic and business groups, public and private social-service agencies, and government agencies. Combined with an ongoing needs analysis in recognition of constantly changing community dynamics, the partnerships can quickly attack any problem or situation that arises.

A restorative-justice movement has grown rapidly but stayed below the radar screen in the United States. In many communities, civil and criminal incidents are more likely to be handled through mediation or arbitration, restitution, community service, and reformation/reintegration than in civil or criminal courts. The goal, besides justice for all, is the development of a symbolic relationship and reconciliation within the community, since more than 90% of all street offenders return to the same community.

## LESSONS FOR THE FUTURE OF CRIME PREVENTION AND CONTROL

All schools of thought on why street crime is decreasing have a commonality: proactive prevention rather than reactive retribution. Even the method to achieve this goal is not really in question—only the emphasis.

Since the 1980s, progressive police agencies in the United States have adhered to the "Broken Windows" and "Weed and Seed" philosophies taken from the work of criminologists James Q. Wilson and George L. Keeling. Broken windows are a metaphor for failure to establish and maintain acceptable standards of behavior in the community. The blame, according to Wilson and Keeling, lay primarily in the change in emphasis by police from being peace officers who seek to capture criminals. They argue that, in healthy communities, informal but widely understood rules were maintained by citizens and police, often using extralegal ("move on") or arrest for minor infractions (vagrancy, loitering, pandering). It was, then, this citizen-police partnership that worked to stem community deterioration and disorder, which unattended, would lead to crime.

"Weeding" involved using street-sweeping ordinances to clean the streets of the immediate problems (drunks, drug addicts, petty thieves, panhandlers). "Seeding" involved taking a breather while these offenders were in jail and establishing "opportunity" programs designed to make the community viable and capable of self-regulating its behavioral controls (job training, new employers, day care nurseries in schools, after-school programs, tutors and mentors, civic pride demonstrations, tenant management of housing projects). In the early years, the "weed" portion was clearly favored; in the early 1990s, "seed" programs based on analysis of the specific needs of the individual community were developed and spread—about the time the crime rates began to plunge.

The Weed and Seed programs in the United States imparted the following lessons:

- Proactive prevention must be at the core of any successful crime-control strategy.
- Each community must have an ongoing needs assessment carried out by a police-citizen partnership.
- A multitude of factors—from laws and neighborhood standards to demographics and socioeconomic needs—must be considered in the assessment process.
- Weed and seed must be balanced according to specific needs—somewhat different in each community.
- When crime does occur, community-based restorative justice should be used to provide restitution to victims and community while reforming and then reintegrating the offender as a law-abiding citizen of the community.

## NEW APPROACHES FOR THE EMERGING CRIME LANDSCAPE

Twenty-first-century crime is going to require new approaches to prevention and control. Street crime dominated the attention of the justice system in the twentieth century, but recent excesses of corporations, costing stockholders and retirees literally billions of dollars, do not fit into the street-crime paradigm. Nor do political or religious-motivated terrorism, Internet fraud, deception, theft, harassment, pedophilia, and terrorism on an information highway without borders, without ownership, and without jurisdiction. Now attention must—and will—be paid to white-collar crimes, infotech and biotech crimes, and terrorism.

Surveys find that a large majority of corporations have been victims of computer-assisted crimes. Polls of citizens find high rates of victimization by Internet offenses ranging from identity theft to fraud, hacking to harassment. U.S. officials have maintained since the late 1990s that it is just a matter of time until there is a "Pearl Harbor" on the Internet (such as shutting down medical services networks, power grids, or financial services nationwide or even worldwide).

### DOOMSDAY SCENARIOS

Following the attacks by terrorists on September 11, 2001, and later strikes abroad, doomsday scenarios have abounded, with release of radio-active or biological toxins being the most frightening. Attempts to shoot down an Israeli commercial airliner with a shoulder-held missile launcher further increased anxiety.

Clearly these crimes against victims generally unknown to the attacker and often chosen randomly cannot be stopped by community policing alone, although vigilant community partners often can spot suspicious activity and expose possible criminals and terrorists. Early response to this dilemma was to pass more laws, catch more offenders, and thus deter future incidents. This is the same response traditionally taken to street crime—the one being abandoned in preference to proactive prevention methods (COP and restorative justice.) Clearly, prevention has to be the first and most important strategy for dealing with the new threats.

Two major approaches will evolve over the next few years. First, national and international partnerships will be necessary to cope with crimes without borders. In 2000, a task force of agents from 32 U.S. communities, the federal government, and 13 other nations conducted the largest-ever crackdown on child pornography exchanged internationally over the Internet. Coordinated by the U.S. Customs Service, the raid resulted in shutting down an international child-pornography ring that used secret Internet chat rooms and sophisticated encryption to exchange thousands of sexually explicit images of children as young as 18 months. It is this type of coordinated transnational effort that will be necessary to cope with infotech and biotech crime and terrorism.

Second, the focus of prevention must change from opportunity reduction to desire reduction. Crime-prevention specialists have long used the equation, Desire + Opportunity = Crime. Prevention programs have traditionally focused on reducing opportunity through target hardening. Locks, alarms, high-intensity lighting, key control, and other methods have been used, along with neighborhood crime watches and citizen patrols.

Little attention has been paid to desire reduction, in large part because of the atomistic approach to crime. Specifically, an offender's criminal behavior is viewed as a result of personal choice. Meanwhile, criminologists and other social scientists say crime is more likely to be a product of the conditions under which the criminal was reared and lived—yet there were no significant efforts to fix this root of the problem. Instead, the criminal-justice system stuck to target hardening, catching criminals, and exacting punishment.

Quashing conditions that lead to a desire to commit crime is especially necessary in light of the apparent reasons terrorists and international criminals attack: religious fervor heightened by seeing abject poverty, illiteracy, and often homelessness and hunger all around while also seeing others live in seeming splendor.

The opportunity to reduce crime and disorder is at hand. The strategies outlined above will go a long way toward that lofty goal as will new technologies. A boom in high-tech development has brought about new surveillance and tracking gadgetry, security machines that see through clothing and skin, cameras and listening devices that see and hear through walls and ceilings, "bugs" that can be surreptitiously placed on individuals and biometric scanners that can identify suspects in large crowds. On the other hand, there are also the technologies that could take away our freedom, particularly our freedom of speech and movement. Some in high government positions believe loss of privacy and presumption of innocence is the price we must pay for safety.

For many it is too high a price. One group that urges judicious use of technology within the limitations of civil liberties protected by the U.S. Constitution is the Society of Police Futurists International (PFI)—a collection primarily of police officials from all over the world dedicated to improving the professional field of policing by taking a professional futurist's approach to preparing for the times ahead. While definitely interested in staying on the cutting edge of technology and even helping to guide its development, PFI debates the promises and perils of each new innovation on pragmatic and ethical grounds. Citizens need to do the same.

---

*Mr. Stephens is a professor emeritus in the Department of Criminology and Criminal Justice at the University of South Carolina. From "Global Trends in Crime," by Gene Stephens,* The Futurist, *May–June 2003, pages 40–46.*

# The Aggregate Burden of Crime

David A. Anderson

## Introduction

Distinct from previous studies that have focused on selected crimes, regions, or outcomes, this study attempts an exhaustively broad estimation of the crime burden....

Overt annual expenditures on crime in the United States include $47 billion for police protection, $36 billion for corrections, and $19 billion for the legal and judicial costs of state and local criminal cases. (Unless otherwise noted, all figures are adjusted to reflect 1997 dollars using the Consumer Price Index.) Crime victims suffer $876 million worth of lost workdays, and guns cost society $25 billion in medical bills and lost productivity in a typical year. Beyond the costs of the legal system, victim losses, and crime prevention agencies, the crime burden includes the costs of deterrence (locks, safety lighting and fencing, alarm systems and munitions), the costs of compliance enforcement (non-gendarme inspectors and regulators), implicit psychic and health costs (fear, agony, and the inability to behave as desired), and the opportunity costs of time spent preventing, carrying out, and serving prison terms for criminal activity.

This study estimates the impact of crime taking a comprehensive list of the repercussions of aberrant behavior into account. While the standard measures of criminal activity count crimes and direct costs, this study measures the impact of crimes and includes indirect costs as well. Further, the available data on which crime cost figures are typically based is imprecise. Problems with crime figures stem from the prevalence of unreported crimes, inconsistencies in recording procedures among law enforcement agencies, policies of recording only the most serious crime in events with multiple offenses, and a lack of distinction between attempted and completed crimes. This research does not eliminate these problems, but it includes critical crime-prevention and opportunity costs that are measured with relative precision, and thus places less emphasis on the imprecise figures used in most other measures of the impact of crime....

## Previous Studies

Several studies have estimated the impact of crime; however, none has been thorough in its assessment of the substantial indirect costs of crime and the crucial consideration of private crime prevention expenditures. The FBI Crime Index provides a measure of the level of crime by counting the acts of murder, rape, robbery, aggravated assault, burglary, larceny, motor vehicle theft, and arson each year. The FBI Index is purely a count of crimes and does not attempt to place weights on various criminal acts based on their severity. If the number of acts of burglary, larceny, motor vehicle theft, or arson decreases, society might be better off, but with no measure of the severity of the crimes, such a conclusion is necessarily tentative. From a societal standpoint what matters is the extent of damage inflicted by these crimes, which the FBI Index does not measure.

Over the past three decades, studies of the cost of crime have reported increasing crime burdens, perhaps more as a result of improved understanding and accounting for the broad repercussions of crime than due to the increase in the burden itself. Table 1 summarizes the findings of eight previous studies....

## The Effects of Crime

The effects of crime fall into several categories depending on whether they constitute the allocation of resources due to crime that could otherwise be used more productively, the production of ill-favored commodities, transfers from victims to criminals, opportunity costs, or implicit costs associated with risks to life and health. This section examines the meaning and ramifications of each of these categories of crime costs.

### Crime-Induced Production

Crime can result in the allocation of resources towards products and activities that do not contribute to society except in their association with crime. Examples include the production of personal protection devices, the trafficking of drugs, and the operation of correctional facilities. In the absence of crime, the time, money, and material resources absorbed by the provision of these goods and services could be used for the creation of benefits rather than the avoidance of harm. The foregone benefits from these alternatives represent a real cost of crime to society. (Twenty dollars spent on a door lock is twenty dollars that cannot be spent on groceries.) Thus, expenditures on crime-related products are treated as a loss to society.

*Table 1*

| Previous Study | Focus | Not Included | $ (billions) |
|---|---|---|---|
| Colins (1994) | General | Opportunity Costs, Miscellaneous Indirect Components | 728 |
| Cohen, Miller, and Wiersema (1995) | Victim Costs of Violent and Property Crimes | Prevention, Opportunity, and Indirect Costs | 472 |
| *U.S. News* (1974) | General | Opportunity Costs, Miscellaneous Indirect Components | 288 |
| Cohen, Miller, Rossman (1994) | Cost of Rape, Robbery, and Assault | Prevention, Opportunity, and Indirect Costs | 183 |
| Zedlewski (1985) | Firearms, Guard Dogs, Victim Losses, Commercial Security | Residential Security, Opportunity Costs, Indirect Costs | 160 |
| Cohen (1990) | Cost of Personal and Household Crime to Victims | Prevention, Opportunity, and Indirect Costs | 113 |
| President's Commission on Law Enforcement (1967) | General | Opportunity Costs, Miscellaneous Indirect Components | 107 |
| Klaus (1994) | National Crime and Victimization Survey Crimes | Prevention, Opportunity, and Indirect Costs | 19 |

Crimes against property also create unnecessary production due to the destruction and expenditure of resources, and crimes against persons necessitate the use of medical and psychological care resources. In each of these cases, crime-related purchases bid-up prices for the associated items, resulting in higher prices for all consumers of the goods. In the absence of crime, the dollars currently spent to remedy and recover from crime would largely be spent in pursuit of other goals, bidding-up the prices of alternative categories of goods. For this reason, the *net* impact of price effects is assumed to be zero in the present research.

## Opportunity Costs

As the number of incarcerated individuals increases steadily, society faces the large and growing loss of these potential workers' productivity.… Criminals are risk takers and instigators—characteristics that could make them contributors to society if their entrepreneurial talents were not misguided. Crimes also take time to conceive and carry out, and thus involve the opportunity cost of the criminals' time regardless of detection and incarceration. For many, crime is a full-time occupation. Society is deprived of the goods and services a criminal would have produced in the time consumed by crime and the production of "bads" if he or she were on the level. Additional opportunity costs arise due to victims' lost workdays, and time spent securing assets, looking for keys, purchasing and installing crime prevention devices, and patrolling neighborhood-watch areas.

## The Value of Risks to Life and Health

The implicit costs of violent crime include the fear of being injured or killed, the anger associated with the inability to behave as desired, and the agony of being a crime victim. Costs associated with life and health risks are perhaps the most difficult to ascertain, although a considerable literature is devoted to their estimation. The implicit values of lost life and injury are included in the list of crime costs below; those not wishing to consider them can simply subtract these estimates from the aggregate figure.

## Transfers

One result of fraud and theft is a transfer of assets from victim to criminal.…

# Numerical Findings

## Crime-Induced Production

… Crime-induced production accounts for about $400 billion in expenditures annually. Table 2 presents the costs of goods and services that would not have to be produced in the absence of crime. Drug trafficking accounts for an estimated $161 billion in expenditure. With the $28 billion cost of prenatal drug exposure and almost $11 billion worth of federal, state, and local drug control efforts (including drug treatment, education, interdiction, research, and intelligence), the combined cost of drug-related activities is about $200 billion. Findings that over half of the arrestees in 24 cities tested positive for recent drug use and about one-third of offenders reported being under the influence of drugs at the time of their offense suggest that significant portions of the other crime-cost categories may result indirectly from drug use.

About 682,000 police and 17,000 federal, state, special (park, transit, or county) and local police agencies account for $47 billion in expenditures annually. Thirty-six billion dollars is dedicated each year to the 895 federal and state prisons, 3,019 jails, and 1,091 state, county, and local juvenile detention centers. Aside from guards in correctional institutions, private expenditure on guards amounts to more than $18 billion annually. Security guard agencies employ 55 percent of the 867,000 guards in the U.S.; the remainder are employed in-house. While guards are expected and identifiable at banks and military complexes, they have a less conspicuous presence at railroads, ports, golf courses, laboratories, factories, hospitals, retail stores, and other places of business. The figures in this paper do not include receptionists, who often play a duel role of monitoring unlawful entry into a building and providing information and assistance.…

## Table 2

| Crime-Induced Production | $ (millions) |
|---|---|
| Drug Trafficking | 160,584 |
| Police Protection | 47,129 |
| Corrections | 35,879 |
| Prenatal Exposure to Cocaine and Heroin | 28,156 |
| Federal Agencies | 23,381 |
| Judicial and Legal Services—State & Local | 18,901 |
| Guards | 17,917 |
| Drug Control | 10,951 |
| DUI Costs to Driver | 10,302 |
| Medical Care for Victims | 8,990 |
| Computer Viruses and Security | 8,000 |
| Alarm Systems | 6,478 |
| Passes for Business Access | 4,659 |
| Locks, Safes, and Vaults | 4,359 |
| Vandalism (except Arson) | 2,317 |
| Small Arms and Small Arms Ammunition | 2,252 |
| Replacements due to Arson | 1,902 |
| Surveillance Cameras | 1,471 |
| Safety Lighting | 1,466 |
| Protective Fences and Gates | 1,159 |
| Airport Security | 448 |
| Nonlethal weaponry, e.g., Mace | 324 |
| Elec. Retail Article Surveillance | 149 |
| Theft Insurance (less indemnity) | 96 |
| Guard Dogs | 49 |
| Mothers Against Drunk Driving | 49 |
| Library Theft Detection | 28 |
| Total | 397,395 |

## Opportunity Costs

In their study of the costs of murder, rape, robbery, and aggravated assault, Cohen, Miller, and Rossman estimate that the average incarcerated offender costs society $5,700 in lost productivity per year. Their estimate was based on the observation that many prisoners did not work in the legal market prior to their offense, and the opportunity cost of those prisoners' time can be considered to be zero. The current study uses a higher estimate of the opportunity cost of incarceration because unlike previous studies, it examines the relative savings from a *crime-free* society. It is likely that in the absence of crime including drug use, some criminals who are not presently employed in the legal workforce would be willing and able to find gainful employment. This assumption is supported by the fact that many criminals are, in a way, motivated entrepreneurs whose energy has taken an unfortunate focus. In the absence of more enticing underground activities, some of the same individuals could apply these skills successfully in the legal sector....

## Table 3

| The Value of Risks to Life and Health | $ (millions) |
|---|---|
| Value of Lost Life | 439,880 |
| Value of Injuries | 134,515 |
| Total | **574,395** |

## The Value of Risks to Life and Health

Table 3 presents estimates of the implicit costs of violent crime. The value of life and injury estimates used here reflect the amounts individuals are willing to accept to enter a work environment in which their health state might change. The labor market estimates do not include losses covered by workers' compensation, namely health care costs (usually provided without dollar or time limits) and lost earnings (within modest bounds, victims or their spouses typically receive about two thirds of lost earnings for life or the duration of the injury). The values do capture perceived risks of pain, suffering, and mental distress associated with the health losses. If the risk of involvement in violent crime evokes more mental distress than the risk of occupational injuries and fatalities, the labor market values represent conservative estimates of the corresponding costs of crime. Similar estimates have been used in previous studies of crime costs....

The average of 27 previous estimates of the implicit value of human life as reported by W. Kip Viscusi is 7.1 million. Removing two outlying estimates of just under $20 million about which the authors express reservation, the average of the remaining studies is $6.1 million. Viscusi points out that the majority of the estimates fall between $3.7 and $8.6 million ($3 and $7 million in 1990 dollars), the average of which is again $6.1 million. The $6.1 million figure was multiplied by the 72,111 crime-related deaths to obtain the $440 billion estimate of the value of lives lost to crime. Similarly, the average of 15 studies of the implicit value of non-fatal injuries, $52,637, was multiplied by the 2,555,520 reported injuries resulting from drunk driving and boating, arson, rape, robbery, and assaults to find the $135 billion estimate for the implicit cost of crime-related injuries.

## Transfers

More than $603 billion worth of transfers result from crime. After the $204 billion lost to occupational fraud and the $123 billion in unpaid taxes, the $109 billion lost to health insurance fraud represents the greatest transfer by more than a factor of two, and the associated costs amount to almost ten percent of the nations' health care expenditures. Robberies, perhaps the classic crime, ironically generate a smaller volume of transfers ($775 million) than any other category of crime. The transfers of goods and money resulting from fraud and theft do not necessarily impose a net burden on society, and may in fact increase social welfare to the extent that those on the receiving end value the goods more than those losing them. Nonetheless, as Table 4 illustrates, those on the losing side bear a $603 billion annual burden....

## Table 4

| Transfers | $ (millions) |
|---|---|
| Occupational Fraud | 203,952 |
| Unpaid Taxes | 123,108 |
| Health Insurance Fraud | 108,610 |
| Financial Institution Fraud | 52,901 |
| Mail Fraud | 35,986 |
| Property/Casualty Insurance Fraud | 20,527 |
| Telemarketing Fraud | 16,609 |
| Business Burglary | 13,229 |
| Motor Vehicle Theft | 8,913 |
| Shoplifting | 7,185 |
| Household Burglary | 4,527 |
| Personal Theft | 3,909 |
| Household Larceny | 1,996 |
| Coupon Fraud | 912 |
| Robbery | 775 |
| **Total** | 603,140 |

## Table 5

| The Aggregate Burden of Crime | $ (billions) |
|---|---|
| Crime-Induced Production | 397 |
| Opportunity Costs | 130 |
| Risks to Life and Health | 574 |
| Transfers | 603 |
| **Gross Burden** | **$1,705** |
| **Net of Transfers** | **$1,102** |
| **Per Capita (in dollars)** | **$4,118** |

marized in Table 1 included transfers, so the appropriate comparison is to the gross cost estimate in the current study. As the result of a more comprehensive treatment of repercussions, the cost of crime is now seen to be more than twice as large as previously recognized.

There are additional cost categories that are not included here, largely because measures that are included absorb much of their impact. Nonetheless, several are worth noting. Thaler, Hellman and Naroff, and Rizzo estimate the erosion of property values per crime. An average of their figures, $2,024, can be multiplied by the total number of crimes reported in 1994, 13,992, to estimate an aggregate housing devaluation of $28 billion. Although this figure should reflect the inability to behave as desired in the presence of crime, it also includes psychic and monetary costs imposed by criminal behavior that are already included in this [article].

Julie Berry Cullen and Stephen D. Levitt discuss urban flight resulting from crime. They report a nearly one-to-one relationship between serious crimes and individuals parting from major cities. The cost component of this is difficult to assess because higher commuting costs must be measured against lower property costs in rural areas, and the conveniences of city living must be compared with the amenities of suburbia. Several other categories of crime costs receive incomplete representation due to insufficient data, and therefore make the estimates here conservative. These include the costs of unreported crimes (although the National Crime Victimization Survey provides information beyond that reported to the police), lost taxes due to the underground economy, and restrictions of behavior due to crime.

When criminals' costs are estimated implicitly as the value of the assets they receive through crime, the gross cost of crime (including transfers) is estimated to exceed $2,269 billion each year, and the net cost is an estimated $1,666 billion. When criminals' costs are assumed to equal the value of time spent planning and committing crimes and in prison, the estimated annual gross and net costs of crime are $1,705 and $1,102 billion respectively. Table 5 presents the aggregate costs of crime based on the more conservative, time-based estimation method. The disaggregation of this and the previous tables facilitates the creation of customized estimates based on

## Conclusion

Previous studies of the burden of crime have counted crimes or concentrated on direct crime costs. This paper calculates the aggregate burden of crime rather than absolute numbers, includes indirect costs, and recognizes that transfers resulting from theft should not be included in the net burden of crime to society. The accuracy of society's perspective on crime costs will improve with the understanding that these costs extend beyond victims' losses and the cost of law enforcement to include the opportunity costs of criminals' and prisoners' time, our inability to behave as desired, and the private costs of crime deterrence.

As criminals acquire an estimated $603 billion dollars worth of assets from their victims, they generate an additional $1,102 billion worth of lost productivity, crime-related expenses, and diminished quality of life. The net losses represent an annual per capita burden of $4,118. Including transfers, the aggregate burden of crime is $1,705 billion. In the United States, this is of the same order of magnitude as life insurance purchases ($1,680 billion), the outstanding mortgage debt to commercial banks and savings institutions ($1,853 billion), and annual expenditures on health ($1,038 billion).

As the enormity of this negative-sum game comes to light, so, too, will the need for countervailing efforts to redefine legal policy and forge new ethical standards. Periodic estimates of the full cost of crime could speak to the success of national strategies to encourage decorum, including increased expenditures on law enforcement, new community strategic approaches, technological innovations, legal reform, education, and the development of ethics curricula. Economic theory dictates that resources should be devoted to moral enhancement until the benefits from marginal efforts are surpassed by their costs. Programs that decrease the burden of crime by more than the cost of implementation should be continued, while those associated with negligible or positive net increments in the cost of crime should be altered to better serve societal goals.

# Reasonable Doubts

*Crime's down but the system's broken:*
The Monthly's *guide to criminal justice reform*

BY STEPHEN POMPER

CRIME MAY BE DOWN BUT THE CRIMINAL JUSTICE SYSTEM remains something of a mess. If you've ever spent time on a jury, if you've worked in a criminal court, or if you caught even 10 minutes of the O.J. trial on TV, you've seen some of the problems. The system has an Alice-in-Wonderland quality: The guilty are over-protected, the innocent are under-served, and much of the time the public interest simply fails to enter the picture. Jurors spend days in court dozing through endless delays and witnesses who dare come forward find their lives imperiled. When all is said and done, too many violent and dangerous felons wind up with Get-Out-of-Jail-Free cards and too many non-violent and just-plain-innocent people wind up doing time.

How do we make it better? Read on for the Monthly's guide to criminal justice reform.

## Get the Truth Out

Courts are supposed to be finders of fact. Yet there's an awful lot about the criminal justice system that keeps them from ever getting to those facts. Some of the obstacles are straight-forwardly bad laws. Others are more a question of resources and oversight. We could help our courts get past some of these obstacles and here's how:

*1. End "Two Wrongs Make a Right" Criminal Procedure:* The judicial system labors under rules crafted by the Warren Court, which protect defendants even if it's at the expense of the truth. In a 1997 law review article, University of Minnesota law professor Michael Stokes Paulsen casts this as the "Dirty Harry" problem. In the movie of the same name, Detective Harry Callaghan gets increasingly violent as he goes after a serial murderer named "Scorpio." He busts into his place without a warrant, nabs the murder rifle, and savages Scorpio until he spits out the location of a kidnap/rape/murder victim. But here's the kicker: Although Scorpio is a monster, and Harry does some monstrous things, neither of them is actually punished. Scorpio goes free because all the evidence against him is tainted by Harry's antics, and Harry slides by because cops get away with stuff.

Decades later, this lose-lose approach is still at the heart of criminal procedure. To be sure, the failing has noble origins. Back in the Civil Rights era, the Supreme Court, concerned about segregationist states deploying policemen to harass and imprison minorities, developed a set of constitutional principles that stopped them from doing that: Ill-gotten evidence was treated like fruit from a poisoned tree and had to be discarded. If the police ransacked your car without a warrant, the resulting evidence could not be produced at trial.

But the days of officially-sponsored police racism are over. And while there's still racism and police abuse on a different scale, it's hard to see why they are best dealt with by excluding otherwise helpful evidence. It's one thing to say that forced confessions should not be considered: That protects innocent people who might be beaten into confessing crimes they did not commit. But what kind of protection does an innocent person get from an "exclusionary rule" that prevents a court from considering ill-gotten evidence? If Harry busts into an innocent person's apartment and doesn't find anything to seize, then there won't be any evidence for a court to exclude, and there won't be any negative consequence for the police. Not that exclusion is such a negative consequence anyway: when police are evaluated in cities like New York, the emphasis is on the number of arrests to their credit—not convictions. If Scorpio goes free because Harry trashes his place, Harry still may be eligible for a promotion.

Part of the problem with the exclusionary rule is that it assumes that the Bill of Rights is focused on protecting the guilty rather than the innocent. But some leading constitutional scholars have begun to suggest that this assumption is backwards—protecting the innocent is in fact the top priority. The correct way to control police abuse is not by tossing potentially useful evidence onto the compost pile. It is by punishing the policeman or the police department through a lawsuit or through criminal charges. But the court should, by all means, be allowed to consider Scorpio's rifle and any other relevant evidence that Harry has managed to dig up.

In 1995 Congress considered a bill that would have gone in this direction—by getting rid of the exclusionary rule and making it easier to sue delinquent cops—but it fizzled. Supporters of the status quo argue that it doesn't really matter: There are so many exceptions to the exclusionary rule that only a small percentage of arrests are lost as a result. They also argue that the rule is useful because it provides at least some check on police abuse—and that creating an alternate system of checks would be a real challenge. This, however, ignores the problems in the current system. Read the recent coverage about the Los Angeles and New York police departments and you will see that the exclusionary rule is not an especially effective mechanism for controlling police brutality. Meanwhile, courts and lawyers waste their time on motions to suppress evidence that can only undermine the truth-seeking process.

Getting to the truth should be the court's foremost objective. And this principle doesn't apply just to the exclusionary rule. For example, a majority of states have deadlines after which a convict cannot introduce new evidence to prove his innocence. In Virginia, the deadline is a scant 21 days after trial. The idea is to keep appeals from dragging out endlessly, but that's not a good rationale for keeping innocent people in jail. If a convict can present credible new evidence, then a court should review it. But if a case reopens for this reason and the state has come up with new evidence of guilt, the court should look at that too.

It's time to end the lose-lose cycle that we create by excluding evidence. A court must get the information it needs to send Scorpio to Alcatraz. If he can prove his innocence later, it must hear the evidence it needs to spring him. And the Harrys of this world must pay for their brutality through some mechanism that punishes them directly—rather than one that punishes the community by putting guilty people back on the street.

*2. Create a Universal DNA Database.* This is an idea that Rudy Giuliani has endorsed and the ACLU has said could usher in a "brave new world" of genetic discrimination—but looking past the rhetoric, it's a winner.

The idea is to take full advantage of the enormous power of DNA evidence. Because it's so much more reliable at identifying people than eyewitnessing, DNA evidence can keep innocent people from going to death row and guilty people from going free. And because it is such powerful proof, it can help shorten trials, relieve problems with witness intimidation, and generally lend itself to a more efficient and reliable criminal justice system. But in order to maximize its usefulness, you need to be able to check crime scene DNA samples against the biggest possible database. The government is already coordinating a database that will include mostly convicted felons' DNA samples. That's a decent start: Convicted felons have a high probability of returning to their old ways when released from prison. Still, plenty of crime is committed by people who have never spent time behind bars. So why not do it right and create a database that includes everybody?

The idea is simple and non-discriminatory. Upon the birth of any child, a hospital would take a DNA sample using a simple procedure that involves swabbing cells off the inside of a cheek with a bit of cotton and then analyzing their genetic material for patterns at 13 separate points, called loci. The information recorded at these loci is referred to as "junk" by geneticists because it doesn't say anything interesting about whether a person is likely to be an insurance risk, is likely to win a Nobel Prize, is a cat or a dog person, or anything of the sort. Like a fingerprint, it would simply identify who a person is. This information would be sent to a federal database where it could be used only by law enforcement authorities when trying to establish the identity of a criminal.

Civil libertarians get hysterical over the privacy issues, but where's the beef? Given the restricted information that we're talking about, and the limited access that would be afforded, the main privacy right at stake is the right to commit crimes anonymously. It's also worth noting that millions of hospital patients leave blood and tissue samples when they come for treatment. Some hospitals keep these on file. So if your local homicide chief decides that he wants to get a DNA profile on you, he may very well be able to go down to City General, retrieve some old cells of yours, and do his own genetic analysis. This analysis could wind up furnishing information that is much more sensitive than the information that would be recorded in the national database. Wouldn't it be preferable to require the police to limit their DNA sleuthing to one tightly controlled source?

One more point on DNA evidence: It can help us correct past mistakes, and we should use it to do so. States should be required to take DNA samples from all convicts in all cases where it could prove their innocence and the prisoner wants it. Given that no fewer than 67 prisoners have already been found innocent using DNA testing, states should be working overtime to find other innocents who have been wrongly imprisoned. The flip side of this position is that states and courts should do whatever it takes to make certain that statutes of limitations don't stop victims and prosecutors from going after violent offenders where DNA technology for the first time allows guilt to be established.

*3. Save the Witnesses.* If you watch too many movies of the week, you can get a highly distorted view of what this country does to protect its witnesses. There is a romantic idea that once you agree to testify in a dangerous case, the FBI rushes in with a team of plastic surgeons, draws up new papers, and moves you to the furthest corner of the furthest possible state—where it continues to keep a watchful eye on you for the rest of your natural born days. But there's a problem: The FBI program is for federal witnesses—it was designed to help U.S. attorneys bust up organized crime. It doesn't do a thing to help out at the state and local levels where most crime, and most witness intimidation, occurs.

And a shocking amount of witness intimidation does occur at those levels. According to a 1995 report published by the National Institute of Justice (their latest on this subject), some prosecutors were able to identify gang-dominated neighborhoods where between 75 and 100 percent of violent crimes involved intimidation—from knee capping potential witnesses to staring them down in court to actually rubbing them out. That's an unsettling figure when you consider that a court's fact-finding machinery can grind to a halt without witnesses.

Consider the following example: A Baltimore jury recently acquitted three men who had been accused of shooting one Shawn L. Suggs in a street fight that spilled out into rush hour traffic. At first, the prosecution seemed to have a good case—but then the key witnesses started dropping out of the picture: The first was killed in his home. Another disappeared without a trace. And the third (Suggs' former girlfriend) claimed at the last moment to have lost her memory to heroin addiction. "I think she is afraid to tell the truth," Suggs' mother told the *Baltimore Sun*. "I think I would be afraid too."

How do you fight that kind of fear? Many states and communities have created their own witness protection programs that try to offer some measure of security—from posting police cars outside witnesses' homes to moving witnesses out of their old neighborhood until the trial is over. But the programs often lack adequate funding. And on top of that, it can be a lot tougher to protect state and local witnesses than it is to deal with mob rats. Street and gang crime witnesses are frequently reluctant to abandon their homes and neighborhoods. They get bored, lonely, and afraid when they're pulled away from their families. And even if they can be persuaded to move a short distance—say a few towns away—the temptation to look in on friends and relatives back in the old neighborhood can be both irresistible and dangerous.

More could be done. Improving funding and stiffening penalties would be a good start. When prosecutors can persuade a witness to cooperate, they should have the money they need to pay for motel bills, replace locks on doors, and pick up the tab for gas and groceries. Because it can be tough to come up with the scratch to do this on short notice, some states, like California, have set aside funds that communities can use to foot the bill. Other states should follow their lead, and the federal government should set up an emergency fund to help communities pick up the slack when there's a shortfall. And with regard to penalties, states should rank intimidation right up there with the gravest non-capital offenses. Under Washington, D.C. law, intimidators can get up to life imprisonment. That sounds about right.

*4. Police the Prosecutors—As Well As the Police.* Police and prosecutors are the gatekeepers of the criminal justice system. But although police brutality gets a lot of attention—as it has recently in New York and Los Angeles—prosecutors tend to escape scrutiny.

We should pay closer attention to the prosecutors. They, after all, are the ones who decide which cases go to trial and how they're presented. If they misrepresent the facts, they can wind up sending innocents to jail. And that's a problem for two reasons. First, there are a lot of powerful incentives that make prosecutors want to win—sometimes even at the expense of the truth. ("Winning has become more important than doing justice," complained Harvard Law School professor Alan Dershowitz in a 1999 *Chicago Tribune* interview. "Nobody runs for Senate saying 'I did justice.'") Second, when a prosecutor does step over the line, he rarely faces serious punishment.

How do we know? In 1999, *The Chicago Tribune* published a nationwide survey. They looked at all the murder cases in the past 40 years that had to be retried because a prosecutor hid evidence or permitted a witness to lie. They found 381 in all. What happened to the prosecutors in those cases? Almost nothing. About a dozen were investigated by state agencies, but only one was actually fired—and he was eventually reinstated. And not a single one of the offending prosecutors was ever convicted of either hiding or presenting false evidence. Indeed, not a single prosecutor in the history of the Republic has ever been convicted on those grounds—even though they're both felony offenses. As Pace University law professor Bennett Gershman told the *Tribune*: "There is no check on prosecutorial misconduct except for the prosecutor's own attitudes and beliefs and inner morality."

But isn't the defense bar a check on prosecutorial misconduct? Don't count on it. In December 1999, *The New York Times* noted that the number of legal aid lawyers in New York City's Criminal Court had dropped from 1,000 a decade ago to 500 today. And it quoted Manhattan defense attorney Ronald Kuby as saying that "No competent criminal defense lawyer zealously representing his clients can make a living on [legal aid rates]." This problem is obviously not limited to New York.

All this suggests that if we want to make certain prosecutors are doing the right thing, we have to police them more aggressively. That means creating well-muscled independent agencies that have strong incentives to find out when prosecutors misbehave—and to fine, press charges, and/or fire them when they do. Judges should help them out by publishing the names of prosecutors who commit misconduct in their orders and opinions (not a common practice)—and circulating them to the independent watchdogs. And while we're on the subject, states should also set up similar watchdogs to police the police—both for abuse and sheer incompetence. There should be independent civilian commissions that not only have responsibility for overseeing police departments, but that also have the power to impose discipline on the departments when they stray.

*5. Abolish the Insanity Defense.* It is true that you have to be a bit crazy to shoot the President like John Hinckley, or to cut off your husband's penis like Lorena Bobbit—but should that affect the state's ability to keep you separated from the rest of society, where you might do further harm? If you are rich or high profile or just plain lucky enough to find a defense lawyer who can successfully argue the insanity defense on your behalf, it can.

Consider the case of Tomar Cooper Locker, who opened fire on a crowded D.C. hospital ward—killing a boxer named Ruben Bell and wounding five bystanders. The apparent motive for the shooting was that Locker had a vendetta against Bell, whom he thought had killed his girlfriend. But Locker pled insanity based on the claim that he was suffering from a momentary attack of post-traumatic stress disorder—a claim endorsed by the same psychiatrist who testified in the Lorena Bobbit incident. The jury bought it. Locker was then committed to St. Elizabeth's Hospital, where he was treated for two whole months until, earlier this spring, doctors declared him fit to reenter society.

Michael Lazas is another example of someone who slipped through the system as a result of the insanity defense. In 1993, Lazas was found not guilty by reason of insanity for strangling his infant son and sent to Maryland's Perkins Hospital Center. It was his second violent assault; two years earlier he had stabbed a picnic companion in the throat. In 1998, Perkins officials thought Lazas was ready for a group home, so they moved him to an essentially zero-security facility in Burtonsville, Maryland. In February of this year, Lazas simply walked away from the Burtonsville facility. He was reportedly gone for four days before anyone notified the authorities he was missing.

In both cases, the public would have been better served if there were no insanity defense. There is no dispute that Locker and Lazas did what they were accused of doing. As a society, we've made a judgment that people who do these things need to be separated from the rest of us for a certain amount of time. Locker and Lazas should each have been found guilty and served the requisite time for his offenses—in an appropriate treatment facility to the extent necessary. The law should not force chronic schizophrenics to do hard time in maximum-security prisons. But it should be adamant about finding ways to keep those who commit violent crimes at a safe distance from the rest of society.

## Lock up the right people

Politicians who vote for mandatory minimum sentences stake a claim to being tough on crime. Politicians who vote against them run the risk of appearing weak. Of course in a perfect world, "toughness" would be assessed by whether you put the right (i.e., most dangerous) people in jail—rather than how many people you put in jail. But the world of sentencing statutes is far from perfect.

The political blindness that surrounds these laws can be partly traced to the death of Len Bias—a Maryland basketball star who had been the Celtics' first pick in the NBA draft. When Bias overdosed on cocaine in his college dorm room in 1986, he become an overnight poster child for the war on drugs. It was an election year and Beltway legislators, who were close enough to Maryland to be caught up in the public horror at Bias' death, wanted to make a statement. So they replaced a set of temporary federal sentencing guidelines that had been in place with permanent "mandatory minimum" sentencing requirements. States followed suit with their own iterations of these requirements. And in 1994, California and Washington added a new wrinkle when they passed so-called "three strikes laws" that require courts to give 25-year minimum sentences to any two-time felony offender who steps out of line a third time—even if to commit a misdemeanor offense.

These laws have generated some spectacularly unfair results. For example, a California court recently sentenced Michael Wayne Riggs, a homeless man, to 25 years in jail for stealing a bottle of vitamins. His most serious prior offense was snatching a purse.

But if Riggs' story is maddening at the individual level, the major concern at the policy level is what all this chest-thumping legislation is doing to our nation's prison system. There are roughly 2 million Americans behind bars, of whom more than half are there for non-violent (in most cases drug-related) crimes. The country spends $31 billion per year on corrections—twice what it spent 10 years ago. There is still not enough room in America's prisons.

Even looking past the overcrowding issues, however, sentencing laws have proven to be losers. Sending minor drug offenders to jail exposes them to hardened criminals and increases the risk of them committing more serious felonies when they get out. The Rand Corporation has found that mandatory minimums are the least cost-effective way to reduce drug use and crime—as compared to treatment programs and discretionary sentencing. Even White House Drug Czar Barry McCaffery has acknowledged that "we can't incarcerate our way out of the drug problem." It is therefore unsurprising that a dozen or so states have formed commissions to reconsider their rigid sentencing policies and several, like Michigan, have begun to repeal them. And on the progressive front, Arizona recently became the first state to offer the option of drug treatment, rather than prison to its non-violent offenders convicted on drug charges.

Arizona's program is both cost efficient and makes sense. A California study found that one dollar spent on drug treatment saves seven dollars in reduced hospital admissions and law enforcement costs. These savings can be put to better use elsewhere in the criminal justice system. For example, they can be used to help communities develop facilities to siphon off non-violent offenders from the heart of the system. Roughly two percent of the nation's drug offender traffic is processed in special "drug courts," which dole out a combination of light sentencing—such as short jail terms, community service, and probation—plus mandatory drug treatment. More drug courts would almost certainly be a good thing.

Communities also do themselves a service when they set up tough probation programs that actually help minor offenders steer away from trouble. Orange County, California has had substantial success with a program that involves 6 a.m. inspection visits to all participants from program officers, surprise drug testing, counseling, and monthly evaluations by the supervising judge. Anecdotal evidence suggests that in order to work these programs have to be ready to dish out real discipline to participants who fail to live up to their end of the bargain. Orange County participant Dale Wilson, who had been addicted to cocaine for three decades before joining the program, told the *Los Angeles Times* that he was sent to jail for nine days when he had a relapse. "It's a strict program," he said. "But I never would've gotten to the point to keep me sober if I hadn't been faced with these punishments."

## Put More Order in the Courts

Finally, we shouldn't forget that the best laws and policies in the world aren't going to do a whole lot of good unless we have reliable, industrious, and smoothly administered courts. And while there are lots of hard-working judges with the same objective, there are also plenty of clunkers.

In a 1996 San Francisco case, for example, two municipal court judges batted a domestic violence case back and forth on an October Friday. According to *The Recorder*, a legal newspaper, Judge Wallace Douglass was supposed to hear the case—but he double-booked another trial for the same day. So he sent it across the hall to Judge Ellen Chaitin, who held a mid-day conference—and then sent it back to Douglass when it failed to settle by the early afternoon. Douglass then said that he couldn't find a jury to hear the case (it was Friday afternoon, after all) and, because a delay would have violated the defendant's speedy trial rights, he dismissed it. This calls to mind the story of the Manhattan judge who in 1971 adjourned a robbery trial to catch a flight to Europe. Another trial would have violated the defendant's constitutional rights, so he walked away scot-free.

The problem is two-fold. One is that judges don't always push themselves that hard. In 1989, *Manhattan Lawyer* correspondents observed that, on average, the judges in Manhattan's criminal court were in session about four and a half hours a day. Sixty-two percent spent less than five hours in session, and 42 percent started after 10 a.m.

In Baltimore, which has more than 300 homicides per year, you can sometimes walk through a criminal courthouse around 3:30 or 4:00 p.m. and find courtrooms that have adjourned for the day.

But the additional problem is that judges are too often inclined to schedule things first for their own convenience, second for the convenience of lawyers, and last of all for the convenience of the people the system should be bending over to accommodate—jurors and witnesses. One prosecutor said that there are days in D.C. Superior Court that unfold as follows: The jury is instructed to arrive at 10 a.m. and sits for hours while the judge kibbitzes with the lawyers over technical legal issues. Sometimes the kibbitzing runs right into lunch. Then everybody trundles off for a two hour break. The trial starts in earnest at 3 p.m. And court adjourns between 4:30 and 5 p.m.—sometimes earlier.

Lack of organization is another problem. Washington D.C.'s Superior Court has no central scheduling mechanism. Judges control their own dockets and are allowed to book two or three trials for the same day, anticipating that there will be pleas and continuances. Policemen who are supposed to testify wind up milling around the courthouse for days on end, waiting for their trials to be called, and—if they otherwise happen to be off-duty—collecting overtime.

It has to be possible to run a tighter ship because some judges already do. As noted in last month's "Tilting at Windmills," for example, a Tennessee judge named Duane Slone has adopted a policy that he won't hear plea bargains on the day a trial is scheduled to begin. This saves the jury from having to sit and wait while lawyers haggle over a plea and allows trials to start promptly at 9 a.m. Common sense courtesies like this could kill a lot of the inefficiencies that you see in courtrooms today. But more importantly, disciplinary panels need to keep better tabs on the courts and punish (by fines or demotions if necessary) those judges who fail to show up on time, stay all day, and run an orderly docket.

## What Next?

Wholesale reform of the criminal justice system obviously isn't going to happen overnight. Some reforms can only be made by Supreme Court decision. Others will have to be effected through new laws and practices at the federal, state, and local levels. Still, it's a set of tasks well worth facing. It's great that crime is down but if we want it to stay there, and if we want to make sure that we're sending the right people to jail, then we need a system that we can really trust beyond a reasonable doubt.

*Research assistance provided by Elisabeth Frater and Patrick Esposito*

# On Patrol

### The tough job of police officer gets more complicated every day

By Eli Lehrer

**B**ored after writing a few traffic tickets, throwing a foul-mouthed malingerer out of a hospital, and grabbing a bite to eat, Fort Myers patrol officer Rebecca Prince heads toward "the crack McDonald's. " That's what she calls a run-down heap of leaky garden apartments on Bramen Avenue, just off a commercial corridor cluttered with gas stations, rent-to-own furniture stores, and taco stands. Even on a January night just a few degrees above freezing, it takes Prince only five minutes to find a wrongdoer.

On a side street, Christine Bosewell, a prostitute whom Prince has arrested "20 or 30 times, minimum" makes an appearance. Bosewell, a computer check confirms, has a thick pile of warrants—enough for an arrest—for failing to pay the loitering tickets Prince writes. Prince calls another officer for backup and searches Bosewell thoroughly. She finds a crack pipe in Bosewell's bra, a can of mace in her pocket, and a knife in her purse. Prince smashes the pipe and tosses the knife down a sewer, then handcuffs Bosewell and takes her back to the city's police station for booking and lockup.

As the crackling police radio grows silent around 9 p.m., Prince answers a false burglar alarm, yells at a gas station owner who lets drug dealing go on in his parking lot, and takes time to chat with a storekeeper grown weary of his neighborhood addicts.

Around 11, Prince stops a dented maroon Cadillac running a red light. A cloud of marijuana smoke strong enough to make a visitor dizzy hits Prince's face as soon as she opens the door. The smoke provides probable cause for a search. Prince calls for other officers, and four more cruisers soon appear. The search turns up a bag of cocaine, some crack, and a package of marijuana. The drug-using driver goes back to the station.

The evening didn't include the violence or physical danger that cops on TV face nearly every episode. Indeed, because of the unusual cold the night brought less action than typical. But for a good cop like Prince it was a fairly normal turn at the office. And thanks to her efforts, the neighborhood immediately became a little less ugly and dangerous.

**L**ast year marked the ninth consecutive year of declining crime in America, though the drop was the smallest since rates started falling, and in the South crime actually rose. Still, the last decade represents the longest sustained period of crime reduction since our nation started keeping systematic statistics in 1934. Increased imprisonment, successful campaigns against drug use, favorable demographic trends, improvements in urban design, a revival of civil society in some inner cities, the peaking of underclass illegitimacy, and the end of cash-entitlement welfare have all helped to reduce crime. But great strides in the way police operate have also helped.

With an eye toward documenting crime fighting today, *TAE* recently researched the twin cities of Fort Myers and Cape Coral, Florida. Located on opposite sides of the Caloosahatchee River in southwestern Florida, Fort Myers and Cape Coral reveal how American crime is evolving, and how police are responding.

Fort Myers is a fairly typical U.S. city—centralized around a downtown, racially diverse, a bit stressed and chaotic, but fairly prosperous. The town's population of around 48,000 is about 30 percent black and 8 percent Latino, with whites (many of them retirees) making up the balance. Around 15 percent of residents live in poverty.

Florida has the highest crime rate of any American state —about twice the national average. While crime fell in the state during the 1990s, Florida still has a long way to go. Several of its cities rank among America's most dangerous.

Fort Myers in particular is an extremely high-crime area by national standards. In 2000, it experienced 125 serious reported crimes per 1,000 residents. That makes it around three times more dangerous than New York City, about twice as dangerous as Chicago, about the same as St. Louis, the most crime ridden large city (over 100,000 population) in the country. Fort Myers' crime rates are about four times the national average.

Like some other southern cities, Fort Myers de-incorporated certain black areas during the 1950s in order to keep newly enfranchised African Americans out of city politics. The unincorporated areas—poor and crime-ridden—resemble numerous little islands floating deep in-

PBS STUDIO/SAM JOHNSON

**Officer Rebecca Prince**

Yet, like most of Florida, Cape Coral has more crime than comparable communities in other parts of America. It reported 37 serious crimes per 1,000 residents in 2000 (compared to Fort Myers' 125). That puts Cape Coral just about at the national average—which is high for a low-poverty bedroom community. And while crime rates fell a bit last year in Fort Myers, they rose in Cape Coral.

Cape Coral and Fort Myers both have professional police departments with dynamic, well-respected chiefs at the top. Fort Myers Chief Larry Hart is known nationally for urging the use of big-city community policing strategies in mid-sized cities. Cape Coral Chief Arnold Gibbs takes great pride in his department's certification from the Commission on Accreditation for Law Enforcement Agencies. Neither department, however, does anything truly extraordinary. Each has about 160 sworn officers authorized to use weapons and make arrests.

Police work is a helping profession that sometimes involves the use of violence. Police arrest murderers, hunt down missing children, stop unsafe motorists, settle quarrels between neighbors, collar shoplifters, and scatter unruly crowds. They do these things better than other citizens because they are authorized to apply force if necessary. Police must walk a fine line between being gentle enough to inspire trust and confidence while being sturdy enough to deter crime by force if pushed into that. The police thus have a nearly impossible task: They must use fear to mitigate fear.

The latest and most promising attempt to manage this difficult assignment is something called "community policing," which aims to prevent crime by working with the community to keep order. As the twentieth century unfolded, the need for courtesy, pre-emptive problem-solving, and community partnerships tended to get lost in other police priorities. Responding quickly to emergency calls became the chief goal, and so rapid mobility in cars, new technologies, reactive investigations, and paramilitary command structures were emphasized.

Today, police departments again emphasize human skills, for even the most routine police activities can demand a good deal of interpersonal deftness. At 7:30 on a quiet Thursday night, Cape Coral patrol officer Steve Petrovich responds to a radio call about a car accident. A gray-haired man in a sweatshirt has crinkled the sheet metal of his Oldsmobile by pulling in front of a pickup truck. A Taurus, trying to avoid the pile up, has run off the road. Petrovich helps a colleague administer a series of field sobriety tests.

The Oldsmobile driver, obviously inebriated, goes through a long series of kindergarten-like exercises. Asked to count backwards from 76, he recites, "76, 78, 73, 72, 75." He misses several times when asked to touch his finger to his nose. "Those tests must look pretty silly" remarks Petrovich. "But if we don't do them, we don't get the people, or we don't make good arrests. It's that sim-

side city boundaries. They present headaches for the police, because city officers cannot make arrests or conduct investigations in the unincorporated neighborhoods without calling in the Lee County Sheriff. Criminals know this and sometimes conduct their business on the jurisdictional boundaries, fleeing one way if a city cruiser pulls up, and another way if it's a sheriff's car.

Cape Coral is entirely different. It began one day in 1957 when Jack and Leonard Rosen—Baltimore cosmetics manufacturers turned hardball swampland salesmen—staked out a Florida field of dreams. Within ten years a community of 50,000 people grew up; the 100,000th resident moved in last year. Though in population it is now a bigger "city" than neighboring Fort Myers, Cape Coral remains mostly a sprawling bedroom community, with some commercial strip malls strung along the main highways—a classic suburbanized sunbelt creation, full of transplants and retirees occupying low-slung single-family houses that front a grid of numbered streets and canals. The city has little poverty. About 95 percent of residents are white, though an increasing number of blacks have purchased homes in recent years to escape Fort Myers' urban ills. There are no terrible neighborhoods, and the "bad" parts of town consist of short stretches of cheesy tract homes with unkempt lawns and trash in the yards.

ple." As he is being handcuffed, the man quietly admits to drunk driving.

# Policing has become a very complex helping profession, as tricky and demanding as teaching or nursing.

While the procedures of DWI stops can be taught fairly easily, a failure to follow them can cause enormous problems and some aspects of patrol work require far more discretion. Later that evening, Petrovich is called to a subdivided ranch house on a barren lot. A woman and her live-in boyfriend have gotten into a serious fight over his failure to accompany their daughter to receive an award at school. Their well-furnished but messy home, littered with fast-food packages, empty beer cans, and Harlequin romances, smells heavily of alcohol. The woman seems drunker than her boyfriend. Petrovich and another officer who assists refer to everyone as "sir" and "ma'am" and are consistently respectful to the intoxicated couple.

The man and woman tell contradictory stories: She complains he sexually propositioned a neighbor, while he says she hit him in a rage. The officers' professional attitude calms the angry couple and wins the trust of their dark-haired, dark-eyed daughter. Standing a few feet away from her parents in the kitchen, the daughter quickly warms to Petrovich. He questions her gently, sounding more like a teacher than a cop as he gracefully mixes concern and sternness.

The 12-year-old tells Petrovich that her mother, drunk as usual, started the argument, although not the physical violence. Her father, whom she thinks has a criminal record, hits her mother a lot. After talking also with some neighbors, who frequently hear the couple arguing but aren't sure who threw the first punch this time, Petrovich hauls the man off to the police station. "It's often impossible to tell what happened for sure, but you always have to try to make a solid decision," he explains. "I just believed the girl. She's pretty mature." Petrovich's procedures show a good command of police ethics: He starts without any assumption of guilt or innocence, treats people with respect, and shows special deference toward children.

Many times, the most important part of police work is just to be quick. Around 6:30 one evening Fort Myers patrol officer Joseph Schwartz is called to an area behind a notoriously troublesome liquor store where men and women congregate to drink malt liquor. A fight has just occurred as our cruiser pulls up, in a lot littered with 40-ounce malt liquor bottles and cans. Two women eye each other threateningly. An older man lies on the ground twitching, obviously drunk or on drugs. Nobody in the crowd welcomes Schwartz's presence, and dark stares greet him. The crowd claims the man lying on the ground "hit his head on the sign." Schwartz orders people to clear out. By showing the colors, he scatters the crowd and avoids a situation that could have turned ugly fast.

Even in a high-crime city like Fort Myers, officers often go an entire night without making an arrest. Their activities to prevent crime *before* it happens, and to collect problem-solving information about crimes that have taken place earlier, can be just as valuable as a collar, though. Police officers have a tremendous amount of latitude in many aspects of their work, and, in trying to squelch crime before and after the fact, professional training can take an officer only so far. The best ones have strong instincts for fixing problems.

Like other proactive cops, Rebecca Prince uses her powers of observation to fight crime. By paying careful attention to little infractions, she often uncovers big ones. The night after Prince arrested Christine Bosewell and the drug-using Cadillac driver, Fort Myers' police headquarters buzzes with news of a two-man burglary ring that broke into nearly 20 homes and businesses over New Year's weekend. During his roll call briefing, Scott Cain, Prince's watch supervisor, asks officers to look out for two African-American men, one taller than average and the other perhaps 6'7".

Thanks to the freakish cold, things remain slow for Prince on that night's patrol. Once again she cruises the area near the crack McDonald's. Soon she comes upon a hard-looking bleached-blonde woman with sun-leathered skin and missing teeth, clearly intoxicated or on drugs. Prince, who often works this area as a hooker decoy in undercover stings, knows her well, and reports she has a closetful of previous citations for prostitution. Unlike Bosewell, who was resigned to spending an evening in jail, this woman badly wants to stay out of lockup. Prince proves willing to deal. "What can you give me?" she asks, shuffling the prostitute into her patrol car. Prince listens to stories about drug dealing at well-known locations. "Give me something better!" she demands.

Finally, the hooker comes up with some street information Prince can use: a story of two men, one tall and one very tall, who are running a burglary ring out of a white house at the end of a cul de sac. The house backs up onto a wooded strip separating it from a parking lot on the other side. According to Prince's informant, the men unload their booty in the parking lot and use a shopping cart to transport it to the house. Thinking she's hit pay dirt, Prince gives the prostitute a lift to a sleazy bar (even promising to bring her back home at the end of the night), and heads for the dead-end street.

The house comes into view just as Prince's informant described it: a low-lying white residence with a junky yard, backing perfectly up against a strip of no-man's land that leads to the parking lot on the commercial strip. The driveway is empty late at night. But lights burn inside, and the bed sheets which hang over the windows ripple when Prince shines her patrol car's spotlight on the home's exterior.

Calling for backup, Prince decides to investigate. Another officer comes to wait in the street and Prince walks up to the door. When two young women answer the door, Prince launches into a convincing patter about a complaint from neighbors about a loud stereo. The women, who say they're "baby-sitting for a friend" stand firmly in the doorway, blush and fidget as Prince talks with them and looks over their shoulders. There's no noise from a stereo, yet the women apologize anyway. But they stand blocking her entrance to the house.

## They must find crime before it finds them.

Convinced something suspicious is afoot, and hoping her imaginative approach may have broken a bothersome case, Prince calls her supervisor. He has an officer posted on the roof of a nearby building to lie in wait for the burglars to return and start unloading their loot. He also offers a gentle reprimand to Prince: Without knowing it, she had strayed into one of the islands of real estate in the middle of the city that is supposed to be under the sheriff's jurisdiction, not her department's.

In many quiet neighborhoods and towns across America, good policing may just mean carefully training officers, avoiding corruption, and showing up quickly when people call. But police need more creative strategies in areas with high levels of transience or neighborhood decay, areas experiencing cultural dashes between ethnic groups, places poisoned by replacement of the work ethic with a welfare culture, neighborhoods with weak community standards, or streets infested with gangs or drug dealing. In particular, police have learned they need to partner with the community to stop crime *before* it happens.

This is an important principle behind "community policing," which nearly every police department in the country now claims to practice. It involves getting to know local residents; searching for long-term solutions to problems like vagrancy, derelict housing, and unsupervised juveniles; and eventually, teaching neighborhoods to police themselves.

Michael Titmuss is a former restaurant and nightclub owner who decided he wanted to help people, became a cop, and eventually a Fort Myers Community Policing Coordinator. Titmuss epitomizes the new type of officer who fixes local problems that breed crime, rather than simply responding to emergency calls on the radio. While he has the same rank and about the same pay as a patrol officer, Titmuss has a far different way of working. He focuses on making allies among local residents and businesspeople, finding the sources of neighborhood crime spikes, and then formulating solutions.

Titmuss begins by keeping in close touch with the four-square-mile area he's assigned to police. The counterman in a deli greets him by name. When he passes a notorious problem property, he explains chapter and verse the owner's habit of trading sex for rent. Driving through a motel that once provided "offices" for many of the area's prostitutes but now features gurgling fountains, a bronze sculpture of dolphins, and a German-speaking staff catering to tourists, Titmuss launches into a five-minute discourse about an angel developer who has remade many of the worst areas on this beat.

PBS STUDIO/SAM JOHNSON

**Officer Michael Titmuss**

Titmuss doesn't spend all his time on community relations. When a puff of smoke materializes behind railroad tracks, he speeds off to investigate. The fire department takes care of the fire but Titmuss radios in a report on some suspicious-looking youths nearby. "Ultimately, I've got to work with the patrol force," Titmuss says. "If I go to a block-watch meeting and people feel that the police won't do anything, then I can run all the youth programs in the world and it won't make a difference. I've got to know everything a patrol officer does and more."

This philosophy has helped Titmuss mobilize a series of revitalization task forces in his neighborhood. He has spearheaded mass trash pick-ups, set up new programs for children, and gotten abandoned buildings harboring vagrants knocked down. He has spent hundreds of hours compiling lists of the owners and managers of problem properties in the area, many of them out-of-towners. He is currently working to convert a long-closed bowling alley in a commercially critical shopping center into a center for area youth. Inside the mildewed structure he sketches his vision of a police- and city-run activity center with a snack bar, homework rooms, and boxing rings. And with his long background in successful nightclub operations, Titmuss's plans are practical and hard-nosed, not pipe dreams. Describing the uses of high ceilings, he explains "I always liked to use bowling alleys for clubs: lots of floor space with no internal supports."

His approach draws raves from community leaders. "It's a professional effort that does what we need them to," says Tony Corsentino, a former diner owner who heads the Palm Beach Boulevard Development Corporation near Titmuss's home base. "I didn't believe it would work out, but when we got a police officer who could coordinate all the city agencies we really did something about crime. The neighborhood is a lot cleaner and a lot safer." Even ordinary citizens notice the local police seem a little more helpful. "I've had problems with the cops in the past," one woman told *TAE*. "But when I call them, they listen."

## Titmuss epitomizes the new type of officer who fixes local problems that breed crime, rather than simply responding to emergency calls on the radio.

Titmuss argues that this method of policing creates long-term crime solutions. "I can sometimes arrest someone and they're out on the street the next day. That isn't very efficient. Or I can work with property owners to get him evicted. That solves the problem for that one guy pretty much permanently." In a typical afternoon, Titmuss might spend an hour or so on paperwork, a few more working with area kids, a few minutes chatting with local business owners and landlords, and an hour or two helping some patrol officers plan a raid on a gas station where drug sales have surged. He'll also find time to back up his colleagues on a few calls, take four or five radio calls himself, and maybe even collar a vandal.

Most patrol officers seem to respect the community cops. Some have doubts, however. "A lot of them slack off," complained one patrol officer. "They don't need to do anything; so unless they're naturally energetic, they aren't *going* to do anything." Working against this skepticism, both Fort Myers and Cape Coral are now trying to make community policing a department-wide philosophy, not just the work of a few specialized officers.

If these efforts succeed, the benefits could extend to officers as well as the city. Titmuss says he finds his job satisfying on many levels. "I can go home every day knowing I've made a positive difference in somebody's life. You work patrol long enough, and you swear there's not a decent human being on the face of this earth," he sighs. "But I can do this job and be convinced people are basically good."

Many traditional patrol officers admit they know only a handful of people on their beats, most of them bad guys. This is particularly a problem in the anonymous residential suburbia of Cape Coral. Despite the generally excellent relations between residents and the police in Cape Coral, officers *TAE* spoke with struggled to come up with the name of even one citizen in the large swath of tract homes they patrolled each evening.

Poor architecture and city design can do that. The atomized, sidewalk-less world of Cape Coral tends to make casual contact difficult or impossible. Though residential Cape Coral has more neighborhood watches than Fort Myers, its sterile civic grid makes neighborliness difficult. "All over the city we identify neighborhood watches by the chair's home address, because the neighborhoods don't have names," explains Brad Johnson, president of Cape Coral's citywide neighborhood watch federation.

Of course, police-community partnerships can only go so far in preventing crime. When miscreants go on the prowl, the police will still need to respond to protect the population. Finding and eliminating such crimes can be done through conventional sting operations and busts, or through more creative "problem solving" approaches.

Problem-solving policing aims not just to solve individual crimes, but to eliminate conditions that underlie lawbreaking. The focus is not on massive social forces like poverty and racism, which would be fruitless for police to try to battle. Rather, problem-solving police teams attempt to fix localized problems of disorder, decay, idleness, and inadequate oversight. Usually this begins with insights gathered through simple patrol work.

On a quiet Fort Myers side street between an apartment complex and a park lies a small wooden house that has become a hangout for prostitutes. The local community policing coordinator has discovered that the resident owner is a retired New York City cop who is providing a haven in return for sexual favors and drugs. Local officers are keeping a close eye on the place.

When a crowd of cars outside the house attracts her attention during one evening patrol, Rebecca Prince decides to knock on the door and see what happens. The retired cop comes to the door in his bathrobe, trim and courteous. She asks to come in. He isn't obligated to let her, but does anyway. Inside, a surreal scene greets the visitors: Perhaps eight women lie around the house, some of them in strange postures. The rooms are spic and span, but almost devoid of furniture. A couple snuggles under a blanket. Prince strolls around, politely but firmly giving the owner a piece of her mind. "You see those girls over there… they have AIDS!" she exclaims. "I know them to be prostitutes. Are you aware of that?" The man protests that the hookers are simply friends whom he rents rooms to. She berates him for a few more minutes for allowing his house to become a serious neighborhood nuisance, then leaves.

Prince knows that any girl she locked up that night for some minor drug or sex offense would likely return to the house within a few days. Frustrated, she brainstorms for a solution. Soon she radios an older, highly experienced officer, fiftyish, with a bit of a beer belly. Meeting him outside a dark building where he was making a burglary check, Prince explains the situation in her neighborhood, says she wants the owner out, and picks her colleague's brain for advice.

After kicking around some complex nuisance-abatement laws, Prince mentions that the proprietor of the cat house said he is renting rooms. The older officer lights up. "You can get him for that," he says. "If he's running a boarding house without a license you can close the place down this week. It ain't a prostitution or drug conviction, but it'll make the problem go away." Her eyes shining, Prince makes a note to start the paperwork the next day with city housing officials.

The new methods of policing ask a lot of officers. They must be less detached, and much more personally involved with individuals. They must find crime before it finds them. They must work in tandem with many other arms of government, as well as with private businesses and civic organizations. At times it can be like wrestling with jello.

Policing has become a very complex helping profession. It may not match the sophistication of heart surgery, but in its current day-to-day practice, policing is easily as tricky and demanding as teaching or nursing.

But if the police are to become more effective, there is probably no alternative. They must help strengthen the bonds that hold American society together. Healthy civilizations depend on people controlling those impulses that bring them momentary pleasure at the expense of the community's good. The police need to step in when that fails, sometimes with force. But the best cops today use their leverage to help communities heal themselves.

*TAE contributing writer Eli Lehrer, visiting fellow at the Heritage Foundation, has observed at roughly 40 different law enforcement agencies while writing a book on policing.*

# The Terrorism to Come

By WALTER LAQUEUR

TERRORISM HAS BECOME over a number of years the topic of ceaseless comment, debate, controversy, and search for roots and motives, and it figures on top of the national and international agenda. It is also at present one of the most highly emotionally charged topics of public debate, though quite why this should be the case is not entirely clear, because the overwhelming majority of participants do not sympathize with terrorism.

Confusion prevails, but confusion alone does not explain the emotions. There is always confusion when a new international phenomenon appears on the scene. This was the case, for instance, when communism first appeared (it was thought to be aiming largely at the nationalization of women and the burning of priests) and also fascism. But terrorism is not an unprecedented phenomenon; it is as old as the hills.

Thirty years ago, when the terrorism debate got underway, it was widely asserted that terrorism was basically a left-wing revolutionary movement caused by oppression and exploitation. Hence the conclusion: Find a political and social solution, remedy the underlying evil—no oppression, no terrorism. The argument about the left-wing character of terrorism is no longer frequently heard, but the belief in a fatal link between poverty and violence has persisted. Whenever a major terrorist attack has taken place, one has heard appeals from high and low to provide credits and loans, to deal at long last with the deeper, true causes of terrorism, the roots rather than the symptoms and outward manifestations. And these roots are believed to be poverty, unemployment, backwardness, and inequality.

It is not too difficult to examine whether there is such a correlation between poverty and terrorism, and all the investigations have shown that this is not the case. The experts have maintained for a long time that poverty does not cause terrorism and prosperity does not cure it. In the world's 50 poorest countries there is little or no terrorism. A study by scholars Alan Krueger and Jitka Maleckova reached the conclusion that the terrorists are not poor people and do not come from poor societies. A Harvard economist has shown that economic growth is closely related to a society's ability to manage conflicts. More recently, a study of India has demonstrated that terrorism in the subcontinent has occurred in the most prosperous (Punjab) and most egalitarian (Kashmir, with a poverty ratio of 3.5 compared with the national average of 26 percent) regions and that, on the other hand, the poorest regions such as North Bihar have been free of terrorism. In the Arab countries (such as Egypt and Saudi Arabia, but also in North Africa), the terrorists originated not in the poorest and most neglected districts but hailed from places with concentrations of radical preachers. The backwardness, if any, was intellectual and cultural—not economic and social.

## It is no secret that terrorists operating in Europe and America are usually of middle-class origin.

These findings, however, have had little impact on public opinion (or on many politicians), and it is not difficult to see why. There is the general feeling that poverty and backwardness with all their concomitants are bad—and that there is an urgent need to do much more about these problems. Hence the inclination to couple the two issues and the belief that if the (comparatively) wealthy Western nations would contribute much more to the development and welfare of the less fortunate, in cooperation with their governments, this would be in a long-term perspective the best, perhaps the only, effective way to solve the terrorist problem.

Reducing poverty in the Third World is a moral as well as a political and economic imperative, but to expect from it a decisive change in the foreseeable future as far as terrorism is concerned is unrealistic, to say the least. It ignores both the causes of backwardness and poverty and the motives for terrorism.

Poverty combined with youth unemployment does create a social and psychological climate in which Islamism and various populist and religious sects flourish, which in turn provide some of the footfolk for violent groups in internal conflicts. According to some projections, the number of young unemployed in the Arab world and North Africa could reach 50 million in two decades. Such a situation will not be conducive to political stability; it will increase the demographic pressure on Europe, since according to polls a majority of these young people want to emigrate. Politically, the populist discontent will be directed against the rulers—Islamist in Iran, moderate in countries such as Egypt, Jordan, or Morocco. But how to help the failed economies of the Middle East and North Africa? What are the reasons for backwardness and stagnation in this part of the world? The countries that have made economic progress—such as China and India, Korea and Taiwan, Malaysia and Turkey—did so without massive foreign help.

All this points to a deep malaise and impending danger, but not to a direct link between the economic situation and international terrorism. There is of course a negative link: Terrorists will not hesitate to bring about a further aggravation in the situation; they certainly did great harm to the tourist industries in Bali and Egypt, in Palestine, Jordan, and Morocco. One of the main targets of terrorism in Iraq was the oil industry. It is no longer a secret that the carriers of international terrorism operating in Europe and America hail not from the poor, downtrodden, and unemployed but are usually of middle-class origin.

## The local element

*T*HE LINK BETWEEN terrorism and nationalist, ethnic, religious, and tribal conflict is far more tangible. These instances of terrorism are many and need not be enumerated in detail. Solving these conflicts would probably bring about a certain reduction in the incidence of terrorism. But the conflicts are many, and if some of them have been defused in recent years, other, new ones have emerged. Nor are the issues usually clear-cut or the bones of contention easy to define—let alone to solve.

If the issue at stake is a certain territory or the demand for autonomy, a compromise through negotiations might be achieved. But it ought to be recalled that al Qaeda was founded and September 11 occurred not because of a territorial dispute or the feeling of national oppression but because of a religious commandment—jihad and the establishment of *shari'ah*. Terrorist attacks in Central Asia and Morocco, in Saudi Arabia, Algeria, and partly in Iraq were directed against fellow Muslims, not against infidels. Appeasement may work in individual cases, but terrorist groups with global ambitions cannot be appeased by territorial concessions.

As in the war against poverty, the initiatives to solve local conflicts are overdue and should be welcomed. In an ideal world, the United Nations would be the main conflict resolver, but so far the record of the U.N. has been more than modest, and it is unlikely that this will change in the foreseeable future. Making peace is not an easy option; it involves funds and in some cases the stationing of armed forces. There is no great international crush to join

the ranks of the volunteers: China, Russia, and Europe do not want to be bothered, and the United States is overstretched. In brief, as is so often the case, a fresh impetus is likely to occur only if the situation gets considerably worse and if the interests of some of the powers in restoring order happen to coincide.

Lastly, there should be no illusions with regard to the wider effect of a peaceful solution of one conflict or another. To give but one obvious example: Peace (or at least the absence of war) between Israel and the Palestinians would be a blessing for those concerned. It may be necessary to impose a solution since the chances of making any progress in this direction are nil but for some outside intervention. However, the assumption that a solution of a local conflict (even one of great symbolic importance) would have a dramatic effect in other parts of the world is unfounded. Osama bin Laden did not go to war because of Gaza and Nablus; he did not send his warriors to fight in Palestine. Even the disappearance of the "Zionist entity" would not have a significant impact on his supporters, except perhaps to provide encouragement for further action.

## *Osama bin Laden did not go to war because of Gaza and Nablus.*

Such a warning against illusions is called for because there is a great deal of wishful thinking and naïveté in this respect—a belief in quick fixes and miracle solutions: If only there would be peace between Israelis and Palestinians, all the other conflicts would become manageable. But the problems are as much in Europe, Asia, and Africa as in the Middle East; there is a great deal of free-floating aggression which could (and probably would) easily turn in other directions once one conflict has been defused.

It seems likely, for instance, that in the years to come the struggle against the "near enemy" (the governments of the Arab and some non-Arab Muslim countries) will again feature prominently. There has been for some time a truce on the part of al Qaeda and related groups, partly for strategic reasons (to concentrate on the fight against America and the West) and partly because attacks against fellow Muslims, even if they are considered apostates, are bound to be less popular than fighting the infidels. But this truce, as events in Saudi Arabia and elsewhere show, may be coming to an end.

Tackling these supposed sources of terrorism, even for the wrong reasons, will do no harm and may bring some good. But it does not bring us any nearer to an understanding of the real sources of terrorism, a field that has become something akin to a circus ground for riding hobbyhorses and peddling preconceived notions.

How to explain the fact that in an inordinate number of instances where there has been a great deal of explosive material, there has been no terrorism? The gypsies of Europe certainly had many grievances and the Dalets (untouchables) of India and other Asian countries even more. But there has been no terrorism on their part—just as the Chechens have been up in arms but not the Tartars of Russia, the Basque but not the Catalans of Spain. The list could easily be lengthened.

Accident may play a role (the absence or presence of a militant leadership), but there could also be a cultural-psychological predisposition. How to explain that out of 100 militants believing with equal intensity in the justice of their cause, only a very few will actually engage in terrorist actions? And out of this small minority even fewer will be willing to sacrifice their lives as suicide bombers? Imponderable factors might be involved: indoctrination but also psychological motives. Neither economic nor political analysis will be of much help in gaining an understanding, and it may not be sheer accident that there has been great reluctance to explore this political-intellectual minefield.

# The focus on Islamist terrorism

$T$O MAKE PREDICTIONS about the future course of terrorism is even more risky than political predictions in general. We are dealing here not with mass movements but small—sometimes very small—groups of people, and there is no known way at present to account for the movement of small particles either in the physical world or in human societies.

It is certain that terrorism will continue to operate. At the present time almost all attention is focused on Islamist terrorism, but it is useful to remember from time to time that this was not always the case—even less than 30 years ago—and that there are a great many conflicts, perceived oppressions, and other causes calling for radical action in the world which may come to the fore in the years to come. These need not even be major conflicts in an age in which small groups will have access to weapons of mass destruction.

At present, Islamist terrorism all but monopolizes our attention, and it certainly has not yet run its course. But it is unlikely that its present fanaticism will last forever; religious-nationalist fervor does not constantly burn with the same intensity. There is a phenomenon known in Egypt as "Salafi burnout," the mellowing of radical young people, the weakening of the original fanatical impetus. Like all other movements in history, messianic groups are subject to routinization, to the circulation of generations, to changing political circumstances, and to sudden or gradual changes in the intensity of religious belief. This could happen as a result of either victories or defeats. One day, it might be possible to appease militant Islamism—though hardly in a period of burning aggression when confidence and faith in global victory have not yet been broken.

More likely the terrorist impetus will decline as a result of setbacks. Fanaticism, as history shows, is not easy to transfer from one generation to the next; attacks will continue, and some will be crowned with success (perhaps spectacular success), but many will not. When Alfred Nobel invented dynamite, many terrorists thought that this was the answer to their prayers, but theirs was a false hope. The trust put today in that new invincible weapon, namely suicide terrorism, may in the end be equally misplaced. Even the use of weapons of mass destruction might not be the terrorist panacea some believe it will be. Perhaps their effect will be less deadly than anticipated; perhaps it will be so destructive as to be considered counterproductive. Statistics show that in the terrorist attacks over the past decade, considerably more Muslims were killed than infidels. Since terrorists do not operate in a vacuum, this is bound to lead to dissent among their followers and even among the fanatical preachers.

*Over the past decade, more Muslims were killed in terrorist attacks than infidels.*

There are likely to be splits among the terrorist groups even though their structure is not highly centralized. In brief, there is a probability that a united terrorist front will not last. It is unlikely that Osama and his close followers will be challenged on theological grounds, but there has been criticism for tactical reasons: Assuming that America and the West in general are in a state of decline, why did he not have more patience? Why did he have to launch a big attack while the infidels were still in a position to retaliate massively?

Some leading students of Islam have argued for a long time that radical Islamism passed its peak years ago and that its downfall and disappearance are only a question of time, perhaps not much time. It is true that societies that were exposed to the rule of fundamentalist fanatics (such as Iran) or to radical Islamist attack (such as Algeria) have been immunized to a certain extent. However, in a country of 60 million, some fanatics can always be found; as these lines are written, volunteers for suicide missions are being enlisted in Teheran and other cities of Iran. In any case, many countries have not yet undergone such firsthand experience; for them the rule of the *shari'ah* and the restoration of the caliphate are still brilliant dreams. By and large, therefore, the predictions about the impending demise of Islamism have been premature, while no doubt correct in the long run. Nor do we know what will follow. An interesting study on what happens "when prophecy fails" (by Leon Festinger) was published not long after World War II. We now need a similar study on the likely circumstances and consequences of the failure of fanaticism. The history of religions (and political religions) offers some clues, as does the history of terrorism.

These, then, are the likely perspectives for the more distant future. But in a shorter-term perspective the danger remains acute and may, in fact, grow. Where and when are terrorist attacks most likely to occur? They will not necessarily be directed against the greatest and most dangerous enemy as perceived by the terrorist gurus. Much depends on where terrorists are strong and believe the enemy to be weak. That terrorist attacks are likely to continue in the Middle East goes without saying; other main danger zones are Central Asia and, above all, Pakistan.

The founders of Pakistan were secular politicians. The religious establishment and in particular the extremists among the Indian Muslims had opposed the emergence of the state. But once Pakistan came into being, they began to try with considerable success to dominate it. Their alternative educational system, the many thousand madrassas, became the breeding ground for jihad fighters. Ayub Khan, the first military ruler, tried to break their stranglehold but failed. Subsequent rulers, military and civilian, have not even tried. It is more than doubtful whether Pervez Musharraf will have any success in limiting their power. The tens of thousands of graduates they annually produce formed the backbone of the Taliban. Their leaders will find employment for them at home and in Central Asia, even if there is a deescalation in tensions with India over Kashmir. Their most radical leaders aim at the destruction of India. Given Pakistan's internal weakness this may appear more than a little fanciful, but their destructive power is still considerable, and they can count on certain sympathies in the army and the intelligence service. A failed Pakistan with nuclear weapons at its disposal would be a major nightmare. Still, Pakistani terrorism—like Palestinian and Middle Eastern in general—remains territorial, likely to be limited to the subcontinent and Central Asia.

## Battlefield Europe

*E*UROPE IS PROBABLY the most vulnerable battlefield. To carry out operations in Europe and America, talents are needed that are not normally found among those who have no direct personal experience of life in the West. The Pakistani diaspora has not been very active in the terrorist field, except for a few militants in the United Kingdom.

Western Europe has become over a number of years the main base of terrorist support groups. This process has been facilitated by the growth of Muslim communities, the growing tensions with the native population, and the relative freedom with which radicals could organize in certain mosques and cultural organizations. Indoctrination was provided by militants who came to these countries as religious dignitaries. This freedom of action was considerably greater than that enjoyed in the Arab and Muslim world; not a few terrorists convicted of capital crimes in countries such as Egypt, Jordan, Morocco, and Algeria were given political asylum in Europe. True,

there were some arrests and closer controls after September 11, but given the legal and political restrictions under which the European security services were laboring, effective counteraction was still exceedingly difficult.

West European governments have been frequently criticized for not having done enough to integrate Muslim newcomers into their societies, but cultural and social integration was certainly not what the newcomers wanted. They wanted to preserve their religious and ethnic identity and their way of life, and they resented intervention by secular authorities. In its great majority, the first generation of immigrants wanted to live in peace and quiet and to make a living for their families. But today they no longer have much control over their offspring.

## *Non-Muslims began to feel threatened in streets they could once walk without fear.*

This is a common phenomenon all over the world: the radicalization of the second generation of immigrants. This generation has been superficially acculturated (speaking fluently the language of the host country) yet at the same time feels resentment and hostility more acutely. It is not necessarily the power of the fundamentalist message (the young are not the most pious believers when it comes to carrying out all the religious commandments) which inspires many of the younger radical activists or sympathizers. It is the feeling of deep resentment because, unlike immigrants from other parts of the world, they could not successfully compete in the educational field, nor quite often make it at the work place. Feelings of being excluded, sexual repression (a taboo subject in this context), and other factors led to free-floating aggression and crime directed against the authorities and their neighbors.

As a result, non-Muslims began to feel threatened in streets they could once walk without fear. They came to regard the new immigrants as antisocial elements who wanted to change the traditional character of their homeland and their way of life, and consequently tensions continued to increase. Pressure on European governments is growing from all sides, right and left, to stop immigration and to restore law and order.

This, in briefest outline, is the milieu in which Islamist terrorism and terrorist support groups in Western Europe developed. There is little reason to assume that this trend will fundamentally change in the near future. On the contrary, the more the young generation of immigrants asserts itself, the more violence occurs in the streets, and the more terrorist attacks take place, the greater the anti-Muslim resentment on the part of the rest of the population. The rapid demographic growth of the Muslim communities further strengthens the impression among the old residents that they are swamped and deprived of their rights in their own homeland, not even entitled to speak the truth about the prevailing situation (such as, for instance, to reveal the statistics of prison inmates with Muslim backgrounds). Hence the violent reaction in even the most liberal European countries such as the Netherlands, Belgium, and Denmark. The fear of the veil turns into the fear that in the foreseeable future they too, having become a minority, will be compelled to conform to the commandments of another religion and culture.

True, the number of extremists is still very small. Among British Muslims, for instance, only 13 percent have expressed sympathy and support for terrorist attacks. But this still amounts to several hundred thousands, far more than needed for staging a terrorist campaign. The figure is suspect in any case because not all of those sharing radical views will openly express them to strangers, for reasons that hardly need be elaborated. Lastly, such a minority will not feel isolated in their own community as long as the majority remains silent—which has been the case in France and most other European countries.

*Extremists may be repelled by the decadence of the society facing them, but they are also attracted by it.*

The prospects for terrorism based on a substantial Islamist periphery could hardly appear to be more promising, but there are certain circumstances that make the picture appear somewhat less threatening. The tensions are not equally strong in all countries. They are less palpably felt in Germany and Britain than in France and the Netherlands. Muslims in Germany are predominantly of Turkish origin and have (always with some exceptions) shown less inclination to take violent action than communities mainly composed of Arab and North African immigrants.

If acculturation and integration has been a failure in the short run, prospects are less hopeless in a longer perspective. The temptations of Western civilization are corrosive; young Muslims cannot be kept in a hermetically sealed ghetto (even though a strong attempt is made). They are disgusted and repelled by alcohol, loose morals, general decadence, and all the other wickedness of the society facing them, but they are at the same time fascinated and attracted by them. This is bound to affect their activist fervor, and they will be exposed not only to the negative aspects of the world surrounding them but also its values. Other religions had to face these temptations over the ages and by and large have been fighting a losing battle.

It is often forgotten that only a relatively short period passed from the primitive beginnings of Islam in the Arabian desert to the splendor and luxury (and learning and poetry) of Harun al Rashid's Baghdad—from the austerity of the Koran to the not-so-austere Arabian Nights. The pulse of contemporary history is beating much faster, but is it beating fast enough? For it is a race against time. The advent of megaterrorism and the access to weapons of mass destruc-tion is dangerous enough, but coupled with fanaticism it generates scenarios too unpleasant even to contemplate.

# Enduring asymmetry

*T*HERE CAN BE no final victory in the fight against terrorism, for terrorism (rather than full-scale war) is the contemporary manifestation of conflict, and conflict will not disappear from earth as far as one can look ahead and human nature has not undergone a basic change. But it will be in our power to make life for terrorists and potential terrorists much more difficult.

Who ought to conduct the struggle against terrorism? Obviously, the military should play only a limited role in this context, and not only because it has not been trained for this purpose. The military may have to be called in for restoring order in countries that have failed to function and have become terrorist havens. It may have to intervene to prevent or stop massacres. It may be needed to deliver blows against terrorist concentrations. But these are not the most typical or frequent terrorist situations.

The key role in asymmetric warfare (a redundant new term for something that has been known for many centuries) should be played by intelligence and security services that may need a military arm.

As far as terrorism and also guerrilla warfare are concerned, there can be no general, overall doctrine in the way that Clausewitz or Jomini and others developed a regular warfare philosophy. An airplane or a battleship do not change their character wherever they operate, but the character of terrorism and guerrilla warfare depends largely on the motivations of those engaging in it and the conditions under which it takes place. Over the past centuries rules and laws of war have developed, and even earlier on there were certain rules that were by and large adhered to.

But terrorists cannot possibly accept these rules. It would be suicidal from their point of view if, to give but one example, they were to wear uniforms or other distinguishing marks. The essence of their operations rests on hiding their identities. On the other hand, they and their well-wishers insist that when captured, they should enjoy all the rights and benefits accorded to belligerents, that they be humanely treated, even paid some money and released after the end of hostilities. When regular soldiers do not stick to the rules of warfare, killing or maiming prisoners, carrying out massacres, taking hostages or committing crimes against the civilian population, they will be treated as war criminals.

If terrorists behaved according to these norms they would have little if any chance of success; the essence of terrorist operations now is indiscriminate attacks against civilians. But governments defending themselves against terrorism are widely expected not to behave in a similar way but to adhere to international law as it developed in conditions quite different from those prevailing today.

Terrorism does not accept laws and rules, whereas governments are bound by them; this, in briefest outline, is asymmetric warfare. If governments were to behave in a similar way, not feeling bound by existing rules and laws such as those against the killing of prisoners, this would be bitterly denounced. When the late Syrian President Hafez Assad faced an insurgency (and an attempted assassination) on the part of the Muslim Brotherhood in the city of Hama in 1980, his soldiers massacred some 20,000 inhabitants. This put an end to all ideas of terrorism and guerrilla warfare.

Such behavior on the part of democratic governments would be denounced as barbaric, a relapse into the practices of long-gone pre-civilized days. But if governments accept the principle of asymmetric warfare they will be severely, possibly fatally, handicapped. They cannot accept that terrorists are protected by the Geneva Conventions, which would mean, among other things, that they should be paid a salary while in captivity. Should they be regarded like the pirates of a bygone age as *hostes generis humani*, enemies of humankind, and be treated according to the principle of *a un corsaire, un corsaire et demi*—"to catch a thief, it takes a thief," to quote one of Karl Marx's favorite sayings?

## *Should terrorists be regarded, like pirates of a bygone age, as enemies of humankind?*

The problem will not arise if the terrorist group is small and not very dangerous. In this case normal legal procedures will be sufficient to deal with the problem (but even this is not quite certain once weapons of mass destruction become more readily accessible). Nor will the issue of shedding legal restraint arise if the issues at stake are of marginal importance, if in other words no core interests of the governments involved are concerned. If, on the other hand, the very survival of a society is at stake, it is most unlikely that governments will be impeded in their defense by laws and norms belonging to a bygone (and more humane) age.

It is often argued that such action is counterproductive because terrorism cannot be defeated by weapons alone, but is a struggle for the hearts and minds of people, a confrontation of ideas (or ideologies). If it were only that easy. It is not the terrorist ideas which cause the damage, but their weapons. Each case is different, but many terrorist groups do not have any specific idea or ideology, but a fervent belief, be it of a religious character or of a political religion. They fight for demands, territorial or otherwise, that seem to them self-evident, and they want to defeat their enemies. They are not open to dialogue or rational debate. When Mussolini was asked about his program by

the socialists during the early days of fascism, he said that his program was to smash the skulls of the socialists.

Experience teaches that a little force is indeed counterproductive except in instances where small groups are involved. The use of massive, overwhelming force, on the other hand, is usually effective. But the use of massive force is almost always unpopular at home and abroad, and it will be applied only if core interests of the state are involved. To give but one example: The Russian government could deport the Chechens (or a significant portion), thus solving the problem according to the Stalinist pattern. If the Chechens were to threaten Moscow or St. Petersburg or the functioning of the Russian state or its fuel supply, there is but little doubt that such measures would be taken by the Russian or indeed any other government. But as long as the threat is only a marginal and peripheral one, the price to be paid for the application of massive force will be considered too high.

Two lessons follow: First, governments should launch an anti-terrorist campaign only if they are able and willing to apply massive force if need be. Second, terrorists have to ask themselves whether it is in their own best interest to cross the line between nuisance operations and attacks that threaten the vital interests of their enemies and will inevitably lead to massive counterblows.

Terrorists want total war—not in the sense that they will (or could) mobilize unlimited resources; in this respect their possibilities are limited. But they want their attacks to be unfettered by laws, norms, regulations, and conventions. In the terrorist conception of warfare there is no room for the Red Cross.

## Love or respect?

*T*HE WHY-DO-THEY-HATE-US question is raised in this context, along with the question of what could be done about it—that is, the use of soft power in combating terrorism. Disturbing figures have been published about the low (and decreasing) popularity of America in foreign parts. Yet it is too often forgotten that international relations is not a popularity contest and that big and powerful countries have always been feared, resented, and envied; in short, they have not been loved. This has been the case since the days of the Assyrians and the Roman Empire. Neither the Ottoman nor the Spanish Empire, the Chinese, the Russian, nor the Japanese was ever popular. British sports were emulated in the colonies and French culture impressed the local elites in North Africa and Indochina, but this did not lead to political support, let alone identification with the rulers. Had there been public opinion polls in the days of Alexander the Great (let alone Ghengis Khan), the results, one suspects, would have been quite negative.

Big powers have been respected and feared but not loved for good reasons—even if benevolent, tactful, and on their best behavior, they were threatening simply because of their very existence. Smaller nations could not feel comfortable, especially if they were located close to them. This was the case even in times when there was more than one big power (which allowed for the possibility of playing one against the other). It is all the more so at a time when only one superpower is left and the perceived threat looms even larger.

There is no known way for a big power to reduce this feeling on the part of other, smaller countries—short of committing suicide or, at the very least, by somehow becoming weaker and less threatening. A moderate and intelligent policy on the part of the great power, concessions, and good deeds may mitigate somewhat the perceived threat, but it cannot remove it, because potentially the big power remains dangerous. It could always change its policy and become nasty, arrogant, and aggressive. These are the unfortunate facts of international life.

Soft power is important but has its limitations. Joseph S. Nye has described it as based on culture and political ideas, as influenced by the seductiveness of democracy, human rights, and individual opportunity. This is a powerful argument, and it is true that Washington has seldom used all its opportunities, the public diplomacy budget being about one-quarter of one percentage point of the defense budget. But the question is always to be asked: Who is to be influenced by our values and ideas? They could be quite effective in Europe, less so in a country like Russia, and not at all among the radical Islamists who abhor democracy (for all sovereignty rests with Allah rather than the people), who believe that human rights and tolerance are imperialist inventions, and who want to have nothing to do with deeper Western values which are not those of the Koran as they interpret it.

## *Big, powerful countries have always been feared, resented, and envied.*

The work of the American radio stations during the Cold War ought to be recalled. They operated against much resistance at home but certainly had an impact on public opinion in Eastern Europe; according to evidence later received, even the Beatles had an influence on the younger generation in the Soviet Union. But, at present, radio and television has to be beamed to an audience 70 percent of which firmly believes that the operations of September 11 were staged by the Mossad. Such an audience will not be impressed by exposure to Western pop culture or a truthful, matter-of-fact coverage of the news. These societies may be vulnerable to covert manipulation of the kind conducted by the British government during World War II: black (or at least gray) propaganda, rumors, half-truths, and outright lies. Societies steeped in belief in conspiracy theories will give credence to even the wildest rumors. But it is easy to imagine how an attempt to generate such propaganda would be received at home: It would

be utterly rejected. Democratic countries are not able to engage in such practices except in a case of a major emergency, which at the present time has not yet arisen.

Big powers will never be loved, but in the terrorist context it is essential that they should be respected. As bin Laden's declarations prior to September 11 show, it was lack of respect for America that made him launch his attacks; he felt certain that the risk he was running was small, for the United States was a paper tiger, lacking both the will and the capability to strike back. After all, the Americans ran from Beirut in the 1980s and from Mogadishu in 1993 after only a few attacks, and there was every reason to believe that they would do so again.

## Response in proportion to threat

*L*IFE COULD BE made more difficult for terrorists by imposing more controls and restrictions wherever useful. But neither the rules of national nor those of international law are adequate to deal with terrorism. Many terrorists or suspected terrorists have been detained in America and in Europe, but only a handful have been put on trial and convicted, because inadmissible evidence was submitted or the authorities were reluctant to reveal the sources of their information—and thus lose those sources. As a result, many who were almost certainly involved in terrorist operations were never arrested, while others were acquitted or released from detention.

As for those who are still detained, there have been loud protests against a violation of elementary human rights. Activists have argued that the real danger is not terrorism (the extent and the consequences of which have been greatly exaggerated) but the war against terrorism. Is it not true that American society could survive a disaster on the scale of September 11 even if it occurred once a year? Should free societies so easily give up their freedoms, which have been fought for and achieved over many centuries?

Some have foretold the coming of fascism in America (and to a lesser extent in Europe); others have predicted an authoritarian regime gradually introduced by governments cleverly exploiting the present situation for their own anti-democratic purposes. And it is quite likely indeed that among those detained there have been and are innocent people and that some of the controls introduced have interfered with human rights. However, there is much reason to think that to combat terrorism effectively, considerably more stringent measures will be needed than those presently in force.

But these measures can be adopted only if there is overwhelming public support, and it would be unwise even to try to push them through until the learning process about the danger of terrorism in an age of weapons of mass destruction has made further progress. Time will tell. If devastating attacks do not occur, stringent anti-terrorist measures will not be necessary. But if they do happen, the demand for effective countermeasures will be overwhelming. One could perhaps argue that further limitations of freedom are bound to be ineffective because terrorist groups are likely to be small or very small in the future and therefore likely to slip through safety nets. This is indeed a danger—but the advice to abstain from safety measures is a counsel of despair unlikely to be accepted.

There are political reasons to use these restrictions with caution, because Muslim groups are bound to be under special scrutiny and every precaution should be taken not to antagonize moderate elements in this community. Muslim organizations in Britain have complained that a young Pakistani or Arab is 10 times more likely to be stopped and interrogated by the police than other youths. The same is true for France and other countries. But the police, after all, have some reasons to be particularly interested in these young people rather than those from other groups. It will not be easy to find a just and easy way out of the dilemma, and those who have to deal with it are not to be envied.

It could well be that, as far as the recent past is concerned, the danger of terrorism has been overstated. In the two world wars, more people were sometimes killed and more material damage caused in a few hours than through all the terrorist attacks in a recent year. True, our societies have since become more vulnerable and also far more sensitive regarding the loss of life, but the real issue at stake is not the attacks of the past few years but the coming dangers. Megaterrorism has not yet arrived; even 9-11 was a stage in between old-fashioned terrorism and the shape of things to come: the use of weapons of mass destruction.

## *The real issue at stake is not the attacks of the past few years but the coming dangers.*

The idea that such weapons should be used goes back at least 150 years. It was first enunciated by Karl Heinzen, a German radical—later a resident of Louisville, Kentucky and Boston, Massachusetts—soon after some Irish militants considered the use of poison gas in the British Parliament. But these were fantasies by a few eccentrics, too farfetched even for the science fiction writers of the day.

Today these have become real possibilities. For the first time in human history very small groups have, or will have, the potential to cause immense destruction. In a sit-

uation such as the present one there is always the danger of focusing entirely on the situation at hand—radical nationalist or religious groups with whom political solutions may be found. There is a danger of concentrating on Islamism and forgetting that the problem is a far wider one. Political solutions to deal with their grievances may sometimes be possible, but frequently they are not. Today's terrorists, in their majority, are not diplomats eager to negotiate or to find compromises. And even if some of them would be satisfied with less than total victory and the annihilation of the enemy, there will always be a more radical group eager to continue the struggle.

This was always the case, but in the past it mattered little: If some Irish radicals wanted to continue the struggle against the British in 1921-22, even after the mainstream rebels had signed a treaty with the British government which gave them a free state, they were quickly defeated. Today even small groups matter a great deal precisely because of their enormous potential destructive power, their relative independence, the fact that they are not rational actors, and the possibility that their motivation may not be political in the first place.

Perhaps the scenario is too pessimistic; perhaps the weapons of mass destruction, for whatever reason, will never be used. But it would be the first time in human history that such arms, once invented, had not been used. In the last resort, the problem is, of course, the human condition.

In 1932, when Einstein attempted to induce Freud to support pacifism, Freud replied that there was no likelihood of suppressing humanity's aggressive tendencies. If there was any reason for hope, it was that people would turn away on rational grounds—that war had become too destructive, that there was no scope anymore in war for acts of heroism according to the old ideals.

Freud was partly correct: War (at least between great powers) has become far less likely for rational reasons. But his argument does not apply to terrorism motivated mainly not by political or economic interests, based not just on aggression but also on fanaticism with an admixture of madness.

Terrorism, therefore, will continue—not perhaps with the same intensity at all times, and some parts of the globe may be spared altogether. But there can be no victory, only an uphill struggle, at times successful, at others not.

*Walter Laqueur is co-chair of the International Research Council at the Center for Strategic and International Studies. He is the author of some of the basic texts on terrorism, most recently* Voices of Terror *(Reed Publishing, 2004). The present article is part of a larger project; the author wishes to thank the Earhart Foundation for its support.*

From *Policy Review*, August/September 2004, pp. 49-64. Copyright © 2004 by Walter Laqueur. Reprinted by permission of Policy Review and the author.

# Understanding the Terrorist Mind-Set

By Randy Borum, Ph.D.

*While nothing is easier than to denounce the evildoer, nothing is more difficult than to understand him.*
—Dostoevsky

The terrorist attacks on America on September 11, 2001, shocked millions who perhaps before did not realize there were people in the world that would take such violent actions, even those resulting in their own deaths, against innocent civilians. It dismayed and puzzled them that such individuals could hate Americans with such fervor that they would commit these large-scale acts of lethal aggression.

After the attacks, many Americans saw terrorism as a real hazard for the first time. However, extremist ideology and its use to justify violence are not at all new. Although the use of the term *terrorism* did not emerge until the late 18th century (identified with the French government's "Reign of Terror"[1]), the idea of terrorizing civilians to further a particular political, social, or religious cause has existed for centuries.[2]

As professionals in the law enforcement and intelligence communities increasingly direct their energies and resources to countering and preventing this type of extreme violence, they are working to acquire new knowledge and skills. In learning about terrorism, they not only should consider the specific ideology of those who commit or advocate acts of terrorism but also gain an understanding of the process of how these ideas or doctrines develop, as well as the various factors that influence the behavior of extremist groups and individuals.[3]

An investigator might reasonably wonder why such an understanding is important. The answer lies in the old military adage "know your enemy." In one of the many translations of *The Art of War*, Sun Tzu, a well-known Chinese general, is quoted as saying, "Know your enemy and know yourself; in a hundred battles you will never be in peril."

## Considering Ideological Origins

There likely is no universal method in developing extremist ideas that justifies terroristic acts of violence. However, four observable stages appear to frame a process of ideological development common to many individuals and groups of diverse ideological backgrounds. This four-stage process—a model designed as a heuristic (trial and error) to aid investigators and intelligence analysts in assessing the behaviors, experiences, and activities of a group or individual associated with extremist ideas—begins by framing some unsatisfying event or condition as being unjust, blaming the injustice on a target policy, person, or nation, and then vilifying, often demonizing, the responsible party to facilitate justification for aggression.

To begin with, an extremist individual or group identifies some type of undesirable event or condition ("it's not right"). This could be, for example, economic (e.g., poverty, unemployment, poor living conditions) or social (e.g., government-imposed restrictions on individual freedoms, lack of order or morality). While the nature of the condition may vary, those involved perceive the experience as "things are not as they should be." That is, "it's not right." Next, they frame the undesirable condition as an "injustice"; that is, it does not apply to everyone ("it's not fair"). For example, members of a police bargaining unit may feel that their low pay scale is "not right"; however, when they learn that other, perhaps less-skilled, city workers are making more money, they also consider the circumstance "unfair." In this regard, some use the United States as a comparison point to create a sense of injustice about economic deprivation; this holds true for some people in Middle Eastern countries who see the United States as a caricature of affluence and wasteful excess. For those who are deprived, this facilitates feelings of resentment and injustice.

Then, because injustice generally results from transgressive (wrongful) behavior, extremists hold a person or group responsible ("it's your fault"), identifying a potential target. For example, racially biased groups in the United States often use this tactic in directing anger toward minority groups. Members of these groups seek out young white men whose families are poor. They then point to examples of minorities receiving economic assistance or preferences in employment as the reason the white family is suffering.

Last, they deem the person or group responsible for the injustice as "bad" ("you're evil"); after all, good

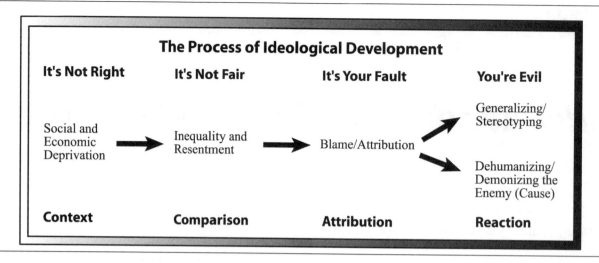

people would not intentionally inflict adverse conditions on others. This ascription has three effects that help facilitate violence.[4] First, aggression becomes more justifiable when aimed against "bad" people, particularly those who intentionally cause harm to others. Second, extremists describe the responsible party as "evil"; dehumanizing a target in this regard further facilitates aggression. Third, those suffering adverse conditions at the hands of others do not see themselves as "bad" or "evil"; this further identifies the responsible person or group as different from those affected and, thus, makes justifying aggression even easier.

When looking at the behaviors of emerging extremists in this way, investigators may better identify persons who represent desirable candidates for recruitment ("it's not fair"), possible sites of indoctrination ("it's not right," and "it's your fault"), and extremists or groups that may use violent tactics ("you're evil"). The operational objective for this analysis and increased understanding is not to sympathize with or excuse terrorism but to comprehend and, thereby, prevent acts of terrorism. Thus, "the challenge for the analyst is to learn why the terrorists are doing what they're doing and how deep it runs, then to look at the moral side and explain why we can't approve of the politics of terrorism even when the motives of some involved are comprehensible."[5]

## Understanding Motive

Fully "knowing one's enemy," specifically, understanding, anticipating, and forecasting another's behavior, demands not only an ideological understanding but a behavioral one as well. Gaining insight as to how someone may resolve a particular dilemma or handle a given situation requires a consideration of the person's entire perspective as influenced not only by their values and beliefs but by other factors, such as the information they have been exposed to, their assumptions, and their life experiences—in short, how they view the world. All people operate on their own internal "map" of reality, not reality itself. This is a mental-behavioral phenomenon that psychologists refer to as "social cognition."[6] If people understand their opponents' "maps," it becomes easier to understand and to anticipate their actions.

### Fully "knowing one's enemy,"...demands not only an ideological understanding but a behavioral one as well.

A good example of how this principle might apply involves considering the common misunderstanding of the tactic of "suicide bombings" used by Islamic extremists. The use of the term *suicide* to characterize these attacks reflects an outsider's view. Those who commit or encourage these attacks do not associate these acts with suicide. Instead, they consider them heroic acts of martyrdom. What is the difference? The motive, thoughts, feelings, responses of others, and preincident behaviors likely will differ for an act of suicide and an act of martyrdom.

People usually associate suicide with hopelessness and depression. The desire to end intense and unbearable psychological pain typically motivates the actor to commit such an act. Others who care for the actor typically view suicide as an undesirable outcome. Family and loved ones attempt to discourage the behavior and often struggle with feelings of shame if suicide does occur.

By contrast, people typically associate martyrdom with hopefulness about afterlife rewards in paradise and feelings of heroic sacrifice. The desire to further the cause of Islam and to answer the highest calling in that religion motivates the actor. Others who care for the actor see the pending act as heroic. Family and loved ones typically support the behavior, and, if the event occurs, the family is honored. Not only does the family of a martyr gain forgiveness of their sins in the afterlife but the supporting community often cares for them socially and financially. If investigators consider these attacks acts of suicide, the result could involve erroneous assumptions about how to anticipate the behavior and misguided ideas about how best to prevent it.

## Attributing Ideology as the Sole Motive

Another investigative issue related to motive is the often-presumed role of ideology as the sole cause for a particular violent act of extremism. Generally, when someone or some group that supports a radical idea commits such an act, the ideology is assumed to be *the* motive. In some cases, this attribution may be overly simplistic. In others, it simply may be wrong.

Some violent people, predisposed to criminality or aggressive behavior, simply use a particular cause or ideology to justify their acts. In the scheme of classifying terrorists as "criminals, crazies, and crusaders," these are the criminals.[7] Threat assessment experts have referred to these individuals as "murderers in search of a cause."[8]

Others truly do believe in extreme ideas, but the motive for a given act or series of acts may be broader. For example, in some Islamic fundamentalist movements, there is significant struggle for power that mixes with the religious ideas; specifically, conflicts exist over establishing the Caliphate that will unite dar al Islam.[9] In this regard, an Islamic fundamentalist leader may wish to support Islam and to defeat those who oppose the kingdom of Allah on earth, but his actions also may insert him in the Caliphate power struggle. From the perspective of strategic intelligence, it would prove inaccurate to see only the "holy warrior" and to miss the influence that the dynamics of this religious power struggle might have on, for example, decisions to act, target selection, and relationships between key figures or groups. Stated simply, the ideology may be *a* factor, but not necessarily *the* factor in determining motive.

## Conclusion

Professionals in the law enforcement and intelligence communities would do well to gain an understanding of how extremist ideas develop. By using a framework to organize behavioral information, counterterrorist analytic and threat assessments can become more accurate and more sophisticated.

Also, it is important to understand that analyzing counterterrorist intelligence requires an understanding of behavior, not just ideology. Investigators and analysts who must attempt to understand and anticipate how a person will act in a given situation should seek to understand that individual's "map," or perception, of the situation. Ideology may be a part of that, but other important dynamics and behavioral factors may contribute as well.

Extremist ideology is not at all new, although many Americans did not give the subject of terrorism proper attention until September 11, 2001. Those facing the task of safeguarding this nation and its interests, particularly important in this day and age, will do so most effectively when armed with a thorough understanding of terrorist ideology and behavior.

---

*Dr. Borum is a forensic psychologist and associate professor in the Department of Mental Health Law and Policy at the University of South Florida in Tampa.*

## Endnotes

1. The Reign of Terror, a period of the French Revolution between 1793 and 1794, was characterized by a wave of executions of presumed enemies of the state.

2. Jonathan White, *Terrorism: An Introduction*, 3rd ed. (Belmont, CA: Wadsworth Publishing, 2002).

3. The author serves on the Forensic Psychology Advisory Board for the Behavioral Science Unit at the FBI Academy and also is an instructor with the State and Local Antiterrorism Training Program (SLATT), a joint effort of the Institute for Intergovernmental Research (IIR) and the FBI.

4. Albert Bandura and others, eds., "Mechanisms of Moral Disengagement in the Exercise of Moral Agency," *Journal of Personality and Social Psychology* 71(2), (1996): 364–374.

5. Stephen Goode, interview by Christopher Harmon, February 5, 2001, "Harmon Details Terrorism Today," *Insight on the News*.

6. S. Fiske and S. Taylor, *Social Cognition*, 2nd ed. (New York, NY: McGraw-Hill, 1991).

7. Frederick Hacker, *Crusaders, Criminals and Crazies: Terror and Terrorism In Our Time* (New York, NY: Norton, 1976).

8. Robert Fein and Bryan Vossekuil, U.S. Department of Justice, Office of Justice Programs, National Institute of Justice, *Protective Intelligence and Threat Assessment Investigations: A Guide for State and Local Law Enforcement Officials* (Washington, DC, 1998).

9. Supra note 2. In this context, the Muslim Khalifa is the successor (in a line of successors) to Prophet Muhammad's position as the political, military, and administrative leader of the Muslims. This definition excludes Muhammad's prophetic role as the Qu'ran clearly states that he was the last of the prophets.

---

From *FBI Law Enforcement Bulletin*, July 2003, pp. 7–10. Published by the Federal Bureau of Investigation.

# UNIT 6

# Problems of Population, Environment, Resources, and the Future

## Unit Selections

34. **Rescuing a Planet Under Stress**, Lester R. Brown
35. **The Pentagon and Climate Change**, Monthly Review
36. **The Future of Humanity**, Colin Tudge
37. **The Secret Nuclear War**, Eduardo Goncalves
38. **The Globalization of Politics: American Foreign Policy for a New Century**, Ivo H. Daalder and James M. Lindsay
39. **Community Building: Steps Toward a Good Society**, Amitai Etzioni
40. **Sleepwalking Through the Apocalypse**, William Van Dusen Wishard

## Key Points to Consider

- What are the advantages of slowing world population growth? How can it be done?

- What is the current state of the world's environment? How can it be improved?

- Are you optimistic or pessimistic about the long-term results of genetic engineering of humans?

- What does your crystal ball say about the future of the world? Which of the assessments of the future that are reviewed in the readings do you find the most plausible?

 **Links: www.dushkin.com/online/**
These sites are annotated in the World Wide Web pages.

**Human Rights and Humanitarian Assistance**
   *http://www.etown.edu/vl/humrts.html*
**The Hunger Project**
   *http://www.thp.org*

The previous units have wrestled with many knotty problems in American society. In this unit the focus is on problems of the future, mostly from a worldwide perspective. Any discussion of the future must begin with a look at present environmental trends. The first subsection in this unit analyzes problems of the environment. The second subsection looks at the problems of new technologies. The final subsection assesses the prospects for the future in very broad terms.

Some scholars are very concerned about the worsening state of the environment, and others are confident that technological developments will solve most of these problems. Since the debate is about the future, neither view can be "proved." Nevertheless, it is important to understand the seriousness of the problems and think about what might be needed to correct them. In the first article Lester Brown reviews the ways that the environment is declining and portrays the planet as a global bubble economy that is based on the over consumption of the Earth's natural capital assets. Unless world consumption and the resulting environmental depletion and damage are reduced the global bubble will burst with severe economic, political, and social consequences. He also provides much advice on how to solve the problems. The second article that focuses on the environment reports on the Pentagon study of the potential severe impacts of global warming that may include economic and political instability and even war. Extreme impacts of global warming may be unlikely but they must not be ignored.

The next subsection looks at technological problems, specifically biological and nuclear technologies. The first deals with issues that have been opened up by DNA research. The beneficial possibilities are enormous; so are the potential dangers and moral questions. For example society must now decide whether to continue to leave the creation of humans to providence and/or evolution or to genetically engineer our offspring. In this article, Colin Tudge presents the issues, options, and debates. In the second article, Eduardo Goncalves evaluates another sophisticated technology—nuclear power. It can win wars and supply useful electrical energy but it may have already killed 175 million people. Furthermore, the way scientists and governments have acted regarding nuclear energy shows that they can not always be trusted to pursue the public good in their decisions regarding new technologies.

The final subsection assesses the prospects for the future. In the first article, the authors argue that global politics has been radically changed since the fall of the Berlin Wall and the September 11, 2001 terrorist attack on the United States. The bipolar world power arrangement has disintegrated and the new world order has not become clear. Politics is becoming globalized with the U.S. at the center but unable to act alone effectively in the long run. In the next article, Amitai Etzioni describes the trends toward greater inequality and diversity in the United States and asks whether these trends threaten the integration of American society. Since the 1960s, identity politics have succeeded in reducing past injustices but also "have divided the nation along group lines." Etzioni draws on sociological theory to propose ways to build community by reducing inequalities, increasing bonds, and generating stronger value commitments. In the last article, William Van Dusen Wishard, a leading world trends expert, describes ten world-wide historical trends that clearly show that the world is presently in a transition period. The world is becoming global; economically, socially, and psychologically. The growth of international travel, migration, and communication are transforming world institutions and cultures. To cope we need a world consciousness.

# Rescuing a planet under stress

## Lester R. Brown

## Understanding the Problem

As world population has doubled and as the global economy has expanded sevenfold over the last half-century, our claims on the Earth have become excessive. We are asking more of the Earth than it can give on an ongoing basis.

We are harvesting trees faster than they can regenerate, over-grazing rangelands and converting them into deserts, over-pumping aquifers, and draining rivers dry. On our cropland, soil erosion exceeds new soil formation, slowly depriving the soil of its inherent fertility. We are taking fish from the ocean faster than they can reproduce.

We are releasing carbon dioxide into the atmosphere faster than nature can absorb it, creating a greenhouse effect. As atmospheric carbon dioxide levels rise, so does the earth's temperature. Habitat destruction and climate change are destroying plant and animal species far faster than new species can evolve, launching the first mass extinction since the one that eradicated the dinosaurs sixty-five million years ago.

Throughout history, humans have lived on the Earth's sustainable yield—the interest from its natural endowment. But now we are consuming the endowment itself. In ecology, as in economics, we can consume principal along with interest in the short run but in the long run it leads to bankruptcy.

In 2002 a team of scientists led by Mathis Wackernagel, an analyst at Redefining Progress, concluded that humanity's collective demands first surpassed the Earth's regenerative capacity around 1980. Their study, published by the U.S. National Academy of Sciences, estimated that our demands in 1999 exceeded that capacity by 20 percent. We are satisfying our excessive demands by consuming the Earth's natural assets, in effect creating a global bubble economy.

Bubble economies aren't new. U.S. investors got an up-close view of this when the bubble in high-tech stocks burst in 2000 and the NASDAQ, an indicator of the value of these stocks, declined by some 75 percent. According to the *Washington Post*, Japan had a similar experience in 1989 when the real estate bubble burst, depreciating stock and real estate assets by 60 percent. The bad-debt fallout and other effects of this collapse have left the once-dynamic Japanese economy dead in the water ever since.

The bursting of these two bubbles affected primarily people living in the United States and Japan but the global bubble economy that is based on the overconsumption of the Earth's natural capital assets will affect the entire world. When the food bubble economy, inflated by the overpumping of aquifers, bursts, it will raise food prices worldwide. The challenge for our generation is to deflate the economic bubble before it bursts.

Unfortunately, since September 11, 2001, political leaders, diplomats, and the media worldwide have been preoccupied with terrorism and, more recently, the occupation of Iraq. Terrorism is certainly a matter of concern, but if it diverts us from the environmental trends that are undermining our future until it is too late to reverse them, Osama bin Laden and his followers will have achieved their goal in a way they couldn't have imagined.

In February 2003, United Nations demographers made an announcement that was in some ways more shocking than the 9/11 attack: the worldwide rise in life expectancy has been dramatically reversed for a large segment of humanity—the seven hundred million people living in sub-Saharan Africa. The HIV epidemic has reduced life expectancy among this region's people from sixty-two to forty-seven years. The epidemic may soon claim more lives than all the wars of the twentieth century. If this teaches us anything, it is the high cost of neglecting newly emerging threats.

The HIV epidemic isn't the only emerging mega-threat. Numerous nations are feeding their growing populations by overpumping their aquifers—a measure that virtually guarantees a future drop in food production when the aquifers are depleted. In effect, these nations are creating a food bubble economy—one where food production is artificially inflated by the unsustainable use of groundwater.

Another mega-threat—climate change—isn't getting the attention it deserves from most governments, particularly that of the United States, the nation responsible for one-fourth of all carbon emissions. Washington, D.C., wants to wait until all the evidence on climate change is in, by which time it will be too late to prevent a wholesale warming of the planet. Just as governments in Africa watched HIV infection rates rise and did little about it, the United States is watching atmospheric carbon dioxide levels rise and doing little to check the increase.

Other mega-threats being neglected include eroding soils and expanding deserts, which jeopardize the livelihood and food supply of hundreds of millions of the world's people. These issues don't even appear on the radar screen of many national governments.

Thus far, most of the environmental damage has been local: the death of the Aral Sea, the burning rainforests of Indonesia, the collapse of the Canadian cod fishery, the melting of the glaciers that supply Andean cities with water, the dust bowl forming in northwestern China, and the depletion of the U.S. great plains aquifer. But as these local environmental events expand and multiply, they will progressively weaken the global economy, bringing closer the day when the economic bubble will burst.

Humanity's demands on the Earth have multiplied over the last half-century as our numbers have increased and our incomes have risen. World population grew from 2.5 billion in 1950 to 6.1 billion in 2000. The growth during those fifty years exceeded that during the four million years since our ancestors first emerged from Africa.

Incomes have risen even faster than population. According to Erik Assadourian's *Vital Signs* 2003 article, "Economic Growth Inches Up," income per person worldwide nearly tripled from 1950 to 2000. Growth in population and the rise in incomes together expanded global economic output from just under $7 trillion (in 2001 dollars) of goods and services in 1950 to $46 trillion in 2000—a gain of nearly sevenfold.

Population growth and rising incomes together have tripled world grain demand over the last half-century, pushing it from 640 million tons in 1950 to 1,855 million tons in 2000, according to the U.S. Department of Agriculture (USDA). To satisfy this swelling demand, farmers have plowed land that was highly erodible—land that was too dry or too steeply sloping to sustain cultivation. Each year billions of tons of topsoil are being blown away in dust storms or washed away in rainstorms, leaving farmers to try to feed some seventy million additional people but with less topsoil than the year before.

Demand for water also tripled as agricultural, industrial, and residential uses increased, outstripping the sustainable supply in many nations. As a result, water tables are falling and wells are going dry. Rivers are also being drained dry, to the detriment of wildlife and ecosystems.

Fossil fuel use quadrupled, setting in motion a rise in carbon emissions that is overwhelming nature's capacity to fix carbon dioxide. As a result of this carbon-fixing deficit, atmospheric carbon dioxide concentrations climbed from 316 parts per million (ppm) in 1959, when official measurement began, to 369 ppm in 2000, according to a report issued by the Scripps Institution of Oceanography at the University of California.

The sector of the economy that seems likely to unravel first is food. Eroding soils, deteriorating rangelands, collapsing fisheries, falling water tables, and rising temperatures are converging to make it more difficult to expand food production fast enough to keep up with demand. According to the USDA, in 2002 the world grain harvest of 1,807 million tons fell short of world grain consumption by 100 million tons, or 5 percent. This shortfall, the largest on record, marked the third consecutive year of grain deficits, dropping stocks to the lowest level in a generation.

Now the question is: can the world's farmers bounce back and expand production enough to fill the hundred-million-ton shortfall, provide for the more than seventy million people added each year, and rebuild stocks to a more secure level? In the past, farmers responded to short supplies and higher grain prices by planting more land and using more irrigation water and fertilizer. Now it is doubtful that farmers can fill this gap without further depleting aquifers and jeopardizing future harvests.

At the 1996 World Food Summit in Rome, Italy, hosted by the UN Food and Agriculture Organization (FAO), 185 nations plus the European community agreed to reduce hunger by half by 2015. Using 1990–1992 as a base, governments set the goal of cutting the number of people who were hungry—860 million—by roughly 20 million per year. It was an exciting and worthy goal, one that later became one of the UN Millennium Development Goals.

But in its late 2002 review of food security, the UN issued a discouraging report:

> This year we must report that progress has virtually ground to a halt. Our latest estimates, based on data from the years 1998-2000, put the number of under-nourished people in the world at 840 million.... a decrease of barely 2.5 million per year over the eight years since 1990–92.

Since 1998–2000, world grain production per person has fallen 5 percent, suggesting that the ranks of the hungry are now expanding. As noted earlier, life expectancy is plummeting in sub-Saharan Africa. If the number of hungry people worldwide is also increasing, then two key social indicators are showing widespread deterioration in the human condition.

The ecological deficits just described are converging on the farm sector, making it more difficult to sustain rapid growth in world food output. No one knows when the growth in food production will fall behind that of demand, driving up prices, but it may be much sooner than we think. The triggering events that will precipitate future food shortages are likely to be spreading water shortages interacting with crop-withering heat waves in key food-producing regions. The economic indicator most likely to signal serious trouble in the deteriorating relationship between the global economy and the Earth's ecosystem is grain prices.

Food is fast becoming a national security issue as growth in the world harvest slows and as falling water tables and rising temperatures hint at future shortages. According to the USDA more than one hundred nations import part of the wheat they consume. Some forty import rice. While some nations are only marginally dependent on imports, others couldn't survive without them. Egypt and Iran, for example, rely on imports for 40 percent of their grain supply. For Algeria, Japan, South Korea, and Taiwan, among others, it is 70 percent or more. For Israel and Yemen, over 90 percent. Just six nations—Argentina,

Australia, Canada, France, Thailand, and the United States—supply 90 percent of grain exports. The United States alone controls close to half of world grain exports, a larger share than Saudi Arabia does of oil.

Thus far the nations that import heavily are small and middle-sized ones. But now China, the world's most populous nation, is soon likely to turn to world markets in a major way. As reported by the International Monetary Fund, when the former Soviet Union unexpectedly turned to the world market in 1972 for roughly a tenth of its grain supply following a weather-reduced harvest, world wheat prices climbed from $1.90 to $4.89 a bushel. Bread prices soon rose, too.

If China depletes its grain reserves and turns to the world grain market to cover its shortfall—now forty million tons per year—it could destabilize world grain markets overnight. Turning to the world market means turning to the United States, presenting a potentially delicate geopolitical situation in which 1.3 billion Chinese consumers with a $100-billion trade surplus with the United States will be competing with U.S. consumers for U.S. grain. If this leads to rising food prices in the United States, how will the government respond? In times past, it could have restricted exports, even imposing an export embargo, as it did with soybeans to Japan in 1974. But today the United States has a stake in a politically stable China. With an economy growing at 7 to 8 percent a year, China is the engine that is powering not only the Asian economy but, to some degree, the world economy.

For China, becoming dependent on other nations for food would end its history of food self-sufficiency, leaving it vulnerable to world market uncertainties. For Americans, rising food prices would be the first indication that the world has changed fundamentally and that they are being directly affected by the growing grain deficit in China. If it seems likely that rising food prices are being driven in part by crop-withering temperature rises, pressure will mount for the United States to reduce oil and coal use.

For the world's poor—the millions living in cities on $1 per day or less and already spending 70 percent of their income on food—rising grain prices would be life threatening. A doubling of world grain prices today could impoverish more people in a shorter period of time than any event in history. With desperate people holding their governments responsible, such a price rise could also destabilize governments of low-income, grain-importing nations.

Food security has changed in other ways. Traditionally it was largely an agricultural matter. But now it is something that our entire society is responsible for. National population and energy policies may have a greater effect on food security than agricultural policies do. With most of the three billion people to be added to world population by 2050 (as estimated by the UN) being born in nations already facing water shortages, child-bearing decisions may have a greater effect on food security than crop planting decisions. Achieving an acceptable balance between food and people today depends on family planners and farmers working together.

Climate change is the wild card in the food security deck. The effect of population and energy policies on food security differ from climate in one important respect: population stability can be achieved by a nation acting unilaterally. Climate stability cannot.

## Instituting the Solution

Business as usual—Plan A—clearly isn't working. The stakes are high, and time isn't on our side. The good news is that there are solutions to the problems we are facing. The bad news is that if we continue to rely on timid, incremental responses our bubble economy will continue to grow until eventually it bursts. A new approach is necessary—a Plan B—an urgent reordering of priorities and a restructuring of the global economy in order to prevent that from happening.

Plan B is a massive mobilization to deflate the global economic bubble before it reaches the bursting point. Keeping the bubble from bursting will require an unprecedented degree of international cooperation to stabilize population, climate, water tables, and soils—and at wartime speed. Indeed, in both scale and urgency the effort required is comparable to the U.S. mobilization during World War II.

Our only hope now is rapid systemic change—change based on market signals that tell the ecological truth. This means restructuring the tax system by lowering income taxes and raising taxes on environmentally destructive activities, such as fossil fuel burning, to incorporate the ecological costs. Unless we can get the market to send signals that reflect reality, we will continue making faulty decisions as consumers, corporate planners, and government policymakers. Ill-informed economic decisions and the economic distortions they create can lead to economic decline.

Stabilizing the world population at 7.5 billion or so is central to avoiding economic breakdown in nations with large projected population increases that are already overconsuming their natural capital assets. According to the Population Reference Bureau, some thirty-six nations, all in Europe except Japan, have essentially stabilized their populations. The challenge now is to create the economic and social conditions and to adopt the priorities that will lead to population stability in all remaining nations. The keys here are extending primary education to all children, providing vaccinations and basic health care, and offering reproductive health care and family planning services in all nations.

Shifting from a carbon-based to a hydrogen-based energy economy to stabilize climate is now technologically possible. Advances in wind turbine design and in solar cell manufacturing, the availability of hydrogen generators, and the evolution of fuel cells provide the technologies needed to build a climate-benign hydrogen economy. Moving quickly from a carbon-based to a hydrogen-based energy economy depends on getting the price right, on incorporating the indirect costs of burning fossil fuels into the market price.

On the energy front, Iceland is the first nation to adopt a national plan to convert its carbon-based energy economy to one based on hydrogen. Denmark and Germany are leading the world into the age of wind. Japan has emerged as the world's leading manufacturer and user of solar cells. With its commercialization of a solar roofing material, it leads the world in electricity generation from solar cells and is well positioned to assist in the electrification of villages in the developing world. The Netherlands leads the industrial world in exploiting the bicycle as an alternative to the automobile. And the Canadian province of Ontario is emerging as a leader in phasing out coal. It plans to replace its five coal-fired power plants with gas-fired plants, wind farms, and efficiency gains.

Stabilizing water tables is particularly difficult because the forces triggering the fall have their own momentum, which must be reversed. Arresting the fall depends on quickly raising water productivity. In pioneering drip irrigation technology, Israel has become the world leader in the efficient use of agricultural water. This unusually labor-intensive irrigation practice, now being used to produce high-value crops in many nations, is ideally suited where water is scarce and labor is abundant.

In stabilizing soils, South Korea and the United States stand out. South Korea, with once denuded mountainsides and hills now covered with trees, has achieved a level of flood control, water storage, and hydrological stability that is a model for other nations. Beginning in the late 1980s, U.S. farmers systematically retired roughly 10 percent of the most erodible cropland, planting the bulk of it to grass, according to the USDA. In addition, they lead the world in adopting minimum-till, no-till, and other soil-conserving practices. With this combination of programs and practices, the United States has reduced soil erosion by nearly 40 percent in less than two decades.

Thus all the things we need to do to keep the bubble from bursting are now being done in at least a few nations. If these highly successful initiatives are adopted worldwide, and quickly, we can deflate the bubble before it bursts.

Yet adopting Plan B is unlikely unless the United States assumes a leadership position, much as it belatedly did in World War II. The nation responded to the aggression of Germany and Japan only after it was directly attacked at Pearl Harbor on December 7, 1941. But respond it did. After an all-out mobilization, the U.S. engagement helped turn the tide, leading the Allied Forces to victory within three and a half years.

This mobilization of resources within a matter of months demonstrates that a nation and, indeed, the world can restructure its economy quickly if it is convinced of the need to do so. Many people—although not yet the majority—are already convinced of the need for a wholesale restructuring of the economy. The issue isn't whether most people will eventually be won over but whether they will be convinced before the bubble economy collapses.

History judges political leaders by whether they respond to the great issues of their time. For today's leaders, that issue is how to deflate the world's bubble economy before it bursts. This bubble threatens the future of everyone, rich and poor alike. It challenges us to restructure the global economy, to build an eco-economy.

We now have some idea of what needs to be done and how to do it. The UN has set social goals for education, health, and the reduction of hunger and poverty in its Millennium Development Goals. My latest book, *Plan B*, offers a sketch for the restructuring of the energy economy to stabilize atmospheric carbon dioxide levels, a plan to stabilize population, a strategy for raising land productivity and restoring the earth's vegetation, and a plan to raise water productivity worldwide. The goals are essential and the technologies are available.

We have the wealth to achieve these goals. What we don't yet have is the leadership. And if the past is any guide to the future, that leadership can only come from the United States. By far the wealthiest society that has ever existed, the United States has the resources to lead this effort.

Yet the additional external funding needed to achieve universal primary education in the eighty-eight developing nations that require help is conservatively estimated by the World Bank at $15 billion per year. Funding for an adult literacy program based largely on volunteers is estimated at $4 billion. Providing for the most basic health care is estimated at $21 billion by the World Health Organization. The additional funding needed to provide reproductive health and family planning services to all women in developing nations is $10 billion a year.

Closing the condom gap and providing the additional nine billion condoms needed to control the spread of HIV in the developing world and Eastern Europe requires $2.2 billion—$270 million for condoms and $1.9 billion for AIDS prevention education and condom distribution. The cost per year of extending school lunch programs to the forty-four poorest nations is $6 billion per year. An additional $4 billion per year would cover the cost of assistance to preschool children and pregnant women in these nations.

In total, this comes to $62 billion. If the United States offered to cover one-third of this additional funding, the other industrial nations would almost certainly be willing to provide the remainder, and the worldwide effort to eradicate hunger, illiteracy, disease, and poverty would be under way.

The challenge isn't just to alleviate poverty, but in doing so to build an economy that is compatible with the Earth's natural systems—an eco-economy, an economy that can sustain progress. This means a fundamental restructuring of the energy economy and a substantial modification of the food economy. It also means raising the productivity of energy and shifting from fossil fuels to renewables. It means raising water productivity over the next half-century, much as we did land productivity over the last one.

It is easy to spend hundreds of billions in response to terrorist threats but the reality is that the resources needed to disrupt a modern economy are small, and a Department of Homeland Security, however heavily funded, provides only minimal protection from suicidal terrorists. The challenge isn't just to provide a high-tech military response to terrorism but to build a global society that is environmentally sustainable, socially equitable, and democratically based—one where there is hope for everyone. Such an effort would more effectively undermine the spread of terrorism than a doubling of military expenditures.

We can build an economy that doesn't destroy its natural support systems, a global community where the basic needs of all the Earth's people are satisfied, and a world that will allow us to think of ourselves as civilized. This is entirely doable. To paraphrase former President Franklin Roosevelt at another of those hinge points in history, let no one say it cannot be done.

The choice is ours—yours and mine. We can stay with business as usual and preside over a global bubble economy that keeps expanding until it bursts, leading to economic decline. Or we can adopt Plan B and be the generation that stabilizes population, eradicates poverty, and stbilizes climate. Historians will record the choice—but it is ours to make.

---

Lester R. Brown is president of the Earth Policy Institute. This article is adapted from his recently released book *Plan B: Rescuing a Planet Under Stress and a Civilization in Trouble*, which is available for free downloading at www.earth-policy.org

---

# The Pentagon and Climate Change

**THE EDITORS**

**Climate Collapse: The Pentagon's Weather Nightmare**

—*Fortune*, February 9, 2004

**Now the Pentagon Tells Bush: Climate Change Will Destroy Us**

—*Observer* (London), February 22, 2004

**Pentagon-Sponsored Climate Report Sparks Hullabaloo in Europe**

—*San Francisco Chronicle*, February 25, 2004

**The Sky is Falling! Say Hollywood and, Yes, the Pentagon**

—*New York Times*, February 29, 2004

Abrupt climate change has been a growing topic of concern for about a decade for climate scientists, who fear that global warming could shut down the ocean conveyer that warms the North Atlantic, plunging Europe and parts of North America into Siberian-like conditions within a few decades or even years. But it was only with the recent appearance of a Pentagon report on the possible social effects—in terms of instability and war—of abrupt climate change that it riveted public attention. As the *Observer* (February 22) put it, "Climate change over the next 20 years could result in global catastrophe costing millions of lives in wars and natural disasters."

Indeed, widespread public alarm, particularly in Europe, was the predictable response to the Pentagon's October 2003 report, *An Abrupt Climate Change Scenario and its Implications for United States National Security*, once it became available early this year.[1] In an attempt to quiet these fears Defense Department officials and the authors of the report quickly came forward to say that the entire exercise was speculative and "intentionally extreme"; that the whole thing had been misconstrued and overblown in certain press accounts.

Was this then simply a "hullabaloo" about nothing, as the *San Francisco Chronicle* suggested, or are there dangers associated with global warming that have not been sufficiently appreciated thus far? To answer this question it is necessary to approach the issue in stages, by first addressing global warming, then abrupt climate change and its inherent social dangers, and finally how the present system of production constitutes a barrier to any ready solution.

## Global Warming: How Bad Is It?

A natural greenhouse effect is crucial to the earth's atmosphere. As carbon dioxide, methane, and other greenhouse gases accumulate in the atmosphere they trap heat that would otherwise radiate off into space. This natural greenhouse effect along with proximity to the sun serves to warm the earth making it habitable to diverse species. But now, as a result of enhanced greenhouse gas emissions from human production, most notably the burning of fossil fuels, this same life-supporting greenhouse effect is pushing average global temperatures higher and higher. Carbon dioxide concentration in the atmosphere is now at its highest point in the last 420,000 years and likely in the last 20 million years. Rising sea levels, heat waves, crop failures, worsening floods and droughts, and more extreme weather conditions in general are all to be expected as a result of such increases in average global temperature.

Some of the warming to be experienced in coming decades is already locked-in. Greenhouse gases have atmospheric lifetimes of decades to centuries. Even if societies were to cease fossil fuel use and end all other forms of greenhouse gas emissions today the accumulation of such gases in the atmosphere would likely generate further warming on the order of 0.5°C (0.9°F) during this century. While if we do nothing to limit such emissions global average surface temperature could conceivably rise as much as 5.8°C (10.4°F) between 1990 and 2100, exceeding the change in average temperature separating us from the last ice age. Few informed analysts now expect the increase in average global temperature from 1990–2100 to be kept below a 2°C (3.6°F) increase, even with the most concerted social action over the next couple of decades. The main fear at present is that the rise in global temperature will be two or three times as large if human society is unable to act decisively.[2]

Global warming is expected to be a growing factor in coming decades in species extinction, the rate of which at present is higher than at any time since the disappearance of the dinosaurs 65 million years ago. In mountainous regions all around the earth plant and animal species are ascending higher and higher as warming occurs. But mountains only reach so far. Consequently, the species occupying the topmost ecological niches are now in the process of ascending "to heaven."[3] We do not know how many other species will share this fate during this century. But we do know that the earth's species in general will be massively affected, that biological diversity will continue to decrease, and that if we do nothing and average global temperatures rise to the upper levels that leading climate scientists think possible by the year 2100 it could prove catastrophic, seriously threatening ecosystems and destabilizing human society.

Still, the ruling economic and political interests and their attendant elites tell us not to be worried. Never mind the threats to other species. Human society, we are frequently told, is different. It can evolve rapidly by economic and technological means and thus adapt to global warming, which from its standpoint can be viewed as slow, "gradual" change. What is often projected for global society then is increased discomfort rather than massive social upheaval and dislocation. Orthodox economists generally caution that we should do nothing that might limit economic growth. Instead they see the only answer as lying in a bigger economy, which will give us more means of addressing future contingencies.

## Abrupt Climate Change

Nevertheless, there is every reason to believe that placing so much faith in economic growth and technological change as answers to global warming is short-sighted and naive. Considerable uncertainty exists as to how far human society can actually support such "gradual" climate change—since human beings are themselves part of nature and dependent on the world around them in manifold ways. But the problem does not stop there. Scientists are now raising the even more alarming question of abrupt climate change, i.e., climate change of a scale and suddenness—shifting dramatically in years rather than decades or centuries—that would definitely have catastrophic effects for human society.

Abrupt climate change is usually seen as change arising from gradual causes that lead to the crossing of a threshold, triggering a sudden shift to a new state—with the shift determined by the climate system itself and oc-

curring at a rate much faster than the initial cause.[4] Such shifts have occurred numerous times in history, one of the clearest being the abrupt cooling of the Younger Dryas (named after an arctic wildflower that thrived in the climate of the time), which began 12,700 years ago and lasted 1,300 years, interrupting the warming associated with the end of the last ice age. A lesser instance of abrupt climate change occurred 8,200 years ago and lasted around a century. In the worst of all current, plausible scenarios, such "abrupt climate change" could occur sometime over the next couple of decades—though this is still seen by scientists as highly unlikely.

Abrupt climate change is believed to result from disruption of the thermohaline circulation, a global ocean conveyor that moves warm, saline tropical waters northward in the Atlantic with the Gulf Stream as its northern arm, and then loops south. ("Thermohaline" comes from the Greek words for heat "thermos" and for salt "halos.") The heat from this warmer water, when it reaches the North Atlantic, is released into the atmosphere, creating milder winters than would otherwise exist at those latitudes, and allowing the dense surface waters to cool and sink. This draws additional warmer, saline water from the south, helping to keep the conveyor going. Differences in the density of ocean waters associated with the saline content thus drive this ocean conveyor. Abrupt climate change arises from a lessening or collapse of the thermohaline circulation due to increased river runoff, melting ice, and changes in precipitation—all of which serve to increase the amount of freshwater supplied to the North Atlantic. As the salinity of the ocean waters decreases a dramatic lessening or complete collapse of the North Atlantic conveyor circulation can occur. The current global warming is seen as potentially triggering this effect. According to the UN Intergovernmental Panel on Climate Change (IPCC), in *Climate Change 2001*, "beyond 2100, the thermohaline circulation could completely, and possibly irreversibly, shut-down in either hemisphere" if global warming is "large enough and applied long enough" (p. 16).

Two basic scenarios are worth considering. (1) If the ocean conveyor slows down or collapses during the next two decades it could cool the North Atlantic region by as much as 5°C (9°F), creating winters of much greater severity. (2) If, however, the conveyor slows down in a century the drop in temperature in the North Atlantic could temporarily compensate for the rise in surface temperature associated with the enhanced greenhouse effect—though once the thermohaline circulation recovered the "deferred" warming could be delivered within a decade. The second of these two scenarios is viewed as much more likely. Yet, recent scientific studies, including a major report in 2002 by the National Academy of Sciences, have stressed that the thermohaline circulation could possibly "decrease . . . very fast,"—resulting in a sudden switch of climate early this century that although still thought unlikely cannot be ruled out altogether. Seeming to confirm these fears, a report in *Nature* in 2002 concluded that the North Atlantic has been freshening dramatically for 40 years; while a report a year earlier suggested that the ocean conveyor may already be slowing down.[5]

Faced with the uncertain hazards of such a "low probability, high impact" event, scientists associated with the National Academy of Sciences study recommended that society take what steps it could, if not too costly, to protect itself against such an extreme outcome. "If a shutdown were to happen soon," Richard Alley, who chaired the scientific team releasing the National Academy of Sciences study, observed in *The Two-Mile Time Machine*, "it could produce a large event, perhaps almost as large as the Younger Dryas, dropping northern temperatures and spreading droughts far larger than the changes that have affected humans through recorded history, and perhaps speeding warming in the far south. The end of humanity? No. An uncomfortable time for humanity? Yes."[6]

These assessments and recommendations on abrupt climate change were offered with so much caution by climate scientists that they might easily have been ignored altogether by a society that in its upper echelons is devoted to the accumulation of capital and little else. That this did not happen is due to the fact that the issue was taken up and dramatized in the Pentagon report.

## The Pentagon Elevates the Threat

The story behind the Pentagon report on abrupt climate change is almost as remarkable as the contents of the report itself. The National Academy study of this issue crossed the desk of Andrew Marshall, director of the Pentagon's Office of Net Assessment. Marshall, who has worked for every secretary of defense since James Schlesinger in the 1970s, is a legendary "wise man," known as "Yoda," at the Pentagon. When they need someone to think about big things, the Department of Defense turns to Marshall. His most famous achievement was the promotion of missile defense. It was Marshall who authorized the $100,000 grant for Peter Schwartz and Doug Randall of the Global Business Network to analyze abrupt climate change for the Pentagon. The intent was obviously to have economic futurologists visualize the possible effects of such abrupt climate change, since they would be in the best position to speculate on the economic and social fallout of such a catastrophic development, and thus upgrade it to a major Pentagon concern.

Schwartz was a surprising choice for such a task since he was best known previously for his book *The Long Boom* (1999). In the 1990s he was a contributing writer to *Wired* magazine. Together with Peter Leyden, a senior editor of the magazine, and Joe Hyatt of the Stanford University Business School he got caught up in the idea that the New Economy, rooted in today's digital high technology, pointed to a long economic boom stretching from 1980 to at least 2020. During this time the economy would, they argued in the book, simply "grow more" based on the

New Economy model pioneered by the United States, with global growth of "possibly even 6 percent" (p. 266). Their first version of this thesis in their *Wired* article on the long boom came out in July 1997 and created a stir. The article together with the book that followed two years later, constituted the most extreme version of the great millennial celebration. According to Schwartz and his co-authors, who grossly misunderstood the main economic tendencies of the time, the U.S. economy was rocketing throughout the 1990s and was likely to accelerate further in the 2000s. All such New Economy mythology was put to an end, however, by the bursting of the speculative bubble and the dramatic stock market decline of 2000, followed by recession in 2001 and slow growth and employment stagnation ever since. Nevertheless, it was to Schwartz, the failed prophet of a long New Economy boom, to whom Marshall turned to dramatize the consequences of abrupt climate change.[7]

*An Abrupt Climate Change Scenario and its Implications for United States National Security* by Peter Schwartz and Doug Randall begins by challenging the way in which climate change is usually approached:

> When most people think about climate change, they imagine gradual increases in temperature and only marginal changes in other climatic conditions, continuing indefinitely or even leveling off at some time in the future. The conventional wisdom is that modern civilization will either adapt to whatever weather conditions we face and that the pace of climate change will not overwhelm the adaptive capacity of society, or that our efforts such as those embodied in the Kyoto protocol will be sufficient to mitigate the impacts. The IPCC documents the threat of gradual climate change and its impact to food supplies and other resources of importance to humans will not be so severe as to create security threats. Optimists assert that the benefits from technological innovation will be able to outpace the negative effects of climate change.
>
> Climatically, the gradual view of the future assumes that agriculture will continue to thrive and growing seasons will lengthen. Northern Europe, Russia, and North America will prosper agriculturally while southern Europe, Africa, and Central and South America will suffer from increased dryness, heat, water shortages, and reduced production. Overall, global food production under many typical climate scenarios increases (p. 4).

Schwartz and Randall argue against such complacent views of global warming, insisting that they do not take sufficient account of the discontinuities that may arise as warming causes various thresholds to be crossed. More frequent droughts, for example, could have disastrous and cumulative effects. Still, the worst effects from such gradual warming are seen as applying mainly to the poorer countries of the global South rather than the richer countries of the global North—the main source of carbon dioxide emissions. All of this encourages a do-nothing or do-little attitude in the northern centers of world power.

Abrupt climate change alters this picture dramatically. Such change would create catastrophic conditions for human society; and rather than falling first and foremost on the global South the direct effects of a shutdown of the thermohaline conveyor would bear down on the global North—specifically those countries bordering the North Atlantic. Schwartz and Randall are clear that they are not actually predicting such abrupt climate change in the near future (though it is certain to occur in the long-term future). Rather, they offer a "plausible" if unlikely scenario "for which there is reasonable evidence" so as to "explore potential implications for United States national security" (p. 5). They model their scenario on the event of 8,200 years ago rather than on the much worse Younger Dryas. In their scenario a "thermohaline circulation collapse" causes a drop in average surface temperature in northern Europe of up to 3.3°C (6°F) along with severe temperature drops throughout the North Atlantic, lasting about a century. Colder temperatures, wind and dryness in the global North are accompanied by increased warmth and drought in much of the rest of the world.

The picture they paint is one of agricultural decline and extreme weather conditions, stretching energy resources, throughout the globe. Relatively well-off populations with ample natural resources and food producing capabilities, such as the United States and Australia, are seen as building "defensive fortresses" around themselves to keep massive waves of would-be immigrants out, while much of the world gyrates toward war. "Violence and disruption stemming from the stresses created by abrupt changes in the climate pose a different type of threat to national security than we are accustomed to today. Military confrontation may be triggered by a desperate need for natural resources such as energy, food and water rather than by conflicts over ideology, religion, or national honor. The shifting motivation for confrontation would alter which countries are most vulnerable and the existing warning signs for security threats" (p. 14). As the world's carrying capacity declines under harsh climatic conditions, warfare becomes widespread—producing increased dangers of thermonuclear war.

For Schwartz and Randall the lesson is clear. Human society must "prepare for the inevitable effects of abrupt climate change—which will likely come [the only question is when] regardless of human activity" (p. 21). If the scenario that they depict is actually in the cards, it is already too late to do anything to stop it. What can be done under these circumstances is to make sure that the necessary security measures are in place to stave off the most disastrous consequences resulting from social instability. Since this is a report commissioned by the Pentagon, the emphasis is on how to "create vulnerability metrics" to determine which countries are likely to be hit the hardest ecologically, economically, and socially and thus will be propelled in the direction of war. Such information will make it possible for the United States to act in its own security interest. The narrow objective is thus to safeguard fortress America at all cost.

Although the ecological repercussions are supposed to hit the global North the hardest, the scenario provided by the Pentagon report with respect to instability and war follows conventional ideological paths, focusing mostly on the global South. The possibility that the United States itself might in such circumstances attempt to seize world oil supplies and other natural resources is not raised by the report. The U.S. response is depicted as entirely defensive, mainly concerned with holding off unwelcome waves of would-be immigrants, and trying to create an atmosphere of peace and stability in the world under much harsher global conditions.

Given the contents of this report it is not surprising that it initially generated dismay and widespread fears when it was made public in February. At that point the Pentagon quickly stepped in to quiet the alarm that the report had set off. Marshall himself released a statement that the Pentagon study "reflects the limits of scientific models and information when it comes to predicting the effects of abrupt global warming." Although backed up by "significant scientific evidence … much of what this study predicts," Marshall indicated, "is still speculation." Pentagon officials meanwhile declared that the abrupt climate change report, although commissioned by their legendary "Yoda," had not been passed on to Marshall's superiors in the Defense Department and the Bush administration (*San Francisco Chronicle*, February 25, 2004; *New York Times*, February 29, 2004).

Yet the real importance of *An Abrupt Climate Change Scenario* does not lie in its impact on the top brass in the Pentagon much less their envionmentally-challenged superiors in the White House. Instead, its historical significance derives from the more general contention made at the beginning of the report that "because of the potentially dire consequences, the risk of abrupt climate change, although uncertain and quite possibly small, should be elevated beyond a scientific debate to a U.S. national security concern" (p. 3). It is a small step from this view to one that insists that the nature of the threat demands that we begin to consider other, radical social alternatives to business as usual, which must be elevated to the forefront of public discussions.

## Accelerated Climate Change

Here it is crucial to recognize that abrupt climate change as currently modeled by scientists, though the most dramatic, is not the only nongradual outcome possible as a result of global warming. Scientists are even more concerned at present about the potential for positive feedbacks that will greatly amplify global warming, increasing the rate of its advance and the speed with which it crosses various ecological thresholds. According to the IPCC in *Climate Change 2001*, "As the $CO_2$ concentration of the atmosphere increases, ocean and land will take up a decreasing fraction of anthropogenic $CO_2$ emissions. The net effect of land and ocean climate feedbacks as indicated by models is to further increase projected atmospheric $CO_2$ concentrations, by reducing both the ocean and land uptake of $CO_2$" (p. 12). The hydrological cycle (evaporation, precipitation, and runoff) could accelerate as a result of global warming, driving temperatures higher faster. Water vapor, the most potent natural greenhouse gas, could trap additional heat increasing the rate at which average surface temperatures rise. The melting of highly reflective ice and snow could result in further absorbtion of sunlight, leading to additional global warming. The capacity of both forests and oceans to absorb carbon dioxide could decrease, creating a positive feedback loop that accelerates climate change. All of this is taken into account to some extent in the IPCC reports. But given the level of uncertainty the possibility of surprising developments under these circumstances is very great.

The grim reality is that the more threatening scenarios with respect to global warming are becoming increasingly plausible as the data keeps coming in. Carbon dioxide levels in the atmosphere increased at an accelerated level over the past year. The increase of 3 parts per million was well above the 1.8 parts per million annual increase on average over the past decade, and three times the year-to-year increase experienced half a century ago. Although it is too soon to be sure if this means anything or not (it may reflect mere annual variance), this kind of evidence is leading scientists to worry that positive feedbacks may already be at work, serving to accelerate the whole problem (*New York Times*, March 21, 2004).

## Capitalism and Carbon Dioxide

Both the capitalist economy and the world climate represent complex, dynamic systems. The uncertainty with respect to climate change and its economic effects has to do with the interaction of these two complex systems. To make matters worse, both the climate system and the human economy are subsets of the biosphere and are inseparably interconnected in extremely complex ways with innumerable other biogeochemical processes. Many of these other biospheric processes are also being transformed by human action.

It is not uncommon for analyses of climate change to assume that the world economy is essentially healthy except for disturbances that could result from the climate. This, however, is in error and underestimates the economic vulnerability of populations and whole societies. As indicated only a few months ago in this space, at present "half the world's population lives on less than two dollars per day, with most of those either chronically malnourished or continually concerned with where their next meal will come from. Many have no access to clean water (1 billion), electricity (2 billion), or sanitation (2.5 billion)" (Fred Magdoff, "A Precarious Existence," *Monthly Review*, February 2004). Economic growth is slowing in ways that have deepened the economic crisis for human populations. At the same time, "nature's economy" is also in trouble, viewed in terms of the diversity of life on the planet. Economic and ecological vulnerabilities are everywhere.

For the Pentagon, the answer to all of these dangers would seem to be straightforward: arm to the teeth, prepare for greater threats than ever from thermonuclear war, and build an impregnable wall around the United States, closing the global masses out. All of this is depicted by Schwartz and Randall. Yet a more rational response to potential highimpact climate events would be to seek to reorganize society, and to move away from imperatives of accumulation, exploitation, and degradation of the natural environment—the "after me the deluge" philosophy—that lies at the base of most of our global problems.

The truth is that addressing the global warming threat to any appreciable degree would require at the very least a chipping away at the base of the system. The scientific consensus on global warming suggests that what is needed is a 60–80 percent reduction in greenhouse gas emissions below 1990 levels in the next few decades in order to avoid catastrophic environmental effects by the end of this century—if not sooner. The threatening nature of such reductions for capitalist economies is apparent in the rather hopeless state at present of the Kyoto Protocol, which required the rich industrial countries to reduce their greenhouse gas emissions by an average of 5.2 percent below 1990 levels by 2008–2012. The United States, which had steadily increased its carbon dioxide emissions since 1990 despite its repeated promises to limit its emissions, pulled out of the Kyoto Protocol in 2001 on the grounds that it was too costly. Yet, the Kyoto Protocol was never meant to be anything but the first, small, in itself totally inadequate step to curtail emissions. The really big cuts were to follow.

Even if the Kyoto Protocol were to be enacted (its future right now is uncertain and depends largely on whether Russia decides to go along with the climate treaty) this would only open the door to bigger questions: Will the rich countries of the global North agree to cut their carbon emissions to the extent required? How can the poorer countries of the global South be brought into the climate accord? There would be little opportunity for most of these poor countries—still the victims of imperialism—to develop economically if they were forced to cut back sharply in their average level of per capita greenhouse gas emissions at this point. Since the atmosphere cannot support increasing levels of carbon dioxide and most of its capacity to do so without high levels of global warming has already been taken up by the rich countries of the center, countries in the periphery are likely to be severely constrained in their use of fossil fuels unless the countries in the center drastically reduce their levels of emissions—on the order of 80–90 percent.

Third world countries insist that the North has an ecological debt to the South, arising from a history of ecological imperialism, and that the only way to redress this and to create a just and sustainable climate regime is to base any solution on per capita emissions. Such a position is rooted in the recognition that the United States, to take the most notorious example, emits 5.6 metric tons of carbon dioxide per person per year,[8] while the whole rest of the world outside of the G-7 countries (the United States, Canada, Germany, Britain, Japan, Italy and France) releases only 0.7 tons of carbon dioxide per person annually on average.[9] Inequality of this kind is a major barrier to a smooth climate transition and means that the necessary change must be revolutionary in nature. The only just and sustainable climate regime will be one in which there is a contraction of per capita carbon dioxide emissions to levels that are globally sustainable, together with a convergenceof rich and poor countries around these low, globally sustainable emissions levels. Such safe per capita emissions levels would be less than a tenth of what the North currently emits per capita. One estimate claims that "based on the 1990 target for climate stabilization, everyone in the world would have a per capita allowance of carbon of around 0.4 tonnes, per year."[10]

Obviously, equalization of per capita emissions at low levels for all countries is not something that the United States and the other nations at the center of the system will readily accept. Yet third world countries that desperately need development cannot be expected to give up the right to equality in per capita emissions. Any attempt to impose the main burdens for global warming on underdeveloped countries in accordance with past imperialistic practices will thus inevitably fail. To the extent that the United States and other advanced capitalist nations promote such a strategy they will only push the world into a state of barbarism, while catastrophically undermining the human relation to the biosphere.

## Easter Island and the Earth

For environmentalists the destruction of the ecology and civilization of Easter Island around 1400–1600 A.D. has long been both a mystery and metaphor for our times. We now know that the giant stone statues, the erection of which resulted in the destruction of the island's forests and with them a whole ecology and civilization, were the main symbols of the power and prestige of competing chiefs and their clans. As Jared Diamond explains: "A chief's status depended on his statues: any chief who failed to cut trees to transport and erect statues would have found himself out of a job."[11] Due to such a narrow acquisitive logic—an early treadmill of production analogous to our own—the Easter Islanders drove their ecology and society to the point of extinction.

Are we headed for a similar disaster today—only on a planetary scale? To quote Diamond again:

Thanks to globalization, international trade, jet planes, and the Internet, all countries on Earth today share resources and affect each other, just as did Easter's eleven clans. Polynesian Easter Island was as isolated in the Pacific Ocean as the Earth is today in space. When the Easter Islanders got into difficulties, there was nowhere to which they could flee, or to which they could turn for help; nor shall we modern Earthlings have recourse elsewhere if our troubles increase. Those are the reasons why people see the collapse of Easter Island society as a metaphor, a worst-case scenario, for what may lie ahead in our own future.

Easter Island society got into trouble because of a class system. With its island world increasingly under ecological strain, the chiefs and priests were overthrown by military leaders and the society descended into the barbarism of civil war and then declined completely. Here too is a lesson for our time: we need to confront the class system and reorganize society in line with the needs of all of its inhabitants before barbarism descends upon us.

The Pentagon report itself takes on a different meaning here. It depicted abrupt climate change and a descent into internecine war. It was "intentionally extreme." But as the fate of Easter Island suggests, it may not have been extreme enough.

## Notes

10. Available at www.ems.org.
11. Thomas R. Karl & Kevin E. Trenberth, "Modern Global Climate Change," *Science* 302, p. 1721; Intergovernmental Panel on Climate Change, *Climate Change 2001* (Cambridge: Cambridge University Press, 2001), pp. 7, 13; Tom Athanasiou & Paul Baer, *Dead Heat* (New York: Seven Stories, 2002), pp. 43–47.
12. "All Downhill from Here?," *Science* 303 (March 12, 2004).
13. National Research Council, *Abrupt Climate Change: Inevitable Surprises* (Washington, D.C.: National Academy Press, 2002) p. 14.
14. Robert B. Gagosian, "Abrupt Climate Change: Should We Be Worried?," World Economic Forum, Davos, Switzerland, January 27, 2003, http://www.whoi.edu; National Research Council, *Abrupt Climate Change*, pp. 115–16B. Dickson, et. al., "Rapid Freshening in the Deep Atlantic Ocean Over the Past Four Decades," *Nature*, 416 (April 25, 2002); B. Hansen, et. al., "Decreasing Overflow from the Nordic Seas into the Atlantic Ocean Through the Faroe Bank Channel Since 1950," *Nature*, 411 (June 21, 2001).
15. Richard B. Alley, *The Two-Mile Time Machine* (Princeton: Princeton University Press, 2000), p. 184.
16. There were no doubt rational motives to assigning the task of writing such a report to Schwartz, who had shown that he had all the necessary dramatic skills of the professional futurologist. Given his past history, and his absolute faith in the system, he could not be viewed as a prophet of doom and gloom or as an enemy of business. Further, a paragraph of *The Long Boom* (p. 153) had actually pointed to the possibility of a shutdown of the thermohaline circulation and the coming of a "another Ice Age"—though this was introduced in a generally pollyan-

naish view of the ecological crisis in which the "long boom" itself provided all the answers.

17. Measured in carbon units.

18. John Bellamy Foster, *Ecology Against Capitalism* (New York: Monthly Review Press, 2002), p. 18; John Bellamy Foster and Brett Clark, "Ecological Imperialism: The Curse of Capitalism," in Leo Panitch and Colin Leys, ed.,

*The Socialist Register* 2004 (New York: Monthly Review Press, 2004), pp. 186–201.

19. Andrew Sims, Aubrey Meyer, and Nick Robbins, *Who Owes Who?: Climate Change, Debt, Equity and Survival*, http://www.jubilee2000uk.; Athanasiou and Baer, Dead Heat, pp. 63–97.

20. Jared Diamond, "Twilight at Easter," *New York Review* of Books, March 25, 2004, pp. 6–10.

# The future of humanity

"How beauteous mankind is!" said Miranda in *The Tempest*.
But can natural evolution or our own genetic engineering
improve on the present model?

## By **Colin Tudge**

Are we it? Have we already seen the best of humanity? Was Plato or Shakespeare or Einstein or Buddha or Lao Tzu or the prophet Mohammed as clever as any human being is ever likely to be? Modern athletes with their minutely cultured hearts and limbs don't run the 100 metres significantly faster than Jesse Owens did in 1936. So is this as fast as people can ever be? In short: has our evolution stopped: and if so, why, and if not, what lies in store? Or might genetic engineering allow us to breed our own superspecies, if not in God's image, at least according to the demands of market forces?

To begin at the beginning. Darwin's great contribution in *The Origin of Species* was to propose not simply evolution, but a plausible mechanism: it happens, he said, "by means of natural selection". The individuals best able to cope at any one time are those most likely to survive and leave offspring. So as the generations pass, each lineage of creatures becomes more and more closely adapted ("fitted") to its particualr surroundings. Natural selection requires an appropriate mechanism of inheritance—one that ensures "like begets like" (that cats have kittens, and horses give birth to foals), but also provides variation, so that not all kittens and foals are identical. Darwin's near contemporary, Gregor Mendel, working in what was then Moravia and is now the Czech Republic, provided just what was needed: he showed that inheritance works by transmitting units of information, now known as genes. Genes encapsulate the characters of the parents, but they are recombined in the offspring through the machinations of sex and and are also prone to random change, of the kind known as mutation. So they provide all the variation that is required.

Darwin did not know of Mendel's work (he had Mendel's account on his desk, but failed to cut the pages), but 20th-century biologists put the two together and, by the 1940s, generated "neo-Darwinism". Creatures that reproduce through sex continually swap and recombine their genes, so all the genes in all the individuals in a sexually breeding population form one great "gene pool". Natural selection operates on the pool as a whole (these neo-Darwinists said). It knocks out individuals who contain less helpful genes, but favours those whose genes are especially advantageous. Thus the "bad" genes tend to be lost as time goes by, while the ones that promote survival and reproduction spread through the pool. Over time, the composition of the gene pool changes and so the creatures change as well. The neo-Darwinian model has been modified somewhat, but that general picture obtains.

There is no destiny in evolution, Darwinian or neo-Darwinian. Natural selection is opportunist and answers to the here and now; it has no mind for the distant future. The fossils tell us that our ancestors grew taller over the past five million years, from about a metre to nearly two, while our brains have puffed up from an apish 400ml or so to 1,400ml—easily the biggest in proportion to body weight of any animal. Perhaps this has made us more like God. But there is nothing in natural selection to suggest that our ancestors did more than adapt to whatever their surroundings threw at them, or to imply that we will grow more godlike as the future unfolds.

Neither will we go the way of *The Eagle*'s Mekon, arch-enemy of Dan Dare: a green homunculus with a head as big as a dustbin and legs like cribbage pegs. Before Darwin, the Frenchman Jean-Baptiste Lamarck proposed a different mechanism of evolution, through "inheritance of acquired characteristics". He observed rightly enough that bodies adapt to whatever is demanded of them, so that blacksmiths, say, acquire bigger muscles. But he was wrong to propose that a blacksmith passes on his hard-earned biceps to his children. If the children want to be tough, they have to do their own smithing. By the same token, thinking won't make our brains grow bigger, in any heritable way, and physical indolence will not shrink our descendants' legs. So our evolution is not shaped by destiny, nor by our own endeavours, nor by our self-indulgence. Neo-Darwinian mutation and selection (plus large slices of chance) are all there is.

---

# The same techniques that made wheat from wild grasses could transform humanity, too

---

But in us, the neo-Darwinian mechanism seems logjammed. Some genetic variants are being lost, as small tribal groups continue to die out; and others are constantly gained by mutations, some of which persist. There are fluctuations: genes that confer resistance to Aids are gaining ground in Africa, for instance, while Kenyans are currently breeding faster than Italians, so any genetic variants that are peculiar to either group must be increasing or falling. But the permanent losses of genes through extinction of minorities are small compared to the whole pool, and while the particular genes of Kenyans may wax in one century, they may wane in another. Most importantly, there is no consistent pressure to push our gene pool in any particular direction. Nobel prize-winners and professional basketball players are lauded, but do not typically leave more offspring than the ordinary Joe. Infant mortality is still high in some societies but, in genetic terms, it strikes randomly because the poor are not genetically distinct.

Genetic logjams certainly happen, as is clear from the fossils. Some lineages of clams remained virtually unchanged for tens or even hundreds of millions of years. Today's leopards and impala are more agile and brainy than their ancestors of 50 million years ago, but they have not changed much in the past three million years. People anatomically undistinguishable from us were living in Africa at least 100,000 years ago.

Yet the deadlock could be broken. Through global war or some other ecological disaster, human beings could again become isolated into island groups, and natural selection could then go to work on each of them separately to produce a range of neo-humans, each adapted to its own island. We should not assume that any of the islands would especially favour brains, which require a great deal of nourishment. Agile climbers of fruit trees might fare best, and so we might again become more simian.

Or human beings might take their own genetic future in hand—which, in principle, has long been within our gift. The same techniques that made wheat from wild grasses and Aberdeen Angus from aurochs could transform humanity, too, in any direction we might care to prescribe—albeit over longer periods, given that we have such an extended generation interval, and many of the characters we might be most interested in undoubtedly have a complex genetic basis. Eugenics, the deliberate transformation of the human gene pool, was popular 100 years ago through most of Europe, and *de rigueur* in the US. Only the Catholics spoke out consistently against it, and the socialists H G Wells, George Bernard Shaw and Sidney and Beatrice Webb were among its most incongruous advocates. Up-to-date Edwardian matrons spoke approvingly of "eugenic" marriages.

The eugenicists were interested not so much in breeding super-people as in preventing the "decline" of the species through the perceived reproductive prodigality of the "feeble minded" (who were taken to include a great many foreigners and a large section of the working class). Hitler revealed the political perils, however, as he wiped out the people who did not meet his own particular criteria and matched blonds with blondes like prize porkers. So eugenics has gone out of fashion and now is virtually taboo. But in various ways, the new biotechnologies seem to open new possibilities and have concentrated minds afresh: cloning, genomics, genetic engineering.

Genetic engineering is the biggie: the transfer of particular stretches of DNA from one individual to another. The first phase of the Human Genome Project was completed last year, and it is already beginning to show which pieces of DNA correspond to which particular genes and which, therefore, are worth transferring. Cloning *qua* cloning is not directly pertinent, but it does provide techniques that will generally be necessary if genetic engineering is ever to progress beyond its simplest stages. Genetic engineering is already commonplace in bacteria, increasingly in food crops (GMOs), and in laboratory mice. It has at least been essayed in farm livestock and, in principle, is certainly applicable to humans. So where might it lead?

Most simply, doctors already try to repair the affected tissues in people with particular diseases: for example, to correct the damaged genes in the lungs of patients with cystic fibrosis (CF). Genetic changes made to the lungs (if and when this becomes possible) would not be reflected in the eggs and sperm, and so would not be passed on to future generations. Some argue that genetically transformed lung cells could escape, to be breathed in by the rest of us. But apart from this hypothetical hazard, no third parties are involved. The ethical problems therefore seem minimal.

More radical would be to repair the CF gene in a very young embryo, so that the whole person who subsequently develops would be genetically changed. His or her sperms or eggs would develop from cells that were already transformed, so the genetic alteration would be passed down the generations. Biologically and ethically, this is far more heavy-duty than *ad hoc* tissue repair.

Whether CF cells are repaired *ad hoc*, or in a young embryo and so passed on, such procedures are clearly in the realms of therapy. CF is a disease that causes suffering: to correct the gene is to attempt a cure. Western medicine is rooted in the belief that therapy, to correct unmistakable illness, is good.

But some already speak not simply of repairing what is obviously damaged, but of improving (according to their own or their clients' judgement) on what already works well enough. By analogy with traditional medicine, this would move us from physic to tonic—a distinction clearly spelled out by controllers of sports, who allow insulin to correct diabetes (some of the greatest athletes have had diabetes) but forbid steroids to pump up muscles that are already perfectly functional. At the end of the line lies the "designer baby", built to a specification in the way that Ferrari builds motor cars. In *Remaking Eden,* Professor Lee Silver of Princeton University in effect advocates such a course, proposing that "GenRich" (genetically enhanced) individuals, primed to gain honours at Princeton and/or to outreach Michael Jordan at the basketball hoop, will be tomorrow's elite. There are plenty of people with cash to spare for such indulgences, says Silver, and plenty of molecular biologists anxious to oblige; and, he says, where the market presses, reality should and indeed must follow.

Yet for all the hype and hand-wringing, the evolutionary impact of these new technologies will surely be virtually zero. The genetic repair of damaged embryos would affect the future, at least in a few families, but it is very difficult to see why anybody should ever want to do such a thing. A person may carry the CF gene (say) yet half of his or her sperm or eggs will be free of it. Even if a carrier marries another carrier, one in four of their embryos will be totally free of the damaged gene. It would be far easier in principle to induce superovulation, fertilise the eggs in vitro to produce a batch of embryos (as is already standard practice for IVF births), and then select the ones that do not contain the mutant gene at all. Only these healthy embryos would then be implanted into the mother. Techniques of the kind that have been developed largely in the context of genetic engineering are employed for diagnosis, but no actual genetic transformation takes place.

Critics, though, have perceived indirect evolutionary consequences if we contrive to rescue babies with damaged genes who would otherwise have died. Those damaged genes, they argue, would once have been purged from the human lineage, but now they survive, and surely this will weaken the pool as a whole. This argument is similar to that of the old eugenicists

who feared the genes of the "feeble minded", and is at least equally misguided.

Most of the genes that cause "single-gene disorders", including CF, have no adverse effects unless they are inherited from both parents. The unfortunate individuals with a double dose are called "homozygotes". The "heterozygotes"—those who inherit the "bad" gene from only one parent—carry that gene and may pass it on to their offspring, but they are not diseased themselves.

Most "bad" genes are rare, but a few are common. The genes that cause sickle-cell anemia occur frequently in people of African descent, while an astonishing one in 20 Caucasians carries the CF mutant. But assuming random mating (as biologists say), each CF carrier has only a one-in-20 chance of mating with another CF carrier; so only one in 400 Caucasian marriages will bring two carriers together. Only one in four of their offspring will inherit the bad gene from both parents, and so be homozygous for CF; so only one in 1,600 children in a Caucasian population will actually manifest the disease. It would be possible to sterilise those children (as if they did not have problems enough already) or to let them die, as they would do if neglected. But it makes no genetic sense to eliminate one in 1,600 children while leaving the carriers, who are so much more common, intact. Indeed, before modern medicine came along, nature had been assiduously eliminating the unfortunate homozygotes for many thousands of years (ever since the CF mutation first occurred) and yet it is still with us.

# To eliminate all "bad" genes, we would need to wipe out the entire human species

Some eugenic zealots could track down all the carriers, and eliminate them: although, if such zealots were Caucasian, they might well find that they themselves were carriers. It's easy to see intuitively, too, that the rarer the gene—and most are far rarer than CF—the more dramatically the heterozygous carriers outnumber the homozygous sufferers. Besides, at least 5,000 different syndromes have been described that are caused by mutations in single genes, and there must in reality be many more, because all our genes are prone to mutation. Thus it is estimated that every one of us is liable to carry an average of five damaged genes that would cause disease if we had children by some similar carrier. To eliminate all "bad genes", we would need to wipe out the entire human species. In short, genetic zealotry is born of nonsense. Humane, sensible medicine implies no genetic risk for our species as a whole.

The designer baby, however, the child conceived like a custom car, is metaphorical pornography that, we may note in passing, is perpetrated not by the much-maligned "press", but by the scientists themselves, many of whom have their eyes on megabucks and argue the market mantra that what people are prepared to pay for is by definition good. Fortunately, it is also ludicrous. This listing of genes through the Human Genome Project does not "open the book of life" as some idle geneticists (not the Cambridge scientists who actually did the work) have claimed.

If we think of genes as words, then what we have is an incomplete lexicon. An individual's apportionment of genes—the genome—should be construed as an arcane work of literature with its own syntax, puns, allusions, redundancies, colloquialisms and overall "meaning" of which we have almost no inkling, and may never understand exhaustively. On present knowledge, or even with what we are likely to know in the next two centuries, it would be as presumptuous to try to improve on the genes of a healthy human baby as it would be to edit sacred verse in medieval Chinese if all we had to go on was a bad dictionary.

So all in all, human beings seem likely to remain as they are, genetically speaking, barring some ecological disaster; and there doesn't seem to be much that meddling human beings can do about it. This, surely, is a mercy. We may have been shaped blindly by evolution. We may have been guided on our way by God. Whichever it was, or both, the job has been done a million times better than we are ever likely to do. Natural selection is far more subtle than human invention. "What a piece of work is a man!" said Hamlet. "How beauteous mankind is!" said Miranda. Both of them were absolutely right.

# The secret nuclear war

The equivalent of a nuclear war has already happened. Over the last half-century, millions have died as a result of accidents, experiments, lies and cover-ups by the nuclear industry. **Eduardo Goncalves** pulls together a number of examples, and counts the fearful total cost.

Hugo Paulino was proud to be a fusilier. He was even prouder to be serving as a UN peacekeeper in Kosovo. It was his chance to help the innocent casualties of war. His parents did not expect him to become one.

Hugo, says his father Luis, died of leukaemia caused by radiation from depleted uranium (DU) shells fired by NATO during the Kosovo war. He was one of hundreds of Portuguese peacekeepers sent to Klina, an area heavily bombed with these munitions. Their patrol detail included the local lorry park, bombed because it had served as a Serb tank reserve, and the Valujak mines, which sheltered Serbian troops.

In their time off, the soldiers bathed in the river and gratefully supplemented their tasteless rations with local fruit and cheeses given to them by thankful nuns from the convent they guarded. Out of curiosity, they would climb inside the destroyed Serbian tanks littering the area.

Hugo arrived back in Portugal from his tour of duty on 12 February 2000, complaining of headaches, nausea and 'flu-like symptoms'. Ten days later, on 22 February, he suffered a major seizure. He was rushed to Lisbon's military hospital, where his condition rapidly deteriorated. On 9 March, he died. He was 21.

The military autopsy, which was kept secret for 10 months, claimed his death was due to septicaemia and 'herpes of the brain'. Not so, says Luis Paulino. 'When he was undergoing tests, a doctor called me over and said he thought it could be from radiation.'

It was only then that Luis learnt about the uranium shells—something his son had never been warned about or given protective clothing against. He contacted doctors and relatives of Belgian and Italian soldiers suspected of having succumbed to radiation poisoning.

'The similarities were extraordinary', he said. 'My son had died from leukaemia. That is why the military classified the autopsy report and wanted me to sign over all rights to its release.'

Today, Kosovo is littered with destroyed tanks, and pieces of radioactive shrapnel. NATO forces fired 31,000 depleted uranium shells during the Kosovo campaign, and 10,800 into neighbouring Bosnia. The people NATO set out to protect—and the soldiers it sent out to protect them—are now dying. According to Bosnia's health minister, Boza Ljubic, cancer deaths among civilians have risen to 230 cases per 100,000 last year, up from 152 in 1999. Leukaemia cases, he added, had doubled.

Scientists predict that the use of DU in Serbia will lead to more than 10,000 deaths from cancer among local residents, aid workers, and peacekeepers. Belated confessions that plutonium was also used may prompt these estimates to be revised. But while NATO struggles to stave off accusations of a cover-up, the Balkans are merely the newest battlefield in a silent world war that has claimed millions of lives. Most of its victims have died not in war-zones, but in ordinary communities scattered across the globe.

## The hidden deaths of Newbury

Far away from the war-torn Balkans is Newbury, a prosperous white-collar industrial town in London's commuter belt. On its outskirts is Greenham Common, the former US Air Force station that was one of America's most important strategic bases during the Cold War. The base was closed down after the signing of the INF (Intermediate Nuclear Forces) Treaty by Ronald Reagan and Mikhail Gorbachev. The nuclear threat was over. Or so people thought.

In August 1993, Ann Capewell—who lived just one mile away from the base's former runway—died of acute myeloid leukaemia. She was 16 when she passed away, just 40 days after diagnosis. As they were coming to terms with their sudden loss, her parents—Richard and Elizabeth—were surprised to find a number of other cases of leukaemia in their locality.

The more they looked, the more cases they found. 'Many were just a stone's throw from our front door,' says Richard, 'mainly cases of myeloid leukaemia in young people.' What none of them knew was that they were the victims of a nuclear accident at Greenham Common that had been carefully covered up by successive British and American administrations.

> ## 'It is believed that the estimated 1,900 nuclear tests conducted during the Cold War released fallout equivalent to 40,000 Hiroshimas in every corner of the globe.'

On February 28 1958, a laden B-47 nuclear bomber was awaiting clearance for take-off when it was suddenly engulfed in a huge fireball. Another bomber flying overhead had dropped a full fuel tank just 65 feet away. The plane exploded and burnt uncontrollably for days. As did its deadly payload.

A secret study by scientists at Britain's nearby nuclear bomb laboratory at Aldermaston documented the fallout, but the findings were never disclosed. The report showed how radioactive particles had been 'glued' to the runway surface by fire-fighters attempting to extinguish the blazing bomber—and that these were now being slowly blown into Newbury and over other local communities by aircraft jet blast.

'Virtually all the cases of leukaemias and lymphomas are in a band stretching from Greenham Common into south Newbury,' says Elizabeth. However, the British government continues to deny the cluster's existence, whilst the Americans still insist there was no accident.

Yet this was just one of countless disasters, experiments and officially-sanctioned activities which the nuclear powers have kept a closely-guarded secret. Between them, they have caused a global human death toll which is utterly unprecedented and profoundly shocking.

## Broken Arrows

In 1981, the Pentagon publicly released a list of 32 'Broken Arrows—official military terminology for an accident involving a nuclear weapon. The report gave few details and did not divulge the location of some accidents. It was prepared in response to mounting media pressure about possible accident cover-ups.

But another US government document, this time secret, indicates that the official report may be seriously misleading. It states that 'a total of 1,250 nuclear weapons have been involved in accidents during handling, storage and transportation', a number of which 'resulted in, or had high potential for, plutonium dispersal.'[1]

Washington has never acknowledged the human consequences of even those few accidents it admits to, such as the Thule disaster in Greenland in 1968. When a B-52 bomber crashed at this secret nuclear base, all four bombs detonated, and a cloud of plutonium rose 800 metres in the air, blowing deadly radioactive particles hundreds of miles. The authorities downplayed the possibility of any health risks. But today, many local Eskimos, and their huskies, suffer from cancer, and over 300 people involved in the clean-up operation alone have since died of cancer and mysterious illnesses.

We may never know the true toll from all the bomb accidents, as the nuclear powers classify these disasters not as matters of public interest but of 'national security' instead. Indeed, it is only now that details are beginning to emerge of some accidents at bomb factories and nuclear plants that took place several decades ago.

## Soviet sins

In 1991, Polish film-maker Slawomir Grunberg was invited to a little-known town in Russia's Ural mountains that was once part of a top-secret Soviet nuclear bomb-making complex. What he found was a tragedy of extraordinary dimensions, largely unknown to the outside world, and ignored by post-Cold War leaders.

His film—*Chelyabinsk: The Most Contaminated Spot on the Planet*—tells the story of the disasters at the Soviet Union's first plutonium factory, and the poisoning of hundreds of thousands of people. For years, the complex dumped its nuclear waste—totalling 76 million cubic metres—into the Techa River, the sole water source for scores of local communities that line its banks. According to a local doctor, people received an average radiation dose 57 times higher than that of Chernobyl's inhabitants.

In 1957, there was an explosion at a waste storage facility that blew 2 million curies of radiation into the atmosphere. The kilometre-high cloud drifted over three

## The cancer epidemic

Scientists at St Andrew's University recently found that cells exposed to a dose of just two alpha particles of radiation produced as many cancers as much higher doses of radiation. They concluded that a single alpha particle of radiation could be carcinogenic.

Herman Muller, who has received a Nobel Prize for his work, has shown how the human race's continuous exposure to so-called 'low-level' radiation is causing a gradual reduction in its ability to survive, as successive generations are genetically damaged. The spreading and accumulation of even tiny genetic mutations pass through family lines, provoking allergies, asthma, juvenile diabetes, hypertension, arthritis, high blood cholesterol conditions, and muscular and bone defects.

Dr Chris Busby, who has extensively researched the low-level radiation threat, has made a link between everyday radiation exposure and a range of modern ailments: 'There have been tremendous increases in diseases resulting from the breakdown of the immune system in the last 20 years: diabetes, asthma, AIDS and others which may have an immune-system link, such as MS and ME. A whole spectrum of neurological conditions of unknown origin has developed'.[10]

Around the world, a pattern is emerging. For the first time in modern history, mortality rates among adults between the ages of 15 and 54 are actually increasing, and have been since 1982. In July 1983, the US Center for Birth Defects in Atlanta, Georgia, reported that physical and mental disabilities in the under-17s had doubled—despite a reduction in diseases such as polio, and improved vaccines and medical care.

Defects in new-born babies doubled between the 1950s and 1980s, as did long-term debilitating diseases. The US Environmental Protection Agency adds that 23 per cent of US males were sterile in 1980, compared to 0.5 per cent in 1938.

Above all, cancer is now an epidemic. In 1900, cancer accounted for only 4 per cent of deaths in the US. Now it is the second leading cause of premature mortality. Worldwide, the World Health Organisation (WHO) estimates the number of cancers will double in most countries over the next 25 years.

Within a few years, the chances of getting cancer in Britain will be as high as 40 per cent—virtually the toss of a coin.

---

Soviet provinces, contaminating over 250,000 people living in 217 towns and villages. Only a handful of local inhabitants were ever evacuated.

10 years later, Lake Karachay, also used as a waste dump, began to dry up. The sediment around its shores blew 5 million curies of radioactive dust over 25,000 square kilometres, irradiating 500,000 people. Even today, the lake is so 'hot' that standing on its shore will kill a person within one hour.

Grunberg's film tells of the terrible toll of these disasters on local families, such as that of Idris Sunrasin, whose grandmother, parents and three siblings have died of cancer. Leukaemia cases increased by 41 per cent after the plant began operations, and the average life span for women in 1993 was 47, compared to 72 nationally. For men it was just 45.

### The secret nuclear war

Russia's nuclear industry is commonly regarded as cavalier in regard to health and safety. But the fact is that the nuclear military-industrial complex everywhere has been quite willing to deliberately endanger and sacrifice the lives of innocent civilians to further its ambitions.

The US government, for example, recently admitted its nuclear scientists carried out over 4,000 experiments on live humans between 1944 and 1974. They included feeding radioactive food to disabled children, irradiating prisoners' testicles, and trials on new-born babies and pregnant mothers. Scientists involved with the Manhattan Project injected people with plutonium without telling them. An autopsy of one of the victims reportedly showed that his bones 'looked like Swiss cheese'. At the University of Cincinnati, 88 mainly low-income, black women were subjected to huge doses of radiation in an experiment funded by the military. They suffered acute radiation sickness. Nineteen of them died.

## 'Scientists predict that millions will die in centuries to come from nuclear tests that happened in the 1950s and 1960s.'

Details of many experiments still remain shrouded in secrecy, whilst little is known of the more shocking ones to come to light—such as one when a man was injected with what a report described as 'about a lethal dose' of strontium-89.[2]

In Britain too, scientists have experimented with plutonium on new-born babies, ethnic minorities and the disabled. When American colleagues reviewed a British proposal for a joint experiment, they concluded: 'What is the worst thing that can happen to a human being as a result of being a subject? Death.'[3]

They also conducted experiments similar to America's 'Green Run' programme, in which 'dirty' radiation was released over populated areas in the western states of Washington and Oregon contaminating farmland, crops and water. The 'scrubber' filters in Hanford's nuclear stacks were deliberately switched off first. Scientists, posing as agriculture department officials, found radiation contamination levels on farms hundreds of times above 'safety' levels.

But America's farmers and consumers were not told this, and the British public has never been officially told about experiments on its own soil.

## Forty thousand Hiroshimas

It is believed that the estimated 1,900 nuclear tests conducted during the Cold War released fallout equivalent to 40,000 Hiroshimas in every corner of the globe. Fission products from the Nevada Test site can be detected in the ecosystems of countries as far apart as South Africa, Brazil, and Malaysia. Here, too, ordinary people were guinea pigs in a global nuclear experiment. The public health hazards were known right from the beginning, but concealed from the public. A 1957 US government study predicted that recent American tests had produced an extra 2,000 'genetically defective' babies in the US each year, and up to 35,000 every year around the globe. They continued regardless.

Ernest Sternglass's research shows how, in 1964, between 10,000 and 15,000 children were lost by miscarriage and stillbirth in New York state alone—and that there were some 10 to 15 times this number of foetal deaths across America.[4]

# 'Over the years, the Harwell, Aldermaston and Amersham plants have pumped millions of gallons of liquid contaminated with radioactive waste into the River Thames.'

Those who lived closest to the test sites have seen their families decimated. Such as the 100,000 people who were directly downwind of Nevada's fallout. They included the Mormon community of St George in Utah, 100 miles away from 'Ground Zero'—the spot where the bombs were detonated. Cancer used to be virtually unheard of among its population. Mormons do not smoke or drink alcohol or coffee, and live largely off their own homegrown produce.

Mormons are also highly patriotic. They believe government to be 'God-given', and do not protest. The military could afford to wait until the wind was blowing from the test site towards St George before detonating a device. After all, President Eisenhower had said: 'We can afford to sacrifice a few thousand people out there in defence of national security.'[5]

When the leukaemia cases suddenly appeared, doctors—unused to the disease—literally had no idea what it was. A nine-year-old boy, misdiagnosed with diabetes, died after a single shot of insulin. Women who complained of radiation sickness symptoms were told they had 'housewife syndrome'. Many gave birth to terribly deformed babies that became known as 'the sacrifice babies'. Elmer Pickett, the local mortician, had to learn new embalming techniques for the small bodies of wasted children killed by leukaemia. He himself was to lose no fewer than 16 members of his immediate family to cancer.

By the mid-1950s, just a few years after the tests began, St George had a leukaemia rate 2.5 times the national average, whereas before it was virtually non-existent. The total number of radiation deaths are said to have totalled 1,600—in a town with a population of just 5,000.

The military simply lied about the radiation doses people were getting. Former army medic Van Brandon later revealed how his unit kept two sets of radiation readings for test fallout in the area. 'One set was to show that no one received an [elevated] exposure' whilst 'the other set of books showed the actual reading. That set was brought in a locked briefcase every morning.'[6]

## Continuous fallout

The world's population is still being subjected to the continuous fallout of the 170 megatons of long-lived nuclear fission products blasted into the atmosphere and returned daily to earth by wind and rain—slowly poisoning our bodies via the air we breathe, the food we eat, and the water we drink. Scientists predict that millions will die in centuries to come from tests that happened in the 1950s and 1960s.

But whilst atmospheric testing is now banned, over 400 nuclear bomb factories and power plants around the world make 'routine discharges' of nuclear waste into the environment. Thousands of nuclear waste dumping grounds, many of them leaking, are contaminating soil and water every day. The production of America's nuclear weapons arsenal alone has produced 100 million cubic metres of long-lived radioactive waste.

The notorious Hanford plutonium factory—which produced the fissile materials for the Trinity test and Nagasaki bomb—has discharged over 440 billion gallons of contaminated liquid into the surrounding area, contaminating 200 square miles of groundwater, but concealed the dangers from the public. Officials knew as early as the late 1940s that the nearby Columbia River was becoming seriously contaminated and a hazard to local fishermen. They chose to keep information about discharges secret and not to issue warnings.

In Britain, there are 7,000 sites licensed to use nuclear materials, 1,000 of which are allowed to discharge wastes. Three of them, closely involved in Britain's nuclear bomb programme, are located near the River Thames. Over the years, the Harwell, Aldermaston and Amersham plants have pumped millions of gallons of liquid contaminated with radioactive waste into the river.

They did so in the face of opposition from government ministers and officials who said 'the 6 million inhabitants of London derive their drinking water from this source. Any increase in [radio-]activity of the water supply would increase the genetic load on this comparatively large group.'[7] One government minister even wrote of his fears that the dumping 'would produce between 10 and 300 severely abnormal individuals per generation'.

Public relations officers at Harwell themselves added: 'the potential sufferers are 8 million in number, including both Houses of Parliament, Fleet Street and Whitehall'. These discharges continue to this day.

Study after study has uncovered 'clusters' of cancers and high rates of other unusual illnesses near nuclear plants, including deformities and Down Syndrome. Exposure to radiation among Sellafield's workers, in northwest England, has been linked to a greater risk of fathering a stillborn child and leukaemia among off-spring. Reports also suggest a higher risk of babies developing spina bifida in the womb.

Although the plant denies any link, even official MAFF studies have shown high levels of contamination in locally-grown fruit and vegetables, as well as wild animals. The pollution from Sellafield alone is such that it has coated the shores of the whole of Britain—from Wales to Scotland, and even Hartlepool in north-eastern England. A nationwide study organised by Harwell found that Sellafield 'is a source of plutonium contamination in the wider population of the British Isles'.[8]

> **'Study after study has uncovered 'clusters' of cancers and high rates of other illnesses near nuclear plants, including deformities and Down Syndrome. Exposure to radiation among Sellafield's workers, in NW England, has been linked to a greater risk of fathering a stillborn child and leukaemia among off-spring.'**

Those who live nearest the plant face the greatest threat. A study of autopsy tissue by the National Radiological Protection Board (NRPB) found high plutonium levels in the lungs of local Cumbrians—350 per cent higher than people in other parts of the country. 'Cancer clusters' have been found around nuclear plants across the globe—from France to Taiwan, Germany to Canada. A joint White House/US Department of Energy investigation recently found a high incidence of 22 different kinds of cancer at 14 different US nuclear weapons facilities around the country.

Meanwhile, a Greenpeace USA study of the toxicity of the Mississippi river showed that from 1968-83 there were 66,000 radiation deaths in the counties lining its banks—more than the number of Americans who died during the Vietnam war.

## Don't blame us

Despite the growing catalogue of tragedy, the nuclear establishment has consistently tried to deny responsibility. It claims that only high doses of radiation—such as those experienced by the victims of the Hiroshima and Nagasaki bombs—are dangerous, though even here they have misrepresented the data. They say that the everyday doses from nuclear plant discharges, bomb factories and transportation of radioactive materials are 'insignificant', and that accidents are virtually impossible.

The truth, however, is that the real number and seriousness of accidents has never been disclosed, and that the damage from fallout has been covered up. The nuclear establishment now grudgingly (and belatedly) accepts that there is no such thing as a safe dose of radiation, however 'low', yet the poisonous discharges continue. When those within the nuclear establishment try to speak out, they are harassed, intimidated—and even threatened.

John Gofman, former head of Lawrence Livermore's biomedical unit, who helped produce the world's first plutonium for the bomb, was for years at the heart of the nuclear complex. He recalls painfully the time he was called to give evidence before a Congressional inquiry set up to defuse mounting concern over radiation's dangers.

'Chet Holifield and Craig Hosmer of the Joint Committee (on Atomic Energy) came in and turned to me and said: "Just what the hell do you think you two are doing, getting all those little old ladies in tennis shoes up in arms about our atomic energy program? There are people like you who have tried to hurt the Atomic Energy Commission program before. We got them, and we'll get you."'[9]

Gofman was eventually forced out of his job. But the facts of his research—and that of many other scientists—speak for themselves.

## The final reckoning

But could radiation really be to blame for these deaths? Are the health costs really that great? The latest research suggests they are.

It is only very recently that clues have surfaced as to the massive destructive power of radiation in terms of human health. The accident at Chernobyl will kill an estimated half a million people worldwide from cancer, and perhaps more. 90 per cent of children in the neighbouring former Soviet republic of Belarus are contaminated for life—the poisoning of an entire country's gene pool.

Ernest Sternglass calculates that, at the height of nuclear testing, there were as many as 3 million foetal deaths, spontaneous abortions and stillbirths in the US alone. In addition, 375,000 babies died in their first year of life from radiation-linked diseases.[11]

# The final reckoning

How many deaths is the nuclear industry responsible for? The following calculations of numbers of cancers caused by radiation are the latest and most accurate:[*]

from nuclear bomb production and testing:     385 million

from bomb and plant accidents:     9.7 million

from the 'routine discharges' of nuclear power plants
(5 million of them among populations living nearby):     6.6 million

likely number of total cancer fatalities worldwide:     175 million

[Added to this number are 235 million genetically damaged and diseased people, and 588 million children born with diseases such as brain damage, mental disabilities, spina bifida, genital deformities, and childhood cancers.]

[*]*Calculated by Rosalie Bertell, using the official 'radiation risk' estimates published in 1991 by the International Commission on Radiological Protection (ICRP), and the total radiation exposure data to the global population calculated by the UN Scientific Committee on the Effects of Atomic Radiation (UNSCEAR) in 1993.*

Rosalie Bertell, author of the classic book *No Immediate Danger*, now revised and re-released, has attempted to piece together a global casualty list from the nuclear establishment's own data. The figures she has come up with are chilling—but entirely plausible.

Using the official 'radiation risk' estimates published in 1991 by the International Commission on Radiological Protection (ICRP), and the total radiation exposure data to the global population calculated by the UN Scientific Committee on the Effects of Atomic Radiation (UN-SCEAR) in 1993, she has come up with a terrifying tally:

- 358 million cancers from nuclear bomb production and testing
- 9.7 million cancers from bomb and plant accidents
- 6.6 million cancers from the 'routine discharges' of nuclear power plants (5 million of them among populations living nearby).
- As many as 175 million of these cancers could be fatal.

Added to this number are no fewer than 235 million genetically damaged and diseased people, and a staggering 588 million children born with what are called 'teratogenic effects'—diseases such as brain damage, mental disabilities, spina bifida, genital deformities, and childhood cancers.

Furthermore, says Bertell, we should include the problem of nonfatal cancers and of other damage which is debilitating but not counted for insurance and liability purposes'[12]—such as the 500 million babies lost as still-births because they were exposed to radiation whilst still in the womb, but are not counted as 'official' radiation victims.

It is what the nuclear holocaust peace campaigners always warned of if war between the old superpowers broke out, yet it has already happened and with barely a shot being fired. Its toll is greater than that of all the wars in history put together, yet no-one is counted as among the war dead.

## 'It is the nuclear holocaust that peace campaigners always warned of if war between the old superpowers broke out, yet it has already happened and with barely a shot being fired.'

Its virtually infinite killing and maiming power leads Rosalie Bertell to demand that we learn a new language to express a terrifying possibility: 'The concept of species annihilation means a relatively swift, deliberately induced end to history, culture, science, biological reproduction and memory. It is the ultimate human rejection of the gift of life, an act which requires a new word to describe it: omnicide'.[13]

*Eduardo Goncalves is a freelance journalist and environmental researcher. He is author of tile reports **Broken Arrow—Greenham Common's Secret Nuclear Accident** and **Nuclear Guinea Pigs—British Human Radiation Experiments**, published by CND (UK), and was researcher to the film **The Dragon that Slew St George**. He is currently writing a book about the hidden history of the nuclear age.*

## Notes

1. 'Report of the safety criteria for plutonium-bearing weapons—summary', US Department of Energy, February 14, 1973, document RS5640/1035.

2. Strontium metabolism meeting, Atomic Energy Division–Division of Biology and Medicine, January 17,1954.
3. memorandum to Bart Gledhill, chairman, Human Subjects Committee. LLNL, from Larry Anderson, LLNL, February 21,1989.
4. see 'Secret Fallout, Low-Level Radiation from Hiroshima to Three-Mile Island'. Ernest Sternglass, McGraw-Hill, New York, 1981.
5. see 'American Ground Zero; The Secret Nuclear War', Carole Gallagher, MIT Press. Boston, 1993.
6. Washington Post, February 24, 1994.
7. see PRO files AB 6/1379 and AB 6/2453 and 3584.
8. 'Variations in the concentration of plutonium, strontium-90 and total alpha-emitters in human teeth', RG. O'Donnell et al, Sd. Tot. Env, 201 (1997) 235–243.
9. interview with Gofman, DOE/OHRE Oral History Project, December 1994, pp 49-50 of official transcripts.
10. 'Wings of Death—nuclear pollution and human health', Dr. Chris Busby, Green Audit, Wales, 1995
11. see 'Secret Fallout, Low-Level Radiation from Hiroshima to Three-Mile Island', Ernest Sternglass, McGraw-Hill, New York, 1981.
12. from 'No Immediate Danger— Prognosis for a Radioactive Earth', Dr Rosalie Bertell. Women's Press. London 1985 (revised 2001)
13. pers. Comm. 4 February 2001

## Further reading:

'No Immediate Danger—Prognosis for a Radioactive Earth', Dr Rosalie Bertell, Women's Press, London (revised 2001)
'Deadly Deceit—low-level radiation, high-level cover-up', Dr. Jay Gould and Benjamin A. Goldman, Four Walls Eight Windows, New York, 1991
'Wings of Death—nuclear pollution and human health', Dr. Chris Busby, Green Audit, Wales, 1995
'American Ground Zero: The Secret Nuclear War', Carole Gallagher, MIT Press, Boston, 1993
'Radioactive Heaven and Earth—the health effects of nuclear weapons testing in, on, and above the earth', a report of the IPPNW International Commission, Zed Books, 1991
'Secret Fallout. Low-Level Radiation from Hiroshima to Three-Mile Island', Ernest Sternglass, McGraw-Hill, New York, 1981
'Clouds of Deceit—the deadly legacy of Britain's bomb tests', Joan Smith, Faber and Faber, London, 1985
'Nuclear Wastelands', Arjun Makhijani et al (eds), MIT Press, Boston, 1995 'Radiation and Human Health', Dr. John W. Gofman, Sierra Book Club, San Francisco, 1981
'The Greenpeace Book of the Nuclear Age—The Hidden History, the Human Cost', John May, Victor Gollancz, 1989
'The Unsinkable Aircraft Carrier—American military power in Britain', Duncan Campbell, Michael Joseph, London 1984

# The Globalization of Politics

## American foreign policy for a new century

September 11 signaled the end of the age of geopolitics and the advent of a new age—the era of global politics. The challenge U.S. policymakers face today is to recognize that fundamental change in world politics and to use America's unrivaled military, economic, and political power to fashion an international environment conducive to its interests and values.

By Ivo H. Daalder and James M. Lindsay

For much of the 20th century, geopolitics drove American foreign policy. Successive presidents sought to prevent any single country from dominating the centers of strategic power in Europe and Asia. To that end the United States fought two world wars and carried on its four-decade-long Cold War with the Soviet Union. The collapse of the Soviet empire ended the last serious challenge for territorial dominion over Eurasia. The primary goal of American foreign policy was achieved.

During the 1990s, American foreign policy focused on consolidating its success. Together with its European allies, the United States set out to create, for the first time in history, a peaceful, undivided, and democratic Europe. That effort is now all but complete. The European Union—which will encompass most of Europe with the expected accession of 10 new members in 2004—has become the focal point for European policy on a wide range of issues. The North Atlantic Treaty Organization has evolved from a collective defense alliance into Europe's main security institution. A new relationship with Russia is being forged.

Progress has been slower, though still significant, in Asia. U.S. relations with its two key regional partners, Japan and South Korea, remain the foundation of regional stability. Democracy is taking root in South Korea, the Philippines, Indonesia,

and Taiwan. U.S. engagement with China is slowly tying an economically surging Beijing into the global economy.

The success of American policy over the past decade means that no power—not Russia, not Germany, not a united Europe, and not China or Japan—today poses a hegemonic threat to Eurasia. In this new era, American foreign policy will no longer pivot on geography. Instead, it will be defined by the combination of America's unrivaled power in world affairs and the extensive and growing globalization of world politics.

## The Sole Global Power

The United States is today the only truly global power. Its military reach—whether on land, at sea, or in the air—extends to every point on the globe. Its economic prowess fuels world trade and industry. Its political and cultural appeal—what Joseph Nye has called soft power—is so extensive that most international institutions reflect American interests. America's position in the world is unique—no other country in history has ever come close.

But is America's exalted position sustainable? Militarily, the vast gap between the United States and everyone else is growing. Whereas defense spend-

ing in most other countries is falling, U.S. defense spending is rising rapidly. This year's requested increase in defense spending is greater than the entire Chinese defense budget. Most remarkably, America can afford to spend more. Defense spending takes a smaller share of the U.S. gross domestic product than it did a decade ago—and even the Bush administration's projected increases will produce an overall budget equal to only about 3.5 percent of GDP, about half of Cold War highs. There is little prospect of any country or group of countries devoting the resources necessary to begin competing with the United States militarily, let alone surpassing it.

Economically, the United States may not widen its edge over its competitors, but neither is it likely to fall behind. The U.S. economy has proved itself at least as adept as its major competitors in realizing the productivity gains made possible by information technology. Europe and Japan face severe demographic challenges as their populations rapidly age, creating likely labor shortages and severe budgetary pressures. China is modernizing rapidly, and Russia may have turned the corner, but their economies today are comparable in output to those of Italy and Belgium—and they have yet to develop a political infrastructure that can support sustained economic growth.

In this new era, American foreign policy will be defined by the combination of America's unrivaled power in world affairs and the extensive and growing globalization of world politics.

Which brings us to the issue of how to transform this unquestioned power into influence. Unless employed deftly, America's military and economic superiority can breed resentment, even among its friends. A growing perception that Washington cares only about its own interests and is willing to use its muscle to get its way has fueled a worrisome gap between U.S. and European attitudes. European elites increasingly criticize the United States as being morally, socially, and culturally retrograde—especially in its perceived embrace of the death penalty, predatory capitalism, and fast food and mass entertainment. Europe has also begun to exercise diplomatic muscle in international institutions and other arenas, seeking to create new international regimes designed to limit America's recourse to its hard power.

The sustainability of American power ultimately depends on the extent to which others believe it is employed not just in U.S. interests but in their interests as well. Following its victory in World War II, the United States led the effort to create not only new security institutions, such as the United Nations and NATO, but also new regimes to promote economic recovery, development, and prosperity, such as the Marshall Plan, the Bretton Woods monetary system, and the General Agreement on Trade and Tariffs to promote free trade. These institutions and agreements preserved and extended American power— but in a way that benefited all who participated. The challenge for the United States is to do the same today.

## Globalization

Globalization is not just an economic phenomenon, but a political, cultural, military, and environmental one as well. Nor is globalization new; networks of interdependence spanning continents were increasing rapidly in the decades before the First World War as the steam engine and the telegraph reduced the cost of transportation and information. What distinguishes globalization today is the speed and volume of cross-border contacts.

The prophets of globalization have trumpeted its benefits, particularly how the increased flow of goods, services, and capital across borders can boost economic activity and enhance prosperity. During the 1990s the more globalized economies grew an average of 5 percent a year, while the less globalized economies contracted by an average of 1 percent a year. The spread of ideas and information across the Internet and other global media has broadened cultural horizons and empowered people around the world to challenge autocratic rulers and advance the cause of human rights and democracy. Globalization can even lessen the chance of war. Fearing that war with Pakistan would disrupt its ties to U.S.-based multinationals, India's powerful electronic sector successfully pressed New Delhi in mid-2002 to de-escalate its conflict with Pakistan.

But globalization also brings terrible new perils. A handful of men from halfway across the globe can hijack four commercial airliners and slam them into key symbols' of American power, killing thousands. A computer hacker in the Philippines can shut down the Internet and disrupt e-commerce thousands of miles away. Speculators can produce a run on the Thai currency, plunging Russia and Brazil into recession, robbing American exporters of markets, and costing American jobs. Greenhouse gases accumulating in the atmosphere in newly booming economies can raise global temperatures, possibly flooding coastal plains and turning mountain meadows into deserts.

Worse for the United States is that its power makes it a magnet for terrorism. As Richard Betts has argued, America's power "animates both the terrorists' purposes and their choice of tactics. . . . Political and cultural power makes the United States a target for those who blame it for their problems. At the same time, American economic and military power prevents them from resisting or retaliating against the United States on its own terms. To smite the only superpower requires unconventional modes of force and tactics [which] offer hope to the weak that they can work their will despite their overall deficit in power." Worse still, other weak countries might decide to buy their security by turning a blind eye to terrorist activities on their soil, thereby increasing the risk to the United States.

## Americanists versus Globalists: The Utility of Power

Much of the foreign policy debate in the United States today revolves around assessments of the fundamental importance of American primacy and globalization. Americanists, so called because they emphasize American primacy, see a world in which the United States can use its predominant power to get its way, regardless of what others want. They believe the United States must summon the will to go it alone if necessary. Globalists emphasize globalization. They see a world that defies unilateral U.S. solutions and instead requires international cooperation. They warn against thinking that America can go it alone.

Americanists see two great virtues in America's primacy. First, it enables the United States to set its own foreign policy objectives and to achieve them without relying on others. The result is a preference for unilateral action, unbound by international agreements or institutions that would otherwise constrain America's ability to act. As Charles Krauthammer puts it, "An unprecedentedly dominant United States ... is in the unique position of being able to fashion its own foreign policy. After a decade of Prometheus playing pygmy, the first task of the new [Bush] administration is precisely to reassert American freedom of action." The views, preferences, and interests of allies, friends, or anyone else should therefore have no influence on American action.

Second, because American power enables the United States to pursue its interests as it pleases, American foreign policy should seek to maintain, extend, and strengthen that relative position of power. As President Bush told graduating West Point cadets last June, "America has, and intends to keep, military strength beyond challenge, thereby making the destabilizing arms races of other eras pointless, and limiting rivalries to trade and other pursuits of peace." In other words, the United States can achieve its policy objectives best if it can prevent others from acquiring the power necessary to oppose it effectively when interests clash. It is as good a definition of what would constitute an American empire as one can get.

In contrast, Globalists stress how globalization both limits and transforms America's capacity to use its power to influence events overseas. At bottom, the challenges and opportunities created by the forces of globalization are not susceptible to America acting on its own. Combating the spread of infectious diseases, preventing the spread of weapons of mass destruction, defeating terrorism, securing access to open markets, protecting human rights, promoting democracy, and preserving the environment all require the cooperation of other countries. As British Prime Minister Tony Blair put it succinctly following the September 11 attacks, "We are all internationalists now."

But, Globalists argue, it is not simply that the nature of the issues arising from globalization limits the reach of American power and compels international cooperation. Globalization transforms the nature of power itself. No one has grappled with this problem more thoughtfully than Joseph Nye in his latest book, *The Paradox of American Power*. As Nye explains, "Power today is distributed among countries in a pattern that resembles a complex three-dimensional chess game." One dimension is military power, where the United States enjoys an unrivaled advantage, and the power distribution is therefore unipolar. The second dimension is economic, where power among the United States, Europe, and Japan is distributed more equally. The third dimension is transnational relations, where power is widely dispersed and essentially beyond government control. This is the realm of nonstate actors—from multinational companies and money managers to terrorist organizations and crime syndicates to nongovernmental organizations and the international media. "Those who recommend a hegemonic [or power-based] American foreign policy," Nye concludes, "are relying on woefully inadequate analysis. When you are in a three-dimensional game, you will lose if you focus on the interstate military board and fail to notice the other boards and the vertical connections among them."

## Who Is Right?

Both Americanists and Globalists are right in important ways. Take the Americanists first. Despite globalization, power remains the coin of the realm in international politics. Five decades of concerted U.S. and allied efforts may have transformed Europe into a Kantian zone of perpetual peace where the rule of law has triumphed, but in much of the rest of the world military might continues to hold sway. True, no country, not even China, poses the geostra-

tegic threat to the United States that first Germany and then the Soviet Union did in the previous century. Still, lesser-order threats abound, from Pyongyang to Tehran to Baghdad, and U.S. military and economic power will be needed to contain, if not extinguish, them. More broadly, the rule of law demands more than simply codifying rules of behavior. It also requires the willingness and ability to enforce them. But that requirement, as Mancur Olson demonstrated years ago, runs into a fundamental collective-action problem—if the potential, costs of action are great and the benefits widely shared, few will be willing to incur the costs. That is where overwhelming power, and the concomitant willingness and ability to provide for global public goods, makes a crucial difference. So, without American primacy—or something like it—it is doubtful that the rule of law can be sustained.

The wise application of American primacy can further U.S. values and interests. The use (or threat) of American military might evicted Iraqi troops from Kuwait, convinced Haiti's military junta to relinquish power, ended Serbian atrocities in Kosovo, and broke al-Qaida's hold over Afghanistan. Nor does American primacy advance only U.S. interests and values. As the one country willing and able to break deadlocks and stalemates preventing progress on issues from promoting peace in the Balkans, Northern Ireland, and the Middle East to preserving financial stability around the world, the United States frequently advances the interests of most other democratic states as well. Often, the United States is exactly what Madeleine Albright said it was—the indispensable nation that makes it possible to mobilize the world into effective action.

And the United States does differ from other countries. Unique among past hegemons in not seeking to expand its power through territorial gains, it is also unique among its contemporaries. Its primacy and global interests prompt others both to seek its assistance in addressing their problems and to resent it for meddling in their affairs. The ambivalence the world feels about American engagement—as well as the unique nature of that engagement—makes it imperative that the United States not mistake the conduct of foreign policy for a popularity contest. Doing the right thing may not always be popular—but it is vitally important nevertheless.

But Globalists are right that while America is powerful, it is not omnipotent. Far more able than most countries to pro-

tect itself against the pernicious consequences of globalization, it is by no means invulnerable. Some crucial problems do defy unilateral solutions. Global warming is perhaps the most obvious case, but others include stopping the spread of weapons of mass destruction and fighting global terrorism. In other cases, such as protecting the American homeland from terrorist attack, unilateral action can reduce but not eliminate risks.

---

**Creating an international order in which more people are free and prosperous is profoundly in America's self-interest.**

---

Similarly, unilateral American power may not be enough to sustain the benefits of globalization. Globalization is not irreversible. World War I, the Russian Revolution, and the Great Depression combined to strangle the economic and social interactions that emerged early in the 20th century. Economic globalization today rests on an intricate web of international trade and financial institutions. Extending, developing, and improving these institutions requires the cooperation of others. Without it, the benefits of globalization, which help to underwrite American power, could erode.

Globalization has greatly broadened America's foreign policy agenda. Infectious diseases, poverty, and poor governance not only offend our moral sensibilities but also represent potential new security threats. Failed and failing states endanger not just their own citizens but Americans as well. If the United States cannot find ways to encourage prosperity and good governance, it runs the risk of seeing threats to its security multiply. It could eventually find itself harmed not by bears in the woods but by swarms of tiny pests.

Finally, cooperation can extend the life of American primacy. Working with others can spread the costs of action over a wider array of actors, enabling the United States to do more with less. By creating international regimes and organizations, Washington can imbed its interests and values in institutions that will shape and constrain countries for decades, regardless of the vicissitudes of American power. And cooperation can build bonds with other countries, lessening the chances of cultural and political tactics that can over the years sap U.S. power.

# Implications for American Foreign Policy

Both Americanists and Globalists understand essential truths about the world today. Power continues to matter, but power alone will often not be enough to achieve our goals. A pragmatic American internationalism would recognize that we do not need to pick between these two truths. Both should guide American foreign policy.

But what should America seek to accomplish abroad? The indisputable first objective must be to safeguard and enhance our liberty, security, and prosperity. The question is how. In the new age of global politics, the best way to accomplish these goals is to promote an international order based on democracy, human rights, and free enterprise—to extend the zone of peace and prosperity that the United States helped establish in Europe to every other region of the world. Put differently, the United States needs to integrate the world's have-nots into the globalized West. Pursuing that goal is not charity. Creating an international order in which more people are free and prosperous is profoundly in America's self-interest. In a world of market democracies, America and Americans are likely to be both more prosperous and more secure. In such a world we are most likely to realize the promise of globalization while minimizing its dangers.

Ensuring that a commitment to democracy and open markets triumphs on a global scale entails four broad strategies. First, it is necessary to sustain and strengthen the bases of American power. This, most of all, requires ensuring that the fundamentals of the nation's economy remain sound. It is important not to spend today what the country may need tomorrow. It also requires maintaining America's military edge, both technologically and in terms of the overall capacity to bring force to bear at a time and place of America's own choosing. And it requires persistent diplomatic engagement on Washington's part to demonstrate awareness that what happens abroad and matters to others can also have a profound impact on security and prosperity at home.

Second, U.S. policy should seek to extend and adapt proven international institutions and arrangements. NATO's recent transformation is a prime example. During the 1990s, the collective defense organization that had safeguarded the territorial integrity of its members against the Soviet Union for four decades gradually took on a new role: providing security for every state and its citizens in an ever-enlarging north Atlantic area. By taking the lead in stabilizing conflict-ridden regions like the Balkans, as well as by opening its doors to new members, NATO began to do for Europe's east what it had done for Europe's west. The world trading system is also ripe for change. Barriers to the free flow of goods, capital, and services have steadily fallen over the years, and more and more countries have joined the free-trading regime. Now it is time to lower the most pernicious barriers, especially those for agricultural goods, and bring poor countries into the global economic system.

Third, U.S. policy should enforce compliance with existing international agreements and strengthen the ability of institutions to monitor and compel compliance. Too many favor the negotiation of new sets of rules or new institutions for their own sake, and too few pay attention to making sure that new rules are upheld and new institutions function effectively. Iraq is a case in point. Even if one believes that Iraq can be contained and deterred and that therefore forcible regime change is neither necessary nor advisable, Baghdad's refusal to comply with UN Security Council resolutions (including the critical terms of the Gulf War cease-fire resolution) means that the threat and possible use of force must be in play. A willingness to use force is no doubt necessary (though by no means sufficient) to persuade Saddam Hussein to allow UN inspectors to re-enter Iraq and permit them to carry out the mandate of the international community. If he refuses, the United States must be prepared to use force, preferably with others but alone if necessary, to compel compliance. Bad behavior that produces no consequences gets emulated.

Finally, U.S. policy must take the lead in creating effective international institutions and arrangements to handle new challenges, especially those arising from the downside of globalization. The United States must lead not only because it alone can help the international community overcome its collective-action problems, but because it is most likely to be hurt by inaction. Just as one example, an international system for reporting and monitoring research in dangerous pathogens could provide early warning if biotechnologists create such pathogens either deliberately or inadvertently.

As these strategies make clear, promoting an international order based on market democracies will require the United States to lead as well as listen, to give as well as take. Arguing that American foreign policy should be either unilateral or multilateral is to posit a false choice and also confuse means with ends. Unilateralism can be put to good or bad uses. The flaw in the Bush administration's decision to withdraw the United States from the Kyoto Treaty was not so much that Washington went its own way—though the peremptory manner of the withdrawal maximized bad feelings—but that it has failed to propose a better strategy for dealing with a rise in global temperatures that its own EPA scientists acknowledge. In this case, what is needed is not more multilateralism, but more unilateral action on the part of the United States to curtail its greenhouse gas emissions. Likewise, multilateralism can produce a modern-day Kellogg-Briand Treaty just as easily as it produces a Gulf War coalition or a World Trade Organization.

Can U.S. foreign policy promote a liberal world order in the new age of global politics? In many ways it has no other choice. The pernicious effects of globalization, which empower tiny groups of people to inflict grievous harm, make it essential to create a world community that shares American values. But there is also good reason to believe that the United States can succeed in integrating the rest of the world into the Western world order. Immediately after World War II, the United States forged a series of bold political, economic, and military arrangements that made allies of former enemies and set the stage for victory in the age of geopolitics. U.S. policymakers at the time took a broad view of American interests and understood that their efforts would be for naught if America's partners did not see them as being in the interest of all. U.S. policymakers in the age of global politics must do likewise.

Ivo H. Daalder and James M. Lindsay are senior fellows in the Brookings Foreign Policy Studies program.

From *Brookings Review*, Winter 2003, pp. 12, 14-17. Copyright © 2003 by Brookings Institution Press. Reprinted by permission.

# COMMUNITY BUILDING
## STEPS TOWARD A GOOD SOCIETY

*AMITAI ETZIONI*

**W**ell-formed national societies are not composed of millions of individuals but are constituted as communities of communities. These societies provide a framework within which diverse social groups as well as various subcultures find shared bonds and values. When this framework falls apart, we find communities at each other's throats or even in vicious civil war, as we sadly see in many parts of the world. (Arthur Schlesinger Jr. provides an alarming picture of such a future for our society in his book, *The Disuniting of America*.)

Our community of communities is particularly threatened in two ways that ought to command more of our attention in the next years. First, our society has been growing more diverse by leaps and bounds over recent decades, as immigration has increased and Americans have become more aware of their social and cultural differences. Many on the left celebrate diversity because they see it as ending white European hegemony in our society. Many on the right call for "bleaching out" ethnic differences to ensure a united, homogenous America.

A second challenge to the community of communities emanates from the fact that economic and social inequality has long been rising. Some see a whole new divide caused by the new digital technologies, although others believe that the Internet will bridge these differences. It is time to ask how much inequality the community of communities can tolerate while still flourishing. If we are exceeding these limits, what centrist corrections are available to us?

## DIVERSITY WITHIN UNITY

As a multiethnic society, America has long debated the merit of unity versus pluralism, of national identity versus identity politics, of assimilation of immigrants into mainstream culture versus maintaining their national heritages. All of these choices are incompatible with a centrist, communitarian approach to a good society. Assimilation is unnecessarily homogenizing, forcing people to give up important parts of their selves; unbounded racial, ethnic, and cultural diversity is too conflict-prone for a society in which all are fully respected. The concept of a community of communities provides a third model.

The community of communities builds on the observation that loyalty to one's group, to its particular culture and heritage, is compatible with sustaining national unity as long as the society is perceived not as an arena of conflict but as a society that has some community-like features. (Some refer to a community of communities as an imagined community.) Members of such a society maintain layered loyalties. "Lower" commitments are to one's immediate community, often an ethnic group; "higher" ones are to the community of communities, to the nation as a whole. These include a commitment to a democratic way of life, to a constitution and more generally to a government by law, and above all to treating others—not merely the members of one's group—as ends in themselves and not merely as instruments. Approached this way, one realizes that up to a point, *diversity can avoid being the opposite of unity and can exist within it.*

Moreover, sustaining a particular community of communities does not contradict the gradual development of still more encompassing communities, such as the European Union, a North American community including Canada and Mexico, or, one day, a world community.

During the last decades of the 20th century, the U.S. was racked by identity politics that, in part, have served to partially correct past injustices committed against women and minorities, but have also divided the nation along group lines. Other sharp divisions have appeared between the religious right and much of the rest of the country. One of the merits of the centrist, communitarian approach has been that it has combined efforts to expand the common ground and to cool intergroup rhetoric. Thus communitarians helped call off the "war" between the genders, as Betty Friedan—who was one of the original endorsers of the Communitarian Platform—did in 1997.

New flexibility in involving faith-based groups in the provision of welfare, health care, and other social services, and even allowing some forms of religious activities in public schools, has defused some of the tension between the religious right and the rest of society. The national guidelines on religious expression in public schools, first released by the U.S. Department of Education on the directive of President Clinton in August of 1995, worked to this end. For example, in July of 1996, these guidelines spurred the St. Louis School Board to implement a clearly defined, districtwide policy on school prayer. This policy helped allay the confusion—and litigation—that had previously plagued the role of religion in this school district.

The tendency of blacks and whites not to dialogue openly about racial issues, highlighted by Andrew Hacker, has to some degree been overcome. The main, albeit far from successful, effort in this direction has been made by President Clinton's Advisory Board on Race. And for the first time in U.S. history, a Jew was nominated by a major political party for the post of vice president.

In the next years, intensified efforts are called for to balance the legitimate concerns and needs of various communities that constitute the American society on one hand, and the need to shore up our society as a community of communities on the other. Prayers truly initiated by students might be allowed in public schools as long as sufficient arrangements are made for students who do not wish to participate to spend time in other organized activities. There are no compelling reasons to oppose "after hours" religious clubs establishing themselves in the midst of numerous secular programs. Renewed efforts for honest dialogues among the races are particularly difficult and needed. None of these steps will cause the differences among various communities—many of which serve to enrich our culture and social life—to disappear. But they may go a long way toward reinforcing the framework that keeps American society together while it is being recast.

## UNIFYING INEQUALITY

Society cannot long sustain its status as a community of communities if general increases in well-being, even including those that trickle down to the poorest segments of the society, keep increasing the economic distance between the elites and the common people. Fortunately, it seems that at least by some measures, economic inequality has not increased in the United States between 1996 and 2000. And by several measures, the federal income tax has grown surprisingly progressive. (The opposite must be said about rising payroll taxes.) About a third of those who filed income tax returns in 2000 paid no taxes or even got a net refund from the Internal Revenue Service (IRS). However, the level of inequality in income at the end of the 20th century was substantially higher than it was in earlier periods. Between 1977 and 1999, the after-tax income of the top 1 percent of the U.S. population increased by 115 percent, whereas the after-tax income of the U.S. population's lowest fifth decreased by 9 per-

cent. There is little reason to expect that this trend will not continue.

### SOCIAL JUSTICE

We may debate what social justice calls for; however, there is little doubt about what community requires. If some members of a community are increasingly distanced from the standard of living of most other members, they will lose contact with the rest of the community. The more those in charge of private and public institutions lead lives of hyper-affluence—replete with gated communities and estates, chauffeured limousines, servants and personal trainers—the less in touch they are with other community members. Such isolation not only frays social bonds and insulates privileged people from the moral cultures of the community, but it also blinds them to the realities of the lives of their fellow citizens. This, in turn, tends to cause them to favor unrealistic policies ("let them eat cake") that backfire and undermine the trust of the members of the society in those who lead and in the institutions they head.

The argument has been made that for the state to provide equality of outcomes undermines the motivation to achieve and to work, stymies creativity and excellence, and is unfair to those who do apply themselves. It is also said that equality of outcomes would raise labor costs so high that a society would be rendered uncompetitive in the new age of global competition. Equality of opportunity has been extolled as a substitute. However, to ensure equality of opportunity, some equality of outcome must be provided. As has often been pointed out, for all to have similar opportunities, they must have similar starting points. These can be reached only if all are accorded certain basics. Special education efforts such as Head Start, created to bring children from disadvantaged backgrounds up to par, and training for workers released from obsolescent industries are examples of programs that provide some equality of results to make equality of opportunity possible.

Additional policies to further curb inequality can be made to work at both ends of the scale. Policies that ensure a rich basic minimum serve this goal by lifting those at the lower levels of the economic pyramid. Reference is often made to education and training programs that focus on those most in need of catching up. However, these work very slowly. Therefore, in the short run more effects will be achieved by raising the Earned Income Tax Credit and the minimum wage, and by implementing new inter-community sharing initiatives.

The poor will remain poor no matter how much they work as long as they own no assets. This is especially damaging because people who own assets, especially a place of residence (even if only an apartment), are most likely to "buy" into a society—to feel and be part of a community. By numerous measures, homeowners are more involved in the life of their communities, and their children are less likely to drop out of school. Roughly one-third of Americans do not own their residence; 73 percent of whites do, compared to 47 percent of African Americans and Hispanics.

*MORTGAGES*

Various provisions allowing those with limited resources to get mortgages through federally chartered corporations like Fannie Mae, which helps finance mortgages for many lower-income people, have been helpful in increasing ownership. More needs to be done on this front, especially for those of little means. This might be achieved by following the same model used in the Earned Income Tax Credit in the U.S. and the Working Families Tax Credit in the United Kingdom: providing people who earn below a defined income level with "earned interest on mortgages," effectively granting them two dollars for every dollar set aside to provide seed money for a mortgage. And sweat equity might be used as the future owner's contribution—for instance, if they work on their own housing site. (Those who benefit from the houses that Habitat for Humanity builds are required to either make some kind of a financial contribution themselves or help in the construction of their homes.) Far from implausible, various ideas along these lines were offered by both George W. Bush and Al Gore during the 2000 election campaign, as well as by various policy researchers.

Reducing hard core unemployment by trying to bring jobs to poor neighborhoods (through "enterprise zones") or by training the long-unemployed in entrepreneurial skills is often expensive and slow, and is frequently unsuccessful. The opposite approach, moving people from poor areas to places where jobs are, often encounters objections by the neighborhoods into which they are moved, as well as by those poor who feel more comfortable living in their home communities. A third approach should be tried much more extensively: providing ready transportation to and from places of employment.

Measures to cap the higher levels of wealth include progressive income taxes, some forms of inheritance tax, closing numerous loopholes in the tax codes, and ensuring that tax on capital is paid as it is on labor. Given that several of these inequality curbing measures cannot be adopted on a significant scale if they seriously endanger the competitive state of a country, steps to introduce many of them should be undertaken jointly with other Organization for Economic Cooperation and Development (OECD) countries, or better yet, among all the nations that are our major competitors and trade partners.

One need not be a liberal—one can be a solid communitarian—and still be quite dismayed to learn that the IRS audits the poor (defined as income below $25,000) more than the rich (defined as income above $100,000). In 1999, the IRS audited 1.36 percent of poor taxpayers, compared to 1.15 percent of rich taxpayers. In 1988, the percentage for the rich was 11.4. In one decade, there was thus a decline of about 90 percent in auditing the rich. This occurred because Congress did not authorize the necessary funds, despite the General Accounting Office's finding that the rich are more likely to evade taxes than are the poor. This change in audit patterns also reflects the concern of Republican members of Congress that the poor will abuse the Earned Income Tax Credit that the Clinton administration has introduced. It should not take a decade to correct this imbalance.

Ultimately, this matter and many others will not be properly attended to until there is a basic change in the moral culture of the society and in the purposes that animate it. Without such a change, a major reallocation of wealth can be achieved only by force, which is incompatible with a democratic society and will cause a wealth flight and other damage to the economy. In contrast, history from early Christianity to Fabian socialism teaches us that people who share progressive values will be inclined to share their wealth voluntarily. A good society seeks to promote such values through a grand dialogue rather than by dictates.

## THE NEW GRAND DIALOGUE

The great success of the economy in the 1990s made Americans pay more attention to the fact that there are numerous moral and social questions of concern to the good society that capitalism has never aspired to answer and that the state should not promote. These include moral questions such as what we owe our children, our parents, our friends, and our neighbors, as well as people from other communities, including those in far away places. Most important, we must address this question: What is the ultimate purpose our personal and collective endeavors? Is ever greater material affluence our ultimate goal and the source of meaning? When is enough—enough? What are we considering the good life? *Can a good society be built on ever increasing levels of affluence? Or should we strive to center it around other values, those of mutuality and spirituality?*

The journey to the good society can benefit greatly from the observation, supported by a great deal of social science data, that ever increasing levels of material goods are not a reliable source of human well-being or contentment—let alone the basis for a morally sound society. To cite but a few studies of a large body of findings: Frank M. Andrews and Stephen B. Withey found that the level of one's socioeconomic status had meager effects on one's "sense of well-being" and no significant effect on "satisfaction with life-as-a-whole." Jonathan L. Freedman discovered that levels of reported happiness did not vary greatly among the members of different economic classes, with the exception of the very poor, who tended to be less happy than others. David G. Myers reported that although per capita disposable (after-tax) income in inflation-adjusted dollars almost exactly doubled between 1960 and 1990, 32 percent of Americans reported that they were "very happy" in 1993, almost the same proportion as did in 1957 (35 percent). Although economic growth slowed after the mid-1970s, Americans' reported happiness was remarkably stable (nearly always between 30 and 35 percent) across both high-growth and low-growth periods.

## HAPPINESS

These and other such data help us realize that the pursuit of well-being through ever higher levels of consumption is Sisyphean. When it comes to material goods, enough is never enough. This is not an argument in favor of a life of sackcloth and ashes, of poverty and self-denial. The argument is that once basic material needs (what Abraham Maslow called "creature comforts") are well sated and securely provided for, additional income does not add to happiness. On the contrary, hard evidence—not some hippie, touchy-feely, LSD-induced hallucination—shows that profound contentment is found in nourishing ends-based relationships, in bonding with others, in community building and public service, and in cultural and spiritual pursuits. Capitalism, the engine of affluence, has never aspired to address the whole person; typically it treats the person as *Homo economicus*. And of course, statist socialism subjugated rather than inspired. It is left to the evolving values and cultures of centrist societies to fill the void.

Nobel laureate Robert Fogel showed that periods of great affluence are regularly followed by what he calls Great Awakenings, and that we are due for one in the near future. Although it is quite evident that there is a growing thirst for a purpose deeper than conspicuous consumption, we may not have the ability to predict which specific form this yearning for spiritual fulfillment will take.

There are some who hold firmly that the form must be a religious one because no other speaks to the most profound matters that trouble the human soul, nor do others provide sound moral guidance. These believers find good support in numerous indicators that there was a considerable measure of religious revival in practically all forms of American religion over the last decades of the 20th century. The revival is said to be evident not merely in the number of people who participate in religious activities and the frequency of their participation in these activities, but also in the stronger, more involving, and stricter kinds of commitments many are making to religion. (Margaret Talbot has argued effectively that conservative Christians, especially fundamentalists, constitute the true counterculture of our age; they know and live a life rich in fulfillment, not centered around consumer goods.) Others see the spiritual revival as taking more secular

forms, ranging from New Age cults to a growing interest in applied ethics.

## PRIORITIES

Aside from making people more profoundly and truly content individuals, a major and broadly based upward shift on the Maslovian scale is a prerequisite for being able to better address some of the most tantalizing problems plaguing modern societies, whatever form such a shift may take. That is what is required before we can come into harmony with our environment, because these higher priorities put much less demand on scarce resources than do lower ones. And such a new set of priorities may well be the only conditions under which those who are well endowed would be willing to support serious reallocation of wealth and power, as their personal fortunes would no longer be based on amassing ever larger amounts of consumer goods. In addition, transitioning to a knowledge-based economy would free millions of people (one hopes all of them, gradually) to relate to each other mainly as members of families and communities, thus laying the social foundations for a society in which ends-based relationships dominate while instrumental ones are well contained.

The upward shift in priorities, a return to a sort of moderate counterculture, a turn toward voluntary simplicity—these require a grand dialogue about our personal and shared goals. (A return to a counterculture is not a recommendation for more abuse of controlled substances, promiscuity, and self-indulgence—which is about the last thing America needs—but the realization that one can find profound contentment in reflection, friendship, love, sunsets, and walks on the beach rather than in the pursuit of ever more control over ever more goods.) Intellectuals and the media can help launch such a dialogue and model the new forms of behavior. Public leaders can nurse the recognition of these values by moderating consumption at public events and ceremonies, and by celebrating those whose achievements are compatible with a good society rather than with a merely affluent one.

But ultimately, such a shift lies in changes in our hearts and minds, in our values and conduct—what Robert Bellah called the "habits of the heart." We shall not travel far toward a good society unless such a dialogue is soon launched and advanced to a good, spiritually uplifting conclusion.

*Mr. Etzioni is editor of* The Responsive Community. *From "Next: Three Steps Towards A Good Society," by Amitai Etzioni,* The Responsive Community, *Winter 2000–01, pages 49–58.*

Reprinted from *Current,* January 2001, pp. 29-33. Originally printed in *The Responsive Community,* Vol. II, No. 1, Winter 2000/01, pp. 49-58, which was adapted from the author's book *Next: The Road to the Good Society* (New York: Basic Books, 2001). Copyright © 2000 by Communitarian Network. Reprinted by permission.

# Sleepwalking Through The Apocalypse THE FUTURE DEPENDS ON US

Wm. Van Dusen Wishard

How are we to make sense of how the world is changing? Jihad vs. McWorld. Nukes in North Korea. A potential India-Pakistan nuclear shoot-out. The merger of human and artificial intelligence creating the "post-human" epoch. We seem to have come to the end of the world, as we've known it. The next three decades increasingly loom as the most decisive 30-year period in history.

Within this context, I've been invited to offer some thoughts on how the world is changing, and what it may mean for us.

Let me start by offering the view of one of the world's most experienced observers of global events. For over sixty years, Peter Drucker has studied how the world has been changing. In 1957 he wrote, "No one born after the turn of the 20th century has ever known anything but a world uprooting its foundations, overturning its values and toppling its idols." If Drucker's right, and I personally think he is, despite all the political, social and technical advances of the past century, basically the story of the 20th century was about a world where the historic social arrangements, spiritual underpinnings and psychological moorings that had anchored nations for centuries, have been in a transition of epochal proportions. The underpinnings of life as we've known it are shifting.

With Drucker's comments in mind, I want to begin by briefly suggesting ten trends that suggest how the entire context of human existence is changing. After that, I'll focus more in depth on two particular trends.

First, science is in the process of redefining our understanding of terms first given us at the dawn of human consciousness: such terms as "nature," "human," and "life." Increasingly, scientists are subordinating humans to technology. In essence, we may be abdicating our own psychological center of being and handing it over to the computer. Within the next three decades we'll have reached the point where the question will be, "What are humans for in a world of completely independent technological capability?"

Second, due to accelerating technology development, so much is happening so fast in every part of the world, we no longer have any frame of reference within which to understand contemporary events. Life has become a passing blur. Yesterday's crisis has not been resolved, but we can't think about it any more because we've got to confront today's crisis. Thus leaders lack any larger order of purpose and significance, any guiding narrative that transcends separate cultures, any pattern of meaning that could give collective human existence coherence and intelligibility.

Third, for the first time in history, the Caucasian race is no longer reproducing itself. No European country is reproducing its population; nor are Caucasians in North America reproducing themselves. The implications of this are so far-reaching that it's difficult even to speculate what they might be.

Fourth, future ages may view man's seeing the Earth from the Moon as the defining event of all subsequent history. Joseph Campbell clearly considered it the most significant psychological event of the past several thousand years. Seeing Earth from the Moon vastly accelerated the collapse of all the boundaries that provide identity-boundaries of nation, race, religion, class and gender. Thus everyone, to some degree or other, faces a crisis of identity. This crisis feeds much of the fundamentalist sentiment, whether religious, political or ethnic. People reach back for the security of past expressions of identity, which, outdated by a new understanding, now need reinterpretation for a completely new phase of human experience.

Fifth, for the first time in history, what constitutes a family is being redefined. This has profound implications for government, education, social cohesion and what we broadly term "civil society".

Sixth, some anthropologists consider the Internet to be the most significant social development since the invention of language. Once again, we have minimal comprehension of how this will affect the structure of human communication and knowledge, our social arrangements, and individual psychology.

Seventh, as Richard Tarnas suggests, we are in the midst of rethinking the role of the human being in nature and the cosmos, rethinking the dilemmas of a world community, the use of knowledge, the basis of moral values, the subjective schism separating the modem human being from the rest of nature, and the direction and meaning-if any-of history and evolution.

Eighth, the ability to create change, as well as the attitude that change is desirable, is now a global possession. Throughout history, in all civilizations, continuity rather than change has been the desired state of affairs. No society on the planet knows how to live with constant, radical change. Thus for the first time in history, every nation is, concurrently with all other nations, in a state of profound crisis as we try to adjust to an ever-accelerating pace of change.

Ninth, for thousands of years the issue was how to protect humans from the ravages of nature. But just in our lifetime, the issue has become how to protect nature from the excesses of humans.

Tenth, our whole symbolic language has been devalued. For example, "Heaven" used to carry a sacred meaning. It was the dwelling place of the gods; a place people hoped to go when they died, our link with eternity. Now we speak simply of "space," an endless void. Similarly, we used to speak of "Mother Earth," which gives the earth a creative, nurturing implication. Now we speak only of "matter," an abstract, lifeless substance. In this way, our symbolic language has been diminished. The function of symbolic language is to infuse into our conscious life some of the transcendent meaning that emanates from the unconscious realm, from the depths of our inner being. That connection has been weakened, so there's far less transcendent vitality brought into our conscious life.

All these trends—and more—will be shaping the global context for the rest of our lives. What these trends portend is one reason I suggest we've come to the end of the world, as we've known it.

Now, let's focus in more tightly on two other trends.

Globalization. We all have some idea of what globalization means. In my view, globalization represents the world's best chance to enrich the lives of the greatest number of people.

Globalization, however, is far more than just economics; more than non-western nations adopting free markets and democratic political systems. The essence of globalization is greater communication between peoples and cultures, and the subsequent merging of beliefs and modes of life. This began in the early 16th century with European exploration and colonialization of Africa, South America and Asia. It expanded in the 1840s with the invention of the telegraph, the world's first electronic information communication system. Clearly, in the 20th century globalization has moved at an exponential pace. In its present phase, it means that western social, cultural and philosophical ideas are gradually seeping into the fabric of the rest of the world, and a reciprocal transfer of culture and lifestyles from non-Western nations to the West.

Look at what's happening. Nations are adopting such ideas as the sanctity of the individual, due process of law, universal education, the equality of women, human rights, private property, legal safeguards governing business and finance, science as the engine of social growth, concepts of civil society, and perhaps most importantly, the ability of people to take charge of their destiny and not simply accept the hand dealt them in life. Equally, African and Latin rhythms infuse American music, while Asian religions and philosophies find an ever-widening Western receptivity.

We take Western ideas for granted, but for millions of people such concepts are new modes of thought and behavior. While we Americans believe what's works for America will work for others, we're sometimes unaware that the cultural differences between the U.S. and the rest of the world represent significant psychological differences. Take some contrasts between America and Asia. America prizes individuality, while Asia emphasizes relationships and community. Americans see humans dominating nature, while Asians see humans as part of nature. In the U.S. there is a division between mind and heart while in Asia mind and heart are unified.

I mention this to illustrate the deep psychological trauma nations are experiencing as they confront the effects of globalization. We Americans, raised on the instinct of change, say, "Great. Let tradition go. Embrace the new." But much of the world says, "Wait a minute. Traditions are our connection to the past; they represent our psychic roots. If we jettison them, we'll endanger our social cohesion and psychic stability." Many thoughtful Muslims clearly fear that the Western model of globalization, based on secular, scientific rationalism, will eventually bring about the destruction of Islam.

The point is this. The pace of globalization is driven by the increase in the pace of technology development in America. No nation today can develop without adjusting to the global economic system anchored in American information technology. Just look at global financial flows and how they operate. Thus all nations struggle as they try to adjust to the new global system—a system for which there is no operating theory that provides guidance. It's a psychological as well as structural crisis.

Part of globalization is the fact that the world is in the midst of the largest migration in history. In China alone, there are one hundred million people on the move from the countryside to the cities. Not only is this causing huge urban problems, but demographers are concerned that if this trend continues, the historic village culture on which China has existed for centuries could eventually disappear.

In the West, migration is changing the face of Europe and North America. The European Union will need 180 million immigrants in the next three decades simply to keep its population at 1995 levels, as well as to keep the current ratio of retirees to workers. In Brussels, over fifty percent of the babies born are Muslim. In Germany, the death rate has exceeded the birth rate for decades, so they now have to fly in planeloads of technicians from India just to maintain their high tech structure. The demographers estimate that the German population will drop by twelve million by 2030. In England, there are now more practicing Muslims than Anglicans. In Russia, the population has dropped three million in the past decade, and demographers estimate a possible drop of another forty million by 2050. In general, present patterns point to a decline in the population of 20 million in Western Europe by 2025. Here at home, while the population continues to increase, 80% of that increase is due to immigration. The U.S. has more immigration than the rest of the world combined. The remainder of the U.S. increase is due to African-American and Hispanic births, while none of the increase is due to Caucasians.

As immigration increases, the historic legends that are the basis of national identities tend to wane. As one British historian put it, "A white majority that invented the national mythologies underpinning modern European culture lives in an almost perpetual state of fear that it and its way of life are about to disappear." In Italy, the Archbishop of Bologna recently warned that Italy is in danger of "losing its identity" due to the immigration from North Africa and Central Europe. The Catholic Church is facing the distinct possibility of Islam becoming the largest European faith. The fear of such demographic shifts and their potential consequences is the subtext for everything else happening in Europe today. It's far more traumatic than adjusting to the euro.

In the coming years, the face of nations will be very different from today. Traditional images of what it means to be French, German, Italian or English are going to change just as radically as the image of what it means to be American has changed in recent decades. It may take longer in various Asian countries such as Japan, but even Japan is increasing immigration from other nations. In sum, it seems to me we are much more in a clash within civilizations than between civilizations.

At the end of the day, for globalization to succeed, if we're going to build a global age, it's got to be built on more than free markets and the Internet. It's got to be built on some common view of life far more inclusive than "my nation," "my race" or "my religion" is the greatest. Such views gave identity and dynamism to the nations of the past. But the task now is to see the world whole, and act in accord with that awareness. To be legitimate, globalization must validate itself in terms of equitable benefits for all nations, and sensitivity to other nations need for social and political stability.

Globalization is part of a profound process taking place. We're living through a period of disintegration, as well as of a new integration. We see the evidence of this new integration in the reconciliation between long-standing schisms that have defined the modern age: between mind and body, science and religion, conscious and unconscious, human beings and nature, the individual self and objective world, spirit and matter. Globalization is part of that new integration. It's part of the expression of a larger human identity that's trying to come into being. To offer an oversimplified metaphor, globalization is humanity's response to seeing Earth from the Moon.

To consider the second trend, I want to quote Adlai Stevenson, who had the unfortunate luck of twice being the Democratic presidential candidate chosen to oppose Dwight Eisenhower. In a 1954 speech at Columbia University, Stevenson asked, "Are America's problems but surface symptoms of something even deeper, of a moral and human crisis in the Western world which might even be compared to the fourth, fifth and sixth-century crisis where the Roman Empire was transformed into feudalism and primitive Christianity? Are Americans," Stevenson queried, "passing through one of the great crises of history when man must make another mighty choice?"

A decade later, Joseph Campbell, perhaps the world's foremost authority on the symbolic and psychological meaning of myths, noted in a New York speech that every one of "the world's great spiritual traditions is in profound disorder. What has been taught as their basic truths seem no longer to hold." The world, he concluded, "is passing through perhaps the greatest spiritual metamorphosis in the history of the human race."

Stevenson and Campbell—two of the most thoughtful Americans of the mid-20th century—comparing the condition of America and the Western world to that of Rome during the end of the ancient world and the emergence of Christianity and feudal Europe. I want to explore the ramifications of their remarks a bit, for this issue has become a dominant driving force not only in America 's spiritual life, but also in our culture, our politics, and international affairs. This represents the most fundamental change a people can experience.

What actually happened when the Greco-Roman world was transformed into early Christianity? The history books tell a certain amount—the corruption of Rome, the severe decline in population, the neglect and even collapse of the Roman aqueducts, roads and farms.

Those were the outer manifestations, but what happened to the inner life of the people? We get some sense from the Roman poet Lucretius who summed up the temper of the times when he wrote of "aching hearts in every home, racked incessantly by pangs the mind was powerless to assuage." There was a loss of collective meaning; a disappearance of what had represented life's highest value. The God-image that had informed the inner life and culture of the Greco-Roman world for a thousand years lost its compelling force, especially for the leadership class. This led to a breakdown of the historic psychic structures that had been the source and container of Greco-Roman morals and beliefs. A collapse of the ethical and social guidelines underlying civilized order took place.

The history books speak of the "decline" of Rome. But at its heart, it was a long-term—at least four or five centuries-psychological shift of the prevailing God-image from the multiple gods of the Greco-Roman period, to a new spiritual dispensation. A new God-image emerged for a new phase of psychological maturation and human experience. From Ireland to Italy, Europe went through a prolonged period of the transformation of underlying principles and symbols. What emerged we know as Christendom.

What Stevenson and Campbell—and others—have suggested is that America and the West have been experiencing at least a similar long-term spiritual and psychological reorientation today. This is what Drucker was referring to when he talked about a world uprooting its foundations, overturning its values and toppling its idols. What, in fact, this would mean is that for some time now we have been living through the Apocalypse. Let me emphasize that in talking about the Apocalypse, I'm not making any metaphysical statements about God; this is strictly commentary on the psychological significance of the Apocalypse.

For those who may be uncertain as to the relevance of this subject, let me quote Walter Russell Mead, a senior fellow at the Council on Foreign Relations, author of several books and countless articles on global issues. Last February Mead wrote an op-ed piece in The Washington Post that carried the headline, "It's the Dawning Age of the Apocalypse." After surveying what he considers to be the retreat of progress, Mead noted, "apocalypse anxiety has moved into the mainstream of American politics and culture… a line has been crossed… The Age of Progress is in the past and this is the era of Shiva, destroyer of worlds." The Council on Foreign Relations and The Washington Post—you don't get more Establishment than that.

Add to that the fact that 60% of Americans believe the prophecies in the Book of Revelation will come true; that 48 million Americans believe the world will come to an end in their lifetime; that over 50% of the fundamentalists supporting the administration's position on Israel believe Israel must control all of Palestine before Christ will return; that a well-known senator said on the floor of the Senate that Israel should control all of Palestine "because God said so. Look it up in the book of Genesis"; put all that together and it becomes clear just what a critical role apocalyptic thinking plays in immediate political and international affairs.

Generally speaking, the Apocalypse as presented in the Book of Revelation is misunderstood, a misunderstanding arising from two different ways of interpretation. One is the literal interpretation, which is the fundamentalists view. The other is a symbolic interpretation, which was St. Augustine's belief. Thus the fundamentalists see the Apocalypse as the literal end of the world. The symbolic interpretation sees the Apocalypse as the end of the Christian epoch, and a protracted time of some new spiritual dispensation coming into being.

The word "apocalypse" comes from the Greek, meaning "revelation, an uncovering of what has been hidden." There are four features of the image of the Apocalypse: revelation, judgment, destruction and renewal. Revelation discloses new truth about how life and the universe function. Judgment assesses the state of contemporary beliefs and social arrangements in light of this new truth. Destruction is the collapse of old institutions and relationships that are no longer effective within the context of the new truth. Renewal is the recreation of civilization according to the requirements of the new truth. If one carefully considers the 20th century, all four of these trends operating simultaneously are visible.

When we speak of the end of the Christian eon, what we're suggesting is that while there are millions of Christians in America, the spiritual impulse that gave highest value and meaning to Western civilization is no longer the inner dynamic of the collective Western psyche. It's no longer the informing force in the soul of America and Europe's "creative minority" who give us our literature, theater, science, technology, education, cinema and music. In this sense, the character of our culture is the best indication of what is emanating from the depths of the Western soul. For culture is to a nation what dreams are to an individual—an indication of what's going on in the depths of the inner life.

Such epochal changes as the Apocalypse don't take place out in the cosmos somewhere. They take place in the collective psyche of us as human beings. As the collective psyche is by definition unconscious, we're usually unaware of the inner psychological dynamics of this change, even though we see its outward manifestations in both culture and contemporary events.

When a shift takes place on the scale we're suggesting, when the God-image changes, that's an epochal experience. For what's happening is that part of the collective unconscious within us is seeking to become conscious, to find a flesh expression. Such a process has happened before. It's exemplified by the differences between the polytheism of Homer's Iliad and monotheism of Exodus in the Old Testament. Indeed, the differences between the Old and New Testaments suggests another such change in the God-image. Such developments represent a significant evolution of consciousness. The underlying continuity of that process must be taken into account as we evaluate our own era. For at the heart of history is a sacred continuity of life, and right now we're in the traumatic throes of taking the next steps of that evolutionary process.

The issue of the Apocalypse affects each of us, whether we're aware of it or not. But it's such a large topic, I've only been able to touch on it just enough to bring it to your attention. For those who wish to explore it further, I suggest reading The New God-Image by Edward F. Edinger. Until his untimely death in 1998, Dr. Edinger was considered to be the dean of Jungian analysts in America. In my view, his book is an essential text for evaluating the most basic change taking place in the world today.

The question remains, given all we've discussed thus far, how do we respond to such a historic moment? We must respond on at least two levels. The first is the level of our collective life, and here we're already undertaking the most sweeping redefinition of life in our history. All our institutions are being redefined and restructured. Corporations are redefining their mission, structure and modus operandi. In education, countless new experiments are underway, from vouchers to charter schools to home schooling. The legal system is assisted by the increasing use of alternative dispute resolution (ADR). Functions formerly executed by local governments are now undertaken by civic and charitable organizations. Numerous steps have been taken to redress the severe environmental imbalance we've created. More citizens are involved in efforts to help the elderly and those in poverty. In fact, it's estimated that well over fifty percent of all adult Americans donate a portion of their time to nonprofit social efforts. Perhaps most importantly, we're gradually integrating a global perspective into the fabric of our education, culture, and international relations. Take West Point, for example. All the cadets at West Point learn a foreign language such as Chinese, Arabic or Russian, and they take a year's course in some foreign culture. So on one level, we're already at grips with some of the manifestations of the reorientation that engulfs us.

The second level is the individual level. How do we respond in our personal lives?

I suggest the key to this is understanding; understanding how change is reshaping our world, and how these changes affect us both collectively and individually. And I suggest it's helpful to move in two directions—seek breadth and depth. Widen and deepen our frame of reference. In my view, it's extremely difficult to truly comprehend what's happening to the world if one's frame of reference is any shorter than a century, and preferably longer. Second, get beneath the surface changes, the economic, social and political factors that are the usual stuff of history. How has psychological maturation created new epochs of history? For example, from a psychological perspective, the Renaissance was not a return to the glory of Greco-Roman times, but a move forward out of the psychic mentality that had produced the Middle Ages. Understanding such a development is key to evaluating what the world is experiencing today.

One place to start could be with the issues we've discussed this afternoon. Take the trends outlined earlier. Look into the whole discipline of Media Ecology. Initially based on the works of Lewis Mumford and Marshall McLuhan, Media Ecology has grown into a wide-ranging consideration how rapid change and technology affect both our social arrangements and us as individuals. Read Neil Postman, who is probably the present-day McLuhan.

There's another aspect of the individual level of understanding—what's going on in us as individuals as we pass through this epochal transition? If we don't comprehend what's happening on the level of the soul, we will not have a basic understanding of what's happening to our world. For in the end, it's the individual that makes history; it's the individual psyche that produces all our philosophies, art, economic and educational theories, technology and all else. The individual psyche is the engine of history, and right now the greatest change in the world is taking place in our collective psyche.

Some people get nervous when they hear the word "psyche." But it's the Greek word for "soul." "The study of the soul" is actually the older meaning of the word "psychology." In talking about psychology, I'm not talking about navel gazing or curing neurosis. I'm talking about gaining essential self-understanding of what makes me what I am; how my unconscious and conscious aspects of life relate to each other; how archetypes determine my conduct as much—or perhaps even more—than does ego-consciousness; and how my shadow side relates to my daily activity. How does our collective shadow relate to America's differences with other nations and peoples? How does our awareness of the shadow side of the Industrial Age help us cope with the shadow side of the Information Age? We are at a point in history where such self-understanding is critical to how the future will unfold.

How do I know what does my shadow really looks like? A British psychologist once said if you really want to know the answer to that question, just draw up a list of the characteristics you most react to in other people, and there you have a picture of your shadow. The point about seeing my shadow is that the very act of seeing it helps transform it. Understanding at a soul level has a transformative effect. That's why the Scriptures say, "With all thy getting, get understanding." In so doing, I not only become a more complete personality, I leave a creative deposit in the collective soul of humanity. In this manner, I create greater consciousness. We become seeds sown in the collective psyche that can promote the unification of the collective psyche as a whole. We help create the new era that is to come.

This is how we achieve the higher level of consciousness that's so urgently needed. What we're discussing is, in my view, the most vital challenge facing any individual, for it's our personal contribution to the future of humanity.

Critical to all this is the question, "What is my highest value in life?" Each of us must know the answer to that question. Historically for the Western world, "God" would have been the answer for most people. For many, that is still true. For others, they would like it to be true, but it doesn't quite have the ring of authenticity about it. It's more in the nature of reaching back for a lost emotional feeling. For still others, it's a meaningless salute to the past.

For myself, I would say my highest value is "the fullest possible degree of psychological maturity and completeness." This is said keeping in mind what I suggested earlier about the older meaning of the world psychology—"the study of the soul." So my highest value would be the greatest possible maturity and wholeness of the soul. Two crucial features of this would be first, a relationship with that transpersonal dimension of life that's beyond all human comprehension, and second, continuing awareness and integration of my shadow.

Psychological wholeness and wisdom is a condition I will never reach, but always seek. One sign of psychological wholeness might be, "To be able to hold two diametrically opposite views in balance without becoming emotionally attached to either view." Or, as Niels Bohr said about quantum physics, "The opposite of a profound truth is another profound truth." In my opinion, such a condition of completeness includes sensitivity to the sacred mystery of all life, and, above all, that quality of compassion and love best described in St. Paul's letter to the Corinthians.

What we've been talking about involves a degree of awareness of the unconscious impulses that are inside each of us, and thus in our civilization as well. Part of the unconscious person inside our collective soul is seeking fresh expression in a greater consciousness. That's the deeper meaning of an apocalyptic time. It's more than intellectual. It's a psychological and spiritual maturation that is seeking new form. We must now climb to a higher moral level; to a higher plane of consciousness in order to be equal to the superhuman powers science and technology have placed in our hands. In reality, nothing else matters at this point.

Some eternal, infinite power is at work in each of us, as well as in the universe. This power is the source of renewal of all man's most vital and creative energies. With all our problems and possibilities, the future depends on how we—each in his or her own unique way—tap into that eternal renewing dynamic that dwells in the deepest reaches of the human soul. Thank you.

# Index

## A

Abrupt climate change, 188–193
*An Abrupt Climate Change Scenario and its Implications for United States National Security,* 189
Abuse, 95–100, 150–153
Adaptive function, and education, 126
Adjustive function, and education, 126
Administrators, and public education, 129–134
Admission standards, higher education, 83–90
AFCD; *See* Aid to Families with Dependent Children (AFDC)
Affirmative action, 2, 63, 83–90
Africa, and AIDS, 139–147, 182
Aggression, 91–94, 150–153, 169–179
Aid to Families with Dependent Children (AFDC), 17, 77–82
AIDS, 139–147, 182
Allen, Arthur, 109, 135–138
Alter, Jonathan, 89
*The American Mercury,* 125
Americanists, versus globalists, 206–207
America's heartland, 54–56
Anderson, David A., 149, 154–157
Antimarriage culture, 116
Apocalypse, 216–218
Assimilation, 57–61, 209–212
Asymmetric warfare, 173–174
Auditing patterns, 211

## B

Babies, and AIDS, 145–146
Bad jobs, and welfare, 80
Barlett, Donald L., 35–37
Benefits, and welfare, 80
Bennett, William J., 16
Bollinger, Lee C., 84
Borum, Randy, 149, 177–179
Botswana, and AIDS, 141
Boys, 106–107
Braverman, Amy M., 109, 115–118
Brewster, Melissa, 120
Brodkin, Evelyn, 63, 77–82
Broken arrows, 199
Broken windows, and crime, 151–152
Brown, Lester, 181, 182–186
Business, and globalization, 39–40
Business and the market, 38–53, 119–123, 135–138

## C

Cairncross, Frances, 57–61
Campaign contributions, and special interest groups, 35–37
Campaign-finance reform, 35–37
Cancer epidemic, 200
Cape Coral, Florida, 163–168
Capitalism, 38–45, 65–72
Capitalism, and carbon dioxide, 191–192
Carbon dioxide, 191–192
Carbon-based energy, 184

*The Case for Marriage: Why Married People Are Happier, Healthier, and Better Off Financially,* 115–118
Caseloads, reducing of, 79–80
Catholicism, 3
Change, reshaping our world, 214–218
*Chelyabinsk: The Most Contaminated Spot on the Planet,* 199–200
Childhood, 57–61, 115–118, 124–134
Children, 57–61, 115–118, 124–134, 145–147
China, and grain imports, 184
Christendom, 216
Chronically ill homeless, 73–76
Civil liberties, 29–34
Civil rights, 29–34, 83–90, 95–107
Class conflicts, 26
Classroom violence, 129–134
Climate change, 187–193
Clinton, President William Jefferson, and welfare, 78
Cloud, John, 63, 101–105
Coercive interrogation, 31–33
Coleman, James, 17
College; *See* Higher education
Communitarian approach, 209–214
Community, 54–61, 209–212
Community building, 209–212
Community of communities, 209–212
Community Health Care Act, 74
Community policing, 166–168
Community-based approach, and crime, 151
Community-oriented policing (COP), 151, 166–168
Computer science, and outsourcing, 48–53
Conflict, 2–15, 35–37, 83–105, 169–179
Conflicts, rights in, 7–9; *See also* Values
Conflict theory, 1
Conflict theory, versus functionalism, 5–6
Constitutional Amendment, gay marriage, 101–105
Consumer economy, 46–48
Consumer spending, 46–48
Consumption, consumer spending, 46–48
Consumption, credit and debt, 48
Consumption, faltering of, 47–48
Consumption, over, 47–48
Coontz, Stephanie, 109
COP; *See* Community-oriented policing (COP)
Corporal punishment, 132
Corporate community, 25, 65–72
Corporate culture, 65–72
Corporate rich, 25, 65–72
Corporate salaries, 65–72
Corporate welfare, 35–37
Corporate-conservative coalition, 26
Costs, and crime, 154–157
Courts, and criminal justice reform, 162
Credit and debt, 48
Crime, 95–100, 149, 150–179
Crime trend, U.S., 151
Crime-induced production, 154–156
Criminal justice system, reform, 149, 158–162

Cubberley, Ellwood P., 127
Culture, 16–22, 101–118, 124–134, 177–179, 213–218
Cystic fibrosis (CF), and genetic engineering, 195–197

## D

Daalder, Ivo H., 205–208
Darwinism, 194
*Debt and Dispossession: Farm Loss in America's Heartland,* 55
Delaney, H. Richard, 1, 2–10
Demographics rule, and crime, 151
Demography, 54–56, 194–197
Depleted uranium (DU), 198–199
Desire reduction, and crime, 152
Detention, preventive, 33–34
Deveny, Kathleen, 109, 119–123
Devolution, and welfare, 79
Diagnostic function, and public education, 126
Dialysis, 137
Differentiating function, and public education, 126
Directive function, and public education, 126
Discrimination, 83–107
Disintegration and integration, 11–15, 54–56, 139–147, 209–212
Disorganization and organization, 11–15, 54–56, 139–147, 209–212
District of Columbia Appropriations Act, 35
Diversity, 83–90
Divorce, 115–118
DNA database, universal, 159
Dollar, 48
Domhoff, G. William, 24, 24–28
Domination, 26, 27
Drugs, and crime, 161–162
Dudley, Kathryn Marie, 55

## E

Easter Island, 192
Ecology; *See* Ecology and environment
Ecology and environment, 182–193
Economic change, and globilization, 41–45
Economic inequality, 13–14
Economy, 35–56, 65–76
Economy, consumer, 46–48
Economy, evaluating change, 41–45
Economy, global, 38–40
Economy, inequality, 13–14
Education, 83–90, 106–107, 124–134
Education, and outsourcing, 48–53
Educational system, 124–134
Effects of crime, 154–157
Eitzen, D. Stanley, 1, 11–15
Employment, men and women, 106–107
Environment; *See* Ecology and environment
Equal Credit Opportunity Act of 1974, 48
*Equality of Educational Opportunity,* 17
Equality of opportunity, 210
Estate tax, 71–72

# Index

Ethnic divide, 14–15
Etzioni, Amitai, 209–212
EU; See European Union (EU)
Eugenic; See Genetic engineering
Europe, and terrorism, 172–173
European Union (EU), 39
Evidence, ill-gotten, 158
Evolution, 194–195
Exclusionary rule, 158–159
Executive salaries, 65–72
Extremist ideology, and terrorism, 177–179
Extremist individual, and terrorism, 177–178

## F

Fair Housing Act of 1968, 48
Family, 18, 73–76, 101–123, 198–204
Fanaticism, 171
Farm economy, 54–56
Finances, and hospitals, 135–138
Food, and the environment, 183–184
Foreign Intelligence Surveillance Act, 30
Foreign policy, future of, 205–208
Fort Myers, FL, 163–168
Fossil fuels, and ecology and environment, 183
Frank, Robert H., 47
Fraud, and hospitals, 135–138
Fukuyama, Francis, 1, 16–22
Functionalism, 1, 5–6
Functionalism, and conflict theory, 5–6
Future, 11–15, 119–123, 169–176, 182–197, 213–218

## G

Gatto, John Taylor, 109
Gay marriage, 101–105
Gay marriage history, 102
Gender gap, 106–107
Gender inequality, 63
Gender roles, 101–123
Genes; See Genetic engineering
Genetic engineering, 194–197
Geopolitics, 205–208
Gilded Ages, 65–66
Glasser, Jeff, 24, 54–56
Global bubble economy, 182–186
Global economy, 38–45
Global marketplace, 38–45
Global power, and the United States, 205–208
Global sourcing, 52; See also Outsourcing
Global warming, 187–188
Globalists, versus Americanists, 206–207
Globalization, 38–45, 49–53, 67, 205–208, 213–218
Goncalves, Eduardo, 198–204
Government, 25–37, 65–76, 83–90, 158–162, 169–176, 205–208
Government appointees, 27
Grain production, 183–184
Great Disruption, 18
Greenhouse effect, 187–188
Growing up with a Single Parent, 17
Growth coalitions, 25

## H

Hanford plutonium factory, 201
Harm, consequences of, 8
Harm, defined, 6

Health, 11–15, 135–147
Higher education, and affirmative action, 83–90
HIV virus, 139–147, 182
Homelessness, 73–76
Homicide, World Crime Survey, 150
Homosexuality, 101–105
Hospitals, 135–138
Housing, for homeless, 73–76
Human rights, 95–100
Hydrogen-based energy, 184–185
Hydrological cycle, and CO2, 191

## I

Ideological development, and terrorism, 177–178
Ideology, and terrorism, 179
Immigration, 57–61, 209–212, 214–215
Impact of crime, 154–157
Implicit Association Test, 93
Income inequality, 210
The Index of Leading Cultural Indicators, 16
India, and outsourcing, 49–53
Individualism, excessive, 11–15
Individualism, fragmentation of social life, 11–15
Inequality, 13–14, 65–72
Inequality gap, widening of, 13–14
Infants, and AIDS, 145–146
Inglis, Alexander, 126
Insanity defense, abolishment of, 161
Integrating function, and public education, 126
Integration, and immigration, 57–61
Interest groups, 35–37
International Labor Organization (ILO), and prostitution, 98–99
International marketplace, 38–45
International partnerships, and crime, 152
Interrogation, 31–33
Investment, 47
Islamist terrorism, 171–172
Isolation, 12–13

## J

Jobs, and welfare, 80
Judges, and criminal justice reform, 162

## K

Kantrowitz, Barbara, 63, 83–90
Kaplowitz, Joshua, 109, 129–134
Kidney dialysis, 137
Krugman, Paul, 63, 65–72
Kyoto protocol, 191–192

## L

Laqueur, Walter, 149, 169–176
Law enforcement, 29–34, 83–90, 95–100, 149, 150–179
Lehrer, Eli, 149, 163–168
Lesotho, and AIDS, 141
Leuchtag, Alice, 63, 95–100
Liberal-labor coalition, 26
Liberty, 29–34
Life and health, value of, 155, 156
Lifestyles, 65–76, 101–123
Lindsay, James M., 205–208
Losing Ground, 17

Lower class, 73–76
Luxury Fever: Money and Happiness in an Era of Excess, 47

## M

Mandatory minimum sentencing, 161–162
Mandatory schooling, 124–128
Manhattan Project, 200
Marriage, 115–118
Marriage and divorce, 101–105, 110–123
Marriage and family, 111–115
Marriage and sex, 119–123
Martyrdom, 178–179
McGeary, Johanna, 139–147
McLanahan, Sara, 17
MCP; See Medical College of Pennsylvania Hospital (MCP)
Medicare, 136–138
Medical College of Pennsylvania Hospital (MCP), 135–138
Men, 106–107
Men and women, 106–107
Mencken, H. L., 125
Mental health, insanity defense, 161
Michigan, University of, and affirmative action, 83–90
Middle-class America, 65–72
Migration, and immigration, 57–61
Miranda rights, 32–33
Monteith, Margo, 91–94
Moral renewal, 16–22
Morals; decline of, 16–22; and globilization, 41–45; regeneration of, 16–22; social, 16–22
Mortgages, and low income, 211
Moussaoui, Zacarias, 30–31
Moynihan, Daniel Patrick, 17
Multiculturalism, 83–94, 209–212
Murray, Charles, 17

## N

NAFTA; See North American Free Trade Agreement (NAFTA)
Namibia, and AIDS, 141
National partnerships, and crime, 152
Natural selection, 194–195
The Negro Family: The Case for National Action, 17
Neo-Darwinism, 194–195
Nevada's fallout, 201
Newbury, England, 199
No-fault divorce, 116–117
North American Free Trade Agreement (NAFTA), 49
Nuclear accidents, 198–204
Nuclear cover-ups, 198–204
Nuclear experiments, 198–204
Nuclear war, silent, 198–204

## O

Ocean conveyor, 188–189
Omnibus Consolidated and Emergency Supplemental Appropriations Act, 36
Opportunity costs, and crime, 155, 156
Outlier payments, 136–138
Outsourcing, 49–53
Over-consumption, 47–48
Ownership, and the poor, 210–211

## P

Parental conflict, 117
Patrol, 163–168
Pentagon, and climate change, 187–193
Personal Responsibility and Work
    Opportunity Reconciliation Act, 78–82
Place entrepreneurs, 25
Pluralism, 26–27
Police officers, 163–168
Police work, 163–168
Police-community partnerships, 166–168
Policy-formation network, 25
Political economy, 24
Politics, 25–37, 77–90, 95–100, 169–176,
    205–208
Pomper, Stephen, 149, 158–162
POP; *See* Problem-oriented policing (POP)
Population, and globilization, 214–215
Population growth, and ecology and
    environment, 183, 184
Poverty, 73–82, 95–100, 169–170
Power and class, 25–28
Power elite, 25–26
Prayer, and public education, 209–210
Prevention programs, and crime, 152
Preventive detention, 33–34
Prince, Rebecca, 163–168
*Principles of Secondary Education,* 126–127
Proactive prevention, and crime, 151–152
Problem-oriented policing (POP), 151
Propaedeutic function, and public
    education, 126
Property ownership, and low income, 210–
    211
Prosecutors, criminal justice reform, 160–161
Prostitution, 95–100, 143–145
Protestantism, 3
Prussian, educational system, 125–126
Public education, 124–134
*Public Education in the United States,* 127
Public schools, 124–134

## R

Race and ethnic relations, 11–15, 83–94
Racial and ethnic inequality, 63
Racism, 91–94
Radiation, exposure to, 198–204
Radiation risk, 203
Randall, Doug, 189
Rape, World Crime Survey, 150
Reactive retribution, and crime, 151
Reallocation of wealth, 211
Reform, criminal justice system, 149
*Regents of the University of California v.
    Bakke,* 83
Religion, 3, 20–21, 104, 215–216
Religious divide, 14–15
Re-moralization, 16–22
Rights, 7–8, 29–34
Right-versus-right moral conflict, 7
Robbery, World Crime Survey, 150

## S

Salary, men and women, 106–107
Salvage Motor Vehicle Consumer
    Protection Act, 36

Samuelson, Robert J., 24, 46–48
Sandefur, Gary, 17
Scams, and hospitals, 135–138
Schwarts, Peter, 189
Searches, 30–31
Searches and seizures, 30
Secular humanism, 18
Security, 29–34
Selective function, and public education, 126
Sex, 119–123, 139–147
"Sex and the Century: A History", 120
Sex slavery, 95–100
Sex tourism, 96
Sex trafficking, 95–100
Sexism, 95–100, 106–107
Sexless marriage, 119–123
Sexuality divide, 14–15
Shelters, 73–74
Single-parenthood, 17
Skill-biased technological change, 67
Slavery, 95–100
Small towns, 54–56
Social change, 11–22, 38–56, 65–90, 101–
    123, 150–153, 169–179, 194–197, 205–
    208, 213–218
Social control, 150–162, 177–179
Social identity theory, 63, 92–93
Social justice, 210–211
Social life, fragmentation of, 11
Social order, 19
Social problems, definition and analysis, 6–7
Social problems, introduction to, 2–3
Social relationships, 11–15, 91–94, 101–
    123, 209–212
Social security, 63
Social stratification and inequality, 11–15,
    25–28, 65–90, 95–107, 209–212
Social theory, 2–10, 25–28, 209–212
Social upper class, 25
Social values, 16–22
Socialization, 91–94, 129–134, 177–179
Society, steps toward a good, 209–212
Soil, stabilizing of, 185
Song, Sara, 112
South Africa, and AIDS, 139–147, 182
Soviet Union, nuclear accidents, 199–200
Special interest groups, 35–37
St. George, UT, 201
Steele, James B., 35–37
Stein, Joel, 63, 73–76
Stephens, Gene, 149, 150–153
Stiglitz, Joseph, 24, 41–45
Strickland, Leif, 87
Suicide attacks, 178–179
Superstar hypothesis, 67
Surveillance, 30–31
Swaziland, and AIDS, 141
Symbolic interactionism, 1, 4–5

## T

TANF; *See* Temporary Assistance to Needy
    Families (TANF)
Tax-free profits, 36
Taylor, Stuart Jr., 24, 29–34
Teach for America (TFA), 129–134
Technology, 48–53, 194–204, 213

Temporary Assistance to Needy Families
    (TANF), 78–82
Tenet Healthcare Corp., 135
Terrorism, 29–34, 91–94, 149, 152, 169–179
Terrorism, rights, liberty, and security, 29–34
TFA; *See* Teach for America (TFA)
Thalidomide, and symbolic interaction, 4
Thermohaline circulation, 188–189
Thottam, Jyoti, 24, 49–53
Three strikes laws, 161
Ticket to Work and Work Incentives
    Improvement Act, 36
Towns, small, 54–56
Trafficking, 95–100
Tudge, Colin, 194–197

## U

Unemployment, reducing of, 211
U. S. crime trend, 151
Unreasonable searches and seizures, 31
Upper class, 25–28, 65–72
Uranium, depleted, 198–199
Urban institute, and welfare, 80–81

## V

Values, 16–22, 101–105, 110–118, 177–
    179, 194–197, 209–218; American, 2–3;
    conflict of, 6; and globalization, 41–45;
    versus duties, 6–7
Van Biema, David, 104
Vehicle theft, World Crime Survey, 150
Victims of Trafficking and Violence
    Protection Act of 2000, 98
Vietnam war, and symbolic interaction, 4
Violence, 150–157, 169–179, 198–204

## W

Warren court, 158
Water, and ecology and environment, 183,
    185
Wealth, 25–28, 41–48, 65–72
Weed and Seed, and crime, 151
Weidenbaum, Murray, 24, 38–40
Welfare, 77–82
Wendland, Joel, 64, 106–107
Widdison, Harold, 1, 2–10
Williams, Armstrong, 84
Wingert, Pat, 83–90
Winters, Jeffrey, 91–94
Wiretapping, 31
Wishard, Wm. Van Dusen, 213–218
Witness, protection of, 159–160
Women, 95–100, 106–107, 119–123
Work and employment, 38–45, 49–53, 73–
    90, 106–107, 110–114, 119–123
Working women, 112–113
World War, silent, 198–204

## X

Xenophobic, 91–94

## Z

Zambia, and AIDS, 141
Zimbabwe, and AIDS, 141

# Test Your Knowledge Form

We encourage you to photocopy and use this page as a tool to assess how the articles in *Annual Editions* expand on the information in your textbook. By reflecting on the articles you will gain enhanced text information. You can also access this useful form on a product's book support Web site at *http://www.dushkin.com/online/*.

NAME: _____     DATE: _____

TITLE AND NUMBER OF ARTICLE: _____

BRIEFLY STATE THE MAIN IDEA OF THIS ARTICLE:

LIST THREE IMPORTANT FACTS THAT THE AUTHOR USES TO SUPPORT THE MAIN IDEA:

WHAT INFORMATION OR IDEAS DISCUSSED IN THIS ARTICLE ARE ALSO DISCUSSED IN YOUR TEXTBOOK OR OTHER READINGS THAT YOU HAVE DONE? LIST THE TEXTBOOK CHAPTERS AND PAGE NUMBERS:

LIST ANY EXAMPLES OF BIAS OR FAULTY REASONING THAT YOU FOUND IN THE ARTICLE:

LIST ANY NEW TERMS/CONCEPTS THAT WERE DISCUSSED IN THE ARTICLE, AND WRITE A SHORT DEFINITION:

# We Want Your Advice

ANNUAL EDITIONS revisions depend on two major opinion sources: one is our Advisory Board, listed in the front of this volume, which works with us in scanning the thousands of articles published in the public press each year; the other is you—the person actually using the book. Please help us and the users of the next edition by completing the prepaid article rating form on this page and returning it to us. Thank you for your help!

## ANNUAL EDITIONS:   Social Problems 05/06

### ARTICLE RATING FORM

Here is an opportunity for you to have direct input into the next revision of this volume.
We would like you to rate each of the articles listed below, using the following scale:

1. **Excellent: should definitely be retained**
2. **Above average: should probably be retained**
3. **Below average: should probably be deleted**
4. **Poor: should definitely be deleted**

Your ratings will play a vital part in the next revision.
Please mail this prepaid form to us as soon as possible.
Thanks for your help!

| RATING | ARTICLE |
| --- | --- |
| | 1. Social Problems: Definitions, Theories, and Analysis |
| | 2. The Fragmentation of Social Life |
| | 3. How to Re-Moralize America |
| | 4. Who Rules America? |
| | 5. Rights, Liberties, and Security: Recalibrating the Balance After September 11 |
| | 6. How the Little Guy Gets Crunched |
| | 7. Surveying the Global Marketplace |
| | 8. Evaluating Economic Change |
| | 9. Shopping and Prosperity: The Consumer Economy |
| | 10. Is Your Job Going Abroad? |
| | 11. A Broken Heartland |
| | 12. The Longest Journey |
| | 13. For Richer: How the Permissive Capitalism of the Boom Destroyed American Equality |
| | 14. The Real Face of Homelessness |
| | 15. Requiem for Welfare |
| | 16. What's At Stake |
| | 17. Why We Hate |
| | 18. Human Rights, Sex Trafficking, and Prostitution |
| | 19. The Battle Over Gay Marriage |
| | 20. Reversing the "Gender Gap" |
| | 21. The American Family |
| | 22. Living Better: Get Wed |
| | 23. We're Not in the Mood |
| | 24. Against School: How Public Education Cripples Our Kids, and Why |
| | 25. How I Joined Teach for America—and Got Sued for $20 Million |
| | 26. Whose Hospital Is It? |
| | 27. Death Stalks a Continent |
| | 28. The Criminal Menace: Shifting Global Trends |
| | 29. The Aggregate Burden of Crime |
| | 30. Reasonable Doubts |
| | 31. On Patrol |
| | 32. The Terrorism to Come |
| | 33. Understanding the Terrorist Mind-Set |
| | 34. Rescuing a Planet Under Stress |
| | 35. The Pentagon and Climate Change |

| RATING | ARTICLE |
| --- | --- |
| | 36. The Future of Humanity |
| | 37. The Secret Nuclear War |
| | 38. The Globalization of Politics: American Foreign Policy for a New Century |
| | 39. Community Building: Steps Toward a Good Society |
| | 40. Sleepwalking Through the Apocalypse |

*(Continued on next page)*

## BUSINESS REPLY MAIL
FIRST CLASS MAIL PERMIT NO. 551 DUBUQUE IA

POSTAGE WILL BE PAID BY ADDRESEE

McGraw-Hill/Dushkin
2460 KERPER BLVD
DUBUQUE, IA 52001-9902

Ialadhallhalhamalllahdahdahmaldahall

## ABOUT YOU

Name

Date

Are you a teacher? ☐   A student? ☐
Your school's name

Department

Address                    City                    State          Zip

School telephone #

## YOUR COMMENTS ARE IMPORTANT TO US!

Please fill in the following information:
For which course did you use this book?

Did you use a text with this ANNUAL EDITION?   ☐  yes ☐  no
What was the title of the text?

What are your general reactions to the *Annual Editions* concept?

Have you read any pertinent  articles recently that you think should be included in the next edition? Explain.

Are there any articles that  you feel should be replaced in the next edition? Why?

Are there any World Wide Web sites that you feel should be included in the next edition? Please annotate.

May we contact you for editorial input?   ☐  yes ☐  no
May we quote your comments?  ☐  yes ☐  no